Prejudice and the Old Politics

Prejudice and the Old Politics

The Presidential Election of 1928

by Allan J. Lichtman

The University of North Carolina Press
Chapel Hill

© 1979 The University of North Carolina Press
All rights reserved
Manufactured in the United States of America
ISBN 0-8078-1358-3
Library of Congress Catalog Card Number 78-26813

Library of Congress Cataloging in Publication Data

Lichtman, Allan J
    Prejudice and the old politics.

    Bibliography: p.
    Includes index.
    1. Presidents—United States—Election—1928.
2. Voting—United States.   I. Title.
E796.L5   329'.023'730915   78-26813
ISBN 0-8078-1358-3

Contents

Tables

Charts

Acknowledgments

Since the inception of this book in 1969, a great many people have ignited my thinking, commented on various drafts, and assisted with the details of manuscript preparation. Frank Freidel helped stimulate an initial interest in political history and encouraged my study of quantitative methods. Charlie Brown served as consultant on statistical matters in the first years of the project. Ivy Broder and David Hoaglin also offered guidance in quantitative techniques.

Chapter 9 appeared in the 1976 *American Historical Review* as an article entitled "Critical Election Theory and the Reality of American Presidential Politics, 1916–1940."

For contributions to the style and substance of the book I am most grateful to J. Morgan Kousser. Others making important contributions include: Robert Beisner, Allan Bogue, Richard Breitman, Roger Brown, Walter Dean Burnham, Stanley Coben, David Fischer, Valerie French, Pat Gudridge, Morton Keller, Ira Klein, Laura Irwin Langbein, Martin Pernick, Robert Shrum, Laurence Tribe, and Glynn Wood.

I am indebted to Katherine Crane, Valerie French, Joel and Susie Lewin, Steven and Ronnie Lichtman, Jack Lord, Daniel Rohrer, and Carolyn and Laurence Tribe for their kind assistance in coping with the details of research and writing. Also helpful in this regard were Mark Arnold, Jane and Bob Baker, Gary Braithwaite, Lonnie Bunch, Keith Ellison, Cindy and Mike Fernandez, Charles Garvin, Don Hornstein, Sarah Krakauer, Mickey Lichtman, Maureen Miller, Eleanor O'Donnell, Peter O'Connell, Greg Rosenbaum, Lynn Steele, Jim Turner, and Debbi Woods.

Above all I would like to thank my parents, Gertrude and Emanuel Lichtman, and my daughter, Kara Lichtman. Without their love and understanding this book would never have been written.

All errors, of course, I claim for myself.

Prejudice and the Old Politics

Chapter 1

Prologue:
Al Smith versus Herbert Hoover

For residents of America's West Coast, suspense created by the presidential contest of 1928 scarcely outlasted an early dinner on election night. At his home in Palo Alto, California, Herbert Hoover, the Republican nominee, gathered with a small group of friends to follow the election returns. By 7:30, Pacific Coast time, the candidate's own carefully kept scorecard already showed a majority of electoral votes safely in the Republican column. Hoover flashed a rare grin, then retired to the privacy of his study, while his guests savored films of his campaign speeches. About an hour and forty-five minutes later, they were interrupted by the arrival of a twenty-seven-word telegram of concession from Al Smith, the Democratic candidate.

The Wednesday morning papers reported that Hoover probably would garner about 60 percent of the popular vote and over 80 percent of the electoral returns. They noted that the most tempestuous campaign in recent memory had produced a record tally, large enough to net the defeated Al Smith more popular votes than any previous candidate, regardless of party. Prepared for a Republican triumph, journalists readily supplied instant explanations. Some commentators stressed the nation's devotion to the GOP, the achievements of the Coolidge administration, the booming national economy, the qualifications of Herbert Hoover, and his dazzling record as secretary of commerce. Other scribes pointed to the reaction against Al Smith —he was not only the first Catholic nominated by a major party, but also an opponent of prohibition and a leader of Tammany Hall, the notorious Democratic machine of New York County. A few observers focused on dissension within the ranks of Democrats and Smith's allegedly blundering campaign.

Responding to the election results, both candidates conformed to a familiar ritual of victory and defeat, assuring the public that conflicts which had erupted during the campaign would not continue to suppurate. Suggesting that his victory transcended partisan politics, Hoover stated that he could "make no adequate expression of gratitude for the overwhelming confidence of our people who without regard to section or interest have selected me for President of the whole United States." The president-elect disclaimed any "feeling of victory or exultation" in this moment of triumph. He confessed only to a "sense of solemn responsibility of the future and of complete dependence upon divine guidance for the task which the greatest office in the world imposes." The popular will, Hoover claimed, now sanctioned both his leadership and the program of his party: "There has been a vindication of great issues and a determination of the true road of progress. The Republican Party has again been assessed with a great responsibility."[1]

Al Smith told his followers that he had "nothing but pleasant memories" of the campaign—no bitterness and no regrets. He suggested that issues which yesterday had seemed mighty must today be put aside because "the American people have rendered their decision" and all must accept "the rule of the majority." Nothing that had surfaced in the campaign, Smith implied, was worth jeopardizing the maintenance of social concord and the smooth transition of government. Conceding the claim of popular assent for Hoover's leadership and policies, Smith reminded fellow Democrats that Hoover "is not the President of the Republican Party, but the President of the United States . . . and as such is entitled to the cooperation of every citizen in the development of a program calculated to promote the welfare and best interests of the country." Smith assured his supporters that they were part of a beneficent social order in which all of them had a secure and honored place. He stressed that "it will not do to let bitterness, rancor or indignation over the results blind us to the one outstanding fact, that above everything else we are Americans."[2]

In the harmony of this ritual, the candidates implicitly affirmed that unusual strife had arisen during the campaign and needed to be defused. Now that the verdict was in, Hoover and Smith would work to end the conflicts that had wracked the campaign and that continue to beguile historians. Persisting interest in the election of 1928 goes beyond fascination with the color and form of a presidential contest. Two generations of scholars have found in the turbulent canvas of 1928 images of life in the decade past and portents of politics in the years to come.

The candidates themselves made this contest exciting to contemporaries and intriguing to historians. No burning issue had to be resolved by the election; no national crisis preoccupied the American public. Rather, the backgrounds of Smith and Hoover, their personalities, their careers in public service, and their approaches to politics gave the campaign its special significance. They both were formidable contenders for the presidency, widely regarded as the best candidates their parties had to offer.

At the peaks of their respective careers in 1928, Hoover and Smith were self-made men noted for their rapid success and solid accomplishments. Herbert Hoover had never run for office before 1928; Al Smith had successfully contested more than a dozen elections, losing only once. Hoover had achieved renown as director of America's food relief efforts during World War I and as the guiding genius of domestic policy during seven years as secretary of commerce. Smith was the nation's most successful Democratic politician of the postwar decade. Between 1918 and 1928, he served four terms as governor of New York State, earning national recognition as an administrator and reformer.

For Herbert Hoover, born to struggling Quaker parents in West Branch, Iowa, education and business led to wealth and fame. An orphan at the age of nine, Hoover spent the rest of his childhood shuttling among relatives for shelter and support.[3] In the late 1880s, Hoover's itinerant life brought him to Oregon. In 1889, at the age of fifteen, he began work for a real estate office that his uncle had just opened in Portland. As jack-of-all-trades for his uncle's concern, Hoover acquired a taste for business life and a yen for mining and engineering. He entered Stanford University in 1891 and two years after his graduation departed for Australia as a mining engineer for a London-based corporation. Hoover spent most of the next seventeen years attending to business overseas. Operating as an administrator, a doctor of ailing organizations, a financier and promoter, as well as a mining engineer, Hoover had amassed a fortune reputed to exceed four million dollars when he retired from business in 1914. He was forty years old.

Hoover retired, in part, because he felt restricted by a life devoted to business. He aspired to public service, seeking both the esteem of his peers and a chance to satisfy the moral yearnings of a Quaker, while using the technical skills of an engineer. The war provided his opportunity. Hoover became administrator of relief to Belgium, then director of America's effort to ship food and supplies to postwar Europe. Fabulously successful in both these positions, he emerged from the war years as one of America's best known and respected public servants.

Following a clumsy effort to attain the Republican nomination for president in 1920, Hoover refused several lucrative offers to reenter private business. Instead, he became secretary of commerce in the administration of Warren G. Harding. Highly regarded by the incoming president, Hoover rapidly maneuvered this traditionally obscure position to a command post in the new administration. He expanded the powers and responsibilities of the Commerce Department, and became a key adviser in domestic and in foreign economic policy. An assiduous public relations staff kept Hoover in the limelight throughout his eight-year tenure. As one observer wryly noted, Hoover was not only secretary of commerce, but was also trying to be "Undersecretary of all other departments." Although generally disliked by both the Old Guard and the insurgents of his party, Hoover's public reputation carried him to the nomination after Calvin Coolidge chose not to run for president in 1928.

Despite his aggressiveness as entrepreneur and administrator, Hoover was reserved, even shy. He kept his private life hermetically sealed from the outside world, forcing journalists to scrape for human interest stories or for appealing anecdotes from his business and public life. Hoover did not get along easily with people he did not know well; he loathed backslapping, handshaking, and small talk. He was dismayed by crowds that sought to cheer him or individuals who tried to shake his hand. Because he was unable to turn memorable phrases or inspire an audience, his public appearances usually were as stiff as the starched collars he still wore in 1928. Hoover's written and spoken prose struggled with abstract ideas, often twisting and coiling into complex sentences. Hoover's metier was command of information, mastery of technique, and control of argument. He did not convey spontaneity, warmth, wit, or passion.

Herbert Hoover was one of the nation's first public officials to muster a staff trained in the new science of public relations. Skillful use of public relations techniques could not only compensate for his forensic deficiencies, but actually turn them to his advantage. The secretary and his staff fashioned a public image consistent with Hoover's own notions about his official role and with beliefs deeply set in the minds of Americans. Hoover became known in the 1920s as a selfless public servant, driven by humanitarian impulses to serve the national interest. He was the impartial expert with mastery over the workings of government. Cooperating with experts from the private economy, he could serve the public without fostering a soulless bureaucracy or challenging American folkways. Hoover did not look forward to an America modeled on the machine or recast according to a utopian dream. Consistently evoking traditional values, he held out the prospect of unlimited progress along familiar pathways.

The secretary and his staff cultivated the image that Hoover was the national leader who knew best how to make government serve individuals. Simultaneously an engineer and a humanitarian, he was the technocrat with a heart. Unbeholden to special interests, free of lust for personal power, Hoover could safeguard everyone's interest. Hoover's reticence, his lack of flamboyance, his penchant for working behind the scenes, his cultivation of privacy befitted his public image. These qualities indicated that he wished only to serve the public and was content to be judged by the objective results of his labors. Hoover's accomplishments proved that he cared about people, proved his competence and ability.

Herbert Hoover represented a public philosophy founded on an evocation of traditional values and a celebration of modern technology. Smoothing over the contradictions emphasized by disenchanted intellectuals of the 1920s, this philosophy reassured Americans that they need not abandon their folkways nor fear that technology would deform their values or coarsen their lives. Hoover's philosophy affirmed that science was a socially neutral force which provided the material foundation of American culture. In this view, American democracy and free enterprise formed a miraculous engine of progress that needed only regular upkeep and protection from malevolent and misguided critics. Hoover personified the notion that continuing progress could be achieved in America through cooperative endeavor guided by a factual analysis of the common good. Directed by impartial experts who understood technology and appreciated American culture, government would provide information and services, foster cooperative activity, and umpire the conduct of business. Eventually the system would eliminate poverty and offer every citizen the leisure and comfort required for moral, spiritual, and intellectual growth. As Hoover proclaimed in his 1922 essay *American Individualism*, material progress advances, rather than threatens, the growth of the mind and the liberation of the spirit. He wrote, "We have long since realized that the basis of an advancing civilization must be a high and growing standard of living for all the people . . . that education, food, clothing, housing and the spreading use of what we so often term non-essentials are the real fertilizers of the soil from which spring the finer flowers of life."[4]

This public philosophy stressed harmony rather than conflict of interest among groups of Americans. No matter how one partitioned the American people, all groups—labor and capital, producer and consumer, white and nonwhite—had a common interest in the efficiency of material production and distribution. No one's interest was advanced by visionary schemes that threatened production by trying to redistribute income or wealth. Everyone would benefit, Hoover insisted, by increasing the size of the pie rather than fretting about reapportioning each slice: "There is a vastly wider field for gains to all of us through cheapening the costs of production and distribution through the eliminating of their wastes, from increasing the volume of product by each and every one doing his utmost, than will ever come to us even if we can think out a method of abstract justice in sharing which did not stifle production of the total product."[5] Faith in the productivity of American business, faith in the unique virtues of American values and culture, faith in science and technology, faith in expertise and objectivity, faith in the common interests of Americans were all part of Herbert Hoover's appeal.

During the campaign of 1928, Hoover did not alter the method of public persuasion that had served him so well and seemed attuned to his personality and consistent with his beliefs. Hoover made few public appearances during the campaign and relied exclusively on prepared speeches. He released no details of his personal life and accorded reporters no intimate interviews. Attempts to fathom the "real" Herbert Hoover became a favorite guessing game of journalists in 1928, adding to his mystique. Although Hoover was now an office seeker rather than a public servant, he maintained the stance of an educator, elevated above the squabbles of politicians. Hoover delivered only eight speeches, all written in his own abstract prose. Rather than developing a single theme, the speeches flitted from topic to topic, expressing Hoover's ideas in the generalities that befitted a front runner. He did not deign to dispute the arguments of his opponent or even refer to him directly.

Only political proxies such as Senators George H. Moses and William E. Borah, Charles Evans Hughes and Mabel Walker Willebrandt actually tangled with Al Smith and his supporters. Dogging Smith around the country, Republican speakers carefully tailored arguments to the preferences of their audiences. For the most part they practiced politics with the gloves off, portraying Smith as irresponsible, unpatriotic, even dangerous. He would bring back the evil saloon, flood the nation with unsavory immigrants, threaten prosperity by slashing the tariff, encourage regimentation through public control of power resources. Only once, late in the campaign, did Hoover step off the high road to warn the public that "our opponents" are abandoning the "American system" and turning instead to "state socialism."[6]

Hoover did not remain aloof from political concerns, however, but tightly controlled his quest for the presidency. He orchestrated the drive for his party's nomination and dictated the strategy and tactics of the fall campaign. He monitored the activities of campaign officials, supervised the dissemination of campaign material, and closely guarded his own powers of decision. The reports of commentators, both friendly and hostile, suggest that even the finer details of the campaign merited his personal attention. After talking with the candidate, Republican politico E. N. Carpenter informed Henry P. Fletcher that "Hoover is dictating the policies of the campaign." Similarly, Brice Clagget confided to alienated Democrat William Gibbs McAdoo, "Dr. Work [chairman of the Republican National Committee] gives the impression of being very inefficient and not having complete control of the situation, particularly since Mr. Hoover seems to have the final say on everything, even the smallest details." In a long article evaluating the performance of Dr. Work, progressive journalist Henry F. Pringle concluded, "Hoover, however, insists on knowing the minute details of everything that is going on—even those unfortunately necessary details regarding which a presidential candidate is supposed to be blissfully ignorant."[7]

Thorough control would, of course, be expected of a candidate who had spent his life reorganizing rickety business firms, running America's food relief programs, and manipulating the machinery of government. Hoover often astounded friends and associates with his memory for facts and figures and his ability to amass and coordinate quantities of information. As secretary of commerce, Hoover had planned and dominated more than 250 conferences on national problems. Within reach of his greatest goal, Hoover would not abandon his wonted control over detail.

If Herbert Hoover often seemed no livelier than an engineering text, Al Smith was among the more colorful politicians of America's Jazz Age.[8] A true New York provincial, Smith flaunted the dress and manners of his city. The derby hat set at a slightly rakish angle, the flashy suits, the big cigar, the slight swagger, the striking pronunciations all bespoke New York specifically, not a blended image of urban America. The Happy Warrior even boasted that his alma mater was F.F.M.—Fulton Fish Market—and bands played "The Sidewalks of New York" as he toured the nation in 1928. Al Smith yearned to be the center of attention, the object of adulation. As governor he loved to hold court in a suite at the Biltmore or at his private club, attended by friends, cronies, and well-wishers. Holding forth with supreme self-confidence, Smith could scathe a ward boss for ignoring people's needs or lecture a social worker on the virtues of party loyalty.

Although identified with the recent immigrant, Al Smith's roots in America stretched beyond the middle of the nineteenth century. Irish on his maternal side, perhaps Italian and German on his paternal side, Smith's Catholic forebears had resided in his Lower East Side neighborhood for two generations. Despite images of an impoverished childhood that have filtered through the years, Smith led a fairly comfortable life that oscillated between the rigid discipline of home, parochial school, and church and the abandon of streets enlivened by sailors, prostitutes, and bands of homeless children. Even his father's death did not bring hunger, cold, or dependence.

Ironically, for one later branded as a patron of gambling and vice, Al Smith was a fiercely respectable homebody, who never strayed from the moral discipline of his parents and pastor. A commitment to hard work, individual responsibility, and Victorian standards of morality were all part of his heritage. In a precampaign biography, published in 1927, Norman Hapgood and Henry Moskowitz described the people of Al Smith's parish as "unquestioning, like the people in the Middle West. A point of view of life had come to them and they accepted it." For Catholics in St. James parish or Presbyterians in the Middle West, they added, "there was no dissent. Virtue was virtue, vice was vice. The ideas of the parents did not differ profoundly from the children." Nobody in Smith's family and "few if any in the neighborhood . . . conceived of life as anything except an existence based on individual effort. Theories about what society owes to the individual were not topics of conversation. Everybody worked, and everybody took work for granted."[9]

When Smith's mother fell ill two years after his father's death, he became the family's mainstay, quitting school in the eighth grade. Al Smith rapidly climbed the occupation ladder of the Lower East Side, earning by age eighteen the relatively munificent sum of $15 per week as a clerk for a firm dealing in wholesale fish. But acting, not work, was Smith's passion. A leading man for an amateur theater group, he dreamed of becoming a Broadway star. Al Smith sought the adoration of those around him. Unlike Hoover, he wanted others to identify with him as a person, to be thrilled by his magnetism and captivated by his warmth. Only when pressed would he play the villain's role in amateur theatricals.

Local politics was as much a part of Al Smith's neighborhood as the parish church, the bars, and the pushcarts. As virtually a dying gesture, Smith's father had struggled to the polls to vote for the candidates of Tammany Hall. Politics was a natural outlet for a frustrated actor, a young man seeking public acclaim. A loyal minion of the local Tammany leader, Smith was rewarded with a post in the municipal court system in 1895, at the age of twenty-one. In 1903, after anxious years of waiting, Tammany called upon him to run for the state assembly. Nomination by Tammany was tantamount to victory in Smith's district, and he easily swamped his Republican opponent.

Al Smith proved to be an effective, if earthy, debater, a fanatical worker who mastered the mechanics of legislative procedures, and an adroit politician who remained loyal to Tammany without sacrificing his integrity. Especially in the years following the Triangle Company fire of 1911 and his service on the subsequent Factory Investigating Commission, Smith also became known for his concern with the plight of poor and working-class people. Within a decade he became Democratic leader of the assembly, retiring in 1915 to run successfully for the office of sheriff of New York County and gain its lucrative fees. In 1918, Smith contended for the first of his four terms as governor of New York State, losing only in the Harding landslide of 1920.

As governor, Smith earned a national reputation as a reformer concerned with both social welfare and the efficiency of government. He advocated measures to curb the use of injunctions against labor organizations. He successfully sponsored legislation regulating women's and child labor, factory safety, and employee compensation. He favored programs of low-cost housing. He strengthened the state's system of public education and supported the movement for the creation of public parks and recreation areas. As his crowning achievement, extending through several administrations, Smith reorganized the state government and overhauled its tax structure.

A professed advocate of temperance, Smith was also a staunch opponent of laws prohibiting the manufacture and sale of alcohol. But he did not oppose, in principle, government intervention in matters of personal morality. Smith supported and signed the "Padlock Law" that authorized the state to close for up to one year theaters that showed lewd or obscene productions. He also signed a bill sponsored by the Catholic church to give juries discretion in obscenity trials and to bar testimony on the literary merits of a work alleged to be obscene.[10]

Smith was an indigenous urban liberal, isolated from the mainstream of progressive politics in the United States. In style and substance, his career reflected his working-class background, his empathy with people in distress, his experience with the pragmatic welfare politics of Tammany Hall. Smith understood that many of the functions once performed by the machine must be translated into public policy. And he appreciated the political value of initiating programs for the welfare of individuals. Yet Smith neither absorbed the writings that animated progressivism nor studied the careers of seminal reformers. Even after his march to national prominence, he never contributed to the debate over progressive philosophy and rarely addressed national issues. He seldom traveled outside his home state and failed to cultivate relationships with progressive politicians from other parts of the nation. Moreover, many of those identified as progressives wanted no part of a New York governor who quaffed beer with the sachems of Tammany Hall.

Al Smith possessed the credentials to challenge Hoover as a consummate technician of government. His greatest accomplishments were not as an innovator of policy, but as a master of government operations. As Democratic leader of the state assembly, Smith had skillfully manipulated the legislative process while serving his colleagues as an oral encyclopedia of state government. As governor, he had nimbly outmaneuvered Republican opposition to put across his schemes for making government more efficient and more responsive to people's needs. Throughout his career, Smith had managed to perform the balancing act needed to keep him in the front ranks of reform without jeopardizing his position in the machine politics of New York City.

Yet Smith's persona was not that of the technocrat. His public image accentuated rather than submerged his personality and was linked to the mythology of upward mobility in America, to the desire for mutual identification with national leaders. In him, many Americans could see the incarnation of their own hopes and dreams. Here was a politician who understood people's everyday concerns, who could empathize with their troubles, and who could clarify the workings of an increasingly remote and complex government. Al Smith had reached prominence without forgetting his origins, without appearing to be above the ordinary citizen. He joked of never having read a single book. He spoke plainly and bluntly, always trying to use simple language and examples that people could understand. Al Smith was the down-to-earth politician who leveled with the people, who stuck to the record, who punctured stuffed shirts, and who cut through the baloney of politics.

If Herbert Hoover inclined to abstractions, Al Smith seemed comfortable only with the concrete. Often extemporized from rough notes scribbled on odd scraps of paper, many of his eighteen campaign speeches focused on a single topic—prohibition, religious toleration, agriculture, the economy, or power resources. He developed his arguments in depth and tried to corroborate them with statistics and examples. Smith quoted Hoover and his boosters and issued specific challenges to the opposition. He attacked Hoover's policies and the record of the Coolidge administration, often using the criticisms of Republican progressives. He tried to exploit his own reputation for candor and straight talk by casting Hoover as a politician who used words to obscure rather than to clarify meanings. As Smith insisted in one speech, "The Republican party is seeking to continue control of this country under false pretenses. It misstates and misrepresents the Democratic attitude; misstates and misrepresents its own attitude; and boasts of accomplishments that in fact never took place."[11] Smith and other Democrats also castigated Hoover and the GOP for advocating one thing and doing another. Hoover and his party applauded prohibition, but failed to enforce the Volstead Act; they espoused toleration, but abetted the whispering campaign against Smith's religion; they promised to aid distressed farmers, but opposed all constructive measures of farm relief; they decried corruption in city machines, but ignored scandal within their own ranks.

Far more than Herbert Hoover, Al Smith relied on personal presence—the melodramatist's ability to interact with an audience, to play upon its emotions and flow with its rhythms. His speeches were ill-suited either to the cold type of printed pages or the disembodied voice of radio. Listened to or read today they may seem more awkward than earthy, more chaotic than spontaneous. Moreover, the actor who shuddered at playing the villain did not adjust well to the chill of a hostile audience. His repertoire lacked the easy charm that could captivate a sullen crowd or the flash of insight that could slice through a leaden atmosphere. Smith's approach was always direct, frontal, without fancy maneuvers.

Al Smith proved to be far more able as a critic than as an architect of policy. He lashed the Republicans for false complacency about the state of society and assailed their solutions to acknowledged national problems. But he neither articulated an alternative vision of America nor challenged the values represented by the candidacy of Herbert Hoover. He failed to develop a coherent theme for his campaign and did not offer the public imaginative, new programs. To win over new Democratic voters, Al Smith relied primarily on dissatisfaction with the Republican regime and his personal appeal to ordinary citizens.

Commentary on the election of 1928 accentuated differences between Al Smith and Herbert Hoover. Most observers matched contrasts in the social origins and associations of the candidates with the lines of stress that divided Americans in the years following World War I. Smith was Catholic; Hoover was Protestant. Smith was against prohibition; Hoover was for it. Smith was from the city; Hoover was from the country. Smith was associated with the immigrant and the urban machine; Hoover was associated with the native-stock American and the business elite. Oppositions of style and personality have also stirred the imagination of scholars. Hoover was the consummate bureaucrat; Smith was the master of party politics. Hoover relied on impersonal persuasion; Smith sought to project his personality and achieve rapport with his audiences. Hoover was reticent and shy; Smith was outgoing and gregarious.

Yet there were equally striking similarities between Smith and Hoover that must be considered in any attempt to interpret the 1928 contest or discern its historical significance. Both candidates represented and defended the American dream of opportunity and mobility. Neither of them would use the government to redistribute wealth or power or to place much restraint on the activities of business. Both Hoover and Smith accepted the prevailing order of the 1920s and sought only modifications to make it function more humanely and efficiently. The candidates agreed on Victorian notions of virtue and vice, the efficacy of electoral politics, and the shared interests of all Americans. The values tapped by Smith and Hoover in their approaches to politics could be fit together without strain. Despite differences in how they sought public acclaim, the candidates evoked aspects of a common tradition.

Although scholars have struggled to understand the presidential contest of 1928, no work has yet achieved the necessary synthesis of sources and methods. Quantitative studies of the election fail to draw upon the primary sources of traditional history and narrative accounts include little or no investigation of statistical data. Yet the full significance of electoral inquiry emerges only from the integration of quantitative and documentary research. The precision of mathematical models is required for reconstructing the behavior of a mass electorate and testing competing theories of political continuity and change. But traditional methods of historical interpretation are necessary for explaining the decisions of voters, reconstructing the episodes of political campaigns, and recovering the contemporary meaning of events.

Chapter 2

Introduction:
Interpretations and Revisions

Interpreting the Presidential Election of 1928

Interest in the presidential election of 1928 has continued despite general agreement that the Democrats had no chance to score an upset and turn the dominant party out of power. In this view, Herbert Hoover, the legatee of Republican prosperity and a formidable candidate in his own right, would have thrashed any nominee of the Democratic party. Given the health of the national economy, scholars have likewise concluded that the class standing of voters was not a central determinant of their choice between the two candidates. Attention has centered instead on social and cultural divisions engendered by the presidential contest and on its meaning for later shifts in the balance of political power.

Although they have eliminated economic class as a primary concern, historians have been reluctant to assess the independent importance of other potential cleavages within the electorate. The main line of scholarship, including the work of Samuel Lubell, William E. Leuchtenburg, Paul A. Carter, and David Burner, suggests that the encounter between Hoover and Smith tapped a fault line in the structure of American society.[1] Pressure on the fault neatly cleaved the polity into two sets of antagonists: Catholic-wet-foreign-urban Americans versus Protestant-dry-native-rural Americans. Voters on each side of the divide responded to multiple cues suggested by each candidate. Democrats who turned against Smith, for example, did not separate fear of his Catholicism from revulsion to his wetness or from alarm at his associations with the metropolis and the immigrant masses. To isolate particular variables would be to destroy the unity of the images projected by the two candidates and to obscure the division of America into two discrete cultures.

An interpretation combining sources of electoral cleavage into a single dimension of conflict appeals to our sense that behavior springs from a plurality of motives that cannot properly be teased apart. To insist that several factors interacted to sway the voters of 1928 seems more sophisticated and subtle than to isolate a single factor—be it religion, prohibition, or ethnic heritage. For historians relying on traditional methods, a unidimensional model becomes a way around the problem of determining the independent effects of attributes that obviously are correlated with one another. Contemporary comment alone cannot reliably be used to separate and weigh influences on the vote, whereas suppositions about motivations, applied to the circumstances of 1928, are not sufficiently powerful to distinguish among different antecedents of the voting decision.

This interpretation of the struggle between Smith and Hoover also conforms to a synthesis of social conflict in which strife between an "old" and a "new" America culminated in the 1920s. The old America, located squarely in the countryside, was peopled by Protestants of native stock. Its denizens sought to defend America's traditional values and beliefs from the alien culture and religion of the immigrant and from the cosmopolitan ethos of the city. According to this account, the boundary between the two Americas was formed by distinctions between the nation's rural and urban traditions. A contemporary observation by Walter Lippmann is the favorite clincher of those endorsing this conclusion: "The Governor's more hasty friends show an intolerance when they believe that Al Smith is the victim of purely religious prejudice. Quite apart even from the severe opposition of the prohibitionists, the objection to Tammany, the sectional objection to New York, there is an opposition to Smith which is as authentic, and, it seems to me, as poignant as his support. It is inspired by the feeling that the clamorous life of the city should not be acknowledged as the American ideal."[2]

Accounts of the 1928 contest as a confrontation of the two Americas closely resemble a later interpretation of American electoral history that has dominated the scholarship of recent years. Historians such as Lee Benson, Paul M. Kleppner, Richard J. Jensen, Ronald P. Formisano, and John Allswang have argued that, for various periods of American history, electoral alignments in the United States mainly reflected conflicts among those with different ethnic and cultural backgrounds.[3] This "ethnocultural" interpretation of voting behavior has appeared with sufficient frequency in quantitative studies of past elections for James E. Wright to observe in a review essay, "The ethnocultural interpretation of political and social conflict has become largely synonymous with . . . the 'new political history.' "[4]

As Richard L. McCormick has noted, those identified as ethnoculturalists have put forth several distinct explanations for the primacy of ethnic and cultural influences on voter choice. Their major hypothesis, however, articulated most forcefully by Jensen, Kleppner, and Formisano to explicate midwestern voting in the nineteenth century, posits that voting reflects a clash of religious values between those dubbed pietists or evangelicals and those dubbed liturgicals or ritualists.[5] Not only Catholics, but also such Protestant groups as German Lutherans and Episcopalians are classified as liturgicals. The distinct values of pietists and liturgicals dictated different approaches to public policy and conditioned a voter's reaction to the symbols of political struggle. Pietists sought to use the government as an instrument of moral reform for quashing sinful behavior—drinking, gambling, and violating the sabbath. Liturgicals, in contrast, saw the fostering of morality as a matter between the communicant and his church, independent of state intervention. Thus people's response to moral reform followed logically from their constellation of value principles. Identify a voter as either a pietist or a liturgical and you should be able to deduce his position on the prohibition of alcohol or the proscription of activity on the sabbath. Not only were issues of moral reform of greatest concern to the voter, but politicians manipulated the discussion of economic issues to fit the cultural biases of their audiences.

Although historians writing about the 1920s do not clearly explain what they mean by culture or how culture translates into political decisions, their work suggests that the systems of contrary values identified by the ethnoculturalists were an important part of what separated the old from the new America. David Burner wrote in 1968 appraising the 1920s, "By the third decade of the century, then, a complex of political, social, and moral attitudes had established itself, compounded of nativism, fundamentalism, prohibitionism, and a conviction that the American character resided in the farm and hinterland town." As in the nineteenth century, it was the moral reform "of prohibition that most broadly realized itself in political action and a legislative program. . . . To understand the special nature of the prohibition movement, one must see that 'Prohibition is part of our religion,' as the leading dry Wayne Williams put it."[6]

Historians who maintain that two American traditions collided in 1928 identify this election as one of those rare turning points in national history that mark the end of one political era and the beginning of another. Ironically, the resounding triumph of Herbert Hoover was the denouement of an age dominated by the old America. Samuel Lubell, in his seminal work *The Future of American Politics*, wrote in 1952, "Before the Roosevelt Revolution there was an Al Smith Revolution. . . . Smith's defeat in 1928, rather than Roosevelt's 1932 victory, marked off the arena in which today's politics are being fought. . . . It was Smith who first slashed through the traditional alignments that had held so firmly since the Civil War, clearing the way for the more comprehensive realignment which came later."[7] The presidential election of 1928 thus becomes a prelude to the New Deal coalition that dominated American politics in the next decade and survived innumerable predictions of its imminent demise. Al Smith, this view suggests, represented the rising underclass of American politics—the Catholic, foreign-stock workers who thronged to the nation's great cities. Although defeated in 1928, the Happy Warrior of New York is said to have generated alliances and antagonisms whose influence is still felt. Following his bid for the presidency, the values of rural America would no longer control the political agenda or guide the cultural life of the nation.

Working within yet another tradition of scholarship, political scientists have endorsed the proposition that 1928 began a new era of political competition. V. O. Key, Jr., in a pioneering article published in 1955, concluded that, for New England, the presidential election of 1928 rather than any of the contests following the crash of 1929 produced a "sharp and durable realignment . . . within the electorate." Echoing language used by Lubell, Key wrote that "in New England, at least, the Roosevelt revolution of 1932 was in large measure an Al Smith revolution of 1928."[8] Key used both this election and the election of 1896 to illustrate a new model of electoral stability and change—termed critical election theory—that has come to dominate the study of electoral change in America. Since 1955, such political scientists as Angus Campbell, Gerald M. Pomper, and Walter Dean Burnham have modified critical election theory.[9]

Critical election theory rests on the premise that American electoral history follows a regular pattern of discontinuous change. Long stretches of stability in the balance of power between competing parties and in the types of voters those parties tend to attract are punctuated periodically by drastic realignments of the American electorate. Key suggested that particular elections—termed critical or realigning elections—constitute the transitions between stable phases of the voting cycle. Critical elections disrupt the continuity of previous electoral eras and initiate new periods of stability characterized by new balances of party power and reconstituted coalitions of voters. Later theorists have modified Key's model by introducing the idea of a critical or realigning era. Most authorities would now agree that realignments of the American electorate may appear not only in a single critical election, but also in a critical era encompassing several elections.[10]

The search for critical elections of the twentieth century has centered on the confrontation between Al Smith and Herbert Hoover. Although scholars are not unanimous in their judgments, they largely agree that 1928 was either a critical election or an important constituent of a realigning era that began the politics of our own time. In a 1975 survey of sixteen history texts (fifteen published from 1971 to 1973) Bernard Sternsher concluded that "ten texts implicitly accept the classification of 1928 as a critical election."[11]

These overlapping interpretations of the presidential election of 1928 ultimately find their synthesis in a pluralist account of the American experience. Pluralist history is part of a general redirection of social science that followed World War II and has become a dominant force in history, political science, and sociology.[12] Pluralism combines an analytic model of American society with a prescriptive ideology of how life ought to be. Pluralist thinkers suggest that, in America, different types of groups compete for places at the springs of prosperity. Individuals have overlapping group memberships, and new groups may be formed at any time. The process of group competition itself determines the allocation of values within the polity; pluralists do not recognize the "public interest" or the "common good" as a category distinct from the outcomes of such competition.

Pluralism survives on the razor's edge between conflict and competition. In a pluralist universe, orderly competition does not degenerate into unchecked conflict because group leaders and their followers agree on rules of the game, respect the legitimacy of those willing to play by the rules, and are committed to bargaining, compromise, and accommodation without coercion. The leaders of groups seek not to promote a general notion of the public interest, to reconstruct American institutions, or to lead a mass movement of the common people. Instead, the role of a group leader is to maximize his group's special interests. According to the pluralists, no group is excluded automatically from access to sources of power. Success in group competition depends on the resources of a group and the skill of its leadership. Although changes in the dynamics of group competition may produce tension and anxiety, the push and pull of compromise and competition should function to maintain a beneficent stability and consensus.

Pluralist historians such as Daniel Boorstin, Richard Hofstadter, and Samuel Lubell deplore what they see as the excesses of radical politics, whatever its ideological cast.[13] They view any mass movement that seeks to reconstitute society as degenerating into either a left-wing or a right-wing version of intolerant, authoritarian politics. America, they argue, has been uniquely successful in steering a middle course between Scylla on the right and Charybdis on the left. Only a few misguided mutineers (for example, agrarian protesters of the late nineteenth and early twentieth centuries) have attempted to divert the ship of state from her steady course. Otherwise, American history has been marked by extraordinary concord and consensus. As John Higham perceptively noted in an early critique of pluralist history, it either denies the very existence of conflict or "trivialize[s] it into a set of psychological adjustments to institutional change."[14]

Not every historian who disputes the prominence of conflict in the American past is properly classified as a pluralist. Rather, pluralist history is a subdivision of what critics have identified as "consensus history." Central to the pluralist vision of American history is the belief that a lack of conflict signifies that the process of group competition has achieved a satisfactory adjustment of people's demands. Yet, other conclusions have been drawn from the same observation of surface consensus in American history. Scholars such as Gabriel Kolko and William Appleman Williams, for example, have argued that consensus may actually reflect the domination of American institutions by unrepresentative elites and the failure of the political process to respond to the interests of less privileged, less vocal groups.[15] Americans may be diverted from their self-interest by false promises, phony panaceas, and fears of reprisal. They may be too weak, scattered, or divided to shape and sustain effective protests.

Although scholars writing about the election of 1928 do not usually relate their work to political theory, pluralism implicitly guides their analysis. To portray the election as a final stage in the conflict between competing systems of values and mores is to slight the significance of religious divisions that transcended the alleged split between rural and urban mentalities in America. Religious strife is transformed by the pluralists into one of the pains of reconciliation between the old and the new America. The repudiation of a Catholic candidate by the old America did not mean that the nation was wracked by religious bigotry. In the pluralistic view America in 1928 was still experiencing the pangs of adjusting to demographic changes of the late nineteenth and early twentieth centuries—most notably the new immigration and the accelerated growth of large cities. Thus the electoral divisions of 1928 were transitional in nature; this critical election marked a crucial stage in the process of incorporating new groups into the pluralist system so that the usual game of politics could proceed on an orderly basis. Rather than evidence of ethnocentric cleavage among Americans, the election of 1928 is seen as a harbinger of a new pluralism in which immigrants from southern and eastern Europe could compete effectively with members of more established ethnic groups. Historians contend that a Catholic candidate like Senator Thomas J. Walsh of Montana, who, unlike Smith, was not associated with liquor, Tammany Hall, and the new immigrant, would not have provoked the enmity of many Protestants. Leuchtenburg, for example, ended his narrative of the 1928 campaign with the judgment that Smith simply had "arrived too early on the political scene to be accepted as a national symbol."[16] And Carter concluded his reflections with the admonition that "conclusions about toleration in American life more optimistic than those which have been customarily drawn for the 1920's would seem to be in order."[17]

Historians, in fact, chide Al Smith for not working harder to obliterate the barriers between the two Americas. Burner believes that Smith bungled the opportunity to reconcile the two cultures during the presidential campaign. Rather than reaching out to "rural and small-town America," Smith flaunted his eastern, urban background and even his Catholicism and disdain for prohibition. Burner concludes that although Smith confronted religious bigotry, he failed to resolve the legitimate concern of rural dwellers that he represented an alien influence on American culture:

The task of squaring a social, ethnic, or regional with a national identity need not be an overwhelming one: Harry Truman and John Kennedy . . . succeeded admirably. But some presidential candidates never transcend the political image that served them in local politics. To this category belongs

Governor Alfred E. Smith of New York. . . . Smith might have tried to make 1928 a year of reconciliation between the two American cultures, but to do so he would have had to reach out beyond the eastern city, to rural and small-town Protestant America, address it and show that he understood its feelings as well as the feelings of the lower East Side and the Bowery.[18]

Pluralist history depends upon this account of the transformations that followed the presidential election of 1928. A pluralist model of society applies neither to a nation polarized into hostile cultures nor to a people riven by ethnic, religious, or racial strife.[19] Tidy competition among groups requires not only a broad consensus on values, but also a tolerance of those with different origins, life styles, or affiliations. Ethnocentric struggle breaks the restraints of benign pluralism and excludes minority groups from the arena of fair competition. Thus pluralist historians are inclined to explain intolerance as a temporary result of adjustments to changes in the process of group competition or as a projection of marginal men isolated from the mainstream of American life.

For pluralist scholarship, 1928 is the critical election of twentieth-century America. Historians such as Hofstadter and Lubell maintain that a shift from the old-style reform tradition of Populism and Progressivism to the new-style reform tradition of the New Deal accompanied the passing of the old politics in 1928.[20] Although preserving much of the earlier tradition, new-style reform no longer looked backward to a more pristine, agrarian America or sought to launch mass-based moralistic crusades against a sinful society. Pluralists celebrate the later tradition as more securely anchored in the realities of modern life. The New Deal, they note, offered the American people pragmatic solutions to immediate economic problems and gave all groups access to the power of government. Indeed, the reconciliation of the two American cultures that fostered the new reform tradition was the common acceptance of pluralist ideology. If the new Americans would reject an assault on traditional values or a leftist alternative to the economic order, the old Americans would forbear from using politics as an agent of moral reform or a means of thwarting the aspirations of newly assimilated immigrants and their children.

As developed by political scientists, the theory of critical elections has become a supporting pillar of pluralist theory. If, over time, competition does not yield satisfactory adjustments of group demands and government fails in its compensatory functions, then realignment

disrupts electoral stability and political institutions become responsive to unmet needs. Critical elections thus serve as the fail-safe
mechanisms of a pluralist democracy. Although a professed critic of
pluralism, Burnham is the political scientist most responsible for explaining how realignment generates responses to political demands.
Burnham's apocalyptic vision of politics in his own time arises from
his understanding of the function performed by critical elections in
the American past. He believes that parties have become progres-
sively weaker in the twentieth century, diminishing the possibility for
yet another decisive realignment of the electorate. Without realignment, however, the preferences of ordinary Americans cannot be
translated into policy and tensions within the polity cannot be resolved. Burnham warned in his influential book, *Critical Elections
and the Mainsprings of American Politics*, published in 1970, "This continuing progression toward electoral disengagement presupposes the
disappearance at some point of system capacity for electoral realignment." Loss of "this dominant system characteristic" would effectively end democracy in America because "the electorate would have
lost what leverage it now possesses on the policy process; and it
presumably would have lost as well its constituent role in the political
system." Burnham saw as a likely possibility the "decisive triumph of
the political right . . . in the near future."[21] Writing in the more
optimistic tradition of American pluralism, Benjamin Ginsberg concluded six years later that critical realignment occurs "approximately
once in a generation," giving voters "the opportunity to alter national
policy significantly." According to Ginsberg, stability follows realignment because of voters' continuing acceptance of choices made during
the critical period. The alternation of stability and change in electoral
history means for him that "public policy is shaped to a significant degree by the behavior of voters" and that "popular majorities appear,
over time, to govern."[22]

The present study disputes these overlapping interpretations of
the encounter between Al Smith and Herbert Hoover. It denies that
prosperity per se guaranteed a Hoover victory, that the class standing
of voters had little effect on their choice of candidates, or that voter
reaction to social issues can be fused into a single dimension of conflict between two American cultures. The study also reexamines the
theory of critical elections and questions the identification of 1928 as a
turning point in political history. Ultimately, the results of my inquiry
challenge the pluralist ideology that dominates current wisdom about
the election and its aftermath.

Chapters 3 through 6 explore each of the antagonisms that allegedly sundered the nation into two Americas during the 1920s: Catholics versus Protestants, wets versus drys, immigrants versus natives, and city versus country. Analysis shows that these divisions within the citizenry were each separate and distinct (if sometimes interacting) influences on the balloting for president. Their indiscriminate combination masks much of what was going on in 1928 and distorts the meaning of the election. Religion, more than any other attribute of voters, made the coalitions supporting Smith and Hoover different from those that coalesced behind candidates in earlier or in later years. But the election cannot accurately be appraised without also grasping the separate significance of a voter's stand on prohibition, his ethnic heritage, and his place of residence.

The next two chapters focus on sources of electoral division that have been omitted from the synthesis of the two Americas. Chapter 7 probes issues relating to the voting of blacks and women, groups that responded strongly to the presidential contest, but have received little attention in accounts of the election. Chapter 8 examines economic concerns, reassessing notions of what prosperity in the 1920s signified for voters and of how economic status affected political decisions in the years before the Great Depression.

The final two chapters focus on broad questions of political theory and historical interpretation. Presidential elections are central events of American politics, often bearing the detailed imprint of the society in which they occur. The careful study of a single election can test theories of social process and illuminate the meaning of a historical era. Chapter 9 explores the origins of contemporary politics, relating critical election theory to the reality of presidential contests from 1916 to 1940. Chapter 10 summarizes the inquiry and suggests new ways of looking at politics in twentieth-century America. If an election can be understood only when projected against the horizon that defines a period of history, so may analysis of an election change our vision of that horizon.

The Strategy of Revision

Since reliable knowledge of how the electorate behaved in 1928 must be sought in the analysis of voting returns and demographic data, the success of any attempt to disclose what influenced the balloting for president is heavily dependent on its statistical methodology. The historian must draw on data that portray an electorate's diversity and deploy techniques that discriminate among disparate influences on voter decisions. Unfortunately, readers often find themselves uncritically rejecting or accepting the conclusions of a quantitative study. Ironically, while those without technical training may become lost in strange jargon and unfamiliar numerics, those with statistical expertise may be unable to mull over the results of analysis and reach independent conclusions. Historians frequently fail to disclose the strategic design of their projects, to explicate their methodology, or to present findings with appropriate indications of probable error. Indeed, some researchers have referred to rather than reported the results of analysis or have mysteriously blended into numerical estimates both statistical inferences and hunches founded on inspection of literary sources.

The remainder of this chapter describes the methodology chosen for the present study and the data that sustain its results. Attention to this discussion should guide a retracing of steps followed in the path of analysis and facilitate an evaluation of the final results. Appendix 1 discusses more technical matters of quantitative methodology.

The execution of statistical research into past politics requires the formulation of detailed plans and procedures. The strategy of historical inquiry, however, is constrained by the quantity and quality of available evidence and by the power of statistical techniques. The research design of a historical study must be adapted to the vagaries of historical data and the limitations of quantitative methodology. Historians exploring popular voting in the 1920s, for example, must rely primarily on data collected for political units.

The present study seeks to determine how different types of voters responded to the candidacies of Al Smith and Herbert Hoover. Its main goal is to reveal cleavages within the electorate and to identify patterns of change and stability. How, for example, did Protestants and Catholics, blacks and whites, city dwellers and country folk respond to the race for president in 1928? How did the divisions of that year compare to those of preceding and subsequent elections?

Unfortunately, the estimation of how voter groups responded to an election is complicated by correlations among the variables that can account for political behavior. In 1928, for example, Catholics were more likely than Protestants to be urban residents, immigrants, or first-generation Americans. Calculation of the simple relationship between religion and voter choice (for example, the proportion of Catholics and Protestants who voted for each candidate) would not disclose how religion influenced the vote for president. The effect of religion would be obscured by the effects of variables correlated with both voting behavior and religious affiliation. Differences discovered in the preferences of Protestants and Catholics could be the result of religion or of the differing ethnic compositions of these two groups. Only multivariate methods of analysis can separate and weigh the independent influences of correlated variables.

Although some previous researchers sought to discover the composition of the vote for president, their work produces substantially different portraits of the coalitions supporting Hoover and Smith. Studies by sociologists William F. Ogburn and Nell Snow Talbot and by historian Ruth Silva are the most ambitious efforts to determine how the characteristics of voters affected the choice between these two candidates. Both studies use the computation of correlation coefficients as a means of weighing the separate influences of the same five attributes—religion, prohibition sentiment, urban-rural residence, foreign-stock heritage, and voting behavior in 1920 or 1924. But the studies yield contrary conclusions. Ogburn and Talbot claim, "The wet influence is the most powerful, nearly three times as great as the Catholic, which ranks second. The Catholic influence is about twice as great as the traditional Democratic party influence, which in turn is twice as great as the rural. The foreign-born influence is quite negligible."[23] Yet Silva maintains that, after controlling for voter decisions in 1924 (Ogburn and Talbot controlled for voting in 1920), only the "foreign-born influence" was of any importance. "Religion, the vote for liquor, and metropolitanism," she insists, "proved to be insignificant correlates of Smith's strength."[24]

A fresh approach to the electorate of 1928 requires better data and more reliable methods. In several ways, my statistical study goes beyond previous efforts to learn about the vote for president. Rather than examining 38 states as does Silva, or a sample of 173 counties as do Ogburn and Talbot, the analysis includes information from all 2,058 counties located outside the formerly Confederate South.[25] This increase in the size of the sample yields more reliable estimates of how variables influenced the vote and permits analysis of regions within the United States and of counties with different levels of urbanization. The study includes many more variables of potential interest, not only expanding the scope of earlier work, but also producing a better separation of variables that are correlated with one another. The study extends from 1916 to 1940, revealing what was special about the ballots cast in 1928. For the first time, nonlinear and interactive models of behavior, voting in primary elections, and registration for parties are examined. Rather than relying on correlation measures, regression analysis, the proper technique for inferring electoral behavior from data collected for political units, is used.

Data from counties is most appropriate for a voting study of national scope. The use of information gathered for states is undesirable because large numbers of individuals are aggregated into a small number of states, producing especially high correlations among the demographic variables measured for each state. High correlations combined with a small sample accentuates the bias produced by excluding relevant variables from the analysis and precludes the reliable estimation of distinctions among the variables that are included. When states are the unit of analysis, voting cannot be compared in different regions or in urban and rural communities. Nor are important variables such as party registration, primary voting, and voter positions on prohibition available for many of the states. For purposes of the present study, county-level data is also preferable to data measured at a lower level of aggregation (for example, information from precincts or townships). Neither voting returns nor many key demographic variables are widely available for units less populous than counties.

The results of an election do not present themselves to an observer neatly carved into forms of action and corresponding sets of explanatory variables. Guided by knowledge of political theory and historical circumstance, a researcher must choose from available data measures of voter behavior and of potentially relevant features of people's background and situation. Variables are usually classified as dependent or response variables and as independent or explanatory variables. Response variables in this study are computations of the vote for president in each county (for example, Al Smith's percentage of the vote cast for president or of the potential voting population). Explanatory variables are characteristics of the counties postulated to explain variations in measures of the vote (for example, the percentage of home owners or of urban residents).

Response variables included in the study express the vote for Smith and Hoover relative to both the total vote cast in the election and the number of potential voters. These variables include the Republican and Democratic percentage of each county's voting-age population and the Democratic percentage of each county's actual voters. The Democratic percentage of the voting-age population is the proportion of adults who voted for Smith rather than voting for Hoover or not voting. The Republican percentage of the voting-age population is the proportion of adults who voted for Hoover rather than voting for Smith or not voting. Analysis of these variables reveals the relative support given to Smith and Hoover by various groups within the potential electorate. Smith's percentage of the vote actually cast measures the relative support given to him by those adults who participated in the presidential election. Analysis of this response variable discloses the preferences of various groups within the actual electorate.

Additional response variables identify the unique features of voting behavior in 1928. Several deviation variables measure differences between the vote for president in 1928 and in the three previous national elections, subtracting from percentage measures of the 1928 vote similar measures computed for one or more earlier elections. Some of the deviation variables portray differences between voting for president in 1928 and in the contiguous election of 1924, using both the percentage of the vote cast and of the potential voting population. To adjust for short-term influences, variables computed for the actual voting population also display differences between the alignments of 1928 and combined measures of the vote for president between 1916 and 1924. For purposes of comparison and contrast, two deviation variables measure differences between voting for president in 1928 and in both 1932 and 1932 to 1940. Insight into changes in voter turnout between 1924 and 1928 is offered by analysis of a response variable showing the difference between the percentage of adults turning out to vote in 1928 and 1924.

Within constraints imposed by the availability of county-level data, explanatory variables represent characteristics of the electorate isolated in models of voting behavior and in earlier exegeses of the 1928 contest. These variables form a far more inclusive set of determinants than has been analyzed in the past, including measures of religious affiliation, ethnic heritage, home ownership, economic status, urban-rural residence, regional location, age, sex, and race. For subsets of counties, explanatory variables also include the results of state-level referenda on prohibition, voting in primary elections, and party registration. Data are unavailable, however, for some variables of interest, including temporal change in economic position. Chart 2.1 reports the variables included in the study.

Chart 2.1. Definition of Variables Used in This Study

Variable Name	Definition
Dem 1928	Al Smith's percentage of the 1928 presidential vote
Dem 1928 total	Al Smith's vote as a percentage of the total adult population
Rep 1928 total	Herbert Hoover's vote as a percentage of the total adult population
Dem 1924	John W. Davis's percentage of the 1924 presidential vote
Prog 1924	Robert M. La Follette's percentage of the 1924 presidential vote
Dem/Prog 1924	Davis's percentage plus La Follette's percentage of the 1924 presidential vote
Dem 1920	James Cox's percentage of the 1920 presidential vote
Dem 1916	Woodrow Wilson's percentage of the 1916 presidential vote
Dem 1924 total	Davis's vote as a percentage of the total adult population
Prog 1924 total	La Follette's vote as a percentage of the total adult population
Dem/Prog 1924 total	Davis's percentage plus La Follette's percentage of the total adult population
Dem 1928 minus mean Dem 1916–20, Dem/Prog 1924	Smith's percentage of the 1928 vote minus the mean percentage for Wilson in 1916, Cox in 1920, and Davis and La Follette combined in 1924
Dem 1928 minus mean Dem 1916–24	Smith's percentage of the 1928 vote minus the mean percentage for Wilson in 1916, Cox in 1920, and Davis in 1924
Dem 1928 minus Dem 1924	Smith's percentage of the 1928 vote minus Davis's percentage of the 1924 vote
Dem 1928 minus Dem/Prog 1924	Smith's percentage of the 1928 vote minus Davis's and La Follette's percentage of the 1924 vote
Dem 1928 minus Prog 1924	Smith's percentage of the 1928 vote minus La Follette's percentage of the 1924 vote
Dem 1928 total minus Dem 1924 total	Smith's vote as a percentage of the total adult population minus Davis's vote as a percentage of the total adult population
Dem 1928 total minus Dem/Prog 1924 total	Smith's vote as a percentage of the total adult population minus Davis's and La Follette's percentages of the total population

Chart 2.1, continued

Variable Name	Definition
Dem 1928 total minus Prog 1924 total	Smith's vote as a percentage of the total adult population minus La Follette's vote as a percentage of the total adult population
Rep 1928 total minus Rep 1924 total	Hoover's vote as a percentage of the total adult population minus Coolidge's vote as a percentage of the total adult population
Total vote 1928 minus total vote 1924	The percentage of adults voting in 1928 minus the percentage of adults voting in 1924
Dem 1932	Franklin D. Roosevelt's percentage of the 1932 presidential vote
Dem 1936	Franklin D. Roosevelt's percentage of the 1936 presidential vote
Dem 1940	Franklin D. Roosevelt's percentage of the 1940 presidential vote
Dem 1928 minus Dem 1932	Smith's percentage of the 1928 vote minus Roosevelt's percentage of the 1932 vote
Dem 1928 minus mean Dem 1932–40	Smith's percentage of the 1928 vote minus the mean percentage for Roosevelt in 1932, 1936, and 1940
Antiprohibition	The percentage of those voting against prohibition in statewide referenda between 1926 and 1929, 471 counties
Dem prim 1928	The Democratic percentage of those voting in the primary elections of 1928, 850 counties
Dem prim 1932	The Democratic percentage of those voting in the primary elections of 1932, 850 counties
Dem prim 1936	The Democratic percentage of those voting in the primary elections of 1936, 850 counties
Dem prim 1940	The Democratic percentage of those voting in the primary elections of 1940, 850 counties
Dem prim 1928 minus Dem prim 1932	The Democratic percentage in 1928 minus the Democratic percentage in 1932 of those voting in primary elections
Dem prim 1928 minus Dem prim 1936	The Democratic percentage in 1928 minus the Democratic percentage in 1936 of those voting in primary elections
Dem prim 1928 minus Dem prim 1940	The Democratic percentage in 1928 minus the Democratic percentage in 1940 of those voting in primary elections
Dem reg 1926	The Democratic percentage of the two-party registration 1926, 223 counties

Chart 2.1, continued

Variable Name	Definition
Dem reg 1928	The Democratic percentage of the two-party registration 1928, 278 counties
Dem reg 1930	The Democratic percentage of the two-party registration 1930, 278 counties
Dem reg 1932	The Democratic percentage of the two-party registration 1932, 278 counties
Dem reg 1934	The Democratic percentage of the two-party registration 1934, 278 counties
Dem reg 1936	The Democratic percentage of the two-party registration 1936, 278 counties
Dem reg 1938	The Democratic percentage of the two-party registration 1938, 278 counties
Dem reg 1940	The Democratic percentage of the two-party registration 1940, 278 counties
Catholic	The percentage of Catholics in 1928
Jewish	The percentage of Jews in 1928
Prot church	The percentage of Protestant church members in 1928
Telephones	The percentage of families owning telephones in 1930
Taxes	The percentage of adults filing income tax returns in 1928
Housing values	Median value of homes and rented dwellings in 1930
Retail purchases	Per capita retail purchases in 1929
Radios	The percentage of families owning radios in 1930
H. S. grads	The percentage of high school graduates in 1940
Economic status	An index number measuring economic status, consisting of an unweighted sum of the six previous variables after transformation into common units
Under 35	The percentage of adults under 35 years of age in 1930
Pop change	The percentage change in population from 1920 to 1930
Owners	The percentage of families owning homes in 1930
Female	The percentage of females in 1930
Urban	The percentage of urban dwellers in 1930 (according to the census definition, used here, an urban community has 2,500 or more inhabitants)
Negro	The percentage of Negroes in 1930

Chart 2.1, continued

Variable Name	Definition
Foreign stock	The percentage of those who are white and are either foreign-born or have a foreign-born parent in 1930
Rural farm	The percentage of rural dwellers living on farms in 1930
Scandinavian	The percentage of immigrants from Scandinavia in 1930
German	The percentage of immigrants from Germany in 1930
British	The percentage of immigrants from Great Britain in 1930
British Canadian	The percentage of immigrants from Canada and of British heritage in 1930
French Canadian	The percentage of immigrants from Canada and of French heritage in 1930
Russian	The percentage of immigrants from Russia in 1930
Polish	The percentage of immigrants from Poland in 1930
Italian	The percentage of immigrants from Italy in 1930
Irish	The percentage of immigrants from Ireland in 1930

Unlike the studies by Ogburn and Talbot and by Ruth Silva, I have used regression rather than correlation analysis. Regression coefficients are more appropriate than correlation coefficients for studying voting behavior from a population of political units (in this case, counties). The investigator relying on data collected for aggregate units such as states, cities, or counties must attempt to specify the relationship among variables measured at that level. But the process of aggregating individuals into groups can introduce distortions into the relationships that pertain to individuals forming the group. An incorrect inference from aggregate-level data to individual-level behavior is generally termed an "ecological fallacy." There is no sleight of hand solution to the problems of inference subsumed under the rubric of the ecological fallacy. At best, the investigator can attempt to minimize the distortions of aggregation and assess their likely extent and direction. Regression analysis is used in this study partly because it is less sensitive to these distortions than the correlation measures often used in studies of past elections. The geographic grouping of individuals can influence the relative variation of independent and dependent variables that, in turn, influence the value of the correlation coefficient. Thus correlation measures reflect artifacts of grouping that are unrelated to the actual behavior of voters. Regression coefficients, however, are resistant to changes in relative variation produced by the process of aggregation. Moreover, temporal changes in relative variation may also occur as a result of factors extraneous to the underlying voter coalitions being explored. Again, regression coefficients, unlike measures of correlation, are resistant to such fluctuations and thus offer more accurate measures of change over time in the composition of voter coalitions.[26] Further analysis of how to infer individual-level behavior from group-level data is reserved for Appendix 1.

Multiple regression analysis can dissect the electoral coalitions of 1928 and disclose how correlated explanatory variables influenced the vote for president. For each explanatory variable, this technique generates regression coefficients that measure the amount of change in presidential voting produced by that variable after controlling for the influence of every other explanatory variable included in the analysis. Affording the researcher great flexibility, regression analysis can encompass ratio-scale variables that can be assigned a precise numerical value as well as nominal-scale variables that include only qualitative categories with no numerical designation. It can also portray various functional forms of the relationships between response variables and sets of explanatory variables. Regression models can, for example, be linear or nonlinear, additive or interactive in form.[27]

Technically, regression is the estimation of unknown values of a response variable from known values of one or more explanatory variables. For linear regression, this estimation equation has the following form: $Y = a + b_1 X_1 + b_2 X_2 + \ldots + b_n X_n + e$. Y is the response variable; each X is an explanatory variable; each b is a partial regression coefficient; a is a constant term (the value of Y when each X is set at zero); and e is an error term (representing the accuracy of the prediction equation). Partial regression coefficients are computed so that when the equation is used to estimate values of the response variable, the sum of squared deviations between actual and estimated values is at a minimum. For each observation, the difference between the actual and the estimated value is known as a residual. The examination of residual values is an important means of evaluating the adequacy of a regression equation.[28]

Each partial regression coefficient taken from a multiple regression equation estimates the direct influence of an explanatory variable on the behavior represented by the dependent variable. The values of these coefficients show the responsiveness of the dependent variable to changes from unit to unit in the explanatory variable, exclusive of the influence of other explanatory variables included in the equation. If both the dependent and the explanatory variable are measured in percentages, the partial regression coefficient reveals the percentage of change (measured in percentage points) in the dependent variable produced by a change of 1 percent in the explanatory variable. A coefficient of zero signifies that the dependent variable does not respond in either direction to changes in the explanatory variable. Coefficients greater than zero reflect varying degrees of responsiveness depending on the units of measurement. A coefficient of .37, for example, obtained for the influence of a county's percentage of Catholics on Al Smith's percentage of the presidential vote, would indicate that for every increase of 1 percent in a county's percentage of Catholics, its percentage of Smith voters should increase by .37 percent, controlling for the effects of such variables as the percentage of home owners and the percentage of urban dwellers. Assume, for example, that two counties were identical in demographic composition; if one has 1 percent more Catholics, it should have .37 percent more Democratic voters; if it has 10 percent more Catholics, it should have 3.7 percent more Democratic voters; if it has 100 percent more Catholics, it should have 37 percent more Democratic voters. Thus a regression coefficient of .37 means that when adjusting for the influence of other explanatory variables, the percentage of Catholics voting for Al Smith is 37 percentage points greater than the percentage of non-Catholics opting for his candidacy.

Partial regression coefficients represent the influence on behavior of an explanatory variable, controlling only for the effects of other explanatory variables that are included in the regression equation. If a variable that is correlated both with the response variable and with an explanatory variable is omitted from the equation, the coefficient for the included variable will reflect the influence of the excluded variable. A regression equation that is properly specified leaves out no variable that is correlated with the dependent variable and any of the explanatory variables. Discounting sampling and measurement error, the difference between the value of a regression coefficient computed from a misspecified and a properly specified model is termed specification bias. For any coefficient the magnitude and direction of bias depend on both the magnitude and direction of the relationship between the included and excluded explanatory variables and between the excluded variable and the behavior being studied. The reduction of specification bias is one important reason for including a wide range of explanatory variables in the equations estimating the vote for president.

Even when a regression equation is specified properly, partial regression coefficients calculated from empirical data only estimate the actual relationships between explanatory variables and a dependent variable. Both sampling and measurement error can produce disparities between estimated and actual values of regression coefficients. Standard errors of estimate, reported for each coefficient, permit determination of the probability that the true value of the coefficient is within a given range of the estimated value, provided that the assumptions of regression analysis are not violated by the data. The reporting of standard errors is a necessary check on the false precision that can be conveyed by numerical estimates. As the standard error increases, the likelihood decreases that the estimated value of a coefficient conforms closely to the actual value.

Calculations based on standard errors can be used to test the hypothesis that a given regression coefficient actually has a value of zero, signifying that the explanatory variable has no influence on the behavior being studied. Two types of error can arise from testing hypotheses. The initial hypothesis, termed the null hypothesis, can either be incorrectly rejected or incorrectly accepted. In classical statistics conventional decision rules are established that set the probability of falsely rejecting the null hypothesis at a fixed level, known as the level of significance. If the actual probability that the null hypothesis is true is greater than the level of significance, the null hypothesis is not rejected.

Typical significance levels used in statistical research are .05 and .01; these low probabilities indicate that, in general, null hypotheses are chosen such that their mistaken rejection is the more serious type of error. To test the null hypothesis at the .05 level that a coefficient has a value of zero, rather than a higher or lower value, requires multiplying the standard error by 1.96; if the product of this multiplication is less than the value of the coefficient, the null hypothesis can be rejected. To test the null hypothesis at the .01 level simply requires multiplying the standard error by 2.58 rather than 1.96. Given, however, that a large number of regression coefficients are computed for this study, even a significance level of .01 may not be sufficiently conservative. Obviously, the likelihood of falsely rejecting a null hypothesis increases as a greater number of hypotheses are tested.[29] One might even adopt a level of statistical significance as low as .001, which would require multiplying the standard error by 3.29. Tests of significance do not offer proof of the substantive importance of a regression estimate, but, as David Gold has noted, they are a useful check against drawing conclusions from "an observed association [that] could be generated in a given set of data by a random process."[30] In general, however, with a large number of cases, coefficients large enough to be substantively important will also be statistically significant at levels even more conservative than .001. None of my major conclusions in this study pivot on close calls of statistical significance.

For all 2,058 counties, regression models were fashioned for fifteen measures of the vote for president in 1928 and of the differences between this vote and the vote cast in other presidential years. To adjust for disparities in population, each county included in the analysis is weighted according to the square root of its adult population in 1928.[31] Each of the chapters dealing with particular issues will draw upon the results of this analysis, fully reported in Table A1.2 of Appendix 1.

To probe within these national statistics, I have separately analyzed voting behavior for seven regions of the nation and for three groups of counties with different levels of urbanization—880 counties with no urban population and an approximately equal division of the remaining counties into 591 that are less than 37.5 percent urban and 587 that are more than 37.5 percent urban. The results of these explorations will be discussed in appropriate chapters. In addition, Appendix 2 reports the coefficients for nine selected regression equations computed within each region.

I have also examined samples of counties with data that are not available for all 2,058 cases. These samples include counties from states holding referenda on prohibition between 1926 and 1929, counties from states reporting party registrants, and counties from states reporting the number of those participating in both Democratic and Republican primaries. Scrutiny of the percentage of Democratic registrants and of the percentage of those participating in the Democratic rather than the Republican primaries is especially important for re-evaluating partisan realignment in the 1920s and 1930s.

The analysis presented in Table A1.2 presumes that a regression model can portray the influence of disparate variables on the vote for president in 1928. Yet equations of different functional form may better represent voting behavior in that year. An indefinite number of equations can be fitted to any set of data, and the task of choosing the one with the best fit is extremely difficult. For our purposes we need consider only a limited number of possible forms, corresponding to theories of voter choice and to verbal descriptions of how voters responded to the presidential candidates of 1928. In addition to linear equations that add together the effects of explanatory variables, this study also considers certain nonlinear and multiplicative relationships among variables. Nonlinear relationships can reveal that the ways in which individuals are grouped into counties has a contextual effect on their behavior as voters. Catholics living in relatively homogeneous Catholic communities, for example, may have been more solidly behind Smith than those living in mixed communities of Protestants and Catholics.[32] Examination of relationships that multiply rather than add the influences of explanatory variables affords an opportunity to test the thesis that a voter's response to Smith and Hoover was conditioned by several factors that cannot be separated from one another.

The perception of politicians active in 1928 also provides a useful check on the findings of quantitative study. I have compared statistical results with evidence from surveys conducted by the Democratic National Committee, the Republican National Committee, and Franklin Delano Roosevelt. Use of these surveys liberates the historian from exclusive reliance on quotations culled from assorted manuscripts and publications. The political alignments of 1928 were sufficiently complex so that scholars limited to such quotations could find examples to support virtually any account of how voters behaved.

Anticipating two generations of scholarship, managers of the Smith and Hoover campaigns were the first to analyze divisions within the electorate of 1928. Aware that the contest would probably scramble the usual loyalties of voters, a few weeks before election day, the Democratic National Committee asked county chairmen from Kentucky to forecast the size and composition of the balloting for president. The committee sought specific numerical estimates of both

Republican and Democratic tallies in each county and of how many votes would be won or lost by the issues of religion, prohibition, and farm relief. Reports are still available from seventy-three counties, permitting computation and comparison of predictions for each issue.[33] Shortly after the election, the Republican National Committee launched a survey of its own, requesting state and local politicians throughout the nation to estimate the net gain or loss in Republican votes produced by these same three issues as well as the proportion of Republican support among Negroes, German-Americans, Italian-Americans, other foreign-born voters, women, and first-time voters. Respondents generally submitted detailed analyses of the vote in their respective bailiwicks, demonstrating a sensitivity to the nuances of building electoral coalitions.[34] While the GOP conducted this canvass, Franklin Delano Roosevelt, governor-elect of New York State, dispatched circular letters to men and women prominent in his party asking for comments on his views that an "active and aggressive party organization during the past four years" would have made the election exceedingly close and perhaps even led to a Democratic victory. He also asked for predictions of how the formation of such an organization would affect party prospects in the next congressional and presidential elections. Many of Roosevelt's respondents included in their letters analyses of the past campaign, citing specific causes for Smith's defeat in their localities. Roosevelt received enough replies to his letters so that the reasons mentioned for Smith's defeat can be charted and compared.[35]

My revised account of the contest between Al Smith and Herbert Hoover ultimately seeks to blend forms of thought often regarded as incompatible. As Richard J. Bernstein has recently noted, we often labor under the "illusion that the history of thought proceeds in terms of clearly demarcated intellectual positions—positions that can be characterized in terms of either/or." Rather, Bernstein contends, "the history of culture develops by the assertion and pursuit of what appear to be irreconcilable conflicts and oppositions. . . . In the final analysis, we are not confronted with exclusive choices." In this work, mathematical and interpretative modes of thought are both put to use for evaluating the correspondence between the ideology of American democracy and the actual functioning of the political system. Empirical analysis, interpretation, and critique thus unite to advance the humanistic goal of applying historical knowledge to the project of choosing among our future possibilities.[36]

Chapter 3

Catholics versus Protestants

Senator George W. Norris of Nebraska bolted his party in 1928 to support Al Smith. He later reflected that "close friends of years standing were so bitter" about his defection "that some of them would have delighted to cast me into the bottomless pit if the opportunity had presented itself." Religion, Norris concluded, "was the dominant thing that brought about this bitterness. Religious grievances always do bring bitterness—unreasonable, illogical bitterness. Prohibition brings pointed disagreement, but men do not turn their love of years into hatred because their friends do not agree with them regarding it."[1] Religion was undoubtedly the most sensitive emotional issue of 1928. The nomination of a Catholic by one of the nation's two major parties rekindled religious strife in the United States. Conflicts over the legitimacy of parochial education still smoldered in 1928; the Scopes "monkey" trial had ended just three years before; and at its zenith in 1924, the Ku Klux Klan had claimed several million members. In 1928, Americans avidly followed every twist and turn of what the media dubbed the "religious issue."

Despite the storm and stress produced by religion during the campaign, most historians have not considered it an especially significant influence on the vote for president. Ogburn and Talbot placed religion in second place, well behind prohibition in importance, whereas Ruth Silva concluded that neither religion nor prohibition was of any importance at all. Using literary sources, Robert Moats Miller concluded that prohibition far outweighed religion as a determinant of the vote,[2] and Paul A. Carter suggested that "the Prohibition issue, and the Klan issue, and possibly even the religious issue were surface stirrings of animosities of another kind."[3]

The Influence of Religion on the Vote for President

Contradicting these conclusions, the presidential tally of 1928 mirrors profound differences in the preferences of Catholic and Protestant voters. For all 2,058 counties outside the South, Table 3.1 displays the influence of the percentage of Catholic residents on various measures of voter choice, when controlling for the influence of other variables included in the regression analysis. The coefficients of Table 3.1 disclose that an increase in the percentage of Catholics from one county to another produces a substantial increase in Al Smith's percentage of either the presidential vote cast in each county or the adult population of each county. In contrast, an increase in the percentage of Catholics produces a moderate decrease in Hoover's percentage of the adult population. This latter coefficient indicates, as well, a disproportionately small percentage of Catholic nonvoters in 1928.

Differences in the behavior of Catholics and Protestants were the

Table 3.1. *Influence of Percentage of Catholics on Measures of the Vote for President: 2,058 Counties (in percent)**

	Regression Coefficient b	Standard Error
Dem 1928	.37	.023
Dem 1928 total	.32	.018
Rep 1928 total	−.12	.019
Dem 1928 minus Dem 1924	.11	.021
Dem 1928 minus Dem/Prog 1924	.37	.020
Dem 1928 minus Prog 1924	.62	.075
Dem 1928 total minus Dem 1924 total	.13	.013
Dem 1928 total minus Dem/Prog 1924 total	.26	.013
Dem 1928 total minus Prog 1924 total	.46	.022
Rep 1928 total minus Rep 1924 total	−.15	.014
Dem 1928 minus mean Dem 1916–24	.22	.018
Dem 1928 minus mean Dem 1916–20, Dem/Prog 1924	.31	.017
Dem 1928 minus Dem 1932	.34	.018
Dem 1928 minus mean Dem 1932–40	.39	.018

*Controlling for percentages of Urban, Foreign stock, Owners, Negro, Female, Under 35, Pop change, Jewish, Prot church, and for Economic status.

most important distinction between the alignments of voters in 1928 and in presidential contests before and since. Disparities in the preferences of these religious groups neither reflected the traditional loyalties of voters nor adumbrated their future behavior. No other division within the electorate stands out as prominently in 1928, yawning so much wider in that election than in any other contest.

Table 3.1 reports regression coefficients for deviation variables measuring differences between percentages of the vote cast in 1928 and in other presidential contests. The robust, positive coefficients for variables registering deviations between the Democratic tally in 1928 and the votes cast in other years means that relative to support for Cox, Davis, La Follette, or Roosevelt, support for Smith increased as the proportion of Catholics in any given county likewise increased. Similarly, the robust, negative coefficient for the difference between the Republican percentage of the adult population in 1928 and 1924 means that relative to support for Coolidge, support for Hoover decreased as the proportion of Catholics in any given county increased. The dissension between Catholics and Protestants that emerged in 1928 did not arise to the same extent in either earlier or later contests.

The religious alignments of 1928 may reflect either pro- or anti-Catholic voting. Did Catholics flock to the first of their brethren nominated for president by a major party? Did Protestants turn away from a Catholic aspirant for the nation's highest office? Or did both effects take place, producing a two-way flow of voters? To probe for the presence of pro- and anti-Catholic voting in 1928, the individual-level behavior of Protestants and Catholics must be inferred from the county-level percentages and the influence of religion must be isolated from the influence of such confounding variables as ethnic heritage. These objectives can be achieved by using a technique developed by Leo Goodman to infer the proportions of Catholics and Protestants voting for Smith in 1928 and for either John W. Davis or Robert M. La Follette in 1924.[4]

The results of applying Goodman's technique to the county-level data suggest that both pro- and anti-Catholic voting skewed the distribution of ballots cast for president in 1928. Compared to the combined vote of Davis and La Follette, the vote for Smith declined by approximately 11 percentage points among Protestants and increased by approximately 28 percentage points among Catholics. Catholics as well as Protestants voted their religion in 1928.

Religion powerfully influenced the choice between Herbert Hoover and Al Smith among diverse groups of Protestant voters—those from different regions of the nation, those from city and country, and those with and without formal sectarian affiliations. The analysis of seven regions of the nation, reported in Appendix 2, discloses no clear pattern of interaction between geographic location and the independent influence of Catholic-Protestant divisions on voting for president in 1928. In every region studied, an increase in a county's percentage of Catholics generated an impressive increase in Al Smith's percentage of either the presidential vote or the population of potential voters. This regional consistency prevails as well for the differences between Smith's percentage of the presidential tally and the percentages garnered by candidates in earlier and later elections. When analysis shifts from all northern counties to separate regions of the nation, religion has even a stronger influence on these various measures of the vote for president. The partitioning of counties into regions yields especially striking changes for the effect of religion on the deviation between Al Smith's percentage of the presidential vote and the percentage garnered by Democratic nominee John W. Davis in 1924. For all counties, the difference between the vote for Smith and the vote for Davis increases by .11 percent when the percentage of Catholics increases by 1 percent from one county to another. Yet in every region save the mountain states, a 1 percent increase in the percentage of Catholics results in at least a .28 percent increase in this difference. For the New England, Mid-Atlantic, West North Central, and Pacific regions, a 1 percent increase in the percentage of Catholics generates at least a .36 percent increase in the difference between support for Smith and support for Davis.

Differences in the preferences of Catholics and Protestants persist in both city and country. The study of groups of counties with varying levels of urbanization reveals little change in the regression coefficients estimating the influence of religion on various measures of the vote for president. The analysis considered, in turn, groups of counties with no urban population; with an urban population greater than zero and less than 37.5 percent; and with an urban population of 37.5 percent or more. The regression coefficients of Table 3.2 show that a gulf between Catholics and Protestants opens at every level of urbanization and for all measures of voting for president. Indeed, the only regression coefficients not significant at the .001 level are for Hoover's share of the adult population and for the difference between the vote for Smith and the vote for Davis among highly urban counties.

Table 3.2. *Rural-Urban Influence of Percentage of Catholics on Measures of the Vote for President (in percent)**

	Rural Counties (0% Urban)		Middle Urban Counties (1%–37.5% Urban)		Highly Urban Counties (Over 37.5% Urban)	
	Regression Coefficient b	Standard Error	Regression Coefficient b	Standard Error	Regression Coefficient b	Standard Error
Dem 1928	.36	.036	.49	.048	.31	.040
Dem 1928 total	.32	.028	.43	.037	.26	.033
Rep 1928 total	−.14	.031	−.15	.043	−.08	.033
Dem 1928 minus Dem 1924	.25	.029	.23	.040	.05	.046
Dem 1928 minus Dem/Prog 1924	.24	.030	.36	.041	.43	.039
Dem 1928 minus Prog 1924	.36	.047	.62	.062	.68	.059
Dem 1928 total minus Dem 1924 total	.19	.019	.23	.024	.10	.027
Dem 1928 total minus Dem/Prog 1924 total	.18	.020	.27	.024	.32	.026

Table 3.2, continued

	Rural Counties (0% Urban)		Middle Urban Counties (1%–37.5% Urban)		Highly Urban Counties (Over 37.5% Urban)	
	Regression Coefficient b	Standard Error	Regression Coefficient b	Standard Error	Regression Coefficient b	Standard Error
Dem 1928 total minus Prog 1924 total	.31	.032	.47	.042	.48	.040
Rep 1928 total minus Rep 1924 total	-.14	.023	-.15	.027	-.11	.026
Dem 1928 minus mean Dem 1916–24	.26	.027	.33	.036	.18	.038
Dem 1928 minus mean Dem 1916–20, Dem/Prog 1924	.26	.025	.37	.032	.31	.034
Dem 1928 minus Dem 1932	.16	.022	.35	.038	.40	.034
Dem 1928 minus mean Dem 1932–40	.24	.024	.48	.034	.42	.037

*Controlling for percentages of Urban, Rural Farm (in rural counties), Foreign stock, Owners, Negro, Female, Under 35, Pop Change, Jewish, Prot church, and for Economic status.

Protestants without formal church affiliations seemed to be as moved by the religious issue as members of Protestant churches. Table 3.3 reports how measures of voting for president respond to changes from county to county in the percentage of Protestant church members when controlling for other variables, including the percentage both of Catholics and of Jews. The table reveals that a 1 percent increase in the members of Protestant churches results in a .17 percent increase in Al Smith's percentage of the presidential vote. This finding suggests that Protestants belonging to a church were more likely to vote for Al Smith than their counterparts with no church affiliation. But an increase in the percentage of Protestant church members from one county to another generates no perceptible increase or decrease in the difference between Smith's percentage of the presidential vote and the percentages of earlier Democratic contenders. Rather than showing that nominal Protestants were more

Table 3.3. *Influence of Percentage of Protestant Church Members on Measures of the Vote for President: 2,058 Counties (in percent)* *

	Regression Coefficient b	Standard Error
Dem 1928	.17	.021
Dem 1928 total	.18	.016
Rep 1928 total	.03	.018
Dem 1928 minus Dem 1924	−.02	.019
Dem 1928 minus Dem/Prog 1924	−.02	.019
Dem 1928 minus Prog 1924	.20	.030
Dem 1928 total minus Dem 1924 total	.01	.012
Dem 1928 total minus Dem/Prog 1924 total	−.01	.012
Dem 1928 total minus Prog 1924 total	.17	.020
Rep 1928 total minus Rep 1924 total	.01	.013
Dem 1928 minus mean Dem 1916–24	.03	.017
Dem 1928 minus mean Dem 1916–20, Dem/Prog 1924	.03	.015
Dem 1928 minus Dem 1932	.07	.016
Dem 1928 minus mean Dem 1932–40	.12	.016

*Controlling for percentages of Urban, Foreign stock, Owners, Negro, Female, Under 35, Pop change, Jewish, Catholic, and for Economic status.

hostile to a Catholic candidate than their counterparts who belonged to churches, statistical analysis suggests that church members were more likely than nonmembers to opt for Smith because of a stronger, traditional allegiance to the Democratic party. The negligible values of regression coefficients for the deviation variables indicate little difference in how the two groups reacted to religious turmoil in 1928.

Despite the presence of control variables, regression analysis may still overstate the importance of religious preferences for voter decisions in 1928. The analysis includes no measures of what voters thought about laws imposing abstinence from alcoholic beverages. Several historians have suggested that apparent religious alignments of the election were produced by the proclivity of Catholics to oppose and of Protestants to support national prohibition. Smith, of course, advocated relaxation of the prohibition laws, whereas Hoover defended the status quo.

Data from state-level referenda can be used to assess how religion affected presidential voting independent of the correlation between religious preferences and positions on the continuation of prohibition. To the extent that differences in Protestant and Catholic voting resulted from conflicts over prohibition, controlling for prohibition sentiment should narrow the gap between Protestants and Catholics. Adding to the regression equations a variable measuring the percentage of voters opposing prohibition in state-level referenda should deflate the value of the coefficients that gauge how measures of voting behavior respond to changes from one county to another in the percentage of Catholics. For response variables measuring the vote for Smith or the differences between this vote and that of other candidates, regression coefficients for the percentage of Catholics should become less positive when prohibition is added to the equation. For response variables measuring Hoover's percentage of the adult population and the difference between this percentage and that of Calvin Coolidge in 1924, regression coefficients should become less negative when prohibition is added to the equations.

Using the results of prohibition referenda taken between 1926 and 1929 for all 471 counties in the states of New York, Illinois, Missouri, Wisconsin, Colorado, and California, Table 3.4 reports regression coefficients for the percentage of Catholics, first, when the prohibition variable is omitted from the regression equations, and second, when the prohibition variable is included in the regression equations. The table reveals that although the inclusion of the percentage of those voting against prohibition does cut somewhat into the influence of religion, every measure of the vote for president remains responsive to variations from county to county in the percentage of Catholics. Changes in the values of regression coefficients after addition of the prohibition variable range from .02 to .16, with a mean of .08. Whether controlling for views on prohibition or not,

Table 3.4. *Influence of Percentage of Catholics on Measures of the Vote for President, Including and Excluding the Percentage Opposing Prohibition: 471 Counties (in percent)**

	Antiprohibition Included		Antiprohibition Excluded	
	Regression Coefficient b	Standard Error	Regression Coefficient b	Standard Error
Dem 1928	.39	.045	.50	.043
Dem 1928 total	.29	.034	.38	.033
Rep 1928 total	−.26	.039	−.28	.036
Dem 1928 minus Dem 1924	.19	.045	.24	.043
Dem 1928 minus Dem/Prog 1924	.35	.044	.44	.042
Dem 1928 minus Prog 1924	.55	.075	.71	.072
Dem 1928 total minus Dem 1924 total	.18	.029	.23	.027
Dem 1928 total minus Dem/Prog 1924 total	.28	.032	.36	.031
Dem 1928 total minus Prog 1924 total	.40	.054	.50	.052
Rep 1928 total minus Rep 1924 total	−.19	.027	−.23	.025
Dem 1928 minus mean Dem 1916–24	.24	.035	.34	.034
Dem 1928 minus mean Dem 1916–20, Dem/Prog 1924	.29	.029	.40	.030
Dem 1928 minus Dem 1932	.26	.034	.36	.033

*Controlling for percentages of Urban, Foreign stock, Owners, Negro, Female, Under 35, Pop change, Jewish, Prot church, and for Economic status.

measures of voting for president in these 471 counties generally are more responsive to variation in the percentage of Catholics than in the sample of all northern counties. Even when the percentage of those opposing prohibition is added to the regression equations, comparison of Tables 3.1 and 3.3 discloses that changes from county to county in the percentage of Catholics have a stronger influence on seven of the thirteen dependent variables among the referendum counties than among all 2,058 counties included in the analysis.

As noted in Chapter 2, historians have insisted that researchers cannot separate the variables that influenced the choice between Hoover and Smith. Rather, they maintain that a voter's decision was conditioned by several characteristics that cumulated into an impression of each candidate. These characteristics—urban-rural residence, ethnic heritage, religion, positions regarding moral legislation— divided the nation into two Americas and formed the lines of opposition in the presidential election of 1928. If this model were correct, then the variables measuring these characteristics should cumulate into a single complex in which their individual effects cannot be distinguished.

This verbal model advanced by historians can be tested roughly through the quantitative analysis of election returns. Any one of several results would be consistent with a quantitative interpretation of scholars' accounts of the election. First, each of the variables included in the model could have approximately the same influence on the vote for president in 1928. Second, the variables could be so highly correlated with each other that their separate effects could not be reliably estimated. Third, a representation of voter behavior that multiplies the influences of variables could better explain the election than one that adds their separate effects. Fourth, a quantitative model that incorporates interactions among variables could show that the joint influence of urbanism, religion, ethnic heritage, and prohibition is appreciably greater than would be anticipated from adding their independent effects. In each case, statistical analysis fails to sustain these interpretations of what historians have argued about the presidential election of 1928.

The results of analysis presented thus far are sufficient to reject both the first and second possibilities. Strands of the vote for president can be separated and studied individually. The standard errors of regression coefficients from the various equations of Table A1.2 in Appendix 1 are low and the coefficients vary considerably in value.

Moreover, the coefficients show that measures of the vote for president also respond to several variables not included in versions of the election based upon the thesis of the two Americas. More detailed explication of these findings will be given in each of the following chapters.

To test the third hypothesis that a multiplicative (i.e., $y = ax_1^{b_1}x_2^{b_2}$) rather than an additive equation (i.e., $Y = a + b_1X_1 + b_2X_2$) best portrays the behavior of voters, alternative models were computed and used to predict variation from county to county in all fourteen measures of the 1928 vote and of differences between this vote and the vote cast in other elections. Using logarithmic transformation to estimate coefficients of the multiplicative model, a simplified regression model was computed that included variables measuring economic status, home ownership, Catholicism, ethnic background, and urban-rural residence.[5] The results of analysis are again sufficient to reject the hypothesis. For all 2,058 counties, the additive rather than the multiplicative model better predicts variation in every one of the response variables. When a voter's position on prohibition is added to the equations, analysis further shows that, for all but two of the variables (percent Democratic 1928 minus percent Democratic 1924 and percent Democratic 1928 total minus percent 1924 total), the additive model again proved to be superior.

The fourth hypothesis is the most difficult to test; its evaluation requires fashioning a model of voting for president that accommodates both additive and interactive effects. Since there are several hundred possible interactions among the eleven explanatory variables represented in the equations of Table A1.2, the analysis focuses only on those interactions that would be emphasized in the verbal model now being translated into quantitative form. Looking at Smith's percentage of the presidential vote and the deviation of this vote from the average vote of the three previous Democratic candidates, interaction models were computed that considered all possible interactions between religion, foreign-stock heritage, and urban-rural residence. For the 471 counties with data from state-level referenda, the variable measuring prohibition sentiment was also included. If the hypothesis in question were correct, the joint influences on voter behavior of the potentially interacting variables should be less positive than expected from the additive model when their values are low and more positive than would be expected from the linear models when their values are high. The results of analysis, reported in Appendix 1, Tables A1.3 and

A1.4, fail to sustain this prediction, indicating that these variables do not cumulate into a mutually dependent set of characteristics that conditioned responses to Smith and Hoover. The joint effects of religion, foreign-stock heritage, and urban-rural residence for the entire sample, and of these variables plus opposition to prohibition for referenda counties, are not greater than would be expected from the additive model when they all have high values. Rather, the results suggest only the presence of interaction in the expected direction between religion and foreign-stock heritage.

The tentative nature of the analysis of interaction suggests caution in emphasizing the importance of interaction between religion and ethnic background. Nonetheless, this interaction is not inexplicable; it may derive both from the process by which Catholics were assimilated into American life and from the anti-Catholic heritage of Protestant immigrants to the United States. Catholics with a long lineage in America may have been less responsive to a coreligionist seeking the presidency than were immigrant or first-generation Catholics. Perhaps religion was less central to the identity of Catholics with deep roots in American soil, the Protestant world less strange and foreboding, and the pain of discrimination less immediate and intense. In his now classic study, *Assimilation in American Life*, Milton M. Gordon argues that successively after the first generation, Catholic immigrants became more attuned to the "core culture" of their adopted land and more likely to have personal relationships with those of different religious and ethnic backgrounds.[6] Moreover, many of the Protestant immigrants who continued to pour into the United States in the late nineteenth and early twentieth centuries feared and distrusted Roman Catholics. The anti-Catholicism of the Scandinavians, German Lutherans, Dutch, and English Canadians was grounded in the Old World experience and may have screened out aspects of Al Smith's candidacy that otherwise would have appealed to an immigrant or a first-generation American. Respondents both to Franklin D. Roosevelt's correspondence and to the Republican survey remarked on the anti-Catholic voting of Protestant immigrants. The Republican National Committee, for example, noted in its summary of survey returns, "There was a line of demarcation between German Catholics and German Lutherans, the former being divided and the latter being almost solidly Republican."[7] Chapter 4 will further consider the behavior of individual nationality groups.

Evidence from surveys of individual opinion corroborates the finding that religion was an important voting issue in 1928. David Burner argues persuasively in *The Politics of Provincialism* that survey research, which has documented a notable pro- and anti-Catholic vote in the presidential election of 1960, suggests that similar alignments must have formed in 1928.[8] But a historian need not travel so far afield for survey evidence relevant to deciding how religion affected voting decisions in 1928. The results of small-group surveys roughly contemporary with the election also sustain the conclusion that religion skewed the vote for president in 1928.[9] Moreover, when, in 1940, the Gallup Poll asked a national cross section of likely voters if they would support a qualified Catholic candidate for president, 33 percent said they would not.[10]

Pundits from both parties also testified to the importance of religious differences in 1928. Analyses of the presidential election offered in response to letters dispatched by FDR generally agree that the religious issue undercut support for Smith. Many Democratic politicians insisted that anti-Catholicism robbed Smith of a likely victory in their states and localities. Despite the obvious bias of these sources, in private correspondence Democratic politicians probably would not have fabricated reports of religious conflict. Democrats who, in the aftermath of Hoover's decisive victory, sought to guard against the nomination of another Catholic may, however, have exaggerated the importance of anti-Catholic voting.

Several of the Democratic leaders writing to Roosevelt expressed shock at finding that religious opposition to Smith was not confined to strains of Protestantism traditionally associated with anti-Catholic agitation. W. H. O'Keefe, for example, editor of the *Democratic-Sun* of Greenville, Tennessee, was amazed to find religious prejudice surfacing among members of the more tolerant Protestant sects: "It is our conviction that Governor Smith's prohibition views cut no ice in his defeat, that the objection was solely on account of his religion. This fact was verified through thousands of instances. . . . I was literally knocked flat to find that Episcopalians, of whom I had expected better things, were just as prejudiced and bitter as any Methodist or Baptist could be."[11]

Table 3.5 reports the number of times that Roosevelt's correspondents cited a particular issue as a cause of Smith's defeat. These Democratic politicians clearly point the accusing finger at Al Smith's Catholicism and his opposition to the prohibition laws. Religion and prohibition comprise 88.5 percent of all causes cited by the respon-

Table 3.5. Reasons Cited for Smith's Defeat in Replies to Franklin D. Roosevelt's Circular Letter

State	Religion	Prohibition	Tammany	Prosperity	Other
Arizona	2	2		1	
California	6	5	5	1	
Colorado	8	1			1
Connecticut	2	1	1		
Delaware	1				
Idaho	3	1	1		
Illinois	19	14	1		1
Indiana	3	2			
Iowa	11	7	1		
Kansas	6	7		1	2
Kentucky	7	7			
Maine	2	1			
Maryland	6	3			
Michigan	5	4			2
Minnesota	6	6	1		
Missouri	10	4	2	2	
Montana	5	3	3		
Nebraska	3	7	1		
Nevada		1		1	
New Hampshire	2				
New Jersey	3	3		1	
New Mexico	3	1			1
North Dakota	1				
Ohio	10	3	2		
Oklahoma	7	3		1	2
Oregon	4	2			
Pennsylvania	12	5			1
Rhode Island	3	1			
South Dakota	3	1			
Tennessee	9	7	1		
Utah		1			
Vermont					
Washington	6	2			1
West Virginia	9	4			
Wisconsin	9	1			1
Wyoming	2	2			
Totals	188	112	19	8	12
Percentages	55.5	33.0	5.6	2.4	3.5

dents, with religion alone comprising 55.5 percent. Although these results do not necessarily represent the views of all Democratic politicians, they do reveal the thinking of a large number of those who had worked for the election of Al Smith and were concerned with the party's future. Their conclusions about the 1928 contest are yet another indication that Protestant voters hesitated to support a Catholic candidate for the presidency.

Although the Republican National Committee was most interested in learning how Catholics voted in 1928 and did not ask about the behavior of Protestants, respondents from Indiana, New Jersey, Los Angeles, Missouri, Cleveland, and Rhode Island all mentioned Protestant voting, unanimously concluding that the party received anti-Catholic votes. The report from Missouri, for example, noted that "religion cut a considerable figure in the returns," producing both gains and losses for the party: "In Catholic centers there were many Catholics evidently influenced by the church question. In Protestant centers there was fully as large a percentage influenced by the religious question." The New Jersey report, however, claimed, "The religious issue gave us a big net gain inasmuch as a goodly number of Catholics in both parties voted for Hoover."

A survey of Democratic county chairmen from Kentucky, conducted by state leader Alben W. Barkley, is another contemporary source that helps to untwine religion and prohibition. A few weeks before the election, at the request of the Democratic National Committee, Barkley asked county chairmen to estimate the likely Democratic and Republican vote totals in each of their jurisdictions. He also asked for estimates of the gains and losses that Smith and Hoover could expect from the impact of religion and prohibition. Specifically, Barkley asked the following four questions on these two issues: "How many votes will the Republicans lose on account of religion?" "How many votes will the Democrats lose on account of religion?" "How many votes will Republicans lose on account of Wet and Dry question?" "How many votes will Democrats lose on account of Wet and Dry question?"

Unique among surveys coeval with the election of 1928, the Kentucky canvass reports quantitative estimates of how reactions to religion and prohibition skewed the vote for president. As Chart 3.1 reveals, the Kentucky results accord remarkably well with the statistical findings of this study, showing that independent of prohibition, religion still cost the party a substantial proportion of the voters they

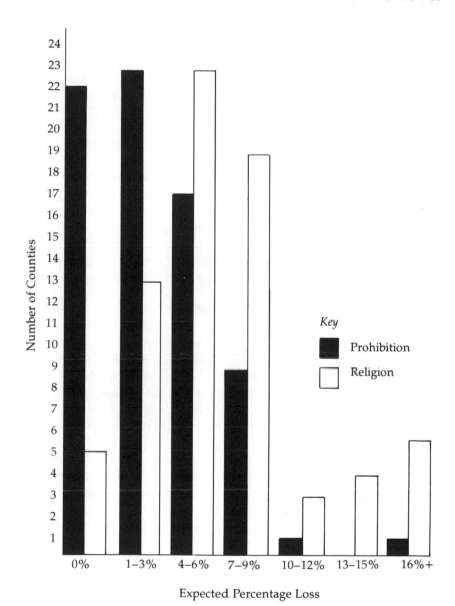

Chart 3.1. Expected Democratic Losses from Religion and Prohibition Reported by 73 County Chairman, Kentucky

otherwise could count on. The chart further discloses that Kentucky leaders expected religion to have a much greater impact on the Democratic vote than the wet and dry question. Of the seventy-three county chairmen whose reports are available, twenty-two expected not to lose a single vote in their county because of prohibition; an additional twenty-three expected losses of between 1 and 3 percent, whereas only two expected losses of 10 percent or more. In contrast, only five of the chairmen expected no losses from the religious issue and only thirteen expected losses of between 1 and 3 percent. Another thirteen expected religion to cost them 10 percent or more of the anticipated Democratic vote. The expected mean loss from prohibition is 3.1 percent with a median loss of 2.3 percent. The expected mean loss from religion is 6.9 percent with a median loss of 6.1 percent. When the estimates of all the chairmen are pooled into a single total, the expected mean loss from prohibition is 3.8 percent of the vote that would otherwise be cast for the Democrats and the expected mean loss from religion is 7.3 percent.

Given the small number of Catholics in Kentucky, the county chairmen agreed that religion would cost the Republicans very few votes. Forty-three of the chairmen expected the GOP to lose not a single vote because of religion; only eleven expected losses of greater than 2 percent. The expected mean loss to the Republicans from religion is 1.2 percent with a median loss of 0.1 percent. When the estimates for all counties are pooled into a single total, the expected mean loss is 1.4 percent of the vote that would otherwise be cast for the GOP.

The chairmen anticipated that the prohibition issue would cut more deeply into the Republican vote. Twenty-four of them expected no Republican losses from this issue, but thirty-one expected losses of greater than 2 percent. The expected mean loss for prohibition is 2.9 percent with a median loss of 2.3 percent. When all reports are pooled, the expected mean loss to the Republicans from prohibition is 3.8 percent of their otherwise anticipated total—the identical percentage loss predicted for the Democrats.[12]

As a counterargument to the assertion that Protestants spurned Smith because he was Catholic, both contemporary observers and historians have claimed that Thomas J. Walsh of Montana, a rural, western, dry Catholic, would have been perfectly acceptable to Protestant voters.[13] Yet Senator Walsh himself privately cast doubt on this idea after his experience with the nominating process: "I am very sincerely appreciative of the opinion you express of my merits, and wish I were altogether worthy of what you say of me. The view that I would have carried every southern state in 1928, had I been the nominee instead of Governor Smith, has often been expressed and it may be that I would. At the same time when I would, as I thought, have made an excellent foil against the onrushing Smith flood in 1928, no southern state exhibited any disposition to send delegates to the convention instructed for me."[14]

The Republican National Committee's canvass of party leaders is the only important source of professional political opinion on pro-Catholic voting in the presidential election of 1928. The Republicans were especially interested in calculating opposition gains among Catholic voters and asked local leaders whether Smith received a "solid Catholic vote." Again, these survey results sustain the findings of statistical study. Although several respondents assured the committee that Smith did not receive a "solid Catholic vote," they virtually all agreed that religion yielded the governor a substantial number of Catholic ballots.

Multiple sources of evidence thus document a notable anti-Catholic and pro-Catholic vote in the presidential election of 1928. The evidence also suggests that religious opposition to Al Smith was not confined to evangelical Protestants, to country folk, or to members of Protestant churches. Although many more evangelical Protestants lived in the border states and the Midwest than in the Northeast, the vote for president in 1928 was strongly responsive to the religious composition of counties in every region studied. The percentage of Catholics in a county actually had a greater effect on the behavior of voters in the New England and Mid-Atlantic states than on those in the border states. Letters from Roosevelt's correspondents and reports to the Republican National Committee indicate that opposition to Smith was not confined to certain types of Protestants, and statistical analysis demonstrates that, independent of control variables, Protestant church members and Protestants without formal church affiliation were equally antagonistic to Smith's bid for the presidency.

Religion as a Campaign Issue

The prominence of religion in the statistical tables is matched by its preeminence in the campaign for president. The prospect of a Catholic seriously seeking the presidency was an intriguing new feature of American politics. For anti-Catholic Protestants, Smith's nomination presented the chance to join a noble crusade against a tangible menace. For Catholics, a Smith victory seemed likely to enhance their prestige, whereas his defeat threatened the status they had already achieved. For civil libertarians, the nomination of a Catholic provided a means of gauging the tolerance of Protestant America. For all Americans, the fusion of religion and politics offered an endless source of fascinating speculation and dispute.[15]

Anti-Catholic opponents of Al Smith were the driving force behind the religious controversies of 1928. Although Protestants agitated against the election of a Catholic president, Catholics did not dare to launch a counteroffensive. Catholic leaders had little to say about how to vote in the presidential campaign, and they invariably denied the relevance of religious considerations.[16]

Even if church leaders yearned for the election of Al Smith, they were wise to refrain from courting Catholic support for the New York governor. Protestants who opposed the election of Roman Catholics to public office frequently contended that the church was an organized political force seeking to dominate America both spiritually and politically. If those identified as Catholic spokesmen had urged their coreligionists to vote for Al Smith, they would have added credibility to this argument and jeopardized the future prospects of Catholic aspirants to public office.

Protestants were far less reluctant to mingle religion and politics. Anti-Catholic arguments against the election of Governor Smith were a common feature of the presidential competition. Both Protestant clergy and laymen argued that Catholics were inherently unfit for the presidency or, at least, that a candidate's Catholicism should be counted heavily against him.

The anti-Catholic campaign against Al Smith had three distinct dimensions. First, it included purely scurrilous propaganda. For professional mongers of hate, the campaign of 1928 offered a unique opportunity to capture a national audience. They invoked images of an army of bloated, liquor-sodden priests tramping into Washington behind Al Smith's inaugural carriage. They portrayed the governor as a willing instrument of the pope: the candidate of the Vatican rather than of the Democratic party. "The real issue in this campaign," thundered James S. Vance, general manager of the *Fellowship Forum*, is "PROTESTANT AMERICANISM VERSUS RUM AND ROMANISM. . . . With righteousness superseded by Rum and Romanism, America becomes a vassal state of the Vatican and a stink-slide of booze and corruption . . . our young men and women will face religious servitude and death dealing poison." America must decide, he admonished, whether "to remain a Nation of thoroughbred Americans or to be turned into a dumping ground of the scum of Europe and Asia."[17] Anti-Catholic propagandists also offered a curious lesson in American history, citing Catholics as the assassins of Abraham Lincoln, James A. Garfield, William McKinley, and a host of lesser-known political figures. And they expertly attempted to arouse the erotic impulse of the rigidly moral Protestant: Catholics in general and Smith in particular were accused of almost every conceivable sexual and moral perversion.

The familiar contingent of anti-Catholic scandal sheets disseminated such propaganda: the *Fellowship Forum*, the *New Menace*, the *Railsplitter*, the *Protestant*, the *Lash*, the *Crusader of Florida*, and others. Warning that Smith's nomination threatened the survival of Protestantism in America, these journals asked their loyal readers for contributions to the crusade against him. Using funds that flowed in during the campaign, the editors greatly increased the circulation of their publications, frequently distributing them free of charge as a public service and sending them through the mails to people in communities considered to be particularly susceptible to their message. A Democratic leader from Fort Dodge, Iowa, reported to Franklin D. Roosevelt that in his state "the *Fellowship Forum*, probably the vilest sheet in existence, flooded the mails for months before the elections." Roosevelt observed a similar situation in his home town of Hyde Park, New York, writing that "practically all" the families served through the local post office "began in early July to receive copies of the *Fellowship Forum*, the *New Menace* and one or two similar publications."[18] The *Commonweal*, which kept track of anti-Catholic agitation, estimated that "the *Fellowship Forum* and the *New Menace*, which under ordinary circumstances lead a precarious hand-to-mouth existence . . . are now circulating upward of 600,000 copies weekly, most of them free."[19]

A profusion of anonymously published leaflets, handbills, placards, posters, and pamphlets supplemented the efforts of established journals to alert America to the menace of Rome. This literature was sent through the mails, passed out from hand to hand, and deposited on doorsteps and porches. Like the anti-Catholic journals, these printed materials were often targeted to areas that seemed particularly receptive to anti-Catholic appeals.[20]

Although impossible to measure, the verbal dissemination of anti-Catholic slander was probably important. Some individuals traveled from community to community inculcating anti-Catholic sentiment; their number is unknown. Even more difficult to assess are the activities of the individuals who voluntarily circulated their ideas within their local communities—the most genuine whispers of the so-called "whispering campaign." Radio joined the bandwagon of religious bigotry to some extent. Under the guise of education and public affairs, a few radio stations broadcast the rankest sort of anti-Catholic propaganda. Finally, in many states Democratic leaders and other observers reported that Protestant ministers were inciting anti-Catholicism from the pulpit.[21]

The second category of anti-Catholic activity during the 1928 campaign was the more temperate, but still primarily emotional, appeals of the Protestant press and clergy. Among the more prominent contributors to this facet of the crusade against Al Smith were four bishops of the Methodist Episcopal church, South; Albert Dieffenbacher, editor of the *Christian Register*; John Roach Straton, pastor of the Calvary Baptist Church in New York City; Reverend Deets Pickett, secretary of the Board of Temperance, Prohibition, and Public Morals of the Methodist Episcopal church, North; Hugh K. Walker, moderator of the General Assembly of Presbyterians; and the Convention of the Lutheran Editors of America. The statement of the Convention of Lutheran Editors illustrates these appeals:

Claims, teachings and principles of the Roman Catholic Church . . . are antagonistic to and irreconcilable with the fundamental principles set forth in the constitution of our country concerning the separation of Church and State, such as the opposition by this Church to the toleration by the state of any religion other than the Roman Catholic; its denial of the right of individual judgement, liberty of conscience and freedom of worship; the claim that the worldly government is in duty bound not only to assist, support and protect exclusively the Roman Catholic Church, but to suppress, if necessary by force every other religion.[22]

The Lutheran Convention represented editors whose publications reached over two million readers.

One Protestant divine, Henry C. Culbertson, even argued that the American people must reject Al Smith to protect the interests of the Catholic church. Were Smith to be elected, Culbertson reasoned, "every fault or failure of his administration would be blamed on that [Catholic] Church." Moreover, because of Smith's opposition to prohibition, the Catholic church would be burdened with "the tremendous odium of having shared in lowering the public standards of our nation on the question of drink." Culbertson called for "prominent Catholic prelates to come out . . . so strongly against Smith on this issue that no one will dare question the good faith and high ideals of that great church."[23]

The third category of anti-Catholic appeals includes arguments founded on a scholarly analysis of what the nation could expect from sending a Catholic to the White House. The only commentaries that clearly fall into this category are the arguments of Charles Marshall following up an earlier exchange of letters with Al Smith, a similar publication by Winfred Ernest Garrison, and some essays appearing in the more scholarly Protestant journals.[24] But these sources did not take the final step of specifically addressing their objections to Al Smith, the Catholic governor of New York State, rather than to the Roman hierarchy or some stereotype of the Catholic layman. Some commentators maintained, however, that despite Al Smith's own views and his record in public life, he still represented Roman Catholicism in the United States. His election, they claimed, would increase the prestige and power of Roman Catholicism, a legitimate concern for those who regarded Catholic doctrine and practice as antithetical to American democracy. In an editorial published on 18 October, the *Christian Century* argued that Protestants had good reasons for rejecting any Catholic candidate for president: "The reasons why Catholics wish to elect Smith are the reasons why Protestant-minded Americans do not wish him elected. They cannot look with unconcern upon the seating of a representative of an alien culture, of a medieval Latin mentality, of an undemocratic hierarchy and of a foreign potentate. . . . How preposterous to call him a 'bigot' who is intelligent enough to let his vote be determined by so deep-going a cleavage in social idealism!"[25]

The campaign organizations could not, of course, remain sheltered from the storms of religious conflict. Although a great many votes may have hinged on reactions to Al Smith's Catholicism, neither party could seek support on explicitly religious grounds. Republicans could not solicit ballots from those hostile to Catholics, and Democrats could not ask Catholics to unite behind the candidacy of a coreligionist. Yet each party was able to devise more subtle strategy for exploiting the passions aroused by the injection of religion into a presidential campaign.

Public statements by Republican politicians, including their presidential candidate, seem to reflect a strategic decision to risk only mild repudiations of religious bigotry, while shifting the onus of intolerance to the opposition party. In his acceptance speech, Herbert Hoover endorsed religious tolerance in the following terms: "In this land dedicated to tolerance we still find outbreaks of intolerance. I come of Quaker stock. My ancestors were persecuted for their beliefs. Here they sought and found religious freedom. By blood and conviction I stand for religious tolerance both in act and in spirit. The glory of our American ideals is the right of every man to worship God according to the dictates of his own conscience."[26] Although Hoover may have been personally tolerant, this general statement only minimally expressed the political necessity to oppose religious bigotry. Hoover could not have sought anti-Catholic support, and silence would have outraged voters committed to religious toleration. Moreover, anti-Catholics could read Hoover's statement as a veiled reference to the supposed threat of a Catholic-imposed state church. The statement affirms religious freedom, but does not specify the source of the present danger to this freedom. Those objecting to Smith's religion had insisted that the threat to tolerance came not from Protestantism, but from Roman Catholicism, an inherently missionary religion. Any faithful Catholic, they warned, would use the presidency to suppress competing religions and advance the spread of Catholicism in the United States.

Hoover planned to say nothing more about religion during the ensuing campaign, but he encountered stiff criticism from those who believed that the situation demanded more forceful and more pointed denunciations of religious bigotry. In a confidential statement to the press corps on 21 September, Hoover justified his restraint by pleading that intolerance "feeds on its own flames" and "the very ventilation of intolerance . . . tends to fan that flame." Reticence was the most effective weapon that could be deployed against Catholic and Protestant zealots. In the same statement, Hoover asserted that he suffered from the whispering campaign "far more than Governor Smith" and that religious intolerance was primarily a manifestation of the internal politics of the Democratic party.[27]

Hoover either had deceived himself or adopted a politically convenient pose. Although the Republican nominee was not immune from obloquy, Al Smith was the target of a far more widespread, intense, and publicized campaign of personal slander. As well as being a dispassionate master of public relations, Hoover possessed a re-markable capacity for self-delusion. Students of Hoover's life have well documented his extraordinary proclivity to recast events to fit his own predilections. Hoover found misjudgment and failure in-tolerable; they had to be exorcised by ingenious explanation or magi-cally transmuted into wisdom and triumph. Nor were achievement and success enough; they had to be ballooned into almost super-human accomplishments. As Joan Hoff Wilson, a generally sympa-thetic biographer, has remarked, "His capacity for self-delusion where failure was involved or exaggeration of what was only average achievement, can be documented in every stage of his private and public development."[28]

Policies of the Republican campaign raise further questions about the sincerity of Herbert Hoover's attempt to dampen the flames of intolerance. Despite the lack of detailed records relating the closed-door activities of Republican strategists, some conclusions can be ex-tracted from available information. The evidence suggests that Hoo-ver and the Republican leadership did not shrink from sponsoring personal attacks on Al Smith and probably took part in efforts to gain anti-Catholic votes.

Although Hoover insisted that the national leadership of the GOP should not be associated with personal innuendo directed against Smith, he did not hesitate to vilify the governor through ostensibly independent spokesmen. Hoover, for instance, ordered that a twelve-thousand-word pamphlet on Tammany Hall prepared by the Repub-lican National Committee be issued instead by a group of bolting Democrats. According to Henry J. Allen, publicity director of the Republican campaign, Hoover had decided that "it would be better to let the attack on Tammany originate elsewhere." Similarly, at Hoover's direction, the national committee provided information and encouragement for William Allen White's attempt to portray Smith as a friend of gambling and prostitution. Publicly, the committee disclaimed "any relationship between the Republican National Com-mittee and the charges levelled against him by William Allen White." The committee asserted that "no member of the Republican National Organization had either communication or knowledge of Mr. White's intention or his action. . . . Instructions of the Republican National Committee are to engage in no personal attack and that Committee or its organization have not done so." White, however, had specifically informed Hoover of his success at "pulling Smith over the first pages by his pants." White disclosed in his private correspondence that "I have a letter from Hoover written after my first blast obviously approving it and a letter from Work after my second barrage saying 'Good, more strength to your elbow.' Also a line saying he had arranged for the expert to get the data I used."[29]

The national committee also sponsored the political sorties of Mabel Walker Willebrandt, assistant attorney general for prohibition enforcement. In 1928, Willebrandt was the highest ranking woman official in the executive branch of the federal government. She had been recommended for placement in the attorney general's office in 1921 by Senator Hiram Johnson of California. After becoming an assistant attorney general, Willebrandt joined forces with Herbert Hoover, helping to manage his campaign for the Republican nomination and serving as a political operative in both official and unofficial capacities. In the summer of 1928, for example, Willebrandt traveled to Mississippi to obtain a federal indictment for corruption against Percy Howard, one of the black Republican leaders Hoover sought to purge from the GOP. Some male politicians felt that the assistant attorney general's ambition and political activism were unseemly for a member of her sex. In 1928, her erstwhile benefactor Senator Johnson wrote that "she is the perfect type of woman as I have found woman in politics—ambitious, mad for publicity, bitter, deceitful, utterly without principle and wholly treacherous."[30] During the 1928 campaign, Willebrandt appeared before Protestant church groups raising a hue and cry against the election of Al Smith. Although she indicted Smith for his wetness rather than his Catholicism, she reviled the governor for cooperating with the underworld, flouting federal law, and nullifying the Constitution.

Willebrandt's correspondence with Hubert Work, chairman of the Republican National Committee, reveals the nature of her relationship to the Republican campaign. In late September, Walter H. Newton, head of the national committee's speaker's bureau, acknowledged the assistant attorney general as "one of the Republican Party's regularly listed speakers," but historians have not clarified her relationship with strategists of the GOP. A confidential letter from Willebrandt to Work reveals that the national committee planned her political junkets and that Republican tacticians scoured her speeches before delivery. Willebrandt complained of Chairman Work's failure to admit her official association with the Republican party: "I have not made a single speech that has not been arranged through your office." Forestalling contradiction, she flourished citations from telegrams dispatched by the national committee informing her of various speaking engagements they had arranged. She also reminded Dr. Work that when she had sought to quit the campaign in early September, because she had "refused to be haggled over and thus contribute to the indecision and confusion of a hard campaign," the chairman had exhorted her "to continue speaking, for reasons you will remember." Finally, she protested that the Republican party had disclaimed any responsibility for a speech she had sent to party headquarters three days before its delivery that had been "modified according to suggestions made" (by Republican officials).[31]

Although none of these solidly documented efforts by the Hoover camp to discredit the moral character of Al Smith focused on his religion, they scarcely sustain Hoover's image as a candidate deeply troubled by the whispering campaign and bent upon silencing all forms of personal slander.

The Republican leadership may also have covertly distributed anti-Catholic propaganda. Alfred M. Landon, 1936 Republican presidential nominee and Republican chairman for the state of Kansas in 1928, recalls that in October 1928 he received from the national committee literature pertaining to Al Smith's religious connections. The material was for his confidential use and was not to be distributed with the imprimatur of the Republican party. Landon, a genuinely tolerant man, claims that he promptly filed all of this literature in his wastebasket.[32] One student of the 1928 campaign in the West also uncovered anti-Catholic material that had been distributed by the Republican leadership.[33]

These findings add plausibility to Democratic Chairman John J. Raskob's accusation that New Hampshire Senator George H. Moses, chairman of the Eastern Division of the Republican National Committee, abetted the anti-Catholic campaign against Al Smith. On 2 November 1928, Raskob released to the press a photostatic copy of the following letter from Moses to Zeb Vance Walser, of Lexington, North Carolina: "I am sending you an article for newspaper publication which is written by a native of South Carolina who is now engaged in editorial work in New York City. It is red hot stuff, and I wish you could get it into some North Carolina papers." The enclosed article was an anti-Catholic polemic, so outrageous that respectable newspapers refused to print it.[34]

Senator Moses denied having sent the enclosure, but did not

flatly deny the authenticity of the letter itself. His response to Raskob's accusation was mainly an effort to turn the tables on the Democratic chairman and blame the Democrats for dragging religion into the campaign. A Moses biographer plausibly claims that the senator was not antagonistic to Catholics, but concedes that Moses might have exploited religious prejudice in an effort to secure Republican votes.[35]

Regardless of the scope of efforts by the Republican National Committee to foment anti-Catholic agitation, local leaders clearly did participate in the religious campaign against Al Smith. In at least three southern states (Louisiana, Alabama, and Virginia) important party officials openly bid for the votes of Protestant bigots. Information regarding the anti-Catholic activities of Republican leaders in other parts of the country can be distilled from the responses to FDR's circular letter of November 1928. The respondents are all Democratic leaders and have an obvious bias; but their letters were for the confidential use of the New York State governor-elect and had no publicity value for the Democratic party. These leaders accused the Republicans in many states of financially supporting purveyors of religious intolerance and of secretly dispensing anti-Catholic propaganda. Their charges were based upon hearsay, deduction, and personal observation. C. M. Haskell of Muskogee, Oklahoma, offered one of the most detailed accounts of Republican complicity in the anti-Catholic campaign:

So far as the South and Southwest were concerned, there was just one issue in the last campaign that influenced voters . . . the religious question, that was the only issue that the opposition promoted.

The Republican State Committees in these several states were merely inactive, quiet, and pretentious. Take our state as an illustration. The Republican Headquarters was the parlor affair, the real place of activity was across the street in the so-called Hoover-Democrat Headquarters, a combination of Ku Klux and ultra-protestants with four times the clerical force and activity of the Republican Headquarters, and every item of expense paid by the Republican Headquarters, numerous paid speakers, big and little, constantly speaking all over the state with the most horrid stories of what the Pope would do to the people of this country. The Republican State Headquarters financed, managed and directed this activity.[36]

Despite a carefully orchestrated campaign that included successful efforts to purge and discredit black party leaders in the South, the Republican National Committee did not attempt to halt anti-Catholic agitation by local politicians. The committee neither disciplined party officials who dispensed anti-Catholic material nor took preventive measures. Directors of the campaign seemed concerned only that the candidate and his prominent supporters not be identified with anti-Catholic agitation. The national committeemen from Louisiana and Alabama and the national committeewoman from Virginia openly distributed anti-Catholic propaganda. Apparently, the national committee reprimanded only Oliver Street, the Alabama official. In September, national committee Chairman Hubert Work released to the press a telegram reproving Committeeman Street and reaffirming the party's commitment to religious toleration. Yet Street regarded the chairman's wrath so lightly that he publicly denied receiving the telegram and continued to maintain that the Catholic church was a "very live and vital issue" in the presidential campaign.[37] Similarly, Henry J. Allen, the official in charge of campaign publicity, seemed to have no control over propaganda emanating from southern members of the national committee. In September, Allen sent George Ackerson, Hoover's secretary and political confidant, five samples of campaign publicity from Louisiana, including an abusive defamation of Catholics, that had been proudly sent to Allen by the national committeeman. Exhibits A and B were standard discussions of economic issues; Exhibit C was an appeal to religious bigotry; and Exhibits D and E were appeals to white supremacy and race prejudice: "It strikes me that Exhibit C transgresses the policy we have been carrying out so carefully in the Campaign. I am sending it to you for two reasons. First, so that Mr. Hoover may have knowledge of this type of publicity which is going out under the National Committeeman in Louisiana. And second, because any word of direction from me on the subject would apparently be without any authority in that section."[38]

In short, the evidence shows that Republicans mounted no campaign against anti-Catholic agitation, even within their own ranks. The party organization neither disciplined those who pandered to religious bigotry nor attempted to police their activities. Until forced by circumstance, Herbert Hoover refused to denounce religious bigotry forcefully; his justifications for this restraint seem implausible when juxtaposed against personal vilification of Smith that was sanctioned by the Hoover campaign. Fragmentary evidence further suggests that the Republican leadership deliberately set out, covertly, to exploit Protestant opposition to the election of a Catholic president.

The Democratic party sought to turn the tide of anti-Catholicism to its own benefit by conflating religious intolerance and support for the GOP. As party leader Breckinridge Long confided to his diary in September, "Religious prejudice has become a major issue and tolerance is on our side." Three weeks later, he noted that "the campaign of 'intolerance' is being waged against the Republicans with real effect."[39]

The "campaign of intolerance," fashioned for those who valued religious toleration for its own sake, rested on several tactical maneuvers. First, the Democrats charged the opposition with at best ignoring and at worst encouraging the anti-Catholic offensive against Al Smith. The governor himself began this phase of the campaign on 20 September with his famous Oklahoma City speech on religious tolerance. Herbert H. Lehman, chairman of the Finance Committee of the Democratic National Committee, recalled, "We all felt that it was very important that he carry the fight in regard to the Ku Klux Klan and the religious issue right into enemy territory. The only question was where he was going to do it. He decided he was going to make it in Oklahoma City."[40] Before a largely hostile audience, on unfamiliar turf, the pugnacious candidate tackled the question of religious bigotry. After scathing those who used other issues to mask their intolerance, defending his record as a public official, and denouncing prejudice as contrary to the spirit of America, Smith turned his fire on the opposition party, claiming, "There is abundant reason for believing that Republicans high in the councils of the party have countenanced a large part of this form of campaign, if they have not actually promoted it. A sin of omission," he charged, "is sometimes as grievous as a sin of commission."[41]

During the remaining weeks before election day, other Democratic spokesmen followed Smith's lead in trying to mark the opposition with the brand of anti-Catholic bigotry. Most spectacular was John J. Raskob's release of the Moses letter just a few days before the election. Raskob may have just received the allegedly incriminating document or he may have deliberately withheld it until the eleventh hour.

The Democrats also sought to equate a vote for Al Smith with a ballot for toleration in matters of religious worship. Unabashedly appealing to guilty Protestants, the Democratic National Committee disseminated a statement in which Henry Van Dyke, former moderator of the Presbyterian General Assembly, plainly argued that his fellow Protestants should reaffirm their commitment to freedom of conscience by supporting Al Smith for the presidency.[42] Democratic campaigners such as John W. Davis, Nellie Tayloe Ross, and Harry B. Hawes—all good Protestants—played variations on this theme in speeches and pamphlets on the religious issue.[43] Other Protestant clergymen indirectly aided the Democratic cause by chiding their colleagues for participating in a misguided effort to deny the White House to a Catholic candidate.[44] The Smith campaign also helped finance the efforts of the Calvert Associates to publicize anti-Catholic activities and to answer the charges made by Protestant critics.[45]

Finally, the Democratic campaigners used the issue of religious toleration as a means of obtaining contributions from wealthy donors. Finance Chairman Lehman recalled that with a few exceptions "it was very difficult to raise money" from businessmen. To loosen the money belts of some potential contributors, Lehman stated, "We had one room that we called the 'Chamber of Horrors,' in which on the wall we had any number of cartoons and editorials, news items of the most vicious character." Lehman added, "When we had somebody who was a little bit hesitant, who we thought would be outraged by the religious issue being brought in the way it was, we'd take him into this room. He usually came out pretty well convinced . . . we took a great many people into the Chamber."[46]

Although individuals on both sides of the religious controversy may have had different attitudes and aspirations, the public manifestation of the debate over Smith's religion revealed no clash of values. The dispute turned instead on the empirical question of how best to protect a shared set of values regarding the relationships between religion, politics, and public policy. It was this consensus on values that gave religious strife its particular character in 1928.

Both anti-Catholic propagandists and their rhetorical opponents of 1928 accepted representative democracy, separation of church and state, toleration of diverse religious beliefs, and clerical abstention from partisan politics. Each side charged the other with trampling upon freedom of conscience, with organizing church members into a political bloc, with allowing policy judgments to be dictated by religious dogma. Those who objected to electing a Catholic president alleged that Smith would obey the edicts of a foreign potentate, that Catholics were organized as a political phalanx to promote their own parochial interests, and that Catholics regarded all other Christian churches as heretical and would use public authority to propagate their faith. Critics also charged that various tenets of Catholicism contradicted venerable principles of American democracy. These arguments, although deformed by exaggeration and factual error, can be found in the most scurrilous of anti-Catholic material. Propaganda disseminated by the Klan, for example, addressed the issue of religious toleration, charging that no sane Protestant could interpret toleration as handing power to representatives of a religion itself intolerant of all other faiths. "Both Catholics and Protestants praise 'tolerance,'" declared J. O. Knott, speaking on the radio station of the Ku Klux Klan: "Here is common ground on which we can stand." According to the *Fellowship Forum*, "The Roman Catholic Church is the most intolerant thing in the world—has been, is now, and forever will be." The *Forum* editorialized, "Years of bloody persecutions, thousands of lives sacrificed is the price Protestantism paid Catholicism for religious freedom. Just because an American happens to think that he should cherish these hardships by our progenitors he is called an intolerant bigot. It is not freedom of Catholic worship that Protestant America is fighting."[47]

Partisans of Al Smith flatly denied that Catholic dogma clashed with the precepts of American democracy or that the pope would sway the judgment of a Catholic president. Affirming religious toleration and the separation of religion and politics, they accused their opponents of forming a cabal designed to promote narrow sectarian interests, of spurning religious toleration, and of repudiating constitutional stipulations on the separation of church and state.

Explanations for the Voting Behavior of Protestants and Catholics

The anti-Catholic reaction against Al Smith may have contained the germ of a realistic clash of opposing interests. Some voters may have rejected Smith on the basis of a reasoned, informed analysis of the dangers posed by his Catholicism. Reasoned opposition to Al Smith, however, was lost in a welter of anti-Catholic prejudice. Inflexible judgments against Catholics as a group were uncritically applied to Al Smith as an individual. Even the learned leaders of American Protestantism generally failed to treat Al Smith as a distinctive individual. They portrayed the threats posed by stereotyped images of Roman Catholics rather than the particular Catholic nominated by the Democratic party. Herbert Hoover, on the other hand, was the beneficiary of an evaluation addressed to him as an individual. Hoover was a Quaker, and during World War I the Quakers were one of the few sects whose pacifist ideology entitled its members to exemption from military service. Yet no critic of consequence seemed to doubt the sincerity of Hoover's pledge to ensure the maintenance of an adequate army and navy and, if necessary, to defend the nation by force of arms. In contrast, eminent churchmen and lay people either ignored or dismissed Smith's claim that he believed in the absolute separation of church and state and would never allow policy decisions to be determined by his loyalty to the Catholic church.[48] They also ignored or distorted his record as governor of New York State. Gordon Allport generalizes the situation that prevailed in 1928: "Realistic conflict is like a note on an organ. It sets all prejudices that are attuned to it into simultaneous vibration. The listener can scarcely distinguish the pure note from the surrounding jangle."[49]

Consistent with interpretations of the presidential election that posit a unidimensional response to Smith and Hoover, historians generally have traced prejudice against Catholics to the fears of rural, Protestant, old-stock Americans that their culture was imperiled by the alien ideology and unsavory habits of the Catholic immigrants flooding into America's large cities. Yet statistical analysis distinguishes religious divisions of the electorate from those founded on ethnic background, prohibition, or urban-rural residence. And analysis reveals that Protestant opposition to Smith's religion was remarkably widespread, extending to all regions of the nation, to city and country, to church members and unaffiliated Protestants. While the traditional paradigm may accurately portray the attitudes of some Protestants, its scope is too narrow; it cannot account for multiple sources of religious animosities in the 1920s.

Anti-Catholicism in the early twentieth century was not a uniquely American phenomenon. Hostility to Catholics was part of the European heritage of Americans who may have opposed prohibition, known nothing of American traditions, and scarcely feared the immigrant or the city. Although the period between 1880 and the passage of restrictive legislation in 1921 commonly is known as the age of the "new immigrant," who came largely from Catholic and Jewish sections of Europe, millions of Protestant immigrants continued pouring into the United States during these years.[50] The Old World heritage of many of these Protestant arrivals, such as German Lutherans, Scandinavians, Dutch, and English Canadians, included a powerful antipathy to Roman Catholics.[51]

Bernhard E. Olson's study of the educational texts used by four types of Protestants (fundamentalists, conservatives, neo-orthodox, and liberals) shows that Protestant religious training was uniquely unfavorable to Roman Catholics. Olson found that each type portrayed Catholics less favorably than non-Christians, Jews, other Christian groups, internationals, other ethnics, and Negroes. Olson devised a scale, ranging in value between −100 and 100, to judge the balance of positive and negative comment on each outside group. The scores attained by each type of Protestant for their image of Catholics were −67 for conservatives, −53 for fundamentalists, +23 for neo-orthodox, and +37 for liberals. All of these scores are minimums—46, 53, 35 and 22 points respectively below the average scores for all rated groups.[52] Olson's ratings apply to materials used after World War II, but there is no reason to assume that Protestant teaching was comparatively more favorable to Catholics in the 1920s.

Analysis of religious prejudice in 1928 also suggests caution in regarding the election as a victory for the spirit of toleration in America. Overt anti-Catholic agitation faded rapidly after Smith's concession in 1928, yet the Gallup Poll of 1940 and surveys for the presidential election of 1960 show that for several decades many Protestants continued to oppose the election of Catholic presidents. Ignoring this later evidence, historians have interpreted the calm aftermath of 1928 as reflecting the onward march of toleration in the United States. A more accurate interpretation that reconciles the evidence draws on a multileveled model of intolerance. Application of the model to 1928 would suggest that prejudice toward Catholics lost its salience with Smith's defeat, but retained the capacity to reappear under comparable conditions.

A multitiered model of prejudice not only accounts for what happened in 1928, but also neatly fits the historical patterns of American nativism sketched most persuasively by John Higham.[53] A growing body of work in social science questions the correspondence between prejudice considered as an individual's attitude toward an out-group and his behavior toward members of the group. Attitudes, the scholars have suggested, must be considered in relation to the dynamics of an individual's personality, to the social structure of his society, to his full complement of values and beliefs, and to components of the specific situations he confronts.[54] Intolerance thus seems responsive to several discrete levels of internal and environmental change. Changes occurring at the different levels may proceed at different rates and may not necessarily affect one another.

A revised interpretation of intolerance calls attention to at least three levels of analysis.[55] At the first level are the components of personality and the interactions between personality and social structure. Study at this level obviously cannot account for prejudice against any particular group, but can explain why, as Allport has observed, "one of the facts of which we are most certain is that people who reject one out-group will tend to reject other out-groups."[56] To explain the targeting of prejudice, analysis must proceed to the second level of attitudes that are conditioned by individuals' culture, history, and current experience. Ascent to this level would be necessary, for instance, to indicate why Americans of the 1920s were more likely to be prejudiced against Catholics than against Quakers. Finally, explanation of how attitudes translate into behavior requires consideration of the salience of prejudice. Eugene L. Hartley observed in his now classic study of American prejudice, "There is not only variation in the degree of prejudice as an abstracted attitude, we may also expect to find the importance of the prejudice varying as a function of factors unrelated to the prejudice itself."[57] The salience of prejudice will depend partly on other values and beliefs held by the individual and partly on the specific situations he confronts. Prejudice that is salient for one situation may not be salient for another.

Since change at each level of analysis is likely to proceed at a different rate, a society should be found to have long-term trends responding to changes in social structure and personality; shorter cycles responding to changes in attitudes; and rapid fluctuations responding to situational changes in the salience of prejudice. Changes in salience, for instance, best explain the repeated rise and fall of nativist agitation in America. Higham has noted that nativist movements have "surged and subsided time and again in American history. Each time the stresses that fostered them had eased in a few years, the agitators had sunk into obscurity, the secret societies had dissolved in factional strife, and the people had recovered their tempers and aplomb." Changes in salience unaccompanied by major changes in attitude can account for the rapidity of these fluctuations, for the frequent reappearance of nativism in much the same form, and for the survival of unfavorable attitudes toward out-groups during the periods of calm.[58]

Changes in salience also explain why agitation against Catholics receded after 1928, although anti-Catholicism seemed to persist. With Al Smith's sound defeat and the belief that no major party would risk nominating another Catholic in the foreseeable future, anti-Catholicism lost its immediate salience. As one correspondent confided to Tom Walsh, the Catholic senator from Montana, "The 'Catholic' question has been settled for good. No party will again risk the chance."[59] But this return to normalcy did not mean that similar anti-Catholic behavior would not reemerge in a similar situation. The evidence suggests that long after the confrontation between Al Smith and Herbert Hoover, many Protestants continued to doubt whether a Catholic should occupy the nation's highest office.

The salience of anti-Catholicism in 1928 related to the special roles of an American president. The president possesses awesome power and has a place in popular lore as the ultimate guarantor of American values and beliefs. In a nation without a separate head of state, he is also a symbol of national unity and popular sovereignty. Issues such as the obedience of individual Catholics to the pope and Catholic doctrine on the relationship between church and state would be given unusual prominence by the publicity of presidential campaigns.[60] Suspicions about Catholics that would not otherwise influence behavior could become reasons for denying a Catholic the presidency. Even the slightest doubt about Smith's susceptibility to antidemocratic and anti-American ideas may have been sufficient impetus for a Hoover vote. The election of a Catholic president would also notably enhance the status and prestige of American Catholics, in effect, recognizing their fitness to hold the nation's most important position and to represent all of America. Protestants who drew distinctions between Catholics and members of their own religion might regard an increase in the status of Catholics as a belittling of themselves.

An analysis of voting for president and for governor in the counties of New York State suggests an intimate relationship between visions of the presidency and the salience of anti-Catholicism in 1928. Regression coefficients computed for the difference between Al Smith's percentage of the 1928 presidential vote and his percentage of the vote cast for governor in 1926 reveal that Smith's race for the presidency opened a wider gulf between Catholic and Protestant voters than had his bid for reelection as governor. Independent of control variables (including a measure of antiprohibition sentiment that is available for the counties of New York State), a 1 percent change in percentage of Catholics yields a .33 percent change in the difference between voting for Smith for president in 1928 and voting for him for governor in 1926 (standard error = .065).

The political realities of 1928 dictated a defensive response by Catholics to the religious conflicts of the time, but for many of them religion was still a voting issue. Some of the same concerns that would move Protestants to reject a Catholic candidate would incline Catholics to favor his election. Despite important divisions of class and ethnic background, Catholics in the 1920s were united by parochial education and religious training; in-group patterns of residence, recreation, and marriage; and discrimination directed against members of their faith. As did many Protestants, Catholics recognized an us-and-them distinction between their coreligionists and those outside the fold.[61] Catholics who linked their own status and prospects to the standing of Catholicism as a whole would find Al Smith's candidacy an irresistible lure. Moreover, Protestant tirades against electing a Catholic president probably strengthened their solidarity during the campaign of 1928. David J. O'Brien, in *American Catholics and Social Reform*, confirms this expectation: "All these sources of conflict were exposed before 1928 and Al Smith's campaign and the accompanying propaganda served to perpetuate and accentuate the isolation and insecurity of American Catholics. . . . For lay people who had grown up in heavily Catholic city ghettoes the challenge to their Americanism in 1928 was the most severe of a number of shocks which retarded their mature emergence into the pluralistic structure of American religious life."[62]

Voting for Smith was also a means of coping with what appeared to be a threat to the status already attained by American Catholics. A Catholic following the presidential competition of 1928 could not fail to note that all the forces of anti-Catholicism had lined up behind the candidacy of Herbert Hoover. Undoubtedly, many Catholics feared that Protestant bigots would regard the election of Hoover as a mandate to persecute Catholics with renewed vigor. Not only did the religious issue stay in the forefront of attention throughout the campaign, but the Democrats sought to demonstrate that a ballot for Herbert Hoover meant a vote for religious prejudice.

Conclusions

Scholarship that downgrades the influence of religion on the distinctive voter alignments of 1928 distorts our understanding of how Americans responded to the candidacies of Al Smith and Herbert Hoover. Differences between Catholics and Protestants best explain the unique shape of electoral politics in the presidential contest. Religious conflict occupied center stage in the competition between Smith and Hoover. Both nationally and regionally, the division between Catholics and Protestants dominates a statistical description of voter decisions; even Protestants without formal church affiliation and those from traditionally tolerant denominations resisted voting for a Catholic presidential contender. Religion also created more interest, excitement, and tension than any other issue that emerged during the months of campaigning in 1928. Anti-Catholic polemics against Al Smith ranged from the scurrilous to the scholarly, and GOP leaders, both directly and indirectly, bolstered the efforts of church groups and private individuals to agitate the religious issue. The political realities of 1928 meant that Catholics could not launch a sectarian campaign on behalf of Al Smith no matter how ardently they may have wanted his election. Instead, Catholic spokesmen denounced the anti-Catholic crusade and insisted that no fair-minded American would let religion become a voting issue. The Democratic high command, following its self-interests, consciously sought to equate voting for Smith with endorsing freedom of religion and to connect the opposition campaign with slanderous attacks on Al Smith.

Anti-Catholic attitudes were not manufactured during the presidential election of 1928. That the campaign newly awakened American Protestants to the menace posed by a Roman Catholic president is unlikely. Rather, hostility to Catholics became politically salient as a consequence of Al Smith's nomination. Anti-Catholicism in the United States was a widespread phenomenon with multiple causes; it was neither the product of a single viewpoint, nor confined to dry, rural, native-stock Protestants. The fading of religious agitation after the 1928 contest did not herald a victory for the spirit of religious tolerance, but only an ebbing of the salience of anti-Catholicism for the behavior of most Americans.

Chapter 4
Wets versus Drys

Al Smith was not only the first Catholic presidential candidate nominated by a major party, but also the first major party candidate to challenge constitutional and statutory restrictions on the manufacture and sale of intoxicants. The passage of the Eighteenth Amendment and the Volstead Act had not led to a stable national consensus on the question of liquor control. Throughout the 1920s, Americans inconclusively debated the moral, political, economic, social, legal, and medical consequences of prohibition. Familiar arguments chased one another in endless circles, providing reams of source material for satirists such as H. L. Mencken and Will Rogers. More than any other policy issue of the 1920s, prohibition commanded public interest and attention.

Religion and prohibition were knotted together in 1928. Protestants were more likely than their Catholic counterparts to favor prohibition,[1] and the most resolute Protestant drys were likely to be among the most vocal opponents of the Catholic church.[2] The prohibition controversy also enabled Protestant leaders to join in the campaign against Al Smith without openly inciting religious animosity. During the campaign, spokesmen for Protestant groups denounced Al Smith as a wet, while disclaiming opposition to his religious affiliation. Later efforts to analyze the vote for president in 1928 and isolate the influence of prohibition from that of religion and other issues have not achieved agreement. The conclusions of researchers using either traditional or quantitative methods have ranged from assurances that prohibition was "an issue of transcendent importance" to pronouncements that prohibition was of no importance at all.[3]

The Influence of Prohibition on the Vote for President

Regression analysis indicates that prohibition was a major if not a transcendent influence on the voting for president in 1928. Although for every measure of voter behavior the effect of prohibition is less than that of religion, prohibition still has a statistically significant (at the .001 level) coefficient for all but two of these measures. Independent of the social and economic composition of counties, the coefficients reported in Table 4.1 show that the percentage of both presidential voters and adult residents voting for Al Smith increased as the percentage of those voting against prohibition in state-level referenda likewise increased. Hoover's percentage of the adult population, however, does not change discernibly in response to changes in sentiment regarding prohibition. This result indicates that those opposing prohibition were more likely than their counterparts favoring liquor control to participate in the election. Prohibition also has a fairly strong positive influence on the deviation variables measuring differences between the vote for Smith in 1928 and the vote for presidential contenders in other elections. Controlling for social and economic variables, the vote for Smith relative to that of other can-

Table 4.1. *Influence of Percentage Opposing Prohibition on Measures of the Vote for President: 471 Counties (in percent)**

	Regression Coefficient b	Standard Error
Dem 1928	.21	.032
Dem 1928 total	.16	.024
Rep 1928 total	−.03	.028
Dem 1928 minus Dem 1924	.09	.032
Dem 1928 minus Dem/Prog 1924	.18	.031
Dem 1928 minus Prog 1924	.30	.054
Dem 1928 total minus Dem 1924 total	.10	.020
Dem 1928 total minus Dem/Prog 1924 total	.14	.023
Dem 1928 total minus Prog 1924 total	.21	.039
Rep 1928 total minus Rep 1924 total	−.07	.019
Dem 1928 minus mean Dem 1916–24	.18	.025
Dem 1928 minus mean Dem 1916–20, Dem/Prog 1924	.21	.021
Dem 1928 minus Dem 1932	.20	.024

*Controlling for percentages of Urban, Foreign stock, Owners, Negro, Female, Under 35, Pop change, Jewish, Prot church, Catholic, and for Economic status.

didates increased as the percentage of voters opposing prohibition likewise increased.

The judgments of political leaders also suggests that the controversy over prohibition affected the behavior of voters in 1928. Most of the Republican politicians canvassed by the national committee believed that prohibition swayed the decisions of many voters and produced net gains for their party. In their synopsis of these reports, the committee optimistically concluded, "The prohibition issues worked tremendously to the advantage of our ticket." The committee claimed that "where we lost in the cities . . . we more than offset the losses in the rural sections. Where we lost foreign groups . . . we more than offset it by gains from the women."[4] Fascinating contradictions appear in these reports, however, illustrating the difficulty of accurately judging political behavior from contemporary comments alone. In both Missouri and New Jersey, for instance, the different leaders asked to evaluate the importance of prohibition submitted remarkably divergent reports. E. B. Clements, Republican national committeeman for Missouri, claimed that the GOP lost very few wet votes and made substantial inroads among the drys. Former Congressman Walter H. Newton, however, averred that although the Republicans gained many dry votes they suffered substantial losses among urban wets. From New Jersey, Senator Walter Edge reported that "there were a great deal of Republicans who voted for Smith because of [the prohibition] issue." But James E. Horne, secretary of the New Jersey Republican State Committee, maintained that the prohibition issue resulted in no Republican losses except among Italians.

Echoing Republican views, Democratic politicians also indicated that voters switched parties because of prohibition. But they clearly accord the controversy over prohibition less importance than the division over Al Smith's religion. Many of the Democrats responding to Roosevelt's circular letter claimed that prohibition was an important reason for the defeat of Al Smith. The prohibition issue constituted 33 percent of the reasons cited by FDR's correspondents for their candidate's defeat (Table 3.5, Chapter 3), placing a strong second to religion with 55.5 percent. All other issues comprised only 11.5 percent of the citations. Corroborating this ranking of religion and prohibition, Kentucky leaders surveyed by State Chairman Alben Barkley expected on the average that prohibition would cost their party 3.1 percent of the vote, compared to an average expected loss of 6.9 percent from religion.

Party and Candidate Positions on Prohibition

Prohibitionists based their opposition to Al Smith on the orations of the two presidential candidates rather than the declarations of their respective party platforms. The Republican and Democratic conventions endorsed virtually identical positions on the regulation of intoxicants. Each platform committed the party's nominee to enforce the Eighteenth Amendment and federal laws relating to the sale and manufacture of alcoholic beverages. The only difference was that the Democrats added a clause attacking the lax enforcement policies of the Coolidge administration. Each party labeled its prohibition plank "Law Enforcement" rather than "Prohibition."[5]

The Democratic statement on prohibition represented a compromise between the party's wet and dry factions. Although the party harbored the staunchest southern drys and the most vociferous northern wets, both groups devoutly wished to avoid a divisive floor fight on prohibition. No Democrat wanted to repeat the disaster of 1924, when the party conclave was ripped apart by a bitter convention-floor controversy over a proposal condemning the Ku Klux Klan. Leading members of the Committee on Platform and Resolutions feared that prohibition could detonate an equally destructive explosion. They sought unanimous agreement on the wording of the prohibition plank they would recommend to the convention; the presentation of a minority report, they believed, could engender the public acrimony that the party desperately wanted to avoid.[6]

Both wets and drys could at least agree on the sanctity of federal law, and they adopted the prohibition enforcement plank framed by Senator Carter Glass of Virginia. Glass explained that his resolution did not commit anyone in the party to support either the maintenance or the modification of the Eighteenth Amendment and relevant federal legislation: "The resolution offered by me does not bind anybody to anything except enforcement—obedience to the Constitution and the enforcement of the law." Glass also maintained that a law enforcement plank would satisfy the Anti-Saloon League and other watchdogs of the Eighteenth Amendment: "All they wanted was for both parties to commit themselves to the Constitution and the enforcement of the law. . . . Bishop Cannon and other speakers . . . stated before this Committee yesterday that they never had asked and do not now ask and will not hereafter ask that any party be committed to prohibition."[7] In offering the proposed prohibition plank to the assembled convention, the platform committee chairman, Senator Key Pittman of Nevada, reiterated Glass's privately stated opinion that the plank "did not prevent an officer or even a President of the United States from recommending the repeal of an amendment or the modification of any act, so long as he supported it while it was a law."[8]

The Glass compromise satisfied every member of the Committee on Platform and Resolutions except Governor Dan Moody of Texas. Moody, a diehard dry, held out for a plank that committed the party to endorsing the Eighteenth Amendment and opposing "any attempt to repeal the same or to weaken or destroy the laws for enforcement."[9] If the committee ratified the Glass plank, he vowed to present a minority report. A substantial proportion of the committee's executive session was consumed by unsuccessful attempts to persuade Governor Moody to change his mind. Moody resisted the entreaties of both wets and fellow drys and presented a brief minority (of one) report to the Democratic convention. Fortunately for the Democrats, Moody declared that in the interests of harmony he would "not carry the minority report to a poll." The prohibition issue provoked only a brief, dignified discussion in which Governor Albert Ritchie of Maryland, representing the wets, and Senator Glass, representing the drys, lauded the law enforcement plank.[10]

Although party platforms gave no hint of differences over prohibition, the two candidates seem to have taken antithetical positions. Immediately after being notified of his nomination, Governor Smith followed a prearranged strategy and snapped off a telegram to the Houston convention that restated his well-known commitment to "fundamental changes in the present provisions for national prohibition" and announced his intention to "point the way to these changes."[11] In his acceptance message to the Republican National Committee, Secretary Hoover refrained from mentioning prohibition, but announced in his acceptance address on 11 August that he favored the Eighteenth Amendment and strict enforcement of the Volstead Act. Hoover also declared that "modification of the enforcement laws which would permit that which the Constitution forbids is nullification." Prohibition, he asserted, could be altered only by constitutional amendment.[12]

The governor's telegram to the Houston convention prompted devout drys to begin an anti-Smith campaign. Despite Glass's assurances that the prohibition plank satisfied the dry forces and Chairman

Pittman's explanation that the plank did not prevent the candidate from advocating changes in the Eighteenth Amendment and the prohibition laws, the drys accused the governor of repudiating the party's platform and of needlessly dragging prohibition into the presidential campaign. How could a loyal dry fail to respond to such a challenge? Bishop James Cannon, Jr., of the Methodist Episcopal church, South, the nation's most famous and influential dry, declared himself "stunned" by Smith's telegram, calling it "a shameless proposition of political double-dealing" and "an action of brazen, political effrontery." Despite ill health, Bishop Cannon, in the words of his biographer, was "galvanized into instant action."[13]

Regarding Smith's "repudiation" of the Democratic platform, Andrew Sinclair's standard work on prohibition misleadingly cites Carter Glass to the effect that Smith's declaration really did conflict with the senator's prohibition plank.[14] Senator Glass, like other dry Democrats, resented the governor's prompt reiteration of his prohibition stance; but he had to admit, however grudgingly, that Smith had not repudiated the party platform. On 3 August, Glass confided his thoughts to bolting Democrat George Fort Milton: "I have not hesitated to say that Governor Smith's telegram to the Houston Convention was amazingly ill-advised and amounted *almost* to a repudiation of the platform, although he could *technically* contend that this is not a fact."[15] Even this admission shifted the emphasis of Glass's assurance to the Committee on Platform and Resolutions that his resolution did "not bind anybody to anything but enforcement."

Apparently, the Democrats' prohibition plank was widely misunderstood. Even some of the convention delegates responding to Franklin Roosevelt's circular letter believed that Smith had repudiated the party's position on prohibition. Mortimer C. Rhone of Pennsylvania, for example, insisted, "No candidate for the Presidency can ever hope to succeed where he is compelled to make a campaign on one or more of the main questions at issue by asserting at the very beginning of the campaign that he himself is not in accord with the party platform." Bolting Democrat Sam T. Spears of West Virginia reported that "had Smith stood on the Houston platform I would have voted for him, yet, in view of his uncompromising position on the Prohibition question I did not vote for him." And C. A. Lord claimed that in Nebraska, Smith's "repudiation of the party's prohibition plank" cost him significant numbers of votes.[16]

The Democratic National Committee was extremely sensitive to the charge that their nominee had spurned the party platform. The Democratic *Campaign Book* for 1928 included a seven-page statement by Senator Pittman explaining how the party platform was compatible with Al Smith's proposals for modifying the prohibition laws. Party publicists devoted only five and a half pages to all other issues raised by the dispute over liquor control.[17]

Church and Voter Interest in the Prohibition Issue

Although a number of respectable Protestant churchmen spoke out against electing a Catholic president, the vast majority of organized Protestant opposition to Al Smith was ostensibly based on Smith's wetness rather than his religion. The Methodist, Baptist, Presbyterian, and Congregational churches had been in the forefront of the prohibition movement and were committed to defending the viability of the Eighteenth Amendment and its enforcement legislation.[18] For many church leaders, prohibition was part of the official Protestant credenda.

As the 1928 campaign progressed, prohibitionists closed ranks against Al Smith. Most notable among the prohibition lobbies opposing the New York governor were the Anti-Saloon League, sponsored by the Protestant denominations, and the Woman's Christian Temperance Union, which claimed the adherence of more than seven hundred thousand drys. Several major Protestant denominations, including the Methodists, Baptists, and Congregationalists, also formally denounced Smith for his opposition to national prohibition. The Presbyterians did not officially oppose Governor Smith, but the moderator of the General Assembly of the Presbyterian church did so on his own.[19] Joining the antiwet campaign against Smith were religious publications representing a wide variety of denominations and thousands of Protestant pastors, who damned repeal, Al Smith, and perhaps Catholics, in a single exhortation.

When challenged to justify their meddling in a contest for the presidency, Protestant clergymen responded with a standard litany that prohibition, unlike the typical political issue, was a moral question, well within the ambit of religious concern. To preserve the sanctity of the Eighteenth Amendment and uphold the morals of the nation, they contended, the church must participate in the presidential campaign. Other members of the clergy, however, opposing sectarian crusaders against Smith, noted that the argument of their fellow clergymen ignored the moral dimensions of all political issues. Every policy decision, they contended, is founded upon judgments about the moral ends or values that government should pursue. Moreover, government decisions on a variety of issues would affect the capacity of individual citizens to follow the paths of sin or salvation. Reverend Rembert Gilman Smith of the Methodist Episcopal church, South, alarmed at the political activities of his colleagues, offered the following criticism of the argument from morality:

The repeated emphasis recently upon the fact that prohibition is a moral issue with the additional statement often made that other issues are political thus seeking to deny their ethical character and empty their moral content have constituted a most alarming moral shrinkage of the body ecclesiastical and prophetical. . . . If this nation should ever become bone dry and yet arid in avarice and confirmed in the corruptions of covetousness, the historians of the future will assess some of the blame on church leaders who cried out in 1928 as though there were but one moral issue before the nation and that the others were merely political.[20]

The attempt to distinguish between moral and nonmoral issues reflects the triumph of a version of Private Protestantism that emphasized the uplifting of personal morality in ways unlikely to affect the distribution of power and wealth in America. Public Protestantism, on the other hand, stressed the need to reform the structure of American society. Cushing Strout, writing in 1974, best expresses the distinctive responses of public and private Protestants to the problem of coping with the evils of society: "Just as ante-bellum reformers had realized slavery was a social system as well as an individual sin, so also the social gospelers, inheriting an evangelical emphasis on the need for individual conversion, were compelled to go beyond it to assess the institutional pattern that had grown up around them and to search for social remedies. The alternative was to rest with the traditional Protestant emphasis on individual conversion and philanthropy or merely to supplement this nonpolitical stand with prohibition as a legislative aim."[21] As Ferenc M. Szasz has demonstrated, these traditions coalesced briefly during the Progressive Era of the early twentieth century: "Historians' traditional separation of the clergy between those concerned with the social gospel and those concerned only with individual salvation does not hold true for this period. From 1900 to about 1917 a liberal-conservative Protestant alliance worked to alleviate social ills, each in its own way." Contradictions among different strains of Protestant thought shattered this reform consensus. During the 1920s, major Protestant denominations narrowed their interpretation of the church's social responsibilities.[22]

Questions concerning the prohibition of liquor also engaged voter attention. If a campaign issue is defined as a question relating to the policy positions of opposing candidates, prohibition undoubtedly stimulated more interest than any other campaign issue. This judgment is supported by virtually every qualitative account of the 1928 campaign, contemporary and historical, public and private. A hitherto neglected survey of newspaper editors conducted by the Republican National Committee in mid-September 1928 provides further evidence of how strongly voters reacted to the controversy over prohibition. The committee asked three thousand editors and other subscribers of the *National Republic* to indicate the issue or issues uppermost in the minds of the voters. Responses were received from 276 localities. Respondents from 219, or 79.3 percent, of these localities, mentioned prohibition as one of the important issues (Table 4.2). No quantitative inferences can be drawn from the data because the sample is unrepresentative of the distribution of population in the United States (it is heavily weighted in favor of rural areas) and the sources are biased. But the results of the survey are nonetheless indicative of the interest generated by the prohibition issue.

Party Responses to the Prohibition Question

Aware that concern with prohibition could swing large numbers of voters in either direction, the parties searched for ways to maximize their gains while minimizing their losses. Directors of the Republican and Democratic campaigns adopted similar stratagems that muddled distinctions between their candidates' positions and perhaps made prohibition less salient as a voting issue.

Following up his telegram to the Houston convention, Al Smith used his acceptance speech to set forth a detailed proposal on the control of alcoholic beverages. First, he vowed to fulfill the party's mandate to enforce the Eighteenth Amendment and the Volstead Act. Second, he recommended "an amendment to the Volstead Law giving a scientific definition of the alcoholic content of an intoxicating beverage. The present definition is admittedly inaccurate and unscientific." Each state would then be allowed to fix its own standard of alcoholic content, subject always to the proviso that that standard could not exceed the maximum fixed by the Congress. Third, he

Table 4.2. Results of the Republican National Committee Questionnaire to Editors and Subscribers to the National Republic, 13–27 September 1928

State	Number of Replies	Issues or Issue Uppermost in the Minds of Voters						
		Prohibition	Religion	Prosperity	Tammany	Farm Rlf.	Tariff	Other
California	17	15	3		3	2	2	3
Colorado	7	6	2		1	1	1	1
Connecticut	2	2					1	
Delaware	1	1						
Idaho	10	8	2			3		1
Illinois	11	7	3			6		
Indiana	8	7	1	1		6	1	1
Iowa	8	5	3	1		6	1	
Kansas	7	6	5					1
Maine	1	1						
Maryland	2	2		1		1		
Massachusetts	2	2				1		
Michigan	7	4	2	1				2
Minnesota	18	11	3			12	2	2
Missouri	5	4	2			3		
Montana	3	3				1		
Nebraska	11	8	2			9		
Nevada	2	1						
New Jersey	5	2	1	1			1	2
New Mexico	1	1	1	1			1	1

Table 4.2, continued

State	Number of Replies	Issues or Issue Uppermost in the Minds of Voters						
		Prohibition	Religion	Prosperity	Tammany	Farm Rlf.	Tariff	Other
New York	10	10		2	1	2		2
North Dakota	10	6	2		1	6		3
Ohio	13	10	4	1		5		
Oklahoma	14	12	7		1	3	1	2
Oregon	38	35	18	1	5	7	4	4
Pennsylvania	13	11	3	4	1	2	5	4
South Dakota	11	9	5			7	1	
Tennessee	3	1	1			1		2
Utah	2	2						
Washington	16	14	8			5		2
West Virginia	5	3	3				1	1
Wisconsin	13	10	4	2		2		4
Total	276	219	85	16	13	91	23	38
Percentage	100	79.3	30.8	05.8	04.7	33.0	08.3	17.8

advocated "an amendment in the Eighteenth Amendment which would give to each individual state itself only after approval by a referendum popular vote of its people the right wholly within its borders to import, manufacture or cause to be manufactured and sell alcoholic beverages, the sale to be made only by the State itself and not for consumption in any public place."[23]

Hoover's position, on the other hand, never evolved beyond the brief statement he had set forth in his acceptance speech. Leaving himself and the party ample maneuvering room, Hoover opposed repeal of the Eighteenth Amendment and modification of the amendment or the enforcement laws that "amounted to nullification," but did not bind himself to the status quo. He termed prohibition an experiment "noble in motive"; but if its motive was temperance, virtually no one, including Al Smith, would disagree.[24]

Analysis of campaign strategy reveals that Smith's apparently well-defined position on the prohibition issue received equal and opposite treatment from Republican and Democratic spokesmen. In this era before national radio and television coverage of campaign activities, the parties could adopt a strategy of calculated contradiction, shaping different appeals for different segments of the electorate. Thus, in dry areas Democratic propagandists downplayed Smith's proposed changes in national prohibition, contending that prohibition was embodied in the Constitution and could not be altered by presidential decree. In the same areas, Republican propagandists took an opposite approach, warning that Smith would surely poison the fruits of America's long and arduous attempt to end the liquor traffic and protect families from the evils of drink. In wet areas, the parties exchanged roles. The Democrats stressed Smith's ability to modify the prohibition laws through presidential leadership, whereas the Republicans pleaded that even presidents cannot change the Constitution. GOP campaigners also exploited the flexibility of Hoover's pronouncements to contend that the secretary of commerce was open to changes in the prohibition laws and would not be handicapped by an allegiance to bone-dry Democrats of the solid South.[25]

The voter was receiving conflicting messages and could not be certain of how prohibition would fare under either Hoover or Smith. Both wet and dry voters may have sought another means of distinguishing between the two candidates. Contemporary political analyst Frank Fabian, for example, believed that prohibition played an important role in the campaign, but admitted that its influence would "have been vastly increased if the election of Smith had meant directly what it probably meant in the long run."[26]

Many defenders of prohibition may have found Al Smith's religion more objectionable than his wetness. Available evidence suggests that opposition to Smith's prohibition policy served as a cloak for opposition to his Catholicism.[27] By focusing on prohibition, vehement opponents of Al Smith could denounce him as immoral, lawless, and godless without raising the religious question. No matter how lurid their rhetoric, defenders of prohibition could claim that they were opposed to Smith's policies and not his religion.[28] Many hard-boiled Democratic politicians reported to FDR that in their localities anti-Catholicism lurked behind the skirts of prohibition. B. E. Haney, for example, Democratic state chairman for Oregon, offered the following assessment of the relationship between religion and prohibition: "I feel that very many women were induced to vote for Hoover upon one or another grounds, who actually were influenced by the religious question. . . . The wet and dry issue, which I have never considered a political question, was, undoubtedly, a very strong factor among the farmers and among the women, though in many instances I suspect that it was but a cover for the religious issue."[29] George N. Peek, director of the Democratic campaign among midwestern farmers, confided to Hugh Johnson that "the sole question remains as to whether the farmers are going to put the religious question and the wet and dry question ahead of their economic interests. In this connection I think the wet and dry issue is the smoke-screen for the whisperers in the religious campaign."[30]

To the confidential disclosures of Democratic politicians may be added the findings of experienced reporters who sought to fathom the sources of anti-Smith sentiment. Consider two reliable reports from the border states. Richard V. Oulahan, special correspondent for the *New York Times*, reported from Missouri that "Democrats in the state have satisfied themselves that while it [Democratic defection] is attributed to the strong dry sentiment among Democratic voters, the underlying cause is that Governor Smith is a Catholic."[31] Robert Barry of the *New York Evening World* filed a similar report from his native state of Kentucky: "It is the religious issue all over again in spite of any perfunctory denials by Republican managers. If Smith were not a Catholic there would not be any resemblance of a 'hoss race'. He would have a walkover. His prohibition views would not matter."[32]

Anti-Catholicism also creeps into the rhetoric of even the most single-minded drys. Bishop James Cannon, Jr., for example, published on the eve of the election a paid newspaper advertisement assailing the Catholic church.[33] Similarly, the official journal of the Anti-Saloon League, the most important prohibition lobby, included the preservation of "Anglo-Saxon Protestant domination" among its reasons for rejecting Al Smith.[34] In 1932, moreover, the even more outspoken wet views of Franklin D. Roosevelt did not inspire dry opposition that was remotely as widespread or as intense as that experienced by Al Smith in 1928.

By unleashing Assistant Attorney General Willebrandt, the Republican party fostered the mingling of religion and prohibition. Willebrandt's one-person crusade against Al Smith sparked a lively controversy. Critics argued that an official of the United States government had no business appearing before church groups and that her speeches were thinly veiled appeals to religious bigotry. But her supporters contended that as long as the assistant attorney general did not mention Smith's religion her call for sectarian support was perfectly legitimate. Objections to Willebrandt's political activities, however, need not be based solely on the issue she raised.

A seemingly realistic conflict—like that of wets versus drys—can be obscured by a host of irrelevant prejudices. An evaluation of Willebrandt's appeal should consider not only the issue she raised, but also the manner in which that issue was discussed. Even a cursory inspection of the assistant attorney general's speeches indicates that her substantive analysis was lost in an effusion of personal slander. Consider, for example, her address to the Ohio Methodist Conference: in the space of three hundred words she associates Smith with the New York underworld; accuses him of violating his gubernatorial oath and of deliberately subverting the Constitution; claims that because of his leadership New York has become the national center of lawlessness; and insists that his election would undermine law and order throughout the country and promote "nullification of the Constitution."

Manhattan is ruled by Tammany, an organization that for underworld connections and political efficiency is matched no place else in America.

Tammany's candidate [in 1924] was the man who had just abandoned the policy of cooperation between the State and national Government provided for in the concurrent clause of the Eighteenth Amendment. He was the one Governor in all the States who, notwithstanding his oath to support the Constitution of the United States, pulled down one of the forty-six pillars the people had erected for its support.

New York, since through Governor Smith's leadership the enforcement act of the State was repealed, has become the center . . . of lawlessness and disregard for the Constitution. . . .

The inevitable result of his [Smith's] leadership would be to increase disregard for law, evasion of responsibility of enforcement, and large avenues of nullification of the Constitution. No dry Congress could prevent that.

There are 2,000 pastors here. You have in your churches more than 600,000 members of the Methodist Churches in Ohio alone. That is enough to swing the election. The 600,000 have friends in other States. Write to them. Every day and every ounce of your energy are needed to rouse the friends of Prohibition to register and vote.[35]

The responses of Chairman Work and candidate Hoover to questions about Willebrandt's activities suggest that they doubted the propriety of her political activities. In light of Willebrandt's letter to Chairman Work, their responses to questions concerning her activities are particularly revealing. On 25 September, there occurred the following brief exchange between Work and members of the press corps:

Question: What is Mrs. Willebrandt's status as far as the Committee is concerned?

Dr. Work: I don't know. She is a sort of free lance, and you of course know she is a Department of Justice official. I don't know where she speaks or when she speaks or anything about it.[36]

The secretary of commerce was scarcely more candid in his comments to reporters:

Press: Would you dispose of Mrs. Willebrandt in a word or two—her connection with you or with the National Committee.

Hoover: I don't think I ought to go into that either. I am not managing this campaign. I'm afraid I can't help you on any of these matters.

Press: Mr. Hoover, you said in connection with Mrs. Willebrandt that you are not managing this campaign. Do you mean it is up to Dr. Work?

Hoover: I would rather you would not bring these things up to me.[37]

Given Hoover's close supervision of the campaign, he could scarcely have been unaware of Willebrandt's activities.

Bootleggers and the Presidential Campaign

An intriguing sidelight on the prohibition issue is the support apparently accorded to the Republican party by the nation's bootleggers. These men credited the Republicans with assuring their prosperity by supporting the continuing existence of national prohibition and failing to enforce the prohibition laws. Writing to Hiram Johnson in early September, progressive Republican Harold Ickes noted ironically, "In this campaign we have the ministers, the Anti-Saloon League and the bootleggers supporting Hoover."[38] In his private correspondence, Senator Key Pittman of Nevada charged that bootleggers in his state favored the Republicans and were intimidating their clients to vote the Republican ticket: "The chief fight being made against Governor Smith is by the boss bootleggers. They are using bribery and intimidation through their control or alleged control of Prohibition enforcement in this state. Except for this we would get 90 percent or more of the Italian vote." Pittman confided to a political associate that similar forms of coercion were being employed by bootleggers in every state.[39]

As the following unsigned memo to A. H. Kirchofer of the Republican National Committee's publicity division reveals, the Republicans were aware of their popularity among bootleggers: "Talked to a big man in the booze racket after my conversation with you in front of the office. This man is for Hoover. Said he had made $150,000 under Republican administrations and has been assured that there can be no change on prohibition that will materially affect his business. Wouldn't say who told him that. 'And if there is, what of it?' he said. 'I have got mine. The Republicans took care of me and I certainly am not going to vote my friends out of office.'"[40] There is no evidence, however, that the Republicans cultivated the support of bootleggers.

A Phony Referendum

Jubilant drys claimed in 1928 that Hoover's decisive victory was tantamount to a successful referendum on national prohibition. More dispassionate observers have justly criticized this claim on the grounds that Hoover's triumph cannot be attributed to any single cause and that prohibition influenced fewer voters than did other issues. Herbert Hoover carried almost every state in the nation, including several that had resoundingly rejected prohibition in state-level referenda.

Chapter 5

Immigrants versus Natives

Few metaphors have been more thoroughly discredited than that of the "Great American Melting Pot." The theory that American society successfully blends the diverse cultures of immigrant peoples has long been the target of scholarly and popular criticism. Rising ethnic consciousness in the 1960s and 1970s has been accompanied by an especially spirited and telling assault on the melting pot metaphor. Although a compelling synthesis of the assimilation experience has yet to be articulated, most scholars would now agree that the communal affiliations, values, and mores of individual nationality groups continue to be notable features of American life.

In 1928, approximately one-third of the American people were foreign-born or had a foreign-born parent. These individuals were more likely than those with extended lineage in America to have been conscious of their heritage and to have been affected by the assimilation process. Foreign-stock Americans included members of the new immigrant groups from southern and eastern Europe and the old immigrant groups from Great Britain, Ireland, Germany, and Scandinavia. A study of ethnic voting should reveal whether or not those of the second and later generations behaved differently from immigrants and their children. If sufficiently refined, it can disclose distinctions in the political preferences of individual ethnic groups.

The Influence of Ethnic Heritage on the Vote for President

Although historians have suggested that Al Smith represented the aspirations of foreign-stock Americans, ethnic voting in the presidential election of 1928 has provoked considerable controversy. Once again, no conventional wisdom dictates how being of foreign birth or of the first generation influenced voting for president in 1928, when controlling for such possibly confounding characteristics as religious affiliation and residence in city or country. Moreover, since the religious commitments of ethnic groups are often a crucial component of group identity, religion and nationality cannot be disentangled completely. Religion, the central motif of the 1928 contest, interacts with the Old World background of American voters.

Samuel Lubell, the first historian to argue persuasively that the presidential election of 1928 began a new era of American politics, claimed that Al Smith's appeal to immigrants and their children was part of the electoral realignment that occurred in 1928: "What Smith really embodied was the revolt of the underdog, urban immigrant against the top dog of 'old American stock.'" Ruth Silva's study seems to support Lubell's contention. She found that only "percent foreign stock" was a significant correlate of Smith's strength. "Religion, the vote for liquor, and metropolitanism" proved to be of no importance. Ogburn and Talbot, however, offer the contradictory finding that independent of religion, urbanism, prohibition, and Democratic voting in the presidential election of 1920, "the foreign-born influence" explained a negligible proportion of Al Smith's vote.[1]

The regression coefficients reported in Table 5.1 disclose that the influence of foreign-stock heritage on the presidential vote of 1928 depends on how that vote is measured. Reflecting profound temporal changes in the behavior of immigrants and first-generation Americans, deviation variables measuring differences between the vote cast for candidates in 1928 and in earlier elections are much more responsive to changes from county to county in the percentage of foreign-stock individuals (those foreign born or with foreign-born parent) than are variables measuring percentages of the 1928 tally. To give perspective on these changes, Table 5.2 reports coefficients for percentages of the presidential tally in the elections of 1916 to 1924 (for ease of reference, 1928 is added as well). The analysis of these elections, however, should be interpreted with caution since demographic data is projected backward from the census of 1930.

Differences from county to county in the percentage of immigrants and first-generation Americans do not produce strong responses in any of the three measures of the 1928 vote. The modest positive regression coefficient for Al Smith's percentage of the presidential vote indicates that foreign-stock Americans were only slightly more likely to opt for the Democratic nominee than were native-stock Americans with similar social and economic characteristics. The coefficient falls to zero for Smith's percentage of the adult population,

Table 5.1. *Influence of Percentage of Foreign-stock Population on Measures of the Vote for President: 2,058 Counties (in percent)**

	Regression Coefficient b	Standard Error
Dem 1928	.09	.013
Dem 1928 total	.01	.010
Rep 1928 total	−.10	.012
Dem 1928 minus Dem 1924	.50	.013
Dem 1928 minus Dem/Prog 1924	.02	.012
Dem 1928 minus Prog 1924	−.38	.019
Dem 1928 total minus Dem 1924 total	.31	.008
Dem 1928 total minus Dem/Prog 1924 total	.05	.008
Dem 1928 total minus Prog 1924 total	−.25	.013
Rep 1928 total minus Rep 1924 total	.01	.008
Dem 1928 minus mean Dem 1916–24	.38	.011
Dem 1928 minus mean Dem 1916–20, Dem/Prog 1924	.22	.010
Dem 1928 minus Dem 1932	−.01	.011
Dem 1928 minus mean Dem 1932–40	−.02	.011

*Controlling for percentages of Urban, Owners, Negro, Female, Under 35, Pop change, Jewish, Prot church, Catholic, and for Economic status.

indicating that foreign-stock voters were less likely to participate in the election than their native-stock counterparts. The negative coefficient for Hoover's percentage of the adult population confirms that immigrants and first-generation Americans were more likely than their native-stock counterparts either to vote for Smith or not to vote rather than to vote for Herbert Hoover.

If the preferences of Catholics and Protestants diverged more widely in 1928 than in elections before and after, the preferences of foreign- and native-stock Americans reached a point of inflection in that election year. The rift between those of foreign and native stock was far less impressive in the election of 1928 than in the elections of 1920 or 1924. But, in 1928, these two groups reversed their positions along the divide between Republicans and Democrats. Controlling for other variables, in the presidential elections of 1920 and 1924, immigrants and their children had been far less likely to vote for a

Democratic candidate than their counterparts of the second generation and beyond. Only with the nomination of Al Smith did presidential candidates of the Democratic party become more attractive to foreign-stock than to native-stock voters. An increase from one county to another in the percentage of foreign-stock residents yields a very substantial increase in deviation variables measuring the difference between the vote for Smith and either the average vote of the three previous Democratic contenders or the vote for John W. Davis in 1924. The regression coefficients for Democratic voting from 1916

Table 5.2. *Influence of Percentage of Foreign-stock Population on Percentages of the Vote for President: 1916–1928: 2,058 Counties (in percent)**

	Regression Coefficient b	Standard Error
Dem 1916	−.12	.014
Dem 1920	−.34	.013
Dem 1924	−.41	.015
Dem/Prog 1924	.08	.017
Prog 1924	.48	.016
Dem 1928	.09	.013

*Controlling for percentages of Urban, Owners, Negro, Female, Under 35, Pop change, Jewish, Prot church, Catholic, and for Economic status.

to 1924 disclose that after 1916 immigrants and their children deserted the Democratic party in far greater proportion than their counterparts of the second generation and beyond. The coefficients are consistently more negative for each election, −.12, −.34, and −.41, respectively. The redirection of this trend in the presidential election of 1928 was no temporary aberration. The new polarity between native- and foreign-stock Americans was about the same in 1932 as it had been in 1928. An increase in the percentage of foreign-stock residents produces virtually no change in the difference between the vote for Smith in 1928 and either the vote for Roosevelt in 1932 or the average vote for Roosevelt from 1932 to 1940.

The failure of Democratic candidates to attract foreign-stock voters prior to 1928 did not necessarily mean that most members of this group rejected Democratic candidates because of hard-core

Republican affiliations. Foreign-stock Americans were more volatile than regular during the 1920s. Progressive party nominee Robert M. La Follette, for example, performed exceedingly well among immigrants and first-generation Americans. An increase from county to county in the percentage of foreign-stock residents produced an extraordinarily large increase in La Follette's percentage of the 1924 vote. The large negative coefficient for the difference between Smith's percentage of the presidential tally and that of La Follette, furthermore, indicates that Smith's support relative to La Follette's declined sharply as a county's percentage of foreign-stock residents increased.

Immigrants and their children, of course, do not form a homogeneous class. Statistics aggregating all nationalities may conceal discrepancies in the behavior of different groups. To portray the political preferences of particular nationality groups, the analysis excises from each regression equation the variable measuring each county's percentage of foreign-stock Americans. In its place are inserted variables measuring the percentage of foreign-born residents from Scandinavia, Germany, Italy, Poland, Great Britain, France, Ireland, Russia, Canada (British), and Canada (French Canadian). The regression coefficients for each of these variables are reported in Table 5.3.

The regression coefficients of Table 5.3 represent both the independent influence of each distinct variable and an indirect influence stemming from correlations with the percentage of first and earlier generations from each immigrant group. The larger this correlation for a given nationality group, the more substantial the indirect effect. Since immigrants and their offspring frequently reside in close proximity to each other, as the percentage of immigrants with a particular ethnic heritage increases, so will the percentage of those from later generations of the same ethnic group. These county-level correlations will obviously affect the value of the regression coefficients reported in Table 5.3. Their influence will be strongest among groups whose ethnic identity continued to influence voter behavior for several generations and groups whose immigration history extends several generations into the American past.

Given these indirect influences and the small variation from county to county in the percentages of county residents from each immigrant group, only limited conclusions can be drawn from the coefficients of Table 5.3. These coefficients cannot be interpreted as the percentage point difference in candidate preference between a particular group of immigrants and the remainder of the population,

Table 5.3. *Influence of Membership in Nationality Groups on Measures of the Vote for President: 2,058 Counties (in percent)**

	Dem 1916		Dem 1920		Dem 1924	
	b	SE	b	SE	b	SE
Scandinavian	− .46	.086	−1.30	.084	−1.74	.097
German	−1.30	.199	−2.81	.192	−2.30	.224
British	− .15	.382	−1.30	.370	−2.17	.431
British Canadian	− .63	.200	−1.03	.195	−1.35	.226
French Canadian	− .25	.202	.05	.196	.26	.228
Russian	− .21	.213	−1.40	.206	−2.12	.240
Polish	− .50	.275	− .62	.266	− .15	.310
Italian	−1.08	.222	− .29	.215	− .10	.251
Irish	1.00	.485	1.57	.470	4.64	.547

*Controlling for percentages of Urban, Owners, Negro, Female, Under 35, Pop change, Jewish, Catholic, Prot church, and for Economic status.

when other variables are held constant. Attention must be focused on the statistical significance of each regression coefficient and changes over time in the magnitude of coefficients for each ethnic group.

Explanations of ethnic voting in 1928 must begin with earlier elections of the decade—the 1920 contest between James Cox and Warren G. Harding and the three-cornered race of 1924 involving Calvin Coolidge, the Republican, John W. Davis, the Democrat, and Robert M. La Follette, the Progressive party nominee. Thus Table 5.3 displays regression coefficients for party percentages from 1916 to 1928. For purposes of comparison, the table also reports coefficients for differences between the vote for Smith and for FDR in 1932.

Ethnic Voting in 1920

Historians have agreed that foreign-stock support for the Democratic presidential candidate sharply tailed off in 1920, but they have disagreed on how to interpret this change. Several interpretations are possible: first, that Democratic losses among immigrant groups were equal to, or less than, their losses overall; second, that Democratic losses among foreign-stock voters were greater than among those of native stock, but for reasons only indirectly related to ethnic back-

Dem/Prog 1924		Prog 1924		Dem 1928		Dem 1928 Minus Dem 1932	
b	SE	b	SE	b	SE	b	SE
.36	.101	2.18	.096	.06	.084	− .15	.062
2.74	.234	4.85	.221	1.97	.193	− .52	.143
−1.42	.449	.84	.425	− .63	.372	.16	.275
−1.53	.236	− .20	.224	− .56	.195	− .27	.144
− .43	.238	− .72	.226	.20	.197	.77	.146
.22	.250	2.05	.237	.44	.207	− .54	.153
−2.33	.323	−2.32	.306	− .97	.267	.82	.198
− .84	.261	− .80	.247	− .16	.216	1.23	.160
1.82	.571	−3.26	.541	3.10	.473	3.27	.350

ground (for example, because foreign-stock Americans tended to earn less income than native-stock Americans); and third, that uniquely ethnic issues produced especially severe losses among immigrants and their children.[2] By determining how changes from county to county in the percentage of foreign-stock residents affected voting for Democratic candidates in 1916 and 1920, when a variety of other variables are held constant, regression analysis can help resolve this dispute. The results suggest that the third interpretation best describes the behavior of foreign-stock voters. Independent of control variables, in both the presidential elections of 1916 and 1920, foreign-stock voters were more inclined to oppose the Democratic candidate than were their counterparts of native stock. By 1920, however, a narrow gap in the preferences of foreign- and native-stock voters had widened substantially. The negative influence of changes in the percentage of foreign-stock residents is almost three times greater for James Cox's percentage of the 1920 vote than for Woodrow Wilson's percentage of the 1916 vote.

At first glance, it seems surprising that Warren Harding could displace the loyalties of immigrants and first-generation Americans. This colorless, stand-pat Republican did not appeal to the special concerns of ethnic Americans in the substance of his policy or in the undercurrents of his rhetoric. One might even expect to find that in 1920 native Americans defected to the Republicans, while immigrants remained fixed in traditional patterns of behavior. Yet the longing for a return to "normalcy," as promised by a Harding presidency, may have been especially poignant for immigrants and their children. America's nationality groups were caught in the riptide of postwar readjustment, for World War I had paradoxically spawned both an increase in ethnic pride and identity and a new movement among native Americans for the rapid and forcible assimilation of immigrants.

During World War I, foreign-stock Americans developed a heightened self-consciousness that was reflected in the formation of nationwide ethnic organizations and a new assertiveness by the foreign-language press. The international ferment of 1914 to 1920 engaged the overseas loyalties of virtually every European nationality group in the United States; as never before, members of ethnic groups united in pursuit of common goals. During the war, the government helped to cement ethnic solidarity through propaganda appeals to ethnic interests and the encouragement of pro-Allied organizations.[3]

Yet the tensions of World War I made Americans more susceptible to demands for "100 percent Americanism"—unstinting national loyalty and conformity to preconceived standards of conduct and belief. A concomitant of 100 percent Americanism was the crusade to Americanize the immigrant—to smelt away his foreign characteristics and blend him into the common coin of American culture. The Americanization movement stimulated by the war abandoned the idea of synthesizing divergent cultures into a new and better hybrid. Instead, the movement sought to compel adherence to visions of a pure American culture, free of alien contaminants. During and after the war, schools, employers, welfare agencies, educational associations, patriotic organizations, and government institutions launched a spirited propaganda campaign against "un-American" styles of life. In some areas these efforts were supplemented by compulsory Americanization programs and discriminatory legislation against aliens.[4] Both parties endorsed measures for drastically curtailing immigration, especially from eastern and southern Europe, and, during the notorious Red Scare of 1919–20, the government even attempted the mass deportation of alien radicals.[5]

Efforts to meld the foreigner into American culture collided head-on with the new strength and solidarity of nationality groups. If the Americanization movement produced some outward conformity to cultural norms, its primary effect was apparently to antagonize the individuals it sought to assimilate. Immigrants recognized the advantages of becoming familiar with American ways, but they resented the smug superiority and bludgeoning tactics of the Americanizers. Edward G. Hartmann, in *The Movement to Americanize the Immigrant*, reports that "editorials appeared in many foreign-language newspapers during the years 1919–20, all expressing their disapproval of various aspects of the Americanization drive; some mildly, almost self-consciously, others frankly and belligerently."[6]

The Democratic administration, of course, was not primarily responsible for fervid Americanism in 1919 and 1920. Nevertheless, President Wilson symbolized the tensions unleashed by World War I, and, in their exasperation over opposition to the Versailles treaty and the League of Nations, Wilson and his followers denounced the "hyphenate Americans" who allegedly placed loyalty to the home country above loyalty to America. "Hyphens," Wilson charged on more than one occasion, "are the knives that are being stuck into this treaty."[7] Most important, members of immigrant groups could welcome a philosophy that meant the cessation of postwar hysteria and the silencing of voices that continued to question their patriotism.

The results of regression analysis, reported in Table 5.3, reveal considerable variation in the behavior of individual nationality groups. This variation can be explained only by pointing to election issues that had differential effects on the groups in question. Explanations citing factors that equally affected all voter groups or even all foreign-stock voters will not suffice. Although the process of waging war and negotiating peace affected members of every ethnic group, different groups were touched in different ways. The burdens of discrimination did not fall uniformly on all, and nationality groups did not share a common response to Wilson's policies. Ethnic voting in 1920 was not a simple response to the tensions of war or the issues raised by settling the peace.

The regression coefficients of Table 5.3 suggest that independent of control variables, some ethnic groups turned from the Democrats in greater proportion than did the rest of the voting population. Democratic losses were especially severe among Americans of German, Scandinavian, British, and British Canadian descent. German-American opposition to the Democratic candidate can be explained as a response to Wilson's approach to negotiating peace. Americans of German extraction welcomed the president's initial postwar procla-

mations and hoped for a peace settlement based on his Fourteen
Points. They were profoundly disillusioned, however, by the actual
terms of the Versailles treaty. German-American leaders charged that
Wilson had discarded the Fourteen Points and sought instead to pun-
ish the German people. German-Americans also expressed dismay
at Wilson's disregard for England's continuing blockade of Germany
and outrage at the administration's denunciation of nationality groups
antagonistic to the agreements reached at Paris.[8]

Governor Cox recognized the futility of seeking to recover German-American support. Instead he sought to rally wartime patriots
by scathing the allegedly disloyal Germans and other "hyphens"
who favored the Republican party. Harding also lashed out against
the spirit of hyphenism, but in less pointed terms than Cox. Other
Republican campaigners sought to convert hostility for Wilson into
votes for Warren Harding.[9]

Scandinavian-Americans joined their German counterparts in
a flight from the Democratic party. The European heritage of the
Scandinavians accustomed them to government activities on behalf
of the individual; although traditional Republicans, they tended to
support progressive reform.[10] During the 1920s, especially in the
Midwest and Far West, battles between conservatives and reformers
were frequently fought within the dominant party or between third
parties and both major parties rather than between the Republicans
and their Democratic rivals. Many Scandinavians may have been
lured by Wilson's progressivism to vote Democratic in 1916, but returned to the Republicans in 1920. In addition, Scandinavians tended
to oppose America's entry into World War I and Woodrow Wilson's
postwar arrangements.[11]

The Democrats also lost support among Russian-Americans in
1920, although these losses probably were not related to Wilson's
sponsorship of the Versailles treaty and the League of Nations. Russian-Americans had little reason to oppose his initiatives; their defection may largely have been a reaction to the activities of the
Democratic administration during the Red Scare of 1919–20. The
Palmer raids had been mainly directed against Russian aliens, and
most Russian-Americans felt that their nationality group had been
shabbily treated by the federal government. Russian-Americans also
resented Wilson's decision to station American troops in Russia
shortly after the end of World War I.[12]

The adverse reaction of Irish-American spokesmen to Wilson's postwar policies might suggest that members of this nationality group would be much less likely to vote for a Democratic candidate in 1920 than in 1916. Spokespersons for the American Irish asserted that the principle of self-determination avowed by the president must be applied to Ireland as well as to continental Europe. They envisaged the peace settlement as a means of securing Irish independence from British rule. Like German-Americans, however, many Irish-Americans seemed dismayed by the results of the Paris deliberations. They believed that Irish independence had been ignored and that the League of Nations had been stacked in favor of Great Britain, which was allotted six votes. Through 1919 and 1920, the Irish press and many leaders of the Irish community crusaded against both the Versailles treaty and the League of Nations. During the presidential campaign of 1920, both parties sought to woo Irish votes by expressing sympathy for the Irish independence movement. But Cox was still the legatee of Wilson's policies.[13]

Yet opposition to Wilson by Irish-American newspapers and leaders preceded Versailles. In 1916, Irish-Americans had condemned President Wilson for his alleged antipathy to the aspirations of the Irish.[14] Independent of control variables, however, changes from county to county in the percentage of Irish-Americans had a positive influence on the county's percentage of Democrats in 1916 and a yet stronger positive influence in 1920. Issues relating to kinfolk overseas apparently were offset by the traditional loyalties of this normally Democratic group. But, in 1924 or 1928, the percentage of Democratic voters in each county was more responsive to changes in the percentage of Irish-Americans than in either 1916 or 1920. This result suggests that ethnic issues may have cut into Irish support for Democratic presidential candidates in both 1916 and 1920.

Although Italian-Americans were staunch supporters of Woodrow Wilson's wartime policies, they were alienated by his peacemaking activities. Many Italian-Americans believed that the president had betrayed Italy at the peace conference by contesting its claim to the Adriatic port of Fiume and other territory eventually ceded to Yugoslavia. Italian-American leaders and newspapers stridently criticized Wilson, claiming that he had cruelly double-crossed the Italian people. Italian animosity against Wilson seemed to persist through the debate over the peace treaty and the League of Nations.[15]

The regression coefficients of Table 5.3 do not reveal, however, that independent of control variables, the Democrats suffered severe losses among Italian-Americans. Indeed, Wilson's percentage of the 1916 vote declined more sharply in response to changes from county to county in the percentage of Italian-Americans than did Cox's percentage of the 1920 vote. This seemingly aberrant result may indicate that Italian-Americans in 1920 may not have been responding primarily to questions of foreign policy. Such a caveat, however, does not explain why the voting of some groups can be explained by reference to foreign policy and that of other groups cannot.

Other immigrant groups included in this study, notably the Polish, British, and both groups of Canadians, tended to favor Wilson's peace plans. The coefficients of Table 5.3 reveal that, independent of control variables, French Canadians may have been more inclined to vote Democratic in 1920 than in 1916. Yet an opposite trend is indicated for the British and the British Canadians. The statistics for the entire period under study in this chapter and for the primary election of 1928 suggest that these latter two groups were normally inclined to vote Republican. Perhaps they were somewhat deflected from their partisan loyalties in 1916 by Wilson's Anglophilism, but were disillusioned with the president by 1920. Primarily concerned with securing American adherence to the League of Nations, British-Americans were willing to accept compromise or reservations.[16]

Ethnic Voting in 1924

John W. Davis, Democratic nominee in 1924, did not recoup the losses suffered by Governor Cox among Americans of foreign stock. Compared to their native-stock counterparts, immigrants and their children were even less likely to vote Democratic in 1924 than in 1920. In 1924, an increase from one county to another in the percentage of foreign-stock Americans produced a decline in Democratic voting that was one-third greater than in 1920. The Republicans, however, were not the major beneficiaries of ethnic opposition to Davis. The most striking feature of ethnic voting in the presidential election of 1924 is the remarkable appeal of Progressive party nominee Robert M. La Follette to immigrants and first-generation Americans. Foreign-stock voters were far more likely than those of native stock from the same social and economic strata to opt for La Follette rather than Coolidge or Davis. The coefficients for individual nationality groups reported in Table 5.3 reveal that La Follette's appeal was concentrated among German, Scandinavian, and Russian voters.

La Follette's war-related activities made him a virtual folk hero among German-Americans. An unremitting advocate of neutrality, La Follette opposed every presidential action that might have promoted involvement in World War I. He voted against the Espionage Acts of 1917 and 1918; after the war he openly expressed sympathy for the plight of the German people and opposed the exclusion of Germany from America's postwar emergency program. The senator flayed the Versailles treaty and personally visited Germany in August 1923.[17]

La Follette's war record was not forgotten during the campaign of 1924. In October the senator again denounced Wilson's policies and America's entry into World War I.[18] The Republicans directed their campaign almost entirely against La Follette rather than Davis and used the senator's war record to cast aspersions on his loyalty. This effort neatly complemented the party's attempt to portray La Follette as a dangerous, irresponsible radical.[19]

La Follette's alleged radicalism seems to have figured in the decisions of some voters. A survey of 1,088 midwestern voters, 875 of whom were university students, found that 202, or 18.6 percent, listed one of the following as their "most important reason for voting for Coolidge": La Follette's policies subversive and dangerous (102); La Follette radical and not constructive (62); did not want La Follette elected because of his association with socialists and reds (38).[20]

Scandinavian-Americans also tended to oppose American involvement in World War I and Wilson's postwar policies. More important, La Follette's progressivism was especially appealing to this group. *New York Times* reporter Richard V. Oulahan found that both German and Scandinavian voters were favorable to La Follette's candidacy.[21]

La Follette's strong showing among Russian Americans cannot be explained by reference to his war record. More likely, La Follette benefited from the socialist orientation of this immigrant group. La Follette was endorsed by the Socialist party and in several states was listed under their label. The senator had also spoken out against the Red Raids and the dispatching of troops to Russia after World War I.[22]

La Follette's war record may also have appealed to voters of Irish-American descent. Although La Follette the dissenter may have been attractive to some Irish-Americans, the statistics of Table 5.3 demonstrate that, in 1924, Irish support for the Democratic party actually increased. Members of this group had powerful Democratic loyalties and were not necessarily motivated by issues relating to the fatherland.

Finally, La Follette was able to cut deeply into the votes of certain immigrant groups, in part because the GOP failed to consolidate or extend their earlier gains among immigrants and first-generation Americans. Despite Harding's success with ethnic voters, the Republican party made no effort to secure the loyalties of ethnic groups by integrating their leaders into the party hierarchy, by granting them a share of the federal patronage, or by showing concern for their special problems. With few exceptions, the Republicans failed to provide the political recognition that, even in the form of token appointments or encouraging rhetoric, was of considerable symbolic importance to groups that were striving to enter the mainstream of American life. Party power and position remained the exclusive province of Protestant, old-stock Americans, who had little sympathy for the aspirations of the immigrant. With respect to the ethnic voter, the 1920s were a period of lost opportunities for the Republican party.[23]

Davis also profited from Republican indifference to the aspirations of ethnic Americans. The Democratic nominee appeared to hold his own among Polish, French, and Italian voters. The value of the regression coefficients for these nationality groups do not change substantially when analysis shifts from Cox's to Davis's percentage of the vote cast for president. Davis performed exceptionally well among the traditionally Democratic Irish-Americans. The strength of the Irish-Americans' commitment to the Democratic party is disclosed by Table 5.4, which records the independent influence of membership in ethnic groups on voting in the Democratic rather than Republican primaries of 1928. The analysis includes statistics on primary voting for only 850 of the 2,058 counties so the standard errors of the coefficients are especially high. But the loyalty of the Irish-Americans stands out. Apparently, the Irish did not find the GOP particularly congenial in the 1920s, and their commitment to the Democratic party solidified in 1924. Table 5.3 demonstrates that changes from county to county in the percentage of Irish-Americans has a stronger positive influence on Democratic voting in 1924 than in 1920 or 1916. A historian of Irish America, William V. Shannon, chronicled the Republicans' failure to pursue the Irish vote: "During the dozen years of normalcy that intervened between Wilson and Franklin Roosevelt, the Irish remained out of the national picture as successive Republican Administrations failed to broaden their party's base."[24]

Public statements denouncing the Ku Klux Klan by Davis and La Follette may also have enhanced their standing with foreign-stock voters. The Klan was a very hot issue in 1924. A proposal to proscribe the Klan was sufficiently controversial to divide the 1924 Democratic convention into warring factions. The hooded order, of course, was the bête noir of most ethnic Americans, who were concerned to know the candidates' views on the Klan. On 8 August, La Follette became the first of the three candidates to condemn the Ku Klux Klan. On 22 August, Davis followed suit. Coolidge never mentioned the Klan throughout the campaign, although in a late gesture, his running mate Charles Dawes spoke out mildly against the Klan.[25]

Ethnic Voting in 1928

In 1928, Al Smith became the first Democratic candidate in four presidential elections to perform better among immigrants and first-generation Americans than among their counterparts of the second and later generations. For the entire collection of counties and for every region except New England, increases from one county to another in the percentage of foreign-stock residents yields substantial increases in the difference between the vote for Smith and the vote for previous Democratic contenders.

Despite these findings, the presidential election of 1928 does not

Table 5.4. *Influence of Membership in Nationality Groups on Voting in the Democratic Primaries of 1928: 850 Counties (in percent)**

	Regression Coefficient b	Standard Error
Scandinavian	− .95	.245
German	− .27	.602
British	− .73	.887
British Canadian	−2.00	.454
French Canadian	−1.32	.510
Russian	− .53	.559
Polish	−2.74	.634
Italian	− .44	.506
Irish	6.10	1.110

*Controlling for percentages of Urban, Owners, Negro, Female, Under 35, Pop change, Jewish, Prot church, Catholic, and for Economic status.

stand out as a confrontation between immigrants and natives. When other variables are held constant, ethnic background is not an especially important influence on any measure of the 1928 vote. Foreign-stock Americans were only slightly more likely than their native-stock counterparts to vote for Al Smith. They were also slightly more likely to refrain from voting at all. When the analysis considers separate regions of the nation, the independent influence of ethnic background on the presidential vote appears even less impressive. Moreover, the vote for Robert M. La Follette in 1924 is much more responsive to changes from county to county in the percentage of foreign-stock residents than is the vote for Al Smith in 1928.

Results of the Republican National Committee's survey of party leaders confirm the movement of foreign-stock voters toward the Democratic party in 1928. The committee asked state and local politicians to evaluate Hoover's performance among German-Americans, Italian-Americans, and other foreign-born voters. In most cases, the respondents reported abnormal Democratic strength among the foreign-born. In its summary report, the national committee acknowledged Smith's appeal to immigrant groups, but predicted that the gains made by Democrats in 1928 would disappear by the next presidential election.[26]

An understanding of foreign-stock voting in 1928 requires explanation of why immigrants and their children turned to the Democratic candidate and of why their political migration did not create more of a gap between foreign- and native-stock voters. Most of those responding to the Republican National Committee's question about the immigrant vote cited the controversy over prohibition as a source of Smith's success with ethnic Americans. With the exception of migrants from Scandinavia, immigrant groups were more likely than their counterparts of native stock to oppose restrictions on the sale and manufacture of intoxicants. Beer and wine were accepted parts of their diet and prohibition seemed an unreasonable response to the abuse of alcohol.[27] The analysis of counties from states holding referenda on prohibition confirms the wetness of foreign-stock Americans. For these counties, a 1 percent increase in the percentage of immigrants and their children produces a .38 percent increase in the percentage of voters rejecting prohibition (standard error = .038).

More refined analysis suggests, however, that the defection of foreign-stock voters to the Democratic candidate in 1928 was not simply a result of the electorate's views about prohibition. A thirst for repeal of the Eighteenth Amendment cannot explain Smith's gain over Davis among those of Scandinavian stock. Moreover, if immigrants and first-generation Americans were responding primarily to candidates' positions on prohibition, changes from county to county in the percentage of foreign-stock residents should have less influence on the difference between the vote for Al Smith and the vote for previous Democratic contenders when the percentage of those opposed to prohibition is added to the regression equations. The deviation variables expressing the difference between the vote for Smith and the vote for Davis and between the vote for Smith and the average Democratic vote from 1916 to 1924 are most responsive to changes from county to county in the percentage of immigrants and their children. Yet the influence of this explanatory variable is not substantially diminished after controlling for the division of opinion over prohibition. Data from the referenda counties reveal that when controlling for social and economic variables other than a voter's stand on prohibition, a 1 percent change in a county's percentage of foreign-stock residents yields a .51 percent change in the difference between the vote garnered by Smith and that garnered by Davis (standard error = .028) and a .32 percent change in the difference between Smith's vote and the average Democratic vote of 1916 to 1924 (standard error = .024). When the percentage of voters opposing prohibition is added to the regression equations, the values of these coefficients decline only slightly to .46 (standard error = .030) and .27 (standard error = .026), respectively.

Laws restricting immigration to the United States were equally or more offensive to foreign-stock Americans than laws establishing national prohibition. Virtually every ethnic group resented the restrictive legislation of 1924, which not only limited European immigration to approximately 150,000 per year, but also favored the British at the expense of other nationality groups. Like the prohibition issue, however, both parties obfuscated the issue of immigration restriction.

The legislation of 1924 had received bipartisan support,[28] and in 1928 both the Republican and Democratic platforms supported continued restriction with the proviso that the law be modified to prevent the permanent separation of family members.[29] The Democratic plank on immigration restriction was melded into the platform with no debate either in the Committee on Platform and Resolutions or in the plenary session of the convention. Despite the impending nomination of a candidate with the potential to cut deeply into ethnic support for the Republican party, the Democrats did not consider altering their position on immigration restriction.

In his acceptance speech, however, Smith ventured a half-hearted appeal to immigrant groups from southern and eastern Europe by criticizing the use of the census of 1890 as a basis for nationality quotas. Unlike his telegram on prohibition, this foray against the Johnson Act provoked no outcry that the Democratic nominee had repudiated the party platform. Moreover, Smith's opposition to the 1890 quotas seemed purely gratuitous, since the Johnson Act mandated that they be replaced by a new quota system based on the national origins of the population. Smith may have been responding to a comment in Hoover's acceptance speech favoring quotas based on the census of 1890 rather than the national origins of the population. Quotas based on the census of 1890 rather than the national origins of the population would mainly benefit Germany and Scandinavia at the expense of Great Britain and Ireland.[30]

In later speeches, Smith further muddled his position on immigration restriction by ignoring his criticism of the 1890 census and claiming to be in complete agreement with Hoover. On several occasions the governor stated, "There is no issue between either the parties or the candidates on the question of sustaining and keeping in full force and effect the restrictive features of the present immigration laws."[31] Smith never explained what manner of fence-straddling would place him in full agreement with Hoover and in opposition to quotas based on the census of 1890.

Although neither party stressed the immigration question during the campaign, both sought to capitalize on Smith's ambiguous position. Ignoring the governor's later protestations, the Republicans courted nativist support by assailing his criticism of the 1890 quota base.[32] Many Americans of the 1920s believed that the so-called Anglo-Saxon and Nordic races were inherently superior to other peoples. Republican spokesmen argued that quotas founded on more recent enumerations of the population would inundate the United States with racially inferior immigrants. The Democrats, on the other hand, communicated through the foreign-language press their willingness to consider more liberal quotas for the "new immigrant" groups.[33]

Responses to the Republican survey and to Roosevelt's circular letter indicate that some voters perceived Smith to be an opponent of the current philosophy of immigration restriction. Although the immigration issue is not separately listed on the chart (Chart 3.1, Chapter 3), a number of Roosevelt's correspondents believed that Smith's position on immigration restriction was an important cause of his defeat.[34] Two of the leaders canvassed by the Republican National Committee claimed that the immigration issue added to Al Smith's popularity among foreign-born voters. Nonetheless, the issue might have become more salient for voter behavior if the Democratic nominee had taken a clear-cut stand against immigration restriction.

Reactions to individuals and groups that coalesced in support of Herbert Hoover may also have swayed the voting decisions of some foreign-stock Americans in 1928. Although Hoover was not widely regarded as an enemy of the immigrant, his most vocal supporters included the self-appointed guardians of pristine Americanism. Despite the important analytic distinctions between hostility to Catholics and to immigrants, these were often complementary aspects of the same world view. Many of the groups and individuals that denounced Al Smith as a Catholic and a wet—the Ku Klux Klan, Mabel Walker Willebrandt, the WCTU, fundamentalist and conservative church organizations—also were noted for their antagonism to immigrants. Smith, of course, had a long record of opposition to the Klan and generally was considered a friend of the immigrant. Given this polarity, some immigrants and their children may have perceived the election as a struggle between the forces of tolerance and bigotry in American life.

Historians have also suggested that Al Smith symbolized the strivings of immigrant Americans. William E. Leuchtenburg, for example, claims that "Smith personified the desire of sons of urban immigrants to make a place for themselves in the world."[35] Smith might have been a more important symbol of success to Catholics who were immigrants or first-generation Americans trying to adapt to America than to their more established brethren. Immigrants of Jewish or Eastern Orthodox heritage may also have linked their aspirations to those of Al Smith. A 1 percent increase in a county's percentage of Jews yields a substantial increase in Al Smith's percentage of the 1928 vote and a more modest increase in his percentage of the potential voting population. Jews also figured more prominently in the vote for Smith than in the average vote of the past three Democratic contenders, the vote for Robert M. La Follette, the combined Davis–La Follette vote, and the vote for Franklin D. Roosevelt in 1932. When other variables are held constant, Jews contributed a proportionately greater vote only to John W. Davis's shrunken coalition of 1924. Given their anti-Catholic animus, however, members of Protestant nationality groups may have found it difficult to envision Smith as a symbol of their hopes and dreams. The statistical analysis suggests that religion may have interacted with ethnic heritage so that support for Smith would be greater than expected among Catholic voters of foreign stock and less than expected among either foreign-stock Protestants or native-stock Catholics.

Like La Follette, Smith benefited from the failure of GOP leaders to integrate foreign-stock Americans into the Republican party during the 1920s. Lacking firm loyalty to the Republicans, foreign-stock voters were susceptible to the appeal of an attractive Democratic candidate. This finding clashes with Lubell's contention that the Democratic party necessarily would benefit from the increasing proportion of foreign-stock Americans in the voting population of the 1920s.[36] National politics during the decade presented opportunities to lure immigrant and first generation voters that the Republicans failed to exploit.

Although foreign-stock voters turned toward the Democrats in 1928, the election is better perceived as a confrontation between Catholics and Protestants than between foreign and native-stock Americans. Immigrants and their children were only slightly more likely to vote for Al Smith than were native-stock Americans from the same social and economic strata. The analysis of deviation variables further suggests that the gap between native- and foreign-stock voters was not at its widest in 1928. Compared to the vote for Al Smith, foreign-stock Americans were a larger component of the vote for La Follette in 1924 and about an equally large component of the vote for Roosevelt in 1932. As the percentage of foreign-stock voters increases from one county to another, the difference between the vote for Smith and the vote for La Follette decreases. Changes in this foreign-stock percentage have virtually no influence on the difference between the vote for Smith and the vote for Roosevelt in 1932 or the difference between the vote for Smith and the average vote for Roosevelt from 1932 to 1940.

Differences in the choices made by foreign- and native-stock Americans undoubtedly were moderated by the anti-Catholicism of some Protestant groups. Possible interaction between religion and ethnic background suggests that religious loyalties may have diluted the appeal of Smith's candidacy to members of predominantly Protestant nationality groups. Anti-Catholicism may also explain why, compared to La Follette and Roosevelt, Table 5.3 reveals that Smith performed much better among predominantly Catholic than among predominantly Protestant groups.

Historians have harped on Al Smith's popularity with foreign-stock Americans, while slighting Herbert Hoover's considerable standing with this same group. Foreign-language newspapers welcomed the nomination of both candidates, applauding their accomplishments in transcending humble origins and achieving national prominence.[37] In addition, members of some nationality groups may have admired Hoover for his role as administrator of food relief to the nations of Europe after World War I. He had been an extraordinarily efficient purveyor of supplies to nations ravaged by wartime conflict and emerged as a hero to Americans grateful for his services to their homelands.[38]

Hoover's strength among those of foreign stock was recognized by Republicans prior to his nomination. In a circular letter sent to all delegates to the Republican convention, William H. Hill, chairman of the New York State Hoover for President Committee, contended that of all GOP aspirants only Hoover could carry the nationality groups of New York State. William Randolph Hearst announced in June 1928 that Hoover would be a particularly formidable Republican candidate "because elements of foreign descent . . . had not forgotten his relief work in the World War."[39]

Hoover was also the beneficiary of a massive publicity campaign organized by the Division for Foreign Language Publicity and Advertising of the Republican National Committee. The division's efforts were summarized in a 1929 report by its director, Frank Little:

> 640 newspapers in 21 languages with 4,000,000 circulation were constantly solicited by this Division both in person and by mail. Every newspaper gave something worthwhile in publicity.
>
> 17 news bulletins were sent out. There were 119 special articles; 700 personal conferences with publishers; 700 telegrams; and 18,300 mailings.
>
> I engaged at a fixed fee for publicity purposes an active commercial publicity and advertising organization—The Inter-Racial Press of America, Inc., of New York.
>
> 1,865,000 booklets were published: 625,000 Polish; 475,000 Italian; 150,-000 Hungarian; 150,000 German; 75,000 French; 50,000 Russian.[40]

The division, however, did not have separately allocated funds to pay for advertising.

The partisan behavior of the foreign-language press both indicated and influenced the mixed response of ethnic Americans to the presidential election of 1928. A nationwide survey by the Foreign Language Information Service revealed that of foreign-language papers taking a stand on the election, 115 supported Smith, 98 supported Hoover, 46 supported Norman Thomas, 3 supported the Socialist Labor party, and 23 the Communist party. The information service concluded that there was no distinctively "foreign vote" in 1928.[41] Table 5.5 reports the preferences of newspapers published in various languages.

Table 5.5. *Presidential Preferences of the Foreign-Language Press in 1928*

	Hoover	Smith		Hoover	Smith
Polish	18	17	Finnish	2	0
Italian	18	22	Czechoslovak	2	19
German	8	20	Yugoslav	4	10
Jewish	2	3	Hungarian	7	16
Scandinavian	26	2	Russian	1	2

Political cues broadcast in the foreign-language press may have figured in the voting decisions of some of those still fluent in their native tongue. Students of the ethnic press have argued persuasively that these journals had wide circulation within their respective nationality groups and influenced their readers' thinking about contemporary affairs. Foreign-language papers printed news of the native land and stories about fellow nationals in the United States. They highlighted issues of special interest to their clientele, played upon the immigrant's sentimental regard for the old country, and offered useful information about the adopted land. Foreign-stock Americans, especially those who used primarily the mother tongue, had fewer sources of information than most Americans and relied on the foreign-language press.[42]

The partitioning of the foreign-stock vote reported in Table 5.3 indicates that, when controlling for social and economic variables, Smith performed better than previous Democratic candidates among members of almost every nationality group. In several instances, however, immigrant groups were a smaller component of Al Smith's voter coalition than of the coalitions put together by Robert M. La Follette in 1924 or Franklin D. Roosevelt in 1932. Inspection of Table 5.3 reveals distinctions among ethnic groups with different religious affiliations.

Compared to earlier nominees of the Democratic party, Al Smith achieved a remarkable turnabout in the voting of German-Americans. Statistics reported in Table 5.3 show that independent of control variables, the difference between the vote for Smith and the vote for Davis, as well as the difference between Smith's vote and the average vote of the past three Democratic candidates, changes in a positive direction as the percentage of German-Americans increases from county to county. For Americans of German descent, memories of World War I did not quickly fade. Throughout the 1920s, Wilson and Wilsonianism continued to be anathema for German-Americans. In 1920, Cox was obliged to defend Wilson's foreign policies, advocating ratification of the Versailles treaty and participation in the League of Nations. In 1924, voters again identified the Democrats with Wilson's brand of internationalism as the party recommended adherence to the World Court and a referendum election on America's joining the League. In 1928, however, the Democratic convention purged from its platform the last traces of Woodrow Wilson's dreams for American participation in world affairs.[43]

Influential members of the Committee on Platform and Resolutions of the 1928 convention sought neither to maintain party traditions nor to present the public with a coherent program for governing the nation. As with policy regarding prohibition, party sachems sought mainly to avoid internecine conflict and to prepare a platform that would not alienate large blocs of voters. In closed session, party leaders expressed admiration for Woodrow Wilson's broad vision and idealism. But, as a matter of practical politics, they argued that the Democrats could no longer continue to be the party of internationalism. With deep regret, the leadership offered a foreign policy plank that omitted any reference to the League of Nations or the World Court and only briefly mentioned the goal of achieving cooperation among nations. Despite the protests of diehard Wilsonians like Newton D. Baker and Josephus Daniels, the committee endorsed the foreign policy plank and the convention ratified its decision.[44] An exchange between Baker and Senator Sam Gilbert Bratton of New Mexico during deliberations of the platform committee illustrates the thinking of those directing the Democratic party:

Mr. Baker: Well, of course, we cannot make a platform that nobody will misunderstand.

Mr. Bratton: That is the very reason I thought we might better remain silent on this subject rather than put the country in the attitude of cooperating with an institution with which many Americans are out of accord.[45]

During the campaign, Smith followed the letter of the platform about foreign affairs, making no attempt to free lance as he had on the subjects of prohibition and immigration restriction. Democratic campaigners, however, privately assured prominent advocates of internationalism that Smith was really more sympathetic than Hoover to American collaboration with the League of Nations and the World Court.[46]

The candidates' positions on prohibition may have influenced German-Americans to vote Democratic in 1928. Of all nationality groups, Germans were probably the most zealous wets. Beyond their love for beer, German-Americans also seem to have regarded the prohibition laws as an attack on the distinctively German life style.[47] Table 5.6 shows that changes from county to county in the percentage of voters opposing prohibition are most responsive to changes in the percentage of German-Americans residing in each county. The same message was given by most of the politicians who reported a loss of German-American support to the Republican National Committee, mentioning prohibition as a major contributing factor.

Smith did not perform nearly as well among German-Americans, however, as did Robert M. La Follette in 1924 or Franklin D. Roosevelt in 1932. An increase from one county to another in the percentage of German-Americans produced a much more striking increase in La Follette's percentage or in Roosevelt's percentage than in the percentage of the vote garnered by Al Smith in 1928. Undoubtedly the anti-Catholicism of Lutheran Germans kept many of them from voting for Smith in 1928. Four years later, the nomination of Roosevelt, a Protestant wet, removed this barrier.

Al Smith performed slightly better than previous Democratic candidates among Scandinavian-Americans. Yet an increase from one county to another in the percentage of Scandinavians in a county still yielded a decrease in the percentage of Democratic voters, and both Robert M. La Follette and Franklin D. Roosevelt were much more successful than Al Smith in luring Scandinavian votes. Disappointed with the conservatism of Republican rule, Scandinavian-

Americans may have been willing to change administrations, but reluctant to install a Catholic in the White House. After studying the campaign in the Midwest, Richard V. Oulahan reported to the *New York Times,* "It comes down to this . . . that Smith would get the bulk of the Scandinavian vote if his religious faith were not involved."[48] The Scandinavian press was solidly behind Hoover in 1928; his candidacy was favored by twenty-eight of the thirty papers canvassed by the Foreign Language Information Service.

As expected, Table 5.3 reveals Smith's great strength among Irish-Americans. The Democratic loyalties of the American Irish were enhanced by the widespread belief that Smith was a fellow Hibernian, the first American of Irish descent with a real chance to win the nation's highest office. Nonetheless, Davis's percentage of the 1924 vote was more responsive to changes from county to county in the percentage of Irish-Americans than was Smith's percentage of the 1928 vote. In 1924, a year of disastrous losses for the Democratic party, Davis's Irish support was an especially large component of his meager accumulation of votes.

The comparative support for Smith among Italian-Americans was greater than that for Wilson in 1916, La Follette in 1924, and Roosevelt in 1932. No clear trend, however, emerges from analysis of the vote for Smith or the differences between this vote and the votes for Cox in 1920 or Davis in 1924. Exclusive of control variables, in-

Table 5.6. Influence of Membership in Nationality Groups on Opposition to Prohibition: 471 Counties (in percent)*

	Regression Coefficient b	Standard Error
Scandinavian	.04	.249
German	4.68	.401
British	1.93	.992
British Canadian	−1.26	.692
French Canadian	3.65	1.354
Russian	− .33	.704
Polish	.90	.542
Italian	.87	.416
Irish	2.90	1.082

*Controlling for percentages of Urban, Owners, Negro, Female, Under 35, Pop change, Jewish, Prot church, Catholic, and for Economic status.

creases from county to county in the percentage of Italians do not yield discernible changes in either direction for any of these variables. The mixed response of Italian-language newspapers to the 1928 contest corroborates this finding. Eighteen of the journals surveyed had endorsed Hoover; twenty-two had endorsed Smith (see Table 5.5).

When controlling for other social and economic variables, Smith is found to have garnered more of his support from Polish-Americans than did La Follette in 1924 or Roosevelt in 1932. But an increase from county to county in the percentage of Polish-Americans still produced a decrease in the vote for Smith and in the difference between this vote and the votes for earlier Democratic nominees. Hoover's record as administrator of war relief was especially important to those of Polish heritage. In early October, the Polish National Alliance endorsed Herbert Hoover, praising him as "alms distributor" to a starving Europe.[49] Several of the local leaders canvassed by the Republican National Committee referred to Hoover's relief efforts as having an impact on the Polish voter. Among the thirty-five Polish newspapers reviewed by the Foreign Language Information Service, a small majority of eighteen opted for Hoover. The journals of no other nationality group except the Scandinavians predominantly favored the Republican nominee.

The voting behavior of Americans with roots in French-speaking Canada closely resembled that of the Italian-Americans. Exclusive of control variables, Smith's support among French-Canadian voters was greater than that of La Follette, La Follette and Davis combined, and Franklin D. Roosevelt in 1932. Again, no clear trend emerges for the difference between the vote for Smith and the vote for earlier contenders nominated by the Democratic party. Smith's percentage of the presidential vote, however, responds positively to changes in a county's percentage of French-Canadian residents.[50]

The vote for Smith, in contrast, responds negatively to changes in the percentage of those from English-speaking Canada. In addition, Roosevelt in 1932 performed much better among members of this group than had Smith in 1928. As with Germans and Scandinavians, the anti-Catholicism of English Canadians probably accounts for these findings. No clear trend, however, emerges for the behavior of English Canadians when the vote for Smith is compared to the vote for previous Democratic contenders or the vote for La Follette.

The separate enumeration by the census of a predominantly Catholic and predominantly Protestant group from the same country provides an extraordinary opportunity to study the relationship between ethnic heritage and religion as determinants of the vote for president. Table 5.7 reports the regression coefficients for the percentage of French and English Canadians, excluding variables measuring religious affiliation. The table discloses notable discrepancies in the preferences of these two immigrant groups when the equations fail to control for religious differences. French Canadians were much more responsive to Smith's candidacy than their English Canadian counterparts; in several instances, the coefficients for these two groups even have opposite signs.

These differences in the voting behavior of French and British Canadians, however, should not be attributed uncritically to their religious loyalties. Because of their culture and language, French Canadians had more difficulty adapting to life in the United States than did the English Canadians. Distinctive experiences with the process of assimilation may also have influenced the voting decisions of the two Canadian groups.

Conclusions

There is no simple answer to the question of how the ethnic heritage of voters affected their response to the presidential competition of 1928. To trace ethnic voting in the 1920s is to encounter an intricate pattern of varied and shifting allegiances. Immigrants and those of the first generation did not vote as a unit for presidential candidates of any party. Rather, the decisions of foreign-stock voters exhibited both change over time and diversity among nationality groups. The German-Americans were the most volatile of all groups. Swayed largely by the pressures of World War I, they were inclined to support the Republicans in 1920, the Progressive party in 1924, and the Democrats in 1928.

Contrasting the four elections from 1916 to 1928, only in the presidential contest of 1928 did immigrants and their children favor the Democratic candidate in greater proportion than native-stock Americans from the same social and economic strata. When compared to their native-stock counterparts, members of virtually every nationality group were more likely to support the Democrats in 1928 than in any of the three previous contests. Yet the gap between native- and foreign-stock voters was modest in 1928. La Follette in 1924 and Franklin D. Roosevelt in 1932 opened up respectively greater

Table 5.7. Influence of Percentage of British Canadians and French Canadians on Measures of the Vote for President, Religious Variables Excluded: 2,058 Counties (in percent)*

	British Canadian		French Canadian	
	b	SE	b	SE
Dem 1928	− .77	.204	1.20	.200
Dem 1928 total	−1.17	.160	.73	.157
Rep 1928 total	− .84	.168	− .70	.164
Dem 1928 minus Dem 1924	.81	.211	1.19	.207
Dem 1928 minus Dem/Prog 1924	.92	.173	1.40	.170
Dem 1928 minus Prog 1924	− .70	.269	1.41	.263
Dem 1928 total minus Dem 1924 total	.21	.137	.99	.134
Dem 1928 total minus Dem/Prog 1924 total	.43	.116	1.10	.114
Dem 1928 total minus Prog 1924 total	− .96	.186	.87	.182
Rep 1928 total minus Rep 1924 total	− .73	.117	− .47	.115
Dem 1928 minus mean Dem 1916–24	.40	.176	1.30	.173
Dem 1928 minus mean Dem 1916–20, Dem/Prog 1924	.44	.157	1.38	.153
Dem 1928 minus Dem 1932	− .43	.147	1.30	.144
Dem 1928 minus mean Dem 1932–40	− .35	.152	1.20	.149

*Controlling for percentages of Urban, Owners, Negro, Female, Under 35, Pop change, and for Economic status.

and equal divisions between these two groups of voters. Despite the interaction between religion and ethnic background, the presidential contest of 1928 can more accurately be viewed as a conflict between Catholics and Protestants than between immigrants and natives.

These results, however, do not sustain the proposition that in the

1920s America was becoming a "triple melting pot" of Catholics, Protestants, and Jews. Deriving primarily from the work of Will Herberg, this theory suggests that by the 1950s, differences among nationality groups in America had melted down to differences among the nation's three major religions. Herberg contends that only the immigrant's religion survived in robust form the process of adjusting to American life:

However important the ethnic group may have been in the adjustment of the immigrant to American society, and however influential it still remains in many aspects of American life, the perpetuation of ethnic differences in any serious way is altogether out of line with the logic of American reality. The newcomer is expected to change many things about him as he becomes American—nationality, language, culture. One thing, however, he is not expected to change—and that is his religion. And it is religion that with the third generation has become the differentiating element and the context of self-identification and social location.[51]

But the evidence presented here does not justify pressing the importance of religion beyond the personalities and issues of 1928. In another context, ethnic background could well overshadow religion as an influence on the behavior of voters. No fixed category like religion or ethnic background can predetermine how people respond to the situations they confront.

Chapter 6

City versus Country

Samuel Lubell, writing in 1952, claimed to have discovered the real significance of the presidential election of 1928. Lubell argued persuasively that Al Smith had effected a revolution in American politics by driving a wedge between city and country. Although Smith lost heavily in small towns and farm areas, he attained a small majority in the nation's largest cities, reversing the substantial Republican majorities of 1920 and 1924. Thus, Lubell contended, Al Smith, not Franklin D. Roosevelt, ended the Republican domination of urban America and paved the way for urban-based Democratic majorities in the 1930s and 1940s.[1] Lubell's analysis of Smith's success in America's cities is now fully established in the historiography of the 1928 election. Historians often portray Al Smith as the "Hero of the Cities," or as the "Symbol of the Urban Masses." Refining and extending Lubell's arguments, such scholars as Richard Hofstadter, Paul A. Carter, William E. Leuchtenburg, John Hicks, and Andrew Sinclair have contended that the split between city and country best represented the clash of cultures that took place in 1928.[2]

A determination of how well the polarity between city and country summarizes the distinctive electoral alignments of 1928 is the first step in understanding the significance of urban-rural conflict. The analysis must then disentangle urban-rural residence from other explanatory variables and, finally, consider why city and country folk might have behaved as they did. Questions relating to the long-term significance of the 1928 contest will be deferred to Chapter 9.

Quantitative Analysis of Urban-Rural Conflict

As stated by Lubell and like-minded historians, theories regarding urban-rural divisions in the presidential election of 1928 are susceptible to conflicting interpretations. First, the division between urban and rural residents may be simply a convenient rubric for expressing the social antagonisms that surfaced during the election. Differences in the voting behavior of city dwellers and country folk may signify only that the types of people most likely to favor Smith (for example, Catholics and foreign-stock Americans) were more likely to reside in cities than the types of people most likely to favor Hoover (for example, Protestants and native-stock Americans). Second, residence in urban or rural communities may have influenced how voters responded to the confrontation between Al Smith and Herbert Hoover, independent of a voter's demographic profile. Although historians have not distinguished clearly between these interpretations, most accounts suggest that urban-rural conflict meant more than the summation of other conflicts and was an important independent influence on voter decisions.

Those historians who discern residence in city or country as having a discrete influence on the vote for president have not clearly shown how the size of a community affected voter behavior. Regardless of his religious and ethnic heritage, was any given urban voter more likely than his rural counterpart to vote for Smith? Or did the size of one's community act to intensify other forces, making nativist opposition to Al Smith more pronounced in rural settings, or making ethnic and Catholic support for the governor more intense in the cities? Perhaps a combination of both these effects shaped the presidential vote? A careful reading of the relevant literature provides no easy answer. Admittedly, the distinction between the direct and interactive effects of variables can be subtle and difficult to detect. Nonetheless, historians should recognize that direct and interactive effects are analytically distinct and can suggest important differences of interpretation.

Zero-order regression coefficients between a county's percentage of urban dwellers and measures of voter behavior provide one indication of how well the split between city and country summarizes the voter alignments of 1928. Unlike the partial regression coefficients computed from multivariate equations, zero-order measures incorporate no controls for the effects of correlated variables. The values of zero-order coefficients include both the independent influence of urban-rural residence and indirect influences flowing from variables correlated with both residence in city or country and responses to Al Smith and Herbert Hoover. For instance, a positive relationship between a county's percentage of urbanites and its percentage of Democratic voters may result entirely or in part from the disproportionate number of Catholics residing in America's cities.

The zero-order regression coefficient registers the amount of change in each response variable produced by a 1 percent change from county to county in the percentage of city dwellers. The larger this regression coefficient, the greater the percentage point difference in the voter preferences of city and country folk. For instance, the regression coefficient of .05 for Smith's percentage of the presidential tally would mean that the proportion of urbanites voting for Smith was 5 percentage points higher than the proportion of rural residents favoring him.

The coefficients reported in Table 6.1 suggest that city dwellers were only slightly more favorable to Al Smith than those who lived in the country. A 1 percent change in a county's percentage of urbanites (census definition) yields only a .05 percent change in the vote for Smith. The coefficients of Table 6.1 also show that city people were

Table 6.1. Zero-Order Regression Coefficients for the Influence of Percentage of Urbanites on Measures of the Vote for President: 2,058 Counties (in percent)*

	Regression Coefficient b
Dem 1928	.05
Dem 1928 total	−.01
Rep 1928 total	−.08
Dem 1928 minus Dem 1924	.14
Dem 1928 minus Dem/Prog 1924	.14
Dem 1928 minus Prog 1924	.04
Dem 1928 total minus Dem 1924 total	.08
Dem 1928 total minus Dem/Prog 1924 total	.11
Dem 1928 total minus Prog 1924 total	.02
Rep 1928 total minus Rep 1924 total	−.06
Dem 1928 minus mean Dem 1916–24	.10
Dem 1928 minus mean Dem 1916–20, Dem/Prog 1924	.10
Dem 1928 minus Dem 1932	.13
Dem 1928 minus mean Dem 1932–40	.04

*No control variables.

less likely to vote in 1928 than were country folk. As the percentage of urbanites residing in any given county increases, both Al Smith's and Herbert Hoover's percentage of a county's potential voting population correspondingly decreases. As would be expected, this relationship is stronger for Hoover's than for Smith's percentage.

The rift between city and country widens only slightly to account for the difference between Al Smith's percentage of the presidential vote and percentages garnered by candidates in other elections. The vote for Smith was more urban-oriented than the vote for previous Democratic contenders, than for Robert M. La Follette in 1924, and for Franklin D. Roosevelt in 1932. A 1 percent change in the percentage of urbanites generates a .14 percent change in the difference between the vote for Smith and the vote for Davis as well as the vote for Davis and La Follette combined in 1924. Moreover, a 1 percent change in the percentage of urban residents yields a .13 percent change in the difference between the vote for Smith and the vote for Roosevelt in 1932. Urban-rural residence, however, has less effect on the difference between the vote for Smith and the average vote for Roosevelt between 1932 and 1940.

Lubell and other historians, of course, were struck primarily by the vote cast for Smith in metropolitan America. As Table 6.2 reveals, Smith performed well in the nation's large cities; but to hail him as the hero of the cities is to exaggerate his appeal. The governor only broke even in large cities, despite a whopping majority of 450,000 in his home city. Eliminating the vote cast in New York City, Smith's percentage declines from 50 to 46 percent. Moreover, Smith received approximately 38.5 percent of the vote cast outside the cities listed in Table 6.2. The gap of 11.5 percent between his percentages in the cities and other communities is the proportion of individual-to-individual variation in voter choice that can be predicted by residence in large cities. Thus, after eliminating metropolitan residence, almost 90 percent of the variation in voting for president remains unexplained. Roosevelt's metropolitan performance in 1932 was not founded upon Al Smith's accomplishments in the great cities. The difference between the vote for Smith and the combined vote for Davis and La Follette in 1924 accounts for a negligible percentage of variation in the vote for Roosevelt.

Multiple regression analysis indicates how urban-rural differences affected voter behavior after controlling for the demography of city and country. The partial regression coefficients reported in Table

Table 6.2. Voting in Major Cities: 1924–1932 (in percent)

	Dem/Prog 1924	Dem 1928	Dem 1932
Baltimore	57	48	67
Boston*	53	67	69
Buffalo	43	49	51
Chicago*	38	47	57
Cincinnati*	39	43	51
Cleveland*	51	46	53
Detroit	20	37	59
Los Angeles*	34	29	60
Newark*	34	41	46
New York	55	62	71
Philadelphia	18	40	56
Pittsburgh	43	47	56
St. Louis	47	52	65
San Francisco*	52	50	67

*Computed for the county in which the city is located.

6.3 suggest that the division between urban and rural residents did not have much of an independent influence on measures of the vote cast for president in 1928. Changes from county to county in the percentage of urbanites have a slightly negative effect on either Smith's percentage of the presidential tally ($b = -.00$) or Smith's percentage of the adult population ($b = -.03$); and a more sizable negative effect on Hoover's percentage of the adult population ($b = -.06$). The negative regression coefficients for both candidates' percentage of potential voters indicate that when controlling for the social and economic composition of city and country, urban residents were still less likely than rural dwellers to vote in 1928.[3]

Multiple regression analysis of deviation variables suggests that independent of control variables, the vote for Smith was not more disproportionately urban than the vote for earlier Democratic candidates. Changes from county to county in the percentage of urban dwellers have virtually no influence on the difference between Smith's percentage of the Democratic vote and either Davis's percentage in 1924 or the average Democratic percentage of 1916 to 1924. Similarly, urban-rural differences have a negligible effect on the differences between 1924 and 1928 in either Democratic or Republican percentages of the potential voting population.

The coalition forged by Al Smith in 1928 was proportionately more urban than the coalitions forged by Robert M. La Follette in 1924 and Franklin D. Roosevelt in 1932. An increase in any given county's percentage of urban residents yields a small increase in the difference between the vote for Smith and the vote for La Follette and a slightly larger increase in the difference between the vote for Smith and the vote for Roosevelt. Apparently, the more urban composition of Smith's support reflected his inability to tap the discontent of farmers as effectively as either La Follette or Roosevelt. Relative to these two candidates, Smith opened a much wider gulf between farmers and residents of rural towns (towns with a population of less than 2,500) than between city and country folk. Thus, differences within rural America were more notable in 1928 than differences between city and country. For entirely rural counties, a 1 percent change in the percentage of those living on farms rather than in towns produces a −.16 percent change in the difference between the vote for Smith

Table 6.3. Influence of Percentage of Urbanites on Measures of the Vote for President: 2,058 Counties (in percent)*

	Regression Coefficient b	Standard Error
Dem 1928	−.00	.010
Dem 1928 total	−.03	.008
Rep 1928 total	−.06	.009
Dem 1928 minus Dem 1924	.02	.010
Dem 1928 minus Dem/Prog 1924	.03	.009
Dem 1928 minus Prog 1924	.04	.015
Dem 1928 total minus Dem 1924 total	−.01	.006
Dem 1928 total minus Dem/Prog 1924 total	.04	.006
Dem 1928 total minus Prog 1924 total	.02	.010
Rep 1928 total minus Rep 1924 total	.02	.006
Dem 1928 minus mean Dem 1916–24	−.02	.008
Dem 1928 minus mean Dem 1916–20, Dem/Prog 1924	−.02	.008
Dem 1928 minus Dem 1932	.07	.008
Dem 1928 minus mean Dem 1932–40	−.07	.008

*Controlling for percentages of Foreign stock, Owners, Negro, Female, Under 35, Pop change, Jewish, Prot church, Catholic, and for Economic status.

and the vote for La Follette and a −.15 percent change in the difference between the vote for Smith and the vote for Roosevelt in 1932. These coefficients are respectively 4 and 2.1 times larger than the corresponding coefficients for a county's percentage of those living in urban communities rather than farms or rural towns. Moreover, the difference between Smith's percentage of the adult population and the percentage garnered by La Follette is not responsive to changes from county to county in the level of urbanization; the regression coefficient is .02, with a standard error of .01.

Although, independent of control variables, the vote for Smith was proportionately more urban than the vote for Roosevelt in 1932, this ordering was reversed in later years. The coefficients of Table 6.3 reveal that the average vote for Roosevelt from 1932 to 1940 was proportionately more urban than the vote for Smith in 1928. The regression coefficients for the difference between Smith's 1928 tally and Roosevelt's 1932 tally and for the difference between Smith's tally and Roosevelt's average tally from 1932 to 1940 have the same magnitude and opposite signs: .07 and −.07, respectively. Both coefficients are statistically significant at a level far more conservative than .001. Further analysis reveals that support for Roosevelt became increasingly urban both in 1936 and 1940. A 1 percent increase in a county's percentage of urban residents yields a −.08 percent change (standard error = .010) in the difference between the vote for Smith and the vote for Roosevelt in 1936 and a −.15 percent change (standard error = .011) in the difference between the vote for Smith and the vote for Roosevelt in 1940. If a revolt of the cities actually occurred in the early twentieth century, these results suggest that historians should look for its origins in the mid-1930s rather than in 1928. Further discussion of what happened in the 1930s is beyond the scope of the present study.

The multiple regression analysis, however, may obscure the real importance of urbanism for the vote received by Smith and the difference between that vote and those garnered by earlier Democratic candidates. Perhaps the distinction between urban and rural communities as defined by the census (any town of 2,500 inhabitants or more is classified as urban) is less important for Smith's accomplishments than the distinction between small cities, suburbs, towns, and farm areas on the one hand and large cities on the other hand.

The hypothesis that residence in large cities had an especially important independent influence on the 1928 presidential vote can be tested against the null hypothesis (of no big city effect) in several ways. The results indicate that the initial analysis did not underestimate the independent influence of urban-rural residence on the vote for president. The first test employs the results of the analysis of covariance performed for counties with different levels of urbanization. If, independent of the other variables included in this study, residence in large cities rather than in small cities and towns was strongly associated with support for Al Smith, urban-rural differences should be greater in the highly urban than in the middle urban groups of counties. The highly urban group includes all the nation's large cities, whereas the urban population of the middle urban group consists of people residing in towns and smaller cities. In the highly urban group, urbanism should have significantly more influence on measures of the 1928 vote and on the difference between Smith's performance and the performances of earlier Democratic combatants.

The results of this first test, reported in Table 6.4, fail to show major differences for the influence of urban-rural residence in the middle urban and the highly urban groups of counties. The coefficients of the table clearly show that, when controlling for the attributes of voters, the split between city and country is not an important influence on the vote for Smith or his lead over previous candidates

Table 6.4. Geographic Influence of Percentage of Urbanites on Measures of the Vote for President (in percent)*

	Middle Urban Counties (1%–37.5% Urban)		Highly Urban Counties (Over 37.5% Urban)	
	Regression Coefficient b	Standard Error	Regression Coefficient b	Standard Error
Dem 1928	.02	.051	.04	.027
Dem 1928 total	−.00	.039	.03	.022
Dem 1928 minus Dem 1924	.06	.043	.08	.031
Dem 1928 total minus Dem 1924 total	.01	.026	.03	.018
Dem 1928 minus mean Dem 1916–24	−.00	.038	.00	.026

*Controlling for percentages of Foreign stock, Owners, Negro, Female, Under 35, Pop change, Jewish, Catholic, Prot church, and for Economic status.

in either group of counties. The magnitudes of the coefficients are too low to indicate substantive significance for the variable measuring urban-rural residence. Despite the moderate values of the standard errors, not one of the coefficients is statistically significant at even the .05 level.

The second test examines regression equations after adding the square of the variable measuring a county's percentage of urbanites. If the influence of urbanism on a given dependent variable increases as a county's percentage of urban residents increases, then the square of percent urban should display a statistically significant regression coefficient. For, in this case, the line representing the influence of urbanism will curve upward and will be best portrayed in nonlinear form. This analysis provides, of course, only a partial check on the hypothesis. A county with a large percentage of urban residents may include a series of towns and small cities rather than one or more large cities. The analyses of nonlinear regression models reported in Appendix 1, pp. 247–64, fail to indicate that the relationship between support for Al Smith and residence in urban communities follows a nonlinear pattern. The independent influence of residence in the city does not seem to increase as counties become more highly urbanized.

The third test of the hypothesis that big city residence rather than residence in urban areas as defined by the census importantly swayed voting behavior in 1928 examines the residuals for individual counties. These residuals are the difference between the vote in a given county predicted by the regression equation and the county's actual vote. If the hypothesis is correct, the regression coefficient computed for the percentage of urbanites will understate the influence of residence in larger cities. Thus, relative to all counties, the regression equations for counties incorporating such cities will underpredict the 1928 Democratic vote and its deviation from the vote of previous Democratic candidates. This should produce residuals that are more positive than those for the entire population of counties. Table 6.5, however, demonstrates that the differences between the means of the residuals for the entire sample and for the ninety-two counties with an adult population of over one hundred thousand are far too small to signify any difference whatever in prediction for these two groups of counties. The largest mean residual in the table is only six-tenths of 1 percent, and the largest difference between residuals for the two groups is but two-tenths of 1 percent. Again, the evidence does not show residence in the metropolis to be an important influence on the vote for president.

Table 6.5. Analysis of Residuals (in percent)

	Mean Residual Complete Sample	Mean Residual 93 Counties: Over 100,000 Adults
Dem 1928	.3	.6
Dem 1928 total	−.3	−.1
Dem 1928 minus Dem 1924	−.6	−.5
Dem 1928 total minus Dem 1924 total	.4	.3
Dem 1928 minus mean Dem 1916–24	0	0

The analysis of groups of counties with different levels of urbanization also indicates how urban-rural residence interacted with nativist opposition to Al Smith. The conventional wisdom suggests that nativism was most intense in the country, implying that rural Protestants and native-stock voters were more repelled by the candidacy of Al Smith than their counterparts in the cities. If this hypothesis were correct, the gap between Protestants and Catholics, or natives and immigrants, would be wider in the country than in the city. The value of regression coefficients for a county's percentage of Catholics and foreign-stock Americans should increase as the analysis moves from rural counties to those with moderate and high levels of urbanization. The only exception would occur if urbanism also affected Catholic and foreign-stock voters so that urban Catholics and immigrants were stauncher friends of Al Smith than their rural counterparts. In this case, the greater inclination of rural rather than urban Protestants and natives to vote for Herbert Hoover would be offset by the greater inclination of urban rather than rural Catholics and immigrants to vote for Al Smith. Depending upon their relative strength, these two patterns of interaction should roughly cancel each other, meaning that the influence of Catholicism and foreign ethnicity on measures of presidential voting should be approximately equal for all three groups of counties.

The results of covariance analysis disclose that the influence of changes in the percentage of Catholics or foreign-stock voters did not systematically increase or decrease as the analysis moved from entirely rural to highly urbanized groups of counties. Although the coefficients were not always equal for all three groups of counties, patterns of change were not consistent from variable to variable. Sometimes the influence of religion or foreign ethnicity was greatest for the rural group of counties, sometimes for the middle group, and sometimes for the highly urbanized group. Urbanism could conceivably be interacting in a complex fashion with religion and ethnic background, but the interaction does not seem to support the conventional wisdom.

The analysis of entirely Protestant counties provides further indication that nativist opposition to Al Smith was not appreciably stronger in the country than in the city. If the conventional wisdom were correct, Protestants living in these overwhelmingly rural, religiously homogeneous counties should have been noticeably less receptive to Al Smith's candidacy than the overall population of Protestants. Yet, when compared to the combined vote for Davis and La Follette in 1924, Smith's losses among Protestant voters were no greater for these counties than for all counties included in the study. Al Smith's percentage of the presidential vote was about 12 percentage points below the combined Davis–La Follette percentage in completely Protestant counties, just 1 percentage point more than the loss in Protestant support estimated for all counties by Goodman's technique for recovering individual-level proportions from multiple regression equations.

The work of some historians implies that Smith was a sectional as well as an urban candidate for the presidency. In this view, he represented, not just the city, but the city of the East. David Burner argued that Smith had failed to "reach out, beyond the *eastern* city, to rural and small-town Protestant America."[4] Again, historians' language about the regional appeal of Smith's candidacy is difficult to interpret precisely. Beyond simply indicating that the types of people tending to live in the East were more likely to respond positively to Smith than the types of people tending to live elsewhere, historians could be suggesting that regional location interacted with urban-rural residence so that urbanism had a stronger positive effect on his candidacy in the East than in other sections. Or scholars could be implying that the regional location of voters was an independent influence on their choice of candidates in 1928.

The results of statistical analysis are sufficient to reject either the supposition that location in the East interacted with residence in the city or the conjecture that, independent of their other characteristics, eastern voters responded more favorably to Smith than did voters in the rest of the nation. The analysis of seven separate regions, reported in Appendix 2, shows that for each region, as for all regions combined, urban-rural residence is not an important influence on measures of the vote for president. In the Mid-Atlantic and New England regions, neither the vote for Smith nor the difference between his vote and votes cast in earlier elections are responsive to changes in the urban composition of counties. The values of the coefficients for this set of variables range from −.03 to .04.

To test the proposition that sectionalism had an independent influence on the vote for president, the qualitative variable of regional location was transformed into a numerical "dummy" variable and entered in the regression equations along with variables portraying the demographic composition of counties. For each of the seven regions, the dummy variable has a value of one for counties within the region and a value of zero for counties outside the region. When six of the seven dummy variables are entered in a regression equation, the intercept (a) of the equation represents the expected value of the response variable in the excluded region, independent of the other variables included in the equation. The regression coefficients for each of the six variables entered in the equation express differences in the expected value of the response variable in the excluded region and in each of the regions represented by the dummy variables. Table 6.6 reports the results of a dummy variable analysis for Smith's vote in 1928 and the differences between his vote and the votes for previous Democratic candidates as well as for Davis and La Follette combined in 1924. In each case, the dummy variable for New England is excluded from the equation and is represented by the intercept. Thus, for Smith's percentage of the vote, the intercept of 54.0 means that the expected value of this variable for New England is 54 percent. Each of the regression coefficients then represents the difference between 54 percent for New England and the expected value of Smith's vote in each of the remaining regions. Thus the coefficient of −2.3 for the Mid-Atlantic region means that, independent of control variables, the expected value of the response variable in the Mid-Atlantic region is 51.7 percent, 2.3 percent less than the 54 percent for New England.

The coefficients displayed in Table 6.6 fail to show that Smith was the candidate of the East. For measures of Smith's vote, of differences between his vote and the vote for Davis, and of differences

Table 6.6. Influence of Regional Location on Measures of the Vote for President: Seven Regions (in percent)*

	Dem 1928		Dem 1928 minus Dem 1924		Dem 1928 minus Dem/Prog 1924		Dem 1928 minus Dem 1916–24		Dem 1928 minus Dem 1916–20, Dem/Prog 1924	
	b	SE	b	SE	b	SE	b	SE	b	SE
Mid-Atlantic	−2.3	1.02	1.6	.92	− 6.1	.90	1.9	.82	− .56	.75
East North Central	3.9	1.02	7.2	.92	− 8.4	.89	5.9	.82	.82	.75
West North Central	4.5	1.05	7.7	.95	−10.5	.92	5.2	.85	− .78	.78
Border	6.1	1.33	2.0	1.23	−12.8	1.18	3.7	1.10	−1.20	1.01
Mountain	5.4	1.25	7.1	1.14	−13.2	1.10	1.4	1.01	−5.24	.93
Pacific	6.1	1.26	15.3	1.13	−13.4	1.11	9.8	1.00	.19	.92
Intercept (New England):	54.0		−5.3		4.9		−16.6		−12.1	

*Controlling for percentages of Urban, Foreign stock, Owners, Negro, Female, Under 35, Pop change, Jewish, Catholic, Prot church, and for Economic status.

between his vote and average vote of the past three Democratic candidates, the expected values of the response variables are smallest for the Mid-Atlantic and New England regions. These results are the opposite of those that would be expected if, independent of other variables, Smith was most appealing to voters in the East. For the difference between Smith's vote and the average vote from the past three elections, using the combined Davis–La Follette vote for 1924, the New England region once again has the lowest expected value. The mountain region has the second lowest value, with the remaining regions about equal. Only for the difference between the vote for Smith and the combined Davis–La Follette vote do the New England and Mid-Atlantic regions have the greatest expected values. Taken together, the results of dummy variable analysis suggest not that Smith was the sectional candidate of the East, but that La Follette was able to gain only limited support in eastern regions of the nation.

Historical Analysis of Urban-Rural Conflict

Statistical analysis indicates that urbanism by itself did not have much influence on the vote for president in 1928. The percentage of urban residents in a county had a very small direct influence on the allocation of the vote between Al Smith and Herbert Hoover. Furthermore, residence in city or country did not have conventionally expected interactive effects on other explanatory variables. The judgments of contemporary politicians seem to verify these findings. The Republican National Committee's canvass of Republican and independent newspapers and observers, despite its heavily rural bias, did not find issues relating to Al Smith's urbanism to be uppermost in the mind of the voter.[5] Smith's Tammany affiliations, the only urban issue cited by the respondents, was deemed important in less than 5 percent of the localities surveyed. Nor did the Democratic leaders who replied to FDR's circular letter generally cite Smith's image as a city man as a reason for his defeat. Again, Smith's Tammany affiliation was the only distinctively urban issue to be cited by respondents, accounting for but 5.8 percent of all citations. James A. Farley recalled that neither Tammany nor any of Smith's other urban connections had much effect on the 1928 election.[6] The Republican National Committee's postelection survey did not ask party leaders to evaluate the role of urban-rural conflict in the campaign; and only a few of the party leaders mentioned Smith's affiliation with Tammany Hall in responding to a question on the behavior of women voters.[7]

These results clash with descriptions of the 1928 contest set forth by most historians. Narrative accounts of the election suggest that even when other factors are controlled, urban voters should have been more inclined to favor Smith than their counterparts from the country. The failure of this distinction to emerge from available data suggests a need to revise prevailing notions of how antagonism between city and country affected the presidential contest. The first task is to consider explanations for the failure of urban-rural differences to interact significantly with the influence of religion and of ethnic origin on the presidential vote.

Deduction from social science theory does not suggest that nativism was likely to be stronger in rural than in urban communities. As is frequently the case in social science research, plausible theoretical arguments can be offered in support of contradictory conclusions. Theories in both science and social science are posited to hold only under certain conditions. Given different conditions, the same situation can produce strikingly different results. Often in social science, however, we do not know precisely the conditions under which one of a number of competing theories properly applies.[8] Thus a historian could argue that whereas residence in the city bred cosmopolitan tolerance, residence in the country led to narrow-minded provincialism. The historian could contend that old-stock Protestants living in the country and having little or no information about foreigners or Catholics were especially susceptible to nativist propaganda. Constrained only by the limits of their imagination, these rural folk could easily be persuaded to believe that immigrants were inveterate criminals and reprobates and that the Ultima Thule of all Catholics was an America governed by the pope. The general argument for rural susceptibility to prejudice was stated in 1929 by sociologists Pitirim Sorokin and Carle C. Zimmerman: *"In so far as the farmer has a very narrow field of indirect knowledge he very easily may be misled or imbued with the most fallacious opinions, superstitions, and prejudices concerning all the phenomena which lie beyond the boundary line of his direct knowledge.* He does not know anything about those phenomena and for this reason may accept any opinion which does not contradict his other opinions. In this respect he is less sophisticated than an urbanite and is more open to propaganda for the most fallacious theories and beliefs."[9]

Yet a historian could argue plausibly that old-stock Protestants living in cities felt immediately threatened by the influx of strangers and thus actively sought to suppress both Catholics and foreigners. Again, Sorokin and Zimmerman state the relevant theory: "Quite different is the situation in a community with heterogeneous religious, political, moral, and social characteristics among its members. Owing to this heterogeneity, a community of beliefs, opinions, and convictions is lacking. Under such circumstances there is an inevitable conflict of ideas, beliefs, and aspirations of the various members."[10]

Beyond the ambiguity of theory, Kenneth T. Jackson's study, *The Ku Klux Klan in the City, 1915–1930,* suggests how widely nativism was distributed in the 1920s. The Klan, the largest and most powerful manifestation of nativism during the period, openly warred against Catholics, foreigners, and Negroes. Jackson assails the usual accounts of the Klan's overwhelmingly rural foundation but does not demonstrate that its power base was in the metropolis. He does show that the Klan was beguiling to Protestants living in large cities as well as to those residing in the country.[11]

Some historians offer a more intricate version of the relationship between nativism and residence in the country. Returning again to the conflict of values that allegedly divided the nation into "two Americas," they argue that nativism was characteristic of both rural dwellers and urban residents who shared rural values and mores. Robert Moats Miller, for example, claims that the Ku Klux Klan was supported in the cities by recent migrants from farms and villages, who "retained their rural mentality and sought desperately to define themselves by clinging to the values of their fathers and perhaps of their own childhood."[12] This argument, however, begs the question of how urban and rural environments influence nativist behavior.[13] Miller assumes that nativism was a manifestation of an "agrarian angle of vision" and that, if urbanites proved to be as nativist as country folk, they must be thinly disguised agrarians. In principle, this proposition can be tested, but neither Miller nor other historians have demonstrated that Protestants with roots in rural America were significantly more nativist than Protestants with several generations of urban background. Even Miller's fairly sophisticated discussion still treats nativism as a single attitude or state of mind with a clear and direct influence on conduct. As was noted earlier, significant new work in social science suggests that nativism must be understood in the context of particular issues and situations. Depending on the question at stake, different groups might vary widely in their relative hostility to immigrants and Catholics.

Additional analysis is required to explain why urban residence per se did not have an important direct influence on the presidential vote of 1928. Arguments offered in support of the traditional thesis that urban-rural conflict was a significant dimension of that contest focus not upon campaign issues, but upon the images evoked by the two candidates. Historians portray Al Smith as the representative urbanite—the first authentic symbol of the city ever to seek the presidency. Smith's cigar, derby hat, flashy suits, East Side accent, affiliation with Tammany Hall, and even his theme song, "The Sidewalks of New York," all linked him with metropolitan America. The governor could establish an instant rapport with his fellow urbanites, but he outraged the many farmers and villagers who feared and resented the big city. In the words of one scholar, "Smith represented the big city, its cosmopolitanism, its impatience with . . . the moral yearnings of the rural communities, its absorption with itself, its failure to think nationally."[14]

Herbert Hoover, on the other hand, seemed able to bridge the gap between urban and rural America. At a speech delivered during the campaign at his hometown of West Branch, Iowa, Hoover appealed to America's idealized image of her rural heritage. He portrayed himself as the poor farmboy who achieved success in the modern world, but still longed for the simple pleasures and virtues of frontier life. Yet Hoover's image as a brilliant engineer, a remarkably efficient administrator of postwar relief, a strikingly successful businessman, and a commanding figure in the national government enhanced his appeal to urban voters. Certainly he was no "country bumpkin" or "rural clod" to be scoffed at by sophisticated residents of big cities.[15]

This argument, of course, is premised on a prior hostility between city and country, not derived solely from differences in the characteristics of urban and rural residents.[16] Historians have suggested that country folk in the 1920s clung to the ancient agrarian myth that rural life uniquely fostered virtue and nobility. The diehard agrarian believed that the city degraded man's physical and spiritual being; it not only attracted the dregs of European civilization, but promoted crime, corruption, and vice. City life sapped the health and vitality of the individual and inured him to the wholesome pleasures of hard work and family life. Prolonged exposure to an urban environment undermined the individual's faith, leaving him prey to the beguiling heresies of "modernism and rationalism."

Historians have traditionally portrayed the 1920s as a period of abnormal tension between city and country. Yet, rather than comparing manifestations of urban-rural antagonism in this and other periods of American history, scholars rely on generalizations about why country folk should have been especially resentful of city dwellers during the 1920s. During this period, many rural areas failed to share the increasing prosperity of the city. The population of urban areas for the first time outnumbered that of the countryside, and country folk feared they were losing their dominance of American society. The despicable urban life style threatened to overwhelm the bastions of rural virtue. Country people also bitterly resented the biting satires of small-town and farm life that flowed from the pens of such cosmopolitan critics as H. L. Mencken and Sinclair Lewis.

The finding that urban-rural differences had little impact on how people decided to vote in the presidential election of 1928 challenges interpretations of the animus between city and country in the 1920s. Although the analysis of elections cannot resolve questions about conflict within a society, election returns do record the attitudes and preferences of ordinary Americans. The failure of city and country folk to diverge widely in their responses to Hoover and Smith suggests that historians may have exaggerated the importance of urban-rural tension as a cause of social conflict in the 1920s.

Residence in city or country did not influence the positions of voters on state-level referenda regarding prohibition, a further indication that traditional interpretations of urban-rural conflict are not tenable. Historians have suggested that voter responses to the question of liquor control reflected separation of the country from the city. No other issue seemed so neatly to divide the cultures of urban and rural America. Yet statistical analysis of 471 counties in states conducting referenda on prohibition discloses no relationship whatever between a county's level of urbanization and the percentage of voters opposing prohibition. The regression coefficients reported in Table 6.7 reveal that primarily religion and ethnic background shaped a voter's position on the prohibition issue. Other studies purporting to demonstrate a correlation between responses to prohibition and residence in city and country do not control for the effects of these additional factors.

Table 6.7. Influence of Explanatory Variables on the Percentage of Voters Opposing Prohibition: 471 Counties (in percent)

	Regression Coefficient b	Standard Error
Catholic	.52	.055
Jewish	.43	.108
Prot church	−.07	.063
Urban	.04	.026
Foreign stock	.38	.038
Economic status	.46	.169
Owners	.01	.061
Female	−.12	.218
Negro	.25	.141
Under 35	.19	.152
Pop change	−.02	.019

Moreover, the rural press, a barometer of public opinion frequently consulted by historians, may have overstated the farmer's hostility to the city. Since the end of World War I, population had been draining from the countryside to the metropolis at an alarming rate; lost to the city were many of the more talented and ambitious members of the younger generation. To preserve their readership, country newspapers and periodicals might have been tempted to portray the city in the bleakest possible terms. The rural press was also overwhelmingly Republican, and political considerations, particularly during the presidential campaign of 1928, may have inspired invidious comparisons between rural and urban life.

Historians of the 1920s have assumed uncritically that demographic and technological trends of the decade exacerbated conflict between city and country. But equally plausible arguments sustain the opposite position—that key developments of the early twentieth century slackened the tension between urban and rural communities. Again, neither common sense nor theory drawn from social science is powerful enough to establish how global changes in urban and rural life affected the attitudes and behavior of individuals residing in each type of community. Thus, a historian could contend that advances in transportation and communication as well as new patterns of community development fostered the nationalization of American culture, eroding cultural differences between city and country folk. Between 1910 and 1930, polar contrasts between urban and rural life became increasingly less accurate descriptions of American society. A much wider range of outside influences penetrated rural regions of the United States. Not only could urban values and culture be transmitted to the countryside through improved means of communication, but the automobile increased the mobility of both farmer and townsman. Furthermore, during this period, new forms of residential development were beginning to obliterate the physical boundaries separating city and country. All of these changes may have tended to integrate the culture of countryside and metropolis and to exert destabilizing influences on rural communities.[17]

Intellectuals of the 1920s had already begun to recognize the futility of describing the United States in terms of a simple urban-rural dichotomy. Sorokin and Zimmerman, for instance, concluded their study of urban-rural sociology with the observation that the United States has "entered the period of 'rururbanization'—a greater and greater obliteration of the rural-urban differences." Rururbanization, they contended, "has progressed already far enough to be quite certain and unquestionable." Similarly, agricultural economist John D. Black argued in 1929 that "farmers are no longer wearing blinders. The time will soon come when our farmers will be as accessible to new ideas as is any group in the nation. That is exactly what rural mail delivery, automobiles, and the radio mean to our country people."[18]

Two urban histories offer a more comprehensive survey of opinion contemporary to the 1920s. Peter J. Schmitt, in *Back to Nature: The Arcadian Myth in Urban America*, found that "nature worship continued in fashion in the 1920's but the urgency with which turn-of-the-century intellectuals resisted the city had begun to evaporate." Schmitt concluded, "The nature movement lingered on, but the desperate vitality that electrified it in 1900 ebbed away." Charles Glaab and A. Theodore Brown, in *A History of Urban America*, noted a related development in the realm of social planning: "Many thinkers and reformers [in the 1920s] abandoned the simple notion of country versus city and began to develop new conceptions of the social environment that emphasized the community, the neighborhood, the region."[19]

Traditional interpretations of urban-rural tension in the 1920s must also be modified by reference to the diversity of both city and country; although crosscutting influences need not obliterate an urban-rural split, they could serve to narrow the gap between city and country. Evidence from contemporary and historical observers suggests that rural residents were not uniformly committed to common "agrarian values." Townsfolk and farmers, for example, cannot be comfortably integrated into a common rural culture. Not only did the interests of the town and countryside often diverge, but scholars have suggested that inhabitants of towns frequently fancied themselves culturally and socially superior to the farmer and were inclined to emulate the sophistication of metropolitan America. As Robert R. Dykstra noted, by the early twentieth century, the "fundamental empathy between farmer and townsmen" had degenerated into "a mutual distrust and hostility."[20] Statistical analysis of the vote for president corroborates this judgment, revealing greater differences between the voting behavior of farmers and townsfolk than between the behavior of urban and rural residents.

A glance at the other half of the urban-rural dichotomy suggests that urban America cannot accurately be portrayed as having a unified state of mind. Social psychologist Anselm Strauss argues in *Images of the American City* that during the 1920s, the meaning of urbanism varied from city to city. Some spokesmen even emphasized the predominantly rural characteristics of their urban communities. Refracted in this spectrum of opinion were differences in the size, composition, location, and historical experience of American cities. These differing views also reflected the proclivity of urban dwellers to become home-town boosters. A prominent example of city booster-ism during the 1920s was the intense intercity rivalry that accompanied the phenomenal growth of professional sports in that decade.[21] Sports rivalries in the 1920s both reflected and augmented home-town loyalty.

Strauss's impressions indicate that Al Smith's accent, his garb, his Tammany affiliations, and his theme song would have identified him as a New Yorker rather than as a representative symbol of urban America. The residents of other cities throughout the nation may have found Al Smith's mannerisms unappealing, and they may have viewed him as the personification of a rival city. Moreover, both urban and rural dwellers appear to have associated New York City with allegedly undesirable aspects of city life.[22] Thus the *Seattle Star* dismissed Al Smith as a candidate with a "typically New York viewpoint,"[23] and the *Kansas City Star* portrayed him as the personification of an especially noxious variety of urban life: "Smith embodies the New York-Baltimore uprising, two centers which due to immigration and various other causes, have become more cosmopolitan in tone, more European in thought. Most American urban life draws from the country and the small town."[24]

Conclusions

To view the presidential election of 1928 as a culmination of strife between urban and rural America is to mislead rather than to enlighten. Historians need to frame hypotheses about urban-rural differences more precisely and to explore multiple influences on the behavior of those who live in each type of community. Although the types of people inclined to favor Smith were more likely to reside in cities than the types inclined to favor Hoover, residence in city or country has only a modest influence on the vote for president. Historians also imply that location in city or country directly influenced voter response to Smith and Hoover or conditioned the influence of religion and ethnic heritage. Yet multivariate analysis demonstrates clearly that after adjusting for the backgrounds of urban and rural folk, residence in city or country had little to do with how people voted for president in 1928. The personal attributes of voters far overshadowed their place of residence. Only in 1936 did urban and rural voters begin to diverge widely in their balloting for president.

A historian's interpretation of urban-rural strife in the presidential election may not be separable from his understanding of how to explain social conflict during the 1920s. Explanations of voting behavior are related dialectically to broader interpretations of social conflict. The prevailing notion that social tension arose from attitudes and interests that were distinctively urban and distinctively rural leads naturally to a similar interpretation of voter behavior in 1928. In turn, explanations of voter reactions to Smith and Hoover as a continuation of an urban-rural feud probably reinforce the notion that antipathy between city and country had been a source of turmoil throughout the 1920s. Similarly, the judgment that urban-rural differences had little effect on voter preferences in 1928 leads to a revised understanding of what residence in city or country meant for Americans of the 1920s. A contest pitting Al Smith against Herbert Hoover would seem likely to crystallize animosity between city and country. The failure of the division between urban and rural America to reveal much about the behavior of voters suggests the need for a more systematic approach to understanding societal conflict and concord in the 1920s.

Chapter 7

Blacks versus Whites
and Men versus Women

The members of any society can be partitioned into an indefinite number of categorical schemes. In analyzing any election, however, only a small proportion of all possible classifications are salient for voting behavior. In addition to the study of the categories that are part of the two Americas thesis, the investigation of divisions between blacks and whites and men and women tells much about the election and its significance.

Although few political contests have inspired a more prolific outpouring of scholarship than the election of 1928, historians have not adequately explored either the race-related issues that emerged during the campaign or the responses of black people to competing candidates and parties. Several studies have examined the voting behavior of relatively homogeneous black communities in northern cities. The findings suggest that a larger proportion of black voters supported the Democratic nominee in 1928 than in earlier contests, but that a majority still favored Herbert Hoover.[1] These studies, however, provide only a limited basis for generalizations about the behavior of northern black voters. Previous work also leaves unanswered many questions about the reactions of black leaders to the presidential campaign and the strategies employed by the parties to deal with matters relating to race.[2]

The Influence of Race on the Vote for President

The scrutiny of black voting in 1928 poses special problems. Not only is there little variation from county to county in the percentage of black Americans, but the presence of large concentrations of blacks in the border states usually inspired white residents to unite behind the Democratic party. Thus the relationship between a county's percentage of Democratic voters and its percentage of blacks will be distorted by the traditional loyalties of whites living in heavily black border state counties. To circumvent this obstacle to analysis, the study explores black voting only for counties outside the border state region.

Regression analysis, reported in Table 7.1, reveals a complex pattern of change in black voting during the 1920s and 1930s. The regression coefficients displayed in the table do not show that, independent of control variables, black and white Americans split decisively over the choice between Smith and Hoover in 1928. The magnitudes of the coefficients for Smith's percentage of the vote, Smith's percentage of the adult population, and Hoover's percentage of the adult population are all low and their standard errors are high. Moreover, regression analysis does not disclose changes in the proportion of blacks in the Democratic coalitions of 1928 and 1924. Whether the

Table 7.1. *Influence of Percentage of Negroes on Measures of the Vote for President: Border State Counties Excluded (in percent)**

	Regression Coefficient b	Standard Error
Dem 1928	.06	.072
Dem 1928 total	.04	.059
Rep 1928 total	−.08	.055
Dem 1928 minus Dem 1924	−.03	.076
Dem 1928 minus Dem/Prog 1924	.34	.072
Dem 1928 minus Prog 1924	.29	.113
Dem 1928 total minus Dem 1924 total	.02	.048
Dem 1928 total minus Dem/Prog 1924 total	.16	.048
Dem 1928 total minus Prog 1924 total	.20	.075
Rep 1928 total minus Rep 1924 total	−.07	.049
Dem 1928 minus mean Dem 1916–24	.12	.066
Dem 1928 minus mean Dem 1916–20, Dem/Prog 1924	.24	.058
Dem 1928 minus Dem 1932	.19	.055
Dem 1928 minus mean Dem 1932–40	−.14	.061

*Controlling for percentages of Urban, Foreign stock, Owners, Female, Under 35, Pop change, Jewish, Prot church, Catholic, and for Economic status.

vote for president or the adult population is used as the base for percentages, the table shows that, when controlling for other variables, differences between Democratic voting in 1928 and 1924 do not respond to changes from county to county in the percentage of blacks.

More decisive results are registered for other deviation variables measuring the difference between the vote for president in 1928 and the vote cast in earlier elections. The relatively large positive coefficients obtained for the differences between the vote for Smith and, respectively, the vote for La Follette, the combined vote for Davis and La Follette, and the average vote between 1916 and 1924 suggest a movement of black voters toward the Democratic party in 1928. Particularly significant is the finding that, independent of control variables, a 1 percent change in a county's percentage of blacks yields a reliably measured (standard error = .072) .34 percent change in the difference between the vote for Smith and for Davis and La Follette combined in 1924. Thus, independent of their social and economic attributes, blacks were more inclined to vote for alternatives to the Republican candidate in 1928 than in 1924. The negative regression coefficient for the difference between the Republican percentage of the adult population in 1928 and 1924 is consistent with this conclusion. The low magnitude of this coefficient, however, reflects an increased turnout rate among blacks in 1928. Independent of control variables, a 1 percent change in a county's percentage of blacks produces a .20 percent change (standard error = .049) in the difference between the turnout of voters in 1928 and in 1924.

When voting for Smith is compared to voting for Roosevelt, the sequence of change is similar to that observed for the rift between city and country. The relative movement of black voters toward the Democrats reverses abruptly in 1932. As the percentage of blacks in a county increases, so does the vote for Smith relative to that of FDR; a 1 percent change from one county to another in the percentage of blacks yields a .19 percent change in the difference between the vote for Smith and the vote for Roosevelt in 1932. Yet black voting seems to have shifted remarkably either in 1936 or 1940. For the difference between the vote for Smith and the average vote for Roosevelt from 1932 to 1940, the sign of the regression coefficient switches; a 1 percent increase in a county's percentage of blacks yields a −.14 percent change in this deviation variable. Analysis of additional deviation variables measuring the difference between the vote cast for Smith and the vote cast for Roosevelt, first in 1936 and then in 1940, shows that a turnabout in black voting occurred in 1936. A 1 percent change in a county's percentage of blacks produces a $-.27$ percent change in the difference between the vote for Smith and the vote for Roosevelt in 1936 (standard error $= .076$) and a $-.34$ percent change in the vote for Smith and the vote for Roosevelt in 1940 (standard error $= .084$).

In their postelection survey of state and local leaders, the Republican National Committee specifically asked about the responses of black voters to Al Smith and Herbert Hoover. The results of this inquiry are reported in Appendix 3, Chart A3.6. Franklin Roosevelt's circular letters, however, elicited no information from Democratic politicians about black voting. Apparently, Roosevelt's correspondents did not consider changes in the preferences of black voters to be sufficiently worthy of mention.

The reports of Republican leaders confirm the findings of statistical studies that black voting shifted in favor of the Democratic party in 1928. But the reports do not indicate that the spectacular transformation of the black voter from a staunch Republican to the most loyal of Democrats occurred in that year. Instead, they suggest that in 1928 a majority of black voters still opted for the Republican presidential candidate.

The Politics of Race in 1928

Traditional historical sources reveal that black leaders far outpaced the rank and file of black voters in their rejection of the Hoover-Curtis ticket in 1928. These sources also permit a reconstruction of the political strategies followed by both parties. In particular, they clarify the "Southern Strategy" whereby Herbert Hoover and the GOP attempted to establish a lily-white Republican party in the deep South and to foster racist opposition to Al Smith. No historical document shows Hoover crisply ordering party leaders to exploit racism in the South or to purge prominent blacks from positions of party leadership. The meticulous and careful Hoover would scarcely be inclined to commit such material to paper or preserve it for the perusal of historians. Yet the hypothesis that Hoover set the Southern Strategy in motion and monitered its operation seems overwhelmingly likely, first, because Hoover closely supervised his presidential campaign, and second, because of revealing statements and activities that can reliably be attributed to Herbert Hoover and his close associates.

A reevaluation of black voting also raises questions about interpretations of black history that emphasize the emergence of a "new Negro" during the 1920s. Such distinguished scholars as Alain Locke, John Hope Franklin, August Meier, Robert A. Bone, and Gilbert Osofsky have argued that during this period northern Negroes became more ambitious, self-conscious, assertive, unified, and proud of their race. A new ethos, they claim, stirred black communities in the North and received artistic expression in the "Harlem Renaissance" of the 1920s.[3] Historians have not, however, carefully differentiated the thoughts and feelings of educated black elites from those of the black masses. Locke's assertion that the Harlem Renaissance represented "the mass movement of the urban immigration of Negroes, projected on the plane of an increasingly articulate elite" has not been directly challenged by more recent scholarship.[4] Election analysis suggests that important distinctions may be obscured by this conventional wisdom. The rank and file of black voters did not follow the path trod by black leaders in 1928.

American blacks were traditionally Republican in the 1920s, with their loyalties traceable to the Civil War and its aftermath. The Republicans had freed the slave, fought for the black man's rights during postwar debates, and sponsored his political ambitions during Reconstruction. The Democrats, on the other hand, had been sympathetic to the Confederacy and had consistently opposed attempts to exert federal power on behalf of liberated slaves. For the first fifteen years after Reconstruction, many Republican leaders strongly spoke out against the oppression of blacks and unsuccessfully sponsored ameliorative measures. Although spirited rhetoric and major legislative efforts ceased after 1893, the Republicans at least continued to pay lip service to black aspirations. Within the South, the Republican party was the only refuge for the few southern blacks who managed to remain politically active. In some cases, blacks even rose to leadership positions in the token Republican organizations that survived the end of Reconstruction.

A black person migrating North in the late nineteenth and early twentieth centuries may no longer have regarded the Republican leaders as the champions of his people, but he probably still respected the traditions of Lincoln's party and undoubtedly considered the Democrats responsible for the worst evils of southern racism. Political scientist Harold F. Gosnell found in 1935 that for members of the older generation of Chicago's Negroes, "Disenfranchisement, lynchings, Jim Crow laws, the cropping system and other social and economic practices were laid at the door of the Democratic Party." Negro writer Wendell Phillips Dabney observed that in Cincinnati prior to the 1920s, "To be a Negro Democrat required courage of a high order, because a great mass of the negroes regarded white Democrats as the Devil's chosen children, and a Negro Democrat was a creature of such depravity that hell was far too good for him."[5]

By November 1928, however, most leaders of the black community had become disillusioned with the Republican party. The GOP seemed responsive to the long memory of black people, but not to their current needs. Although black voters did not massively desert their traditional party until 1936, black leaders did so eight years earlier.

Black leaders in 1928 had little control over black voters. White politicians almost invariably dominated the political machines operating in northern cities. And no charismatic black leader had a sufficiently large and devoted following to be able to swing significant numbers of voters. Any discussion of black leadership in the presidential election of 1928 refers to a diverse group of prominent individuals, whose opinion carried some weight among black Americans.[6]

Black leaders included publishers and editors of black newspapers and periodicals, educators, businessmen, ministers and bishops, fraternal officers, minor government officials, self-proclaimed race leaders, and leaders of organizations such as the NAACP and the National Urban League. Especially important in the realm of politics were black churchmen and fraternal leaders. Far more than their counterparts in white America, black churches and lodges were centers of political activity. As Ralph Bunche noted in 1939, "A good many of the Negro ministers and lodge leaders in the north are important political figures, and during the heat of the campaign, church and lodge meetings are often converted into political forums."[7] Leaders of the black community did not form a cohesive subgroup in 1928. They represented a wide range of ideological positions and advocated conflicting strategies for the advancement of their race. Changes in the political behavior of black leaders in 1928 are inferred from the endorsement practices of black newspapers, newspaper reports on the political activities of black elites, the statements of black leaders themselves, the comments of white politicians, and the experiences of both parties in attempting to recruit prominent blacks for their respective campaign organizations.

The positions taken by black elites in 1928 reflected both their reaction to the presidential campaign and long-term changes in their perceptions of the nation's two major parties. First, the history of the Harding and Coolidge administrations indicated that Republicans as well as Democrats had abandoned the black man. The political recognition so important to blacks was not forthcoming from the Republicans during their years of power. Two Negroes received federal appointments during the Harding and Coolidge years, one less than during Woodrow Wilson's two terms; none of the GOP appointments were above the level of customs collector. The Republican administrations also failed to meet demands for legislative and executive protection of black political and civil rights. Black Americans had long sought federal protection from lynching: of the 1,811 lynchings that had taken place between 1900 and 1928, 1,633 of the victims (90.2 percent) had been Negroes.[8] Warren G. Harding and the Republican platform of 1920 had supported federal antilynching legislation;[9] with the election of Harding and a strongly Republican Congress, black leaders expected the Republicans to redeem their pledges. After eight years of token effort, they had failed to do so by 1928. Republican administrations took no steps to enforce the constitutional amendments guaranteeing black people the full prerogatives of American citizenship. Despite Hoover's eleventh-hour order ending segregation in the Department of Commerce, Republican executives also accepted segregation within many departments and agencies of the federal government and racial discrimination in the selection of federal employees.[10]

Second, black leaders perceived that racial discrimination and oppression were not causally dependent upon the white man's affiliation with the Democratic party. Racial attitudes, they found, no longer followed party lines. In their dealings with local politicians in the North, blacks learned that the Democrats were as willing as the Republicans to grant their demands for recognition and assistance. Similarly, black leaders realized that white southern Republicans in the twentieth century were no more solicitous of black rights than the basest white Democrats. Kelly Miller, eminent black educator, included the following observations in a long and eloquent letter of protest sent to Herbert Hoover on 4 October 1928:

Tradition and inertia impels the Negro to follow the fortune of the party of Lincoln, Grant and Sumner, and at the same time to antagonize the party which espoused slavery, opposed the Civil War amendments and antagonized the Negro's political status in general. But Negroes and whites, Republicans and Democrats are forgetting the things that are past and are pressing forward to the high calling of the present. Favorable or unfriendly attitude towards the Negro is no longer a matter of party creed, but of geographical latitude. Northern Democrats are every bit as favorable to the claims of the race as Northern Republicans. On the other hand, the distinction in racial attitude between a Southern Democrat and a Southern lily white Republican has yet to be isolated and defined.[11]

The growing antagonism of black leaders toward the Republican party surfaced in the presidential election of 1924. A number of prominent blacks supported the election of Democratic candidate John W. Davis, and other leaders declined to support any of the three nominees.[12] Four years later, a much larger number of the black elite defected to the Democratic party. The Republican administration had still not demonstrated any responsiveness to black needs, and the Republican campaign strategy of 1928 seemed a deliberate affront to black voters.

In the late nineteenth century, Republican leaders had flirted with such schemes as internal improvements and favorable tariff legislation to restore party power in the solidly Democratic South.[13] Herbert Hoover, following this tradition, adopted a Southern Strategy in the campaign of 1928. Confronted with a candidate who repulsed most southern whites, Hoover saw a unique opportunity to garner the electoral votes of the normally Democratic South by shrewdly directing appeals to religious bigotry, prohibitionism, and racism. Hoover's actions also suggest that he sought a permanent reorganization of southern Republicanism under the leadership of white racists. Apparently, Hoover realized that his party's association with the Negro was an insurmountable handicap to its political success in the South. He probably hoped to create a southern Republican party that could compete on a fairly equal basis for the votes of white supremacists.

Hoover's Southern Strategy began to unfold in June at the Republican National Convention. There were several credentials disputes at the convention between integrated and lily-white delegations from southern states. In most instances, Hoover's managers supported the lily-whites. The Hoover forces were willing to cooperate with some Negro leaders, such as R. R. Church of Tennessee and

Percy Howard of Mississippi, who favored Hoover's nomination. But they sided with all-white delegations from Florida and Texas and a predominantly white delegation from Louisiana that opposed the integrated delegation led by Walter L. Cohen, longtime leader of the party in Louisiana and the nation's highest black federal appointee.[14] Hoover's supporters in the Resolutions Committee quashed a proposal by black leaders that the party platform advocate enforcement of the Fourteenth and Fifteenth Amendments as well as the Eighteenth Amendment. The committee also spurned other efforts to commit the party to the promotion of racial justice and equality.[15] The Republican platform devoted only thirty-five words to racial issues, repeating the party's empty promise to support antilynching legislation.[16]

Republican leadership in 1928 also purged black Republican leaders in the South. At the party convention, the national committee deposed Cohen and refused to recognize either Ben Davis, national committeeman for Georgia, or his black rival for the post. Shortly after the convention, federal authorities indicted Percy Howard, national committeeman for Mississippi, for accepting bribes in return for political favors, and a Republican-controlled Senate committee chose to begin an investigation of post office corruption with the activities of Ben Davis and his associates. Assistant Attorney General Mabel Walker Willebrandt made a special trip to secure the indictment of Howard. Thus, the three most important black leaders of the deep South (including the only two black members of the Republican National Committee) were neatly disposed of before the campaign began. Finally, Hoover established a lily-white campaign committee for the South under the leadership of Colonel Horace Mann, an obscure politician with alleged close ties to the Ku Klux Klan.[17]

Al Smith's religious preference and his opposition to national prohibition were the major sources of Hoover's appeal to white southerners. But the Republican party also sought to exploit southern racism. Republican leaders in the South circulated racist propaganda and portrayed Smith as favoring complete equality of the races, including sexual relations and miscegenation. Under his sponsorship, Negroes allegedly had been extending their influence throughout New York. Southern Republicans and bolting Democrats disseminated pictures of blacks and whites dancing together in New York clubs and of white people taking orders from black employers.

Herbert Hoover and the national Republican leadership approved and directed this propaganda effort as well as the course taken by the campaign in the South. Hoover closely monitored party strategy and tactics on matters related to race. He guided credentials battles at the Republican National Convention and directed the purge of black leaders from the party's southern wing. He established the southern campaign committee under the leadership of Colonel Mann and personally guided his activities. Apparently, Hoover granted Colonel Mann latitude to operate free of control by officials in the regular chain of command. On 26 September, publicity chief Henry J. Allen wrote to Hoover's secretary, "I have not been in touch with the publicity of the several states [southern], having been informed early that the matter was being taken care of entirely through Colonel Mann's office." Hoover also directed that publicity he did not wish to see associated with the national campaign be released by Colonel Mann's organization.[18]

Although, in 1928, Republicans were not prone to record their closed-door discussions, the private correspondence of Henry J. Allen offers further insight into how Republican campaigners treated issues pertaining to race. On 11 August, a few weeks before serious campaigning was to begin, fellow Kansan Sam Woolard wrote to Allen advocating a "new Republican line in the South." He passed on a comment from a southern Republican friend that "the better class of white people vote the Democratic ticket down here, [because] big *black* Republicans control the offices and tell us who shall go to the National Convention as Delegates." According to Woolard, "this was the cold blooded situation in many of the Southern states." He asserted that "the easiest job in the world would be to win several of the southern states this year with the proper man sent down there to give those people the assurance that Republican politics should be controlled in the south by *white* men and that no negro would be put in office where the principle patrons of such office were white people." Allen responded by return mail. He assured Woolard that he "was in hearty accord with just what you said" and that "an intelligent effort is being made this year to give the white folks down there a chance."[19]

About a month later, Allen received several examples of the publicity being issued by the national committeeman for Louisiana. Two of the statements distributed in Louisiana were standard appeals to economic interests, one appealed to anti-Catholicism, and two others to race prejudice. In a letter to Hoover's secretary, Allen questioned the propriety of the anti-Catholic literature, but did not object to the antiblack material. Early in the campaign, Allen had also proposed to Hoover that they use their apparently declining popularity among northern Negroes to win racist votes in the South: "It seems rather certain for the moment that we are going to lose the colored vote in the north. If this knowledge could be judiciously used in the south, it would be helpful to us. I wonder if you have some connection down there that I might take advantage of, if you think it wise to pass the word along."[20] The later course of the campaign indicates that Hoover followed Allen's advice.

The candidate himself sought in several ways to assure white southerners that he posed no threat to their racial hegemony. He ignored the party's declaration on the need for antilynching legislation and raised no other issues that might antagonize white racists. Responding to fears that a Hoover administration might impose black officials on southern communities, Hoover pledged in a Tennessee speech that he believed "in the merit system of the Civil Service" and believed that "appointive offices must be filled by those who deserve the confidence and respect of the communities they serve."[21] Contradicting claims made in the North, Hoover also informed his southern partisans that he was not responsible for ending segregation in the Department of Commerce. On 28 August 1928, L. M. Osborne of Madrianna, Arkansas, wrote to Hoover, "If it wasn't for the Negro question I feel you would carry the entire south. . . . I deny daily your doing away with negro segregation in your offices when in the Department of Commerce. Have I strained my Quaker training for truth and veracity by doing so?" Hoover responded three days later, assuring Osborne that "as for the colored situation in the Department of Commerce, it is in no way different from conditions during the last thirty years and during the administration of President Wilson." This line remained unchanged throughout the campaign. On 20 October, Hoover's secretary wrote to K. C. Barnard, "I can state to you positively that there has been no change whatever in the Department of Commerce since the Wilson Administration regarding the treatment of colored people."[22]

Responding to contemporary criticisms of Hoover's Southern Strategy, loyalists claimed that Hoover's goal was the elimination of corruption rather than the creation of a segregated Republican party in the South.[23] Despite quarrels with some individual politicians, however, Hoover did not launch a crusade against corrupt or incompetent white politicians either in the South or elsewhere.

Yet Hoover and his advisers failed to pursue fully the goal of founding a competitive, lily-white party in the South. Their putative reorganization of southern Republicanism was a lurching, haphazard endeavor, marked by uncertainty and confusion. Party leaders were unwilling to remain steadfast and to trade off advances in the South against a massive defection of black voters in the North. Confronted in the summer of 1928 with severe criticism from Negro leaders, party managers may have feared that an ongoing purge of Negro politicians would cause unacceptable losses among black voters. After indicting Percy Howard and investigating Ben Davis, the Republicans decided to call off further inquiry into southern corruption until after the election.[24] Alarmed by reaction to the indictments in Mississippi, Hoover suggested to Chairman Work, "It seems to me most imperative that a special campaign committee should be set up in Mississippi with some colored representation and leadership that cannot be questioned."[25] The Hoover forces also persuaded some disaffected black Republicans to remain nominally within the party and refrained from challenging R. R. Church, the powerful black leader in Tennessee. Local lily-white groups, however, encouraged by the policies of the national party, unsuccessfully attempted to unseat Church and replace him with a white man. Church himself became so disgusted with the GOP campaign that he refused to serve on the Executive Committee of the Republican National Committee's Colored Voters Division.[26]

Republican campaigners seem to have hoped for a sufficiently ambiguous situation to attract southern whites without sacrificing the votes of too many northern blacks. This hope proved to be well founded. Hoover became the first Republican candidate since Reconstruction to receive the electoral votes of Florida, North Carolina, Texas, and Virginia, and he lost none of the northern states with substantial populations of blacks. Although Hoover continued a lurching Southern Strategy during his presidential years, the dream of fashioning a genuinely competitive Republican party in the traditionally Democratic South was rudely shattered by the depression. Rather than conquering new territory, the Republicans found themselves in the 1930s scrambling unsuccessfully to defend their northern homeland from the onslaught of a resurgent opposition.

If black leaders were outraged by Hoover's campaign strategy, they were appalled by the support he attracted. Many perceived Hoover to be the candidate of the Ku Klux Klan and other groups of Protestant bigots who hated both Negroes and Catholics. Hoover's failure to denounce the Klan or speak out strongly against intolerance only reinforced this perception. The *Chicago Defender*, for example, supporting a Democratic presidential candidate for the first time, closed its advisory editorial with the following message: "Our readers are entitled to know that the Ku Klux Klan is taking an active part in the campaign and that it is NOT aiding the Democratic candidate. Our readers are entitled to know that the hypocrites and church bigots are taking a more active part in this campaign than they have ever done before. And they are NOT aiding the Democratic candidate. Our readers should know that Senator Tom Heflin, who shot a 'nigger' in Washington years ago and bragged about it, is supporting the Republican candidate."[27]

Rather than making a strong pitch for black votes, the Democratic party maintained its traditionally racist posture in 1928. No black delegates or alternates attended the Democratic convention in Houston and black visitors to Convention Hall were segregated behind a barrier of chicken wire. Fifty black delegates came to the Republican convention in Kansas City, and Convention Hall was integrated.[28] The Democratic platform and the major Democratic campaigners were silent on matters of special concern to blacks. Democratic leaders denied that Smith was responsible for the promotion of racial equality in New York City; and, in some parts of the South, they argued that white supremacy could not be maintained unless voters remained loyal to their traditional party.[29] In a manifesto issued at the height of the campaign, the NAACP complained about the racist tactics of both parties.[30]

Leaders of the Democratic party recognized that the South could be held in line if voters came to realize that ballots for the party would help sustain white supremacy, whereas a resurgence of the GOP would benefit only the Negro. Bernard Baruch, writing to Senator Walter George in late August, insisted, "The real question for the South is to decide whether they are going to secede from the protecting folds of the Democratic Party." Were the South to vote Republican, Baruch predicted, "it will have to face the problem it has been struggling against ever since the slaves were freed." Baruch assured George that "our people" will not "be led astray by intolerance and false issues to destroy themselves."[31]

Al Smith, however, was personally appealing to black Americans. Blacks could empathize with him as a fellow victim of white Protestant bigotry and could admire his forthright and vigorous opposition to the Ku Klux Klan. They could even entertain the hope that his election would lead to increased tolerance in American life. In an editorial published on the eve of the campaign, the *Messenger* detailed some of the attractive features of candidate Smith:

Alfred E. Smith is a Catholic. Fundamentalists and Protestant bigots have asserted that no Catholic can become President of the United States. Because of his religious faith, the Governor of New York will lose many thousands of votes in the Bible Belt where anti-Catholicism flourishes along with color-phobia and a large number of other prejudices. Since it is immaterial to the Negro worker which party gets into office, it would be striking a severe blow at intolerance, prejudice, and bigotry if Negroes should help send this Catholic gentleman to the White House. Whatever sins may be charged against the Catholics, it cannot be said that in this country they have aligned themselves with the Negro baiters and lynchers.[32]

The Democratic "campaign of intolerance," designed to associate the Republicans with anti-Catholic agitation against Al Smith, may have served to heighten the identification of Herbert Hoover with the Ku Klux Klan. The Democrats also made a special effort in 1928 to organize black voters, apparently devoting substantial resources to this end.[33]

Although the defection of black elites from the Republican party cannot be measured precisely, the evidence suggests that it was widespread. The black press carried weekly stories of prominent Negro leaders in business, politics, and religion who had shifted their political loyalties to the Democrats. For the first time, the Republicans had difficulty finding eminent blacks to serve on the Colored Advisory Committee of the Republican National Committee. Five men publicly declined this honor, including with their regrets statements condemning the current policies and leadership of the GOP. Neval Thomas, for example, president of the District of Columbia branch of the NAACP, wrote, "I refuse to allow a crowd of oppressors who are opposed to everything Republican masquerade in its sacred name. This aggregation now parading in its name stands for everything that Republicanism condemned and destroyed. They are in solemn compact with the Bourbon South in their wicked schemes against the Negro."[34] The black press reported that many other well-known citizens privately declined invitations to serve on the Colored Advisory Committee.[35] In contrast, the Democrats succeeded in persuading an especially large and prominent group of black leaders to serve on their colored voters division.[36]

Endorsement policies of the black press in 1928 also point to changes in the political preferences of black leaders. In past years one had to search for black newspapers that supported Democratic candidates. In 1928, the black press was far more favorable to Al Smith than to Herbert Hoover. Virtually none of the major Negro papers supported Hoover; they either endorsed Al Smith or remained neutral.[37]

Although elite blacks in 1928 appear to have deserted the Republican party in greater proportion than the rank and file of black voters, the postelection analyses of Republican politicians, reported in Chart A3.6, Appendix 3, suggest that the same concerns motivated individuals from both groups. Black leaders and black voters were influenced to support Smith by the failure of the Coolidge administration to promote the interests of black people, the tendency of Protestant bigots to support Herbert Hoover, the fear that Hoover was personally hostile to Negroes and sought to expel them from the Republican party, and the personal appeal of Al Smith. The survey responses also suggest that the prohibition issue, which seems to have had little effect on the behavior of black elites, influenced the decisions of some black voters.

Both Hoover and Smith responded to racist cues institutionalized in the presidential politics of 1928. Al Smith and local Democratic leaders loyal to the national ticket sought to preserve as much of the normally Democratic South as possible. Only by waving the banner of white supremacy could they hope to resist formidable Republican challenges in many southern states. Although Al Smith did not need to direct or coordinate the machinations of southern leaders, he did not curtail or control their racist tactics. Herbert Hoover craved the triumph of cracking the solid South and the broader achievement of nationalizing the GOP by resurrecting the two-party South. Whereas Smith's religion and his opposition to national prohibition formed the opening wedge for Republican penetration of the South, Republicans also believed they had to rival the Democrats as champions of white supremacy.

Herbert Hoover was personally in control of the Southern Strategy that helped gain electoral votes in the South, while alienating prominent black Americans. Historians have mistakenly attributed too little practical, political concern to the great engineer. Hoover's activities in 1928 show that he responded as a politician to the opportunities offered by racial issues. As a presidential candidate, Hoover was alert to political opportunity and willing to exploit racial conflict.

Despite many grounds for the defection of black voters, reports submitted to the Republican National Committee along with predictions of politicians and journalists during the campaign suggest that the Republicans lost fewer black votes in 1928 than had been anticipated. These miscalculations probably stemmed, in part, from a proclivity to judge a group's political behavior by the pronouncements of its purported leaders. This same error reappears in historical accounts of the 1920s. Historians need to be more critical of inferences about the lives of rank-and-file blacks that are drawn from elite sources. While it may be heartening to believe that the sophisticated "new Negro" articulated the thoughts and feelings of most black Americans, voting data disclose that, in 1928, arguments that seemed persuasive to educated, outspoken blacks apparently had much less influence on the preponderant majority of black citizens. Traditional political allegiances seem to have survived both the "Negro Renaissance" and the leadership efforts of prominent blacks.

Yet the inclination of Negro leaders to favor the Smith-Robinson ticket in 1928 did not reflect a bright hope that the Democratic party or even a Smith administration would champion the cause of black people. Rather, it revealed the limited political options still available to black Americans in the era of the new Negro. In their quest for equal rights, black people were confronted on the one hand by a Republican party whose friendship for their people was a tarnished memory and, on the other hand, by a Democratic party wedded to southern racism. Thoroughly disgusted with the protracted backsliding of Lincoln's party and the Southern Strategy it pursued in 1928, many among the Negro elite rejected the candidacy of Herbert Hoover. But their positive reasons for supporting Governor Smith were extremely thin. Given the internal structure of the Democratic party, it is inconceivable that the election of Al Smith would have perceptibly altered the status of black people in American society.

The Voting of Women and Men in 1928

No historian or political scientist has yet made a serious effort to quantify the distinctive voting behavior of men and women in the presidential election of 1928. The very enterprise is perilous. Because sex ratios do not vary much from one political unit to another, random error is likely to plague any measurement of differences in the voting decisions of men and women. Fortunately, this study includes a sufficient number of counties to obtain statistically significant indicators of how measures of the presidential vote respond to changes in a county's percentage of women. Nonetheless, variation in the proportion of women residing in American counties may be correlated with such confounding variables as occupational structure. Thus, the results of statistical analysis must be regarded skeptically and special attention paid to documentary evidence.

From fragments of quantitative and literary data, historians have tried to learn how the contest between Al Smith and Herbert Hoover affected the political participation of women. Scholars generally agree that the new turnout of 1928 was disproportionately female and that the new woman voter of that year was typically a Catholic, whose culture had discouraged political participation, but who voted in the election for her coreligionist Al Smith.[38]

The results of regression analysis support the first proposition, but suggest the need to modify the second. These results also indicate how men and women responded to the presidential combatants of 1928. Increases in voter turnout between the presidential elections of 1924 and 1928 were proportionately greater for women than for their male counterparts. Independent of a county's score on control variables, as the percentage of women increases so does the percentage increase in voter turnout over 1924. A 1 percent increase from one county to another in the percentage of women yields a .29 percent increase in the difference between voter turnout in 1928 and 1924 (standard error = .046).

More refined analysis indicates that Catholic women were far more likely than their Catholic male counterparts to become new voters in 1928. To a lesser extent, the same pattern may have prevailed for Protestants, but the statistics are less reliable for Protestant behavior. To test the interaction between religious affiliation and increases in the political participation of women, an analysis of covariance was performed for 367 counties with less than 1 percent of their population listed as members of the Roman Catholic church and the 200 counties with the highest percentage of Catholics. Independent of control variables, a county's percentage of women has appreciably more influence on differences in voter turnout for highly Catholic than for highly Protestant counties. A 1 percent change in the percentage of women residents yields a .29 percent increase in the difference between voter turnout in 1928 and 1924 for predominantly

Protestant counties (standard error = .102) and a .59 percent change for predominantly Catholic counties (standard error = .181). This test, of course, is not definitive because the behavior of individuals residing in religiously homogeneous counties may not match the behavior of their counterparts residing in more heterogeneous communities.

The statistical analysis also sheds light on the candidate preferences of men and women, terra incognita for the election of 1928. The regression coefficients reported in Table 7.2 disclose that women were more likely to vote for Republican candidate Herbert Hoover than were their male counterparts. An increase from county to county in the percentage of women produces a fairly substantial decrease in Al Smith's percentage of the presidential vote, when controlling for the social and economic composition of each county. Similarly, an increase in the percentage of women yields a decrease in Al Smith's

Table 7.2. *Influence of Percentage of Females on Measures of the Vote for President: 2,058 Counties (in percent)**

	Regression Coefficient b	Standard Error
Dem 1928	−.30	.074
Dem 1928 total	−.12	.058
Rep 1928 total	.31	.064
Dem 1928 minus Dem 1924	−.68	.070
Dem 1928 minus Dem/Prog 1924	.21	.067
Dem 1928 minus Prog 1924	.45	.106
Dem 1928 total minus Dem 1924 total	−.16	.043
Dem 1928 total minus Dem/Prog 1924 total	.15	.043
Dem 1928 total minus Prog 1924 total	.19	.070
Rep 1928 total minus Rep 1924 total	.05	.045
Dem 1928 minus mean Dem 1916–24	−.10	.060
Dem 1928 minus mean Dem 1916–20, Dem/Prog 1924	.20	.054
Dem 1928 minus Dem 1932	.21	.058
Dem 1928 minus mean Dem 1932–40	.39	.058

*Controlling for percentages of Urban, Foreign stock, Owners, Negro, Under 35, Pop change, Jewish, Prot church, Catholic, and for Economic status.

percentage of the potential voting population and an increase in Hoover's percentage of this population.

Differences in the voter choices of men and women were not especially marked in 1928. The coefficients reported in Table 7.2 indicate that, relative to their male counterparts, women were even less likely to vote for Robert M. La Follette in 1924 or for Franklin D. Roosevelt from 1932 to 1940, than to vote for Al Smith in 1928. As the percentage of women increases from one county to another so does the difference between the vote for Smith and the vote for La Follette as well as the difference between the vote for Smith and either measure of the vote for Roosevelt. But, relative to men, women were more likely to vote for John W. Davis than for Al Smith. An increase in the percentage of women yields a very substantial decrease in the difference between the vote for Smith and the vote for Davis.

Overall, regression analysis suggests that women were more inclined than men to support presidential candidates who seemed less likely than their opponents to tamper with the status quo. They favored Davis and Coolidge over La Follette, Hoover over Smith or Franklin Roosevelt. These results corroborate the tentative conclusions of political scientists writing in the 1920s.[39]

Both the Republican National Committee's postelection survey and the responses to Franklin D. Roosevelt's circular letters contain information on how women reacted to the presidential competition of 1928. The reports of those who responded to each inquiry sustain the results of statistical analysis. The Republican National Committee specifically asked party leaders to analyze the behavior of women voters; their responses are reported in Appendix 3, Chart A3.7. Virtually every Republican respondent agreed that women experienced a remarkable political renaissance in 1928, voting in unprecedented numbers. Not one of them asserts that this awakening of the female voter was confined to Catholics. Most of the respondents also informed the national committee that women were the most steadfast supporters of Herbert Hoover. They argued that Hoover's image was especially appealing to the woman voter and that women were more likely than males to penalize Smith for his religious affiliations and disdain for prohibition. In its summary of the individual reports, the Republican National Committee reached the following conclusions: "Most conspicuous and important was the support given President-elect Hoover by the women. . . . Indifference or aversion to political activity . . . was overcome, and hundreds of thousands of women who had never participated in politics and never voted were brought into the campaign as zealous workers in behalf of Mr. Hoover. . . . Hoover's support by women was the one constant, dominating factor in every state making a report—in many states women offsetting all losses of normal Republican votes due to variously assigned causes."[40] If Protestant women were beguiled by Hoover and repelled by Smith, it is not surprising that they turned out in large numbers for the 1928 contest.

Many of the Democrats responding to Roosevelt's inquiries bemoaned their candidate's poor showing among female voters, placing the blame on the religiosity of Protestant women and their ardent support for prohibition. Thomas E. Cashman of Michigan, for example, wrote that the party's "worst problem in this midwestern country was the women." He claimed that "Republican farmers by the thousands voted for Governor Smith, but their wives and daughters and the great majority of single women voted against Governor Smith," largely because of the liquor issue but partly because of his religion.[41]

Roosevelt's correspondents also complained that the opposition could turn out the women's vote more effectively than could the Democrats. Upper-class, Republican women, they asserted, controlled most women's organizations in the United States and used their positions to promote the Republican cause. Emma M. May of Terre Haute, Indiana, offered FDR the following analysis of how women fared in the politics of her party. Roosevelt's aides annotated May's letter as "the best woman's letter *received.*"

Now, Governor Roosevelt, why don't they make women a real part of the organization? Why are not women asked to help raise finances, help select party tickets and do all the things that organization requires of the men? Just as long as women will be kept as "auxillaries" you will never get them to organize. . . .

Do you know that the greater part of Federation of Clubs, League of Women Voters, the D.A.R.'s, the Council of Jewish Women, the Business and Professional Women, W.C.T.U., are composed mostly of Republican women throughout the United States? Democrats should organize women into clubs, local luncheon groups, encourage them to become "joiners." There is not the slightest doubt that the Republican Party distributes much political propaganda thru all local women's clubs.[42]

Women became more than nominal participants in party activities only after Roosevelt appointed Mary Dewson chairman of the Democratic National Committee's Women's Division in the early 1930s. But even during the New Deal, women wielded little power within the party.

The behavior of women voters in 1928 is linked dialectically to the decline of the American woman's movement during the 1920s. In time for the presidential election of 1920, Congress and the states had guaranteed woman's suffrage by constitutional amendment, culminating fifty years of struggle. In 1920, the National American Woman's Suffrage Association (NAWSA) claimed several million members; presidential aspirants and party platforms advocated feminist legislation as well as reforms of special interest to the woman's movement. Both parties fashioned schemes for integrating women into their leadership strata, and Congress seemed responsive to feminist demands, passing legislation for maternity and child care, independent citizenship for women, and a constitutional amendment proscribing child labor. By mid-decade, however, the woman's movement had lost both its political influence and its following among the rank and file of American women. Leaders of the movement were fighting among themselves and politicians no longer seemed responsive to feminist demands. Although most feminists sought protective legislation for women and viewed the quest for woman's rights as part of the larger struggle for progressive reform, others insisted on completely equal treatment for men and women and urged women to concentrate on securing their rights. Only a small percentage of NAWSA's membership had enrolled in the League of Women Voters, its successor organization. The Child Labor Amendment died in the state legislatures, and, taking a step backward, Congress voted in 1927 to allow legislation providing aid for mothers and infants to expire after two more years. By the end of the decade, women had achieved no major breakthroughs in their quest for political power or for equal access to jobs, pay, and promotion.[43]

Historians are just beginning to perform a belated autopsy on the woman's movement of the 1920s. Some have argued that the movement destroyed itself by the very means used to win the suffrage fight. Shifting from an earlier emphasis on the equality of the sexes, leaders of the NAWSA argued in the early twentieth century that women were especially sensitive to injustice, to immorality, to simple human misery. As voters and officeholders, the suffragists contended, women would spearhead the reform of society.[44] In a seminal study of American feminism, William L. O'Neill wrote that reliance on this pragmatic argument for suffrage left feminism in an untenable position during the 1920s: "Unfortunately, pragmatism cuts both ways. If the results by which a thing is to be judged are inadequate, then the thing itself is at fault. Social feminists in the post-war era were victims of their own logic. Having failed to deliver the goods as promised, they were in no position to demand that young women rally round a program that was, if not discredited, at least eminently discardable."[45] A more complete analysis, of course, would have to consider matters such as conflicts among feminists; the objectives actually sought by the majority of feminist leaders; the strategic decisions made after the achievement of suffrage; the interests of the male power structure; the social and economic conditions of the 1920s; and the preferences of ordinary women.[46]

The voting behavior of those women who were the potential constituents of a feminist movement helps explain the dwindling momentum of feminism in the 1920s. The results of statistical analysis suggest that women were even more inclined than their male counterparts to opt for the candidates least threatening to the established order. Women, moreover, turned out in large numbers only in response to the issues of religion and liquor, matters not likely to threaten allocations of power or to advance the goal of equal rights for American women. By the late 1920s, male politicians surely realized that the female voter posed no threat to business as usual and need not be granted any special concessions. Putative leaders of the rank and file of American women could not use the political clout of their sisters as a bargaining chip in support of their demands. Women became neither an independent force in American politics nor an interest group within the parties whose loyalty had to be preserved.

Chapter 8

Economic Issues

Analysis of economic issues suggests modifications of cherished dogma concerning the presidential contest of 1928. Historians have paid little attention to the hypothesis that the economic status of voters significantly influenced their presidential preferences in 1928. They have generally assumed that the nation's overall prosperity and the absence of sharply defined economic issues in the election campaign ruled out the possibility that, independent of social divisions, the contest would pit class against class. The nationwide, multivariate studies of the 1928 election fail to include a measure of economic status among their explanatory factors,[1] and historians using traditional methods have not paid much attention to the role of economic class. Virtually all scholars have agreed, however, that regardless of the identity of the Democratic nominee and the strategy of his campaign, economic prosperity guaranteed the victory of Herbert Hoover. David Burner explained: "The Presidential election of 1960, in which a Catholic faced a Protestant for the second time in American history, prompted new interest in the 1928 election and led to an extensive reexamination of the earlier contest. But only one point seems to have been established with finality: that in 1928 Hoover would have won over any Democratic candidate. No Democrat, whatever his faith and whatever his political program, could have vanquished the party that was presiding over the feverish prosperity of the later twenties."[2]

While the ultimate conclusion that Hoover was a sure winner in 1928 may possibly be true, the conventional wisdom underlying this conclusion is too simple. Economic developments during the 1920s did not in themselves guarantee the perpetuation of Republican power. Rather, despite the imperfections of prosperity during this decade, a combination of the reality and mythology of prosperity made the Republicans formidable in 1928. Most middle- and upper-class Americans had reaped tangible benefits from economic change during the 1920s and believed that their good fortune was best protected by Republican presidents. Millions of poor Americans, convinced by the evidence of prosperity seemingly surrounding them and the drumbeat of establishment propaganda, believed that prosperity was also within their reach; they, too, demanded no fundamental changes in the prevailing order. Had the Democratic party been able to win over most of those Americans living at or below contemporary estimates of minimum decency, their candidates would have dominated elections in the 1920s.

Although Democrats failed to lure enough working-class support to avoid lopsided defeat in presidential elections of the 1920s, voters still divided according to their economic position, not only in 1928, but in earlier elections as well. Even though many working-class Americans failed to vote or voted Republican during the 1920s, these citizens joined the minority coalitions of the Democratic party in greater proportion than their wealthier counterparts. It was neither the Great Depression nor the initiatives of Franklin Delano Roosevelt that first opened a gulf between rich and poor voters, independent of their religion, their ethnic heritage, their residence in city or country. Nor did policy differences between Republicans and Democrats in the 1920s generate economic divisions of the electorate. The Democrats never devised a coherent alternative to the economic philosophy of their Republican rivals; and, as a presidential candidate, Al Smith decided not to launch a progressive challenge to the GOP. Persuasive explanations of class voting in the 1920s must focus on neither philosophy nor policy, but on the images projected by parties and candidates.

The Influence of Economic Status on Voting for President

To study class divisions in the electorate, regression coefficients were computed for an index of each county's economic status as well as for the six variables that comprise the index. Table 8.1 reports coefficients for this index and for a slightly modified index that excludes the percentage of high school graduates. Table 8.2 reports coefficients for each of the distinct variables entered separately in the regression equations. The coefficients for these variables combine their direct influence on the dependent variable and an indirect influence stemming from correlations with economic measures not included in the equation. The six variables represent several distinct ways of measuring economic status. They include a measure of consumption in each county (per capita retail purchases in 1929); a measure of the proportion of county residents exceeding a certain income level (the percentage of taxpayers in 1928); a measure of the proportion of county residents achieving a particular level of education (the percentage of high school graduates in 1940);[3] a measure of the value of the housing in which people lived (median housing values for 1930); and two measures of the proportion of county residents possessing a particular item (the percentage of those with telephones and with radios in 1930). The index number constructed from these variables is an equally weighted sum of all variables after they have been transformed into common units (standard deviation units). Unlike individual variables, however, the index number has no clear substantive interpretation. Attention should be focused only on its sign, statistical significance, and comparative magnitude for different measures of voting behavior.

Of the variables included in the index, the four percentage variables represent aggregate-level measures of individual-level characteristics whose values are dichotomous. One either pays taxes or does not, owns a radio or does not. Only a very small percentage of the American people paid income taxes in 1928; more than any other variable, the percentage of taxpayers identifies a small economic elite. Its regression coefficient registers differences in the behavior of taxpayers and the remainder of the population. The two additional variables represent aggregate-level measures of individual-level characteristics whose values are continuous—the cost of one's housing and the amount of money one spends on retail goods. For housing values, the aggregate-level variable is the median or midpoint of the individual-level values. For retail purchases, the aggregate-level variable is the average or per capita measure of individual-level values. Although county-level variables obviously cannot capture distinctions in economic status within a community, they do reveal differences from county to county in the proportion of those possessing a certain product, achieving a particular level of education, and receiving enough income to file a tax return. The variables also register differences from county to county in retail purchases and housing values. To the extent that they omit significant within-county effects of economic distinctions, the measures used in this study should underestimate the importance of economic status for presidential voting.

Table 8.1. *Influence of Economic Status on Measures of the Vote for President: 2,058 Counties (in percent)**

	Economic Index with H.S. Grads		Economic Index without H.S. Grads	
	Regression Coefficient b	Standard Error	Regression Coefficient b	Standard Error
Dem 1928	−.84	.071	−1.03	.087
Dem 1928 total	−.23	.055	− .25	.068
Rep 1928 total	.95	.061	1.20	.074
Dem 1928 minus Dem 1924	.07	.067	− .02	.082
Dem 1928 minus Dem/Prog 1924	.04	.064	.04	.078
Dem 1928 minus Prog 1924	−.97	.101	−1.07	.125
Dem 1928 total minus Dem 1924 total	−.01	.041	− .05	.050
Dem 1928 total minus Dem/Prog 1924 total	−.16	.042	− .16	.051
Dem 1928 total minus Prog 1924 total	−.38	.067	− .35	.083
Rep 1928 total minus Rep 1924 total	.11	.043	.18	.052
Dem 1924 minus mean Dem 1916–24	−.41	.057	− .45	.071
Dem 1928 minus mean Dem 1916–20, Dem/Prog 1924	−.42	.052	− .42	.064
Dem 1928 minus Dem 1932	−.08	.056	− .06	.068
Dem 1928 minus mean Dem 1932–40	−.09	.056	.00	.068

*Controlling for percentages of Urban, Foreign stock, Owners, Negro, Female, Under 35, Pop change, Jewish, Prot church, Catholic.

Table 8.2. Influence of Economic Variables on Measures of the Vote for President, Separately Entered in Regression Equations: 2,058 Counties (in percent)*

	Radio Owners		Telephone Subscribers	
	b	SE	b	SE
Dem 1928	−.23	.021	−.15	.032
Dem 1928 total	−.02	.016	.03	.024
Rep 1928 total	.33	.017	.29	.027
Dem 1928 minus Dem 1924	−.02	.020	.10	.029
Dem 1928 minus Dem/Prog 1924	.11	.019	−.08	.028
Dem 1928 minus Prog 1924	−.09	.030	−.34	.044
Dem 1928 total minus Dem 1924 total	.02	.012	.02	.018
Dem 1928 total minus Dem/Prog 1924 total	.05	.012	−.14	.018
Dem 1928 total minus Prog 1924 total	.03	.020	−.13	.029
Rep 1928 total minus Rep 1924 total	.03	.013	.01	.019
Dem 1928 minus mean Dem 1916–24	−.10	.017	−.03	.025
Dem 1928 minus mean Dem 1916–20, Dem/Prog 1924	−.05	.015	−.09	.023
Dem 1928 minus Dem 1932	.04	.016	−.22	.024
Dem 1928 minus mean Dem 1932–40	.06	.016	.00	.024

*Controlling for percentages of Urban, Foreign stock, Owners, Negro, Female, Under 35, Pop change, Jewish, Prot church, Catholic.

The regression coefficients portrayed in Tables 8.1 and 8.2 disclose that independent of their other demographic characteristics, lower-class Americans disproportionately supported Al Smith. The robust negative coefficient for Smith's percentage of the vote means that as the value of the index decreases, Al Smith's percentage of the presidential vote increases. Similarly, each one of the coefficients for the individual variables also has a negative, statistically significant (at the .0001 level) coefficient, confirming the inverse proportion between economic status and support for Al Smith. Although the negative relationship between economic measures and Democratic voting persists for Al Smith's percentage of the potential voting population, its magnitude is diminished considerably, both for the index number and the individual variables. Along with the especially

Taxpayers		H.S. Grads		Retail Purchases		Housing Values	
b	*SE*	*b*	*SE*	*b*	*SE*	*b*	*SE*
− .80	.085	−.43	.058	−.016	.002	−.018	.002
− .42	.065	−.19	.044	−.007	.002	−.004	.002
.49	.075	.42	.051	.015	.002	.023	.002
− .16	.079	.24	.053	.002	.002	−.008	.002
− .27	.075	.17	.051	−.002	.002	.016	.002
−1.24	.120	−.72	.081	−.021	.003	.009	.004
− .22	.048	.08	.033	−.000	.001	−.002	.001
− .39	.049	−.14	.033	−.003	.001	.013	.002
− .60	.079	−.41	.053	−.010	.002	.012	.003
.25	.050	−.03	.034	.002	.001	.004	.002
− .38	.068	−.32	.046	−.009	.002	−.009	.002
− .41	.061	−.39	.041	−.010	.001	−.001	.002
.15	.065	−.09	.044	−.005	.002	.019	.002
− .33	.066	−.25	.044	−.004	.002	.013	.001

strong positive relationship between economic status and Herbert Hoover's percentage of the potential voting population, these findings indicate that those of lower economic status were less likely to participate in the election than their more substantial counterparts. Again, the individual variables and the index number suggest identical conclusions.

The examination of regression coefficients for variables measured in percentages affords insight into the importance of economic differences for voter decisions in 1928. A county in which all families owned radios, for instance, would be 20 percentage points less Democratic than one with no radio owners but with an otherwise identical demographic profile. A county with all telephone subscribers would be 15 percentage points less Democratic than one with no subscribers;

a county of all taxpayers would be 80 percentage points less Democratic than one in which no person filed a tax return; and a county of all high school graduates would be 43 percentage points less Democratic than one with no high school graduates. The small proportion of those earning enough income to file tax returns in 1928 explains the very substantial difference in voting behavior between this group and the rest of the electorate.

An economic division of the electorate did not first appear in 1928. In previous elections as well, lower-class Americans were especially inclined to vote for Democratic candidates. The index number shows that the regression coefficients for the difference between the vote for Smith and the vote for Davis are not much different from zero, whether the presidential vote or the adult population is used for the computation of percentages. In both cases, for the six individual variables, three of the coefficients for the variable measuring differences between the performances of Smith and Davis are positive; three are negative. All of them have relatively low values. For both the index number and the individual variables, economic status also has little effect on the difference between the Republican proportion of the adult population in 1928 and 1924. Regression coefficients are negative for the difference between Smith's percentage and the average percentage of the three previous Democratic contenders. In each case, however, the magnitude of the coefficient is less than half that of the corresponding coefficient for Al Smith's percentage of the presidential vote. Similar relationships hold for each of the individual variables, with the exception of the percentage of taxpayers.

The economic divisions generated by the candidacy of Al Smith in 1928 were wider than those created by protest candidate Robert M. La Follette in 1924 and about equal to those generated by Franklin D. Roosevelt, whether in 1932 or from 1932 to 1940. As the difference between the vote for Smith and the vote for La Follette increases, the value of the index of economic status decreases, as do values for all other variables except for housing. For the index numbers, the coefficients for the differences between Al Smith's percentage of the vote and either Roosevelt's 1932 percentage or his average percentages from 1932 to 1940 are not significantly different from zero. In each case, of the six remaining variables, three of the coefficients for this difference are positive; three are negative. These findings suggest that the impact of the Great Depression and the New Deal did not appreciably widen the gap between economic classes that already existed in the 1920s.

The class divisions of 1928 were not confined to counties with particular levels of urbanization. Table 8.3 reveals remarkable consistency in the influence of the economic index on measures of the 1928 vote in rural, moderately urban, and highly urban counties. For all three variables and all three groups of counties, the regression coefficients for the index number offer the same conclusions. These coefficients again show that support for Smith decreased as economic status increased and that voter turnout increased as economic status likewise increased.

Analysis of how measures of the vote for president respond to changes from county to county in the percentage of home owners sheds additional light on class voting in 1928 and other presidential contests. Regression coefficients reported in Table 8.4 again disclose the middle- and perhaps upper-class composition of the vote for Republican candidates. After controlling for the influence of other explanatory variables, including economic status, Smith's percentage of either the presidential vote or the adult population of each county decreases as the percentage of home owners increases from one county to another. In contrast, Hoover's percentage of the adult population increases as the percentage of home owners likewise increases. A gulf between those who owned and those who rented their homes, however, did not first appear in 1928. The difference between voting for Smith in 1928 and voting for Democratic candidates in earlier elections is not especially responsive to changes from county to county in the percentage of home owners. The largest value for any regression coefficient from this group of response variables is −.12, about one-third the magnitude of the coefficient for Smith's percentage of the presidential vote. Similarly, changes from county to county in the percentage of home owners have virtually no influence on differences between voting for Smith in 1928 and voting for Franklin D. Roosevelt, either in 1932 or from 1932 to 1940. Once again, the most important distinction is between voting for Smith in 1928 and voting for Robert M. La Follette in 1924. Independent of control variables, those who owned their homes were comparatively much more favorable to La Follette than to Smith. A 1 percent change from one county to another in the percentage of home owners yields a −.41 percent change in the difference between the vote for Smith and the vote for La Follette.

Scattered tidbits of documentary evidence support the finding of an inverse relationship between economic position and voting for Al Smith. Although no group was more responsive to Smith's aspira-

Table 8.3. *Geographic Influence of Economic Status on Percentages of the 1928 Vote (in percent)**

	Rural Counties (0% Urban)		Middle Urban Counties (1%–37.5% Urban)		Highly Urban Counties (Over 37.5% Urban)	
	Regression Coefficient b	Standard Error	Regression Coefficient b	Standard Error	Regression Coefficient b	Standard Error
Dem 1928	–.92	.119	–.98	.151	–.59	.127
Dem 1928 total	–.25	.092	–.30	.115	–.22	.103
Rep 1928 total	1.17	.103	1.11	.137	.71	.103

*Controlling for percentages of Urban, Foreign stock, Owners, Negro, Female, Under 35, Pop change, Jewish, Prot church, Catholic.

Table 8.4. *Influence of Percentage of Home Owners on Measures of the Vote for President: 2,058 Counties (in percent)**

	Regression Coefficient b	Standard Error
Dem 1928	−.35	.024
Dem 1928 total	−.13	.019
Rep 1928 total	.26	.021
Dem 1928 minus Dem 1924	−.02	.023
Dem 1928 minus Dem/Prog 1924	−.06	.022
Dem 1928 minus Prog 1924	−.41	.035
Dem 1928 total minus Dem 1924 total	−.02	.014
Dem 1928 total minus Dem/Prog 1924 total	−.05	.014
Dem 1928 total minus Prog 1924 total	−.16	.023
Rep 1928 total minus Rep 1924 total	.10	.015
Dem 1928 minus mean Dem 1916–24	−.12	.020
Dem 1928 minus mean Dem 1916–20, Dem/Prog 1924	−.13	.018
Dem 1928 minus Dem 1932	.04	.019
Dem 1928 minus mean Dem 1932–40	−.05	.019

*Controlling for percentages of Urban, Foreign stock, Negro, Female, Under 35, Pop change, Catholic, Jewish, Prot church, and for Economic status.

tions than Irish Catholics, a private researcher reported to Secretary Hoover that a majority of young Irish businessmen favored his candidacy. James A. Farley reached a similar verdict when he recalled that in New York State many well-educated and economically successful Catholics voted for Hoover. Farley also indicated that many of the more prosperous Jews supported Hoover, although their less affluent coreligionists overwhelmingly favored Smith.[4] Finally, the Republican National Committee, in their review of the 1928 contest, claimed that Hoover retained the fealty of the "conservative, thoughtful segment" of the groups that defected to the Democrats. Although the committee does not mention the class standing of its loyalists, the statement implies that these voters were the more affluent members of otherwise dissident groups: "Another outstanding fact obtained from these reports is the support given Mr. Hoover by the conservative, thoughtful segment of those groups of voters who, as groups, broke away from their normally Republican allegiance. . . . The appeal of business prosperity and sound economic principles and governmental practices—all of which were embodied in the Hoover candidacy—kept an untold number of German-Americans, Jews, Poles, and other so-called foreign language groups, in line for Mr. Hoover against the pull of such issues as immigration, prohibition and religious prejudice."[5]

Economic Distress in the 1920s

One basis for an economic cleavage in the 1928 presidential election was the persisting poverty of ordinary Americans. Although wages and salaries increased during the "prosperity decade," they still lagged behind contemporary estimates of the minimum necessary for a decent standard of living. For perhaps a majority of Americans, prosperity was a hope, not a reality.

Abraham Epstein, executive secretary of the American Association for Old Age Security, examined sixty estimates of the "minimum sums required by an American family for the maintenance of a decent standard of living." Epstein found that "if the estimates are taken as a whole and on a conservative basis, the average worker's requirement for a standard of minimum decency throughout the decade was between $35 and $40 a week, or from $1,820 to $2,080 a year."[6] Yet, in 1928, the average annual compensation per full-time employee was only $1,428.[7] Of course, in some cases, family income was supplemented by a second wage earner: in 1930, 32 percent of all families had two or more gainful workers. Many of these extra workers, however, may have been employed for no wages on farms or part-time for very low compensation. Moreover, wage rates are not adjusted for unemployment or underemployment. Although employment statistics for the 1920s are very sketchy, an estimated two to four million persons (approximately 4.3 to 8.6 percent of the labor force) were unemployed in October 1928.[8] Economists have estimated that 13 percent of the available work force was underemployed.[9]

Estimates of family income are first available for 1929. Table 8.5, which records these estimates measured in 1950 dollars, demonstrates that 41.5 percent of all American families and unattached individuals in 1929 received before taxes a total income of less than $2,000 per year, well below the official poverty level for a family of four measured in 1950 dollars. In 1935–36 the percentage of families and individuals with this level of income had increased to only 48.7 percent. Substantial changes in the percentage of American households earning less than $2,000 in 1950 dollars occurred only during World War II, declining to 21 percent by 1944.

Although a substantial portion of the American people remained mired in poverty throughout the "prosperity decade," real wages rose during the 1920s, credit was increasingly available to consumers, and the government provided additional services.[10] Those who remained steadily employed during the decade had reason to believe that their prospects were good.

*Table 8.5. Family Personal Income in 1950 Dollars (in percent)**

	1929	1935–36	1941	1944
Under $1,000	15.9	19.5	15.1	7.3
$1,000–$1,999	25.6	29.2	19.9	13.7
$2,000–$2,999	25.7	20.7	18.5	15.5
$3,000–$3,999	12.2	12.3	15.7	17.6
$4,000–$4,999	7.2	7.3	12.3	14.7
$5,000–$7,499	7.4	6.7	12.0	18.4
$7,500–$9,999	3.1	1.8	3.1	7.0
$10,000 and over	2.9	2.5	3.4	5.8

*Source: Selma F. Goldsmith, "The Relation of Census Income Distribution Statistics to Other Income Data," p. 93.

Nonetheless, the economic progress of most Americans was painfully limited. Table 8.6 reveals that the postwar spurt in real wages occurred primarily between 1919 and 1921 (an increase of 25.5 percent). Between 1921 and 1928, wages increased only 6.4 percent and real wages only 10.6 percent (prices fell slightly during this period). This increase in real wages was less than one-third the increase in real per capita Gross National Product (34.6 percent). The chief beneficiaries of wage increases during the 1920s were workers in the upper wage brackets,[11] and unemployment was a serious problem. Not only were many Americans out of work or underemployed, but contemporary studies demonstrate that unemployment was frequently of long duration and often led to reemployment at lower wages.[12]

The economy of the 1920s had several sick industries, including textiles, shipping, mining, and agriculture. Most important politically was the distress suffered by farmers. For agriculture, this was not only a period of inadequate income, but also of declining income and wealth. The return of peace in 1919 had rudely shattered a farm prosperity that had been sustained by wartime demand. Farm income fell precipitously between 1919 and 1921. The parity ratio dropped from 110 to 80, and the index number of per capita income available for farm living from 259.7 to 98.6.[13] During the rest of the decade, farm income increased, but not rapidly enough to end the general depression of agriculture, to halt the erosion of property values, or to stop the escalation of farm bankruptcies.[14]

Leaders of farm organizations, publishers of agricultural journals, congressmen and senators from farm states demanded that the federal government act to bolster the prosperity of farmers. The Harding and Coolidge administrations had responded with several limited measures designed mainly to ease the farmer's access to credit and to improve the efficiency of his marketing operations.[15] Passage of this legislation did not end the outcry for farm relief, and agricultural leaders pressed for direct federal action to increase farm prices. The controversial McNary-Haugen Bill, twice passed by Congress and twice vetoed by Coolidge, mandated such action. Drafted to help

Table 8.6. *Wages, Cost of Living, and Real Wages (Index Numbers: 1913 = 100)**

Year	Wages Per Hour	Cost of Living	Real Wages
1919	184	188.3	97.7
1920	234	208.5	112.2
1921	218	177.3	123.0
1922	208	167.3	124.3
1923	217	171.0	126.9
1924	223	170.7	130.6
1925	226	175.7	128.6
1926	229	175.2	130.7
1927	231	172.7	133.8
1928	232	170.7	135.9

*Source: U.S. Department of Commerce, Bureau of the Census, *Statistical Abstract of the United States*, 1931, p. 347.

farmers reap the benefits of a protective tariff on produce, the bill authorized payment of a subsidy to exporters equal to the amount of the tariff levy added to the world price of an agricultural good. Advocates of the legislation argued that this subsidy would spur exports, thereby reducing domestic supply and raising prices to the level of the world price plus the tariff levy. The president's veto messages criticized this method of raising prices, but offered farmers no other means for increasing their income.[16]

Yet the Democrats failed to take advantage of the economic problems experienced by farmers and workers. Although support for Smith increased as the economic position of voters declined, there was no groundswell of underclass support for his presidential bid. Undoubtedly, many poor Americans voted for Hoover and many others did not vote at all.

Democratic Conservatism in the 1928 Campaign

The Democrats did not emerge as champions of the underprivileged during the campaign of 1928. Instead of exploiting economic distress, they sought to persuade the business community that they were as safe and sound as the GOP. Early in the campaign, Al Smith had decided that he would rely on his personal appeal to working-class Americans rather than on a progressive challenge to positions of the GOP.

The Democratic strategy of appealing to American business began to unfold during the party convention. The Democrats had historically been the low-tariff party, advocating the principle of a tariff for revenue rather than for protection. In 1928, however, many influential Democrats felt that much of the business community would look askance at any attempt to lower tariff rates. Once again seeking to abandon a controversial position, the Democrats obfuscated their party's position on the tariff. The Committee on Platforms and Resolutions recommended and the convention adopted an evasive tariff plank designed to appease the protectionists. The Washington correspondent of the *Protectionist* commented that the plank is "designed to assure business that the party, if returned to power, will not undertake downward revision of a kind to create alarm."[17]

Tradition-minded Democrats were appalled by the party's revision of its low-tariff doctrine, but more practical politicians explained that tariff policy was a lamentable casualty of political necessity. As one party leader commented, "I never thought that the time would come when I would sit silent and see a plank go into a Democratic platform on the tariff such as we read here this morning, taking the exact language that has been in the Republican platform for forty years, but we want to carry the country."[18]

The full platform was scarcely the daring proclamation of a party intent upon reconstructing society. Except for its plank on the public ownership of water power resources, the document was only slightly more progressive than the platform adopted by the Republican party only two weeks previously. The Democratic plank on the antilabor injunction was more specific and forthright than that of the GOP, but fell short of labor's expectations.[19] The agriculture plank was long, rambling, and inconclusive. The platform assailed business concentration in general terms, but failed to bolster its rhetoric with concrete proposals. It did not mention any other programs that were aimed at altering the distribution of wealth and power in American society, and it endorsed two of business's favorite proposals—lower taxes and government economy. Commenting on the Democratic platform in a letter to Oswald Garrison Villard, disgruntled Democrat George Fort Milton plaintively asked, "In what regard do we really afford an economic contrast to the GOP?"[20]

After his nomination, Al Smith continued the party's strategy of attempting to secure the favors of American business. His selections for executive positions on the Democratic National Committee portrayed the party as being no less friendly to business than the GOP. John J. Raskob, chairman of the finance committee of General Motors, was appointed national chairman, and four other millionaires received key appointments. The Democrats also sought the allegiance of prominent businessmen who would testify that Smith did not threaten the nation's prosperity.[21]

Chairman Raskob was a conservative business leader who had contributed heavily to the Republican party. Less than eight months before his appointment as chairman of the Democratic National Committee he had donated $5,000 to the New York State Republican Committee.[22] Raskob's interest in Smith's candidacy stemmed from their common opposition to the continuation of prohibition. In mid-July 1928, Raskob confided to Irenée Du Pont that Smith would protect the interests of big business and that only the prohibition issue divided the two candidates:

Governor Smith's ideas of protecting big business are quite in accord with yours and mine. I have talked with him about this and he believes in a tariff of honesty, that is, to give all the tariff protection that industry that is honestly and efficiently managed needs in order to enable it to pay high wages and meet other conditions. . . . Furthermore, I happen to know that the Governor believes that there is too much interference of the Government in business. . . .

Personally, I can really see no big difference between the two parties except the wet and dry question, and, of course, some people say the religious question, which I think both of us agree should form no part of politics.[23]

In the 1930s, Smith, Raskob, and Du Pont joined with other business-men to assail the New Deal as directors of the Liberty League.[24]

Throughout the campaign, Smith and his retinue avoided posi-tions that might antagonize businessmen. Although Smith denied that prosperity was as widespread as the Republicans would have the nation believe, he did not set forth a bold program for reforming the economic order. Smith ignored the problem of business concentra-tion and downplayed labor issues; throughout the campaign, he left dangling a prolabor declaration that was included in his acceptance speech. Like Hoover, Smith stressed the need for economy in the conduct of government and the application of business methods to the direction of public affairs. Like Hoover, he also affirmed that gov-ernment must not interfere with the distribution of an ever-expanding quantity of goods and services through attempts to redistribute in-come and wealth in America. Only Smith's vaguely defined program of farm relief seemed to promise redistribution, but Smith never clarified how his tactics of distribution would differ from those of his Republican opponent.[25]

Unlike Franklin D. Roosevelt four years later, Smith did not gar-ner much support from prominent third-party or Republican progres-sives. Of this group only Senator George W. Norris of Nebraska and Senator Jonathan J. Blaine of Wisconsin campaigned for the New York governor. Norris was primarily influenced by Smith's position on the public ownership of water power facilities, an issue that otherwise stirred few voters.

Democratic progressives bemoaned the governor's failure to ad-vance genuine alternatives to the economic policies of the Republican party. On 3 August, John Dickinson, assistant professor of politics at Princeton University, confided to William Gibbs McAdoo the disappointment of Smith's liberal friends. The letter indicates how early Smith had resolved to conduct a business-oriented campaign:

There is decided disappointment among some members of the liberal or progressive element among Smith's own immediate circle of advisers with whom I am in touch at the sort of campaign he has decided to carry on—his appointment of Raskob, his appeal to big business, etc. It seems he is convinced that his only chance to win is by carrying the North-East and he figures that his support among the immigrants and labor groups on racial and social grounds is not sufficient to give him those states unless business preserves a benevolent neutrality. He regards the likelihood of carrying the midwest as too problematical to justify him in not playing up to the business support which he needs in the northeast.[26]

Al Smith was ill-equipped for an assault on the economic policies of the GOP. His progressive reputation rested on his reorganization of the state government and his promotion of social welfare measures. Smith had always looked askance at expansive fiscal policy or government intervention in the economy. As governor he had consistently pressed for tax reduction, sometimes in the teeth of Republican opposition. Never had he pushed for an expanded state role in the regulation of economic life. Al Smith was committed to free enterprise, to a system he believed was open to men of talent and perseverance like himself and his friends.

Al Smith had changed since he served on the Factory Investigating Commission of 1911. During his last three or four years as governor, Smith had begun to hobnob with the rich and powerful. The once aspiring thespian became the cynosure of a crowd as fast and high-rolling as the swells of Broadway. Al Smith's crowd gathered in the Tiger Room, William F. Kenny's private club in a penthouse on East Twenty-Third Street. As one Smith biographer put it, "To be admitted [to the Tiger Room] you had to be well heeled, golf happy and political minded; you had to agree to the proposition that Al Smith was the greatest statesman since George Washington."[27] Regulars at the Tiger Room were primarily nouveau riche Catholics or Jews—Kenny, James J. Hoey, Herbert Lehman, Jim Riordin, Tim Mara. Al Smith first met John Jacob Raskob at the Tiger Room.

Economics and Ideology in the 1920s

Franklin D. Roosevelt was one of the Democratic politicians who felt that Smith should battle against the economic philosophy of the

Republican party. FDR favored a campaign that would have concentrated upon "a progressive attack against the Coolidge-Hoover economic program."[28] Even if Smith had followed Roosevelt's advice, however, he might not have inspired a surge of working-class support for his candidacy.

The political culture of the 1920s and the lack of an institutional basis for dissent would have impeded any effort to mobilize a protest vote among working-class Americans. The emergence of lower-class protest depends upon both the consciousness of the poor and their position relative to the institutions of society.[29] Much of the public, at every level of income and wealth, seemed confident in 1928 that decent opportunities were available to them. Many poor Americans probably believed that they or their children could share in prosperity and that failure signified a flaw of character rather than a failing of the system. Protest is unlikely when individuals believe that opportunities are plentiful and that their own actions, rather than social forces beyond personal control, determine their economic prospects. The alternatives to confidence about the future become self-doubt, apathy, and despair.[30]

The vaunted prosperity and confidence of the 1920s were a product of effective socialization and public relations as well as economic progress. The schools, the media, government, and business told the American people that they lived in a nation where a good living would be available to anyone with a modicum of wit and industry. Government tampering would only undermine the balance of the economy, jeopardizing everyone's prospects. The actual increase in real wages, consumer purchases, and government services during the decade was sufficiently encouraging to reinforce these assumptions. Although the top 5 percent of the population garnered 30 percent of the national income and the upper 20 percent received over half of all income in 1928, many impoverished Americans believed that the system operated in their favor. As Will Rogers put it, "Prosperity—millions never had it under Coolidge, never had it under anybody, but expect it under Hoover."[31]

Faith in the beneficence of the American economic system had been instilled by the schools and was reinforced during the 1920s by propaganda emanating from other institutions of society. Social scientists have suggested that the most effective propaganda plays upon both the hopes and fears of a target population.[32] Such communication arouses tension and anxiety while simultaneously offering simple and compelling solutions to the problems portrayed. During America's prosperity decade, establishment propaganda painted a glowing portrait of the nation's economy and suggested that all Americans had a common interest in maintaining the status quo. It labeled dissent as dangerous and subversive, intimating that if the public remained vigilant it would reap the rewards of universal prosperity and well-being. If necessary, dissent would have to be stifled by repressive and coercive measures.

Throughout the nineteenth century, American schools had instilled respect for law and authority and inculcated values and beliefs that fostered the interests of dominant social and economic groups. By the 1920s, these educational functions had become firmly institutionalized and bureaucratically regulated. Both the length and frequency of school attendance significantly increased in the late nineteenth and early twentieth centuries. Thus from their days in grade school, the voters of 1928 had been socialized to believe that their society offered unparalleled opportunity for the hardworking and responsible individual. This belief neatly dovetailed with the ideas about America shared by many European immigrants.[33]

Information disseminated by the government during the 1920s seemed to corroborate the most optimistic opinions about the American economy. Successive Republican administrations assured the public that the economy was fundamentally sound and that citizens could anticipate the abolition of poverty in their time. Government officials added to these assurances, statistical reports of the nation's soaring economy. Potentially embarrassing statistics on unemployment, underemployment, and the gap between earnings and subsistence were not distributed to the American people. These facts were themselves branded as subversive.

American businessmen delivered essentially the same message. Members of the business community were often perceived as the wise guardians of a boundless prosperity, and their views were heard and respected. During the Progressive Era, business leaders had frequently initiated and supported reform measures. They had sought to turn economic regulation to their own advantage and forestall the adoption of genuinely radical proposals. Changing tactics in the 1920s, business spokesmen attempted to persuade the public that the productive genius of American industrialists guaranteed a continuing material progress that could be threatened only by undue government interference.[34] What was good for business was good for John Q.

Public as well. All Americans, business leaders averred, would suffer from any attempt to pit class against class.

The nation's press shared in the efforts of business and government to foster optimism and complacency. Throughout the 1920s only a minority of families possessed radios; newspapers were still the major source of news and opinion. Both dailies and weeklies were overwhelmingly probusiness and pro-Republican, serving as willing boosters of business and party ideology. Democrats in virtually every state of the union reported to Franklin Roosevelt that Smith's candidacy was severely hampered by the orientation of the press. They referred not only to newspapers' electoral partisanship, but also to the attitudes inculcated by the press over extended periods of time.[35] John W. Davis, Democratic candidate for president in 1924 and campaigner for Smith in 1928, echoed these views in his analysis of the 1928 contest: "Unless we can stiffen the Democratic press, I don't see how we can ever hope to indoctrinate the country with Democratic ideas. After all, it is the day to day dripping that wears away the stone of opposition."[36]

Economic developments of the 1920s reinforced the public's faith in the prevailing system. Individuals could be persuaded by the surface prosperity and conspicuous consumption visible around them that their personal prospects must be bright. Some opportunity to share in the rewards of prosperity helped keep these hopes alive. Real wages crept upward during the decade, consumer goods were more readily available, and government services more plentiful.

The weakening of institutional support for dissent during the 1920s also helps to explain the quiescence of American voters. Revisionist historians have argued persuasively that reports of the death of progressivism in 1920 were greatly exaggerated. Yet progressivism remained in poor health throughout the prosperity decade. In the first two decades of the twentieth century, Theodore Roosevelt and Woodrow Wilson had rallied the public in support of reform. No comparable national leaders assumed this role during the 1920s. Progressive-minded politicians served in the House and Senate, but were divided among themselves, lacking in original ideas, and wary of further tinkering with the American economy. Contradictions in their own thinking also stymied these latter-day progressives. On the one hand, many progressives favored limited government, low taxes, and restrained spending. On the other hand, they realized that further reform would probably lead to an expansion of government power and additional financial commitments. By 1920, the major Protestant denominations had either abandoned the goal of reforming American society or narrowed their focus to the maintenance of prohibition. Private organizations and local politicians remained interested in reform throughout the 1920s, but their efforts were limited in scope and depth, fragmented, and highly specialized.[37]

Events of the late 1910s and early 1920s had sapped the organizational strength of American radicalism. Radical unionism, best represented by the International Workers of the World, was crushed by the dual impact of wartime patriotism and government repression. The dominant unions of the 1920s abandoned even the pretense of class struggle and sought instead partnership and cooperation with business leaders. The Socialist party of the United States, a formidable political organization for more than a decade, splintered into competing factions in the years following World War I. By the mid-1920s the socialist movement had little political clout and commanded the loyalties of very few voters. Organizations that were both progressive and radical in outlook had coalesced behind the candidacy of Robert M. La Follette in 1924, but these groups were divided among themselves over how to recast society and how to approach political action. La Follette had run in 1924 as an independent progressive rather than as the representative of an established political movement; no third party arose from the ashes of his candidacy.[38]

During the 1920s, businessmen also sponsored company unions and implemented elaborate welfare schemes. Linking workers to their bosses, welfare capitalism became another means of undermining the solidarity and class consciousness of employees.[39] It promoted a dependency on the part of employees that businessmen could exploit to manipulate their political decisions. Workers were warned that their wages, benefits, and even jobs depended upon the continuation of Republican rule. In his analysis of labor's response to the 1928 campaign, George Berry, chairman of the Democratic National Committee's Labor Division, claimed that many workers were "subject to intimidation and coercion by the management of certain industries."[40]

The strength of the forces binding Americans to the status quo is illustrated by the failure of those left behind by prosperity to become agents of political protest. As Caroline Bird pointed out in *The Invisible Scar*, "Farmers, seamen, textile workers, coal miners had hard going all through the prosperous Twenties, but many believed that soon all this would change."[41] Those without work were equally quiescent during the 1920s. Despite the severity of unemployment, the jobless seemed to be quiet, invisible Americans. They generated pitifully little protest and were conveniently ignored by most of society.

Not simply economics, but a combination of the reality and mythology of prosperity made the Republicans formidable in 1928. Perhaps a more progressive campaign by Al Smith would have sacrificed few votes while cutting into working-class support for the GOP and motivating more working-class Americans to vote in the election. Yet the data suggest that the Democrats would have been hard pressed to overcome the ideology of prosperity in a single presidential campaign. Although economic developments did not make the Republicans invincible in 1928, the Democrats' past failure to challenge Republican ideology created difficulties for any Democratic nominee. As Democratic leader E. H. Casterlin confided to FDR, the party needed to reeducate the American public in favor of progressive reform:

I am thoroughly convinced that no candidate can be sold to the public, outside of his immediate locality, without a campaign of education. . . . The Democratic party . . . should be in the hands of its friends constantly, with publicity that is constructive in character. Since the days of the "Full Dinner Pail," "Infant Industries," and "Republican Prosperity," the Republican Party has been constantly hammering into the minds of the voters, not the educated and well-read voter, necessarily, these slogans, backed up with constant reference in the press to "good times," until many, many people really believe that they are living in an age of prosperity excelling all expectations, whether or not they have in the bank their per capita portion of hard money fixed by statisticians.[42]

Beginning in late 1928, the Great Depression and the superb propaganda efforts of the Democratic National Committee reeducated the public more quickly than Casterlin or Roosevelt would have dreamed possible.

Regression analysis reported earlier in the chapter shows that, prior to the depression, the working class opted for Al Smith and earlier Democratic candidates in greater proportion than their wealthier counterparts. The remainder of this chapter evaluates competing explanations for this finding. The first few hypotheses, relating to the impact of issues relevant to organized workers and farmers, fail to explain class divisions in 1928. Better explanations are provided through an examination of party and candidate images.

Organized Labor's Reaction to the Presidential Campaign

During the early twentieth century, the American Federation of Labor was by far the nation's largest and most important labor organization. In 1928, 2,896,000 of the nation's 3,567,000 organized workers belonged to unions affiliated with the AFL. The federation had officially supported Democratic presidential candidates between 1900 and 1920,[43] but in 1924, it had supported Progressive party nominee Robert M. La Follette.[44]

In 1928, the American Federation of Labor remained nonpartisan throughout the campaign, endorsing none of the presidential competitors. Most members of the Executive Committee of the AFL, meeting in early August at Atlantic City, were favorably impressed by Al Smith's prolabor record as governor of New York State.[45] But after the crushing defeats of James Cox and Robert M. La Follette, AFL leaders were unwilling to stake their organization's prestige on yet another underdog candidate. They also feared that endorsement of Smith would precipitate internecine conflict within the federation and would imply support for the unsatisfactory Democratic platform.[46]

Most important, unlike previous Republican candidates, Herbert Hoover could not be identified as an enemy of labor. As John P. Frey, president of the Ohio Federation of Labor, recalled, "Hoover—not warmly a friend, you know, but certainly not unfriendly."[47] Not confronted with a clear-cut distinction between friend and foe, labor leaders were reluctant to act. Before entering the Harding cabinet as secretary of commerce, Hoover was regarded as a mild progressive and was considered for the Democratic presidential nomination until, in March 1920, he declared himself a Republican. Hoover's progressive reputation was somewhat tarnished during his years with the administrations of Warren Harding and Calvin Coolidge, but union leaders still did not view him as being antilabor.[48]

During the late 1920s, the Republican party muted its image of implacable hostility to the aspirations of organized labor. Many Republicans supported the Railway Labor Act of 1926, which generally favored the railroad unions and defused a potentially explosive labor issue. Conservative Republican legislators criticized the use of court injunctions to control labor disputes and suggested ameliorative legislation. Under Hoover's leadership the party also seemed to be less closely allied with diehard antiunion bosses and projected a more balanced image of its position on the relationship between labor and capital. Finally, in the fall of 1928, Republican Senator James E. Watson drafted legislation that guaranteed unions in the strife-ridden soft coal industry the right of collective bargaining and provided for the regulation of wages, prices, and profits.[49]

The militancy of labor reached a nadir in the late 1920s. Rather than expanding the scope of union organization, the AFL sought to conserve its strength among the skilled workers, who were already tightly organized. Instead of mounting an offensive against the bosses, it tried to become a useful "auxiliary of business."[50]

Like the American Federation of Labor, the Railroad Brotherhoods, with a combined membership of approximately five hundred thousand, and the international unions associated with the AFL refused in 1928 to endorse any of the presidential aspirants. But not all labor organizations and leaders followed suit. A few AFL state federations voted to endorse Al Smith, and many local unions, city centrals, and individual labor leaders abandoned neutrality, in most cases to support Governor Smith.

In his study of labor activity in the 1928 campaign, Vaughn Davis Bornet concluded that "the amount of union money spent, quantity of partisan material printed, numbers of speeches made, and degree of general effort exerted were infinitely smaller in proportion to union membership than would be true in years to come." Bornet believed, however, that labor support for Smith was sufficiently widespread to justify the conclusion that "substantial elements in the American trade union movement supported in 1928 the candidate of one party —the Democratic Party."[51]

Bornet correctly observed that available evidence affords no means of judging the transformation of leadership support for Smith into the votes of rank-and-file members.[52] Organized labor put forth no sustained effort on behalf of the Democratic nominee. Its major organs were nonpartisan; local support for Smith was not backed up by the concerted canvassing of union members. But the same concerns that motivated labor leaders to endorse Al Smith may have swayed the votes of union members. George L. Berry claimed in a postelection letter to Chairman Raskob that 90 percent of union members who participated in the presidential election voted for Al Smith.[53] Since data on union membership are not available at the county level for the 1920s, quantitative analysis offers no test of Berry's assertion.

Even a strong positive association between union membership

and support for Al Smith would have made but a small contribution to the economic cleavage found within the electorate of 1928. Only a small minority of workers belonged to unions in 1928 (approximately 3,567,000 out of 47,000,000), and they were mainly skilled workers from relatively high-paying industries. Masses of unskilled workers were not organized until the 1930s.[54]

The Farmer's Reaction to the Presidential Campaign

Al Smith vigorously campaigned for the allegiance of discontented farmers in 1928. Many proponents of agricultural relief within the Republican party were dissatisfied with the party's platform and presidential nominee. They did not regard Hoover as a trustworthy ally of the farmer and had been unable to persuade the GOP to endorse the McNary-Haugen Bill.[55] The Democrats hoped to use the agricultural issue to attract the support of progressive Republican leaders and of midwestern farmers who usually voted Republican.

Al Smith devoted the first speech of his campaign to farm relief (Omaha, Nebraska, 18 September). He disparaged the administration's record, belittled the promises of Herbert Hoover, and sought to advance proposals of his own. Smith supported the principles, though not necessarily the details, of the McNary-Haugen legislation. To aid in the actual development of a farm relief program, he promised to form a "non-partisan commission of farm leaders and students of the problem."[56]

Smith, however, was better able to criticize than to formulate agricultural policy. He effectively exposed the dismal record of the past four years, quoting administration statements and the criticisms of Republican progressives. He argued persuasively that Hoover's proposals, while commendable, fell far short of a solution to the farm problem. Yet his own suggestions were vague. Did he or did he not favor the equalization fee (the key feature of the McNary-Haugen Bill)? If not, what substitute measure did he have in mind? Was the shaping of specific legislation to be left to the omniscient bipartisan committee? Under the questioning of reporters, Smith failed to clarify his position.[57]

Hoover's remedy for the ills of agriculture reflected his philosophy of "cooperative individualism." Hoover advocated the formation of a federal farm board to assist the farmer in marketing his products. The board was designed "especially to build up with federal finance, farmer-owned and farmer-controlled stabilization corporations which will protect the farmer from the depressions and demoralization of seasonal gluts and periodical surpluses." Like Smith's nonpartisan committee, Hoover's farm board was to be given a broad mandate to deal with "the variable problems of agriculture."[58] Hoover never clarified, however, exactly how improved marketing would significantly increase agricultural income. Improved marketing was a laudable goal (even Smith was for it), but few believed it to be the farmer's panacea.

Despite his reluctance to espouse specific legislation, Smith's support for McNary-Haugen principles was more acceptable to proponents of farm relief than Hoover's plan for improved farm marketing. A number of agricultural leaders from the Midwest joined the Smith bandwagon, or at least indicated that they favored the Democratic nominee. Under the leadership of veteran farm leader George N. Peek, who bolted the Republican party after vainly seeking to persuade Republican leaders to accept McNary-Haugen principles, the Democrats undertook a well-financed effort to win over the midwestern farmer. They established a separate campaign organization and appropriated several hundred thousand dollars from central headquarters.[59] Peek sought to convince the farmer that despite Smith's public diffidence, he really did favor the equalization fee. But the governor's vagueness was very difficult to explain away, for it seemed to confirm the Republican contention that Smith was ignorant of farm problems.[60]

Other factors undermined the selling of Al Smith to the American farmer. Democratic leaders were bitterly disappointed that few of the important Republican politicians joined their campaign. With the exception of Senators Norris and Blaine, these men remained within their party and worked for the election of Herbert Hoover. Smith also received very limited active support from the heads of farm organizations or from prominent third-party leaders.[61]

In many agricultural counties, Democratic organizations had long been dormant or nonexistent. The Republicans, on the other hand, generally had maintained ongoing organizations in rural America. Several Democratic leaders from farming regions reported to Franklin Roosevelt that it was extremely difficult to mobilize a Democratic vote in their localities with a makeshift organization of only a few months' duration.

The rural press was overwhelmingly Republican and served as a valuable adjunct to the efforts of party politicians. The press played a particularly important role during the 1920s because rural dwellers had fewer sources of politically relevant information than their urban counterparts. Republican-oriented newspapers supported individual candidates and policies and, over the long run, insinuated support for Republican leadership and ideology.[62]

The anti-Catholicism of rural dwellers further impeded the Democratic campaign. Intense anti-Catholicism among farmers may have acted as a filter, screening out the attractive features of candidate Smith. Scandinavian farmers, for example, were especially suspicious of Herbert Hoover and receptive to the agricultural policies of Al Smith. But they were very reluctant to vote for a Catholic. Visiting the Midwest, *New York Times* correspondent Richard Oulahan reported the attitudes of Scandinavian-Americans: "Mostly farming people, most of them are more taken with Smith's ideas of how to accomplish farm relief than those of Mr. Hoover. . . . Smith would get the bulk of the Scandinavian vote if his religious faith were not involved."[63] A disgruntled George Peek blamed religion and to a lesser extent prohibition for thwarting his efforts to sell Al Smith and his programs to midwestern farmers. "I had hoped that the great silent vote would find expression for Governor Smith," Peek wrote to Hugh Craig on 13 November, "although I realized the danger of the insidious propaganda based on religion and wet and dry, but primarily religion."[64]

Moreover, the McNary-Haugen principles advocated by Al Smith were not universally popular among the nation's farmers. The McNary-Haugen Bill was geared to the staple farmers of the Midwest and, to a lesser extent, the mountain and Pacific regions. The products of most eastern farms would not be covered by the act. Reports to the Republican National Committee from the editors and other subscribers of the *National Republic* (Table 4.2, Chapter 4) disclose that most of the interest in proposals for farm relief was centered in the Midwest, although in this region, too, there were pockets of opposition. In response to a direct question about the impact of the farm relief issue, politicians from eastern and Pacific states surveyed by the Republican National Committee uniformly dismissed this issue in a single sentence (Appendix 3, Chart A3.5). Similarly, reports to Alben Barkley from the Democratic chairmen of Kentucky suggest that a negligible proportion of votes would be gained from the issue of farm relief.[65]

The results of the Republican National Committee's postelection survey further suggest that the struggle for agricultural relief had slight impact on the decision to vote for Smith or Hoover. Although respondents from the Midwest felt compelled to offer more lengthy analyses of this issue than those from the East and West Coasts, only the report from Illinois claims that the question of farm relief influenced more than a negligible number of voters. In their summary of these reports, the Republican National Committee concluded, "A very notable feature of the reports is the general statement that the so-called 'farm issue' which was supposed to be the trump card of the opposition, was practically lost sight of in the campaign."[66]

Finally, even if Smith's campaign had made significant inroads into the farm vote, he may not thereby have generated an economic cleavage of the electorate. First, changes over time in the prosperity of farmers may have had more influence on their political behavior than static measures of their economic condition. Poorer farmers whose lot was improving may have been more likely to vote Republican than wealthier farmers whose prosperity was in jeopardy. Second, the McNary-Haugen Bill tended to be supported primarily by farm groups representing middle-class farmers. The legislation was not likely to assist farmers eking out a subsistence living or serving as tenants on the land of others.

Party Images and the Economic Division of the 1928 Electorate

The image of the two major parties helps to explain why voters split according to their economic positions in 1928 and earlier contests for the presidency. Recent political science has demonstrated that party images may persist for many years and have an important influence on voting in particular elections.[67]

In the 1920s, Republican chief executives were regarded as the special paladins of American business. Business spokesmen articulated a coherent and commonly held set of beliefs about the proper relationship between government and business. In their view, the government should not upset the economy's natural balance, either by artificially improving the status of the masses or by unduly restricting the businessman.

Although the Democratic presidential nominees of the twentieth century were far from radical, Republican presidents still seemed to be the safest repositories of business values and policies. Despite the blusterings of Theodore Roosevelt and the progressive inclinations of some GOP legislators and governors, Republicans at the presidential level had been stalwart defenders of business interests. The national Democratic party, on the other hand, had harbored both the agrarian insurgency of William Jennings Bryan and the urbane progressivism of Woodrow Wilson. The Democratic party had also tinkered with such economically irresponsible schemes as tariff reduction and labor legislation.[68]

Of course, the strong Republicanism of the numerically insignificant business elite could not in itself create a statistically discernible economic cleavage of the American electorate. However, a large number of middle-class Americans emulated the politics of business leaders. Although the perceptions and ideology of businessmen permeated all strata of society, they were likely to be more widely accepted among members of the middle class than among those of lesser means. The superior economic status of the middle class, and their particularly bright economic prospects in the decade, tended to make them more ardent and consistent supporters than lower-class Americans of a philosophy that called for maintaining the status quo. Given the less secure foundations of their prosperity, many middle-class people may have been even more suspicious of government tampering with the economy than were some of the magnates of business.[69]

In trying to convince business and its middle-class boosters that he was as safe and sane as any Republican, Smith was fighting a losing battle. In the lexicon of argumentation, he adopted a strategy termed the "no-need need." This strategy seeks to convince a listener to abandon an established position not because an alternative is better, but because the rationale of the original position has disappeared. Smith sought to gain business support on the grounds that there was no longer any need to vote Republican in order to sustain business prosperity. But voting Republican was a confirmed practice of businessmen in the 1920s, and people tend to resist changes that are perceived to offer no benefits. Moreover, Smith was unable to convince the average businessman that he actually was as safe as his Republican counterpart. Ingrained beliefs are not easily altered by verbal persuasion, especially when the speaker may lack credibility. Social scientists have found that the impact of communication depends, in part, on the credibility of its source. Based on past experiences, Hoover could more credibly claim to continue policies favored by American business interests. Republican propaganda in 1928 stressed that the Democrats could not be trusted to fulfill the promise of their conservative rhetoric. In his 1929 study of businessmen and presidential elections, Arthur Burns found that the rank and file of the business community were unwilling to risk the possible shenanigans of a Smith administration. "Armed with inveterate convictions, the rank and file of the business community continued to cling to their shibboleths. Even the examples of their pecuniary idols—the Raskobs and the Du Ponts—left them undisturbed. They knew full well that men of big business venture occasionally on social and political experiments, but as merchants and dentists they could afford no such luxury."[70] The day that returns were in, Newton D. Baker reflected on the futility of Smith's "no-need need": "The results of this election make a fairly clear case against the Democratic Party's trying to be more Republican than the Republican Party. The Houston platform got us nowhere. As a matter of fact, I think it hurt us very badly, for in effect it was a concession that the Republicans had created and maintained the country's prosperity and that we . . . were going to try to do it the same way. Naturally the people who were voting on the prosperity plea would rather have experienced experts rather than amateurs do the job."[71]

Smith's strategy, of course, was designed to do more than win over successful businessmen. As John Dickinson's letter indicated, Smith also sought to dampen business hostility. The governor apparently hoped that business could be sufficiently mollified so that its wealth and power would not be fully deployed against his presidential aspirations. No evidence has been uncovered, however, to indicate that this feature of Smith's strategy was notably successful. Democratic labor leader George Berry believed that industrialists continued to intimidate their employees during the election of 1928; and the Republicans raised sufficient funds to finance an adequate campaign.

Smith did succeed, however, in attracting sufficient big business support to finance his campaign. The Democrats reported spending $7,152,512 in 1928; the Republicans reported $9,433,604. In 1924, the Republicans had outspent the Democrats nearly four to one and in 1920 nearly three to one. Seventy percent of all contributions to the Democratic National Committee were in amounts of $1,000 or more; the corresponding statistic for the Republican committee was 68 percent. A significant proportion of the Democratic funds came from businessmen opposed to prohibition;[72] but if Smith had appeared unduly progressive, they might have been reluctant to bankroll his campaign.

Status Striving and the Economic Division of the 1928 Electorate

In addition to shared material interests, the status concerns of many middle-class Americans led them to emulate the behavior and attitudes they saw as typical of the business elite; status striving helps explain the economic division that marks every election from 1916 to 1928. During the 1920s, middle-class Americans identified with successful businessmen. In an age of material values, the magnates had the wit, wisdom, and energy to achieve material success. Big businessmen likely represented the ideals of success, accomplishment, and service to significant numbers of middle-class Americans. Those of moderate means sought to be included among the elite, striving for the same kinds of accomplishments, while seeking to achieve some sense of belonging by adopting the modes of behavior, values, and beliefs thought to be characteristic of elevated society.

Not only would the internalization of upper-class values and standards have motivated middle-class Americans to vote Republican, but by voting Republican, these individuals may also have been seeking symbolic identification with the "better sort of people," whose Republicanism was a matter of common knowledge.[73] Voting is more than a choice between alternative policies and leaders. It is also an affirmation of group affiliation and an attempt to define one's identity. By voting Republican, just as by adopting certain modes of dress and deportment, one could achieve a sense of kinship with the elite. More concretely, overt Republicanism may have been a prerequisite for participation in some circles. The Lynds, for example, reported in *Middletown*, "In view of the fact that very few of the city's business leaders are Democrats, it is decidedly 'good business' to be Republican, and this consideration in certain cases overrides the accident of birth."[74]

The candidacy of Al Smith may have accentuated elements of presidential politics relevant to middle-class status concerns, accounting for the slightly negative influence of economic status on the deviation of Smith's vote from the vote for previous Democratic candidates. Hoover superbly personified the successful, socially impeccable businessman; his wife typified the ideal of respectable American womanhood. Smith, on the other hand, could have seemed shoddy and suspect. His clothes were a bit too flashy, his accent too crude, his manners too rough, and his wife too common. These factors might not have much impeded his gubernatorial aspirations, but the presidency has a special symbolic importance for the American people.

Smith's social disabilities were a subject of the underground campaign conducted by Republican leaders and anti-Smith forces outside the party. Smith was charged with being an inveterate drunkard; a friend of organized vice, including gambling and prostitution; and an uncouth ignoramus, who regularly butchered the English language and would disgrace any polite drawing room. Mrs. Smith was portrayed as a dowdy, ignorant woman, with no social graces, who would humiliate the nation in her capacity as First Lady and hostess of the White House.[75]

The recollections of James A. Farley attest to the importance of the Smiths' social qualifications in the minds of status-conscious voters. Farley recounted that upper- and middle-class people whom he canvassed during the campaign felt that Mr. and Mrs. Smith were simply "not fit" to occupy the White House.[76] Many of the politicians reporting to the Republican National Committee after the election asserted that similar prejudices cost Smith votes in their localities, especially among women.

*A Reinterpretation of Economic Developments
and Presidential Voting in 1928*

Much of the new political history, as already noted, would have us believe that the class standing of voters had little to do with their responses to parties and candidates. Lee Benson sounded the keynote for a generation of scholars when he wrote: "At least since the 1820s, when manhood suffrage became widespread, ethnic and religious differences have tended to be *relatively* the most important sources of political differences." In the work of ethnocultural historians, class generally is regarded as being of little consequence for voting, except perhaps during periods of economic crises.[77] Similarly, historians writing about the presidential election of 1928 have focused on social and cultural issues, paying little attention to economic matters. The results of multivariate analysis, however, show an economic division of the 1928 electorate, independent of religion, ethnic heritage, or place of residence. Yet no economic crisis confronted the nation in 1928 and the candidates did not differ sharply on issues of economic policy. Moreover, economic divisions, keynoted by a positive relationship between economic status and voting for Republican candidates, was not unique to 1928, but prevailed in earlier elections as well. Further analysis suggests that explanations for class voting can be sought not only in economic interests, but also in levels of commitment to prevailing ideology, in perceptions of economic prospects, and in the status strivings of voters. These may be reasons both for preferring one candidate or party over the other and for deciding whether to vote at all.

Despite the appearance of an economic division within the electorate, many working-class Americans voted for Hoover or did not vote in 1928. The ideology of prosperity was widespread in the 1920s, and Al Smith never sought to rally voters around particular issues that challenged Republican policy. Neither the parties nor other institutions of the late 1920s offered a base for the development of dissenting views. Little effort to "reeducate" the public came from the Democratic party until depression produced demands for changes in policy. As will be argued later, however, those demands were for restoration as well as for revision of the order prevailing in the 1920s.

Chapter 9

Change and Continuity
in Presidential Politics, 1916–1940

In 1957, William L. Langer, president of the American Historical Association, exhorted his fellow historians to enrich their discipline with insights drawn from social science theory.[1] Historians have recently sought to follow this advice, guiding their work not only by the traditional historiographic principles of common sense, honest presentation, and individual inspiration, but also by formal models of man and society drawn from other disciplines.[2] The trend toward interdisciplinary history is particularly evident in the analysis of American elections. The theory of critical elections, long the conventional wisdom in political science, has profoundly influenced historical studies of electoral change in the United States. This theory suggests that American political history follows a regular pattern of discontinuous change. Stable periods in partisan competition periodically are interrupted by critical elections that realign the electorate and begin new eras of stability.

Using both quantitative and traditional methods, this chapter applies critical election theory to presidential contests from 1916 to 1940. Focusing on the encounter between Al Smith and Herbert Hoover, it reinterprets electoral politics during these years. The study also questions the logical and empirical validity of critical election theory and argues for a broader vision of electoral change and stability in the United States.

Since publication in the 1950s of Samuel Lubell's account of the "Al Smith Revolution" and V. O. Key's seminal article identifying 1928 as a critical election, scholars have devoted considerable energy to quantitative analysis of electoral change in the 1920s and 1930s. The findings of nationwide studies generally have been consistent with the notion that 1928 was either a critical election or an important constituent of a critical era; the findings of more microscopic studies at the state and local levels have been mixed. Irving Bernstein and Carl Degler have examined patterns of urban voting and strongly reaffirmed the thesis of the "Al Smith Revolution." Gerald M. Pomper, in a more elaborate analysis of state-level voting returns, concluded that 1928 was the "most critical" election of a realigning era. W. Phillips Shively, examining the bias in *Literary Digest* polls from 1924 to 1936, argued that two realignments occurred, one in 1924 and 1928 and one in 1936. William H. Flanigan and Nancy H. Zingale, applying new methods of electoral analysis to state-level data, found that a "substantial" realignment of the Democratic vote occurred in 1928. Duncan MacRae, Jr., and James A. Meldrum, in a pioneering study of Illinois counties, concluded that 1928 was the focal point of a realigning period, and John M. Allswang found that for ethnic voters in Chicago, 1928 was a classic critical election. Marc Levine concluded that in Maryland, the election of 1928 "disrupted the standing [political] decision and initiated a *critical period* of realignment." Walter Dean Burnham argued that in Pennsylvania, the 1928 election was part of a complex process of realignment, a judgment corroborated by John L. Shover's study of Philadelphia. Yet in an earlier study of California, Shover claimed that the Smith-Hoover confrontation did not play an important role in realigning the Golden State's electorate. Similar negative results are reported by Charles M. Dollar for Oklahoma, David J. Alvarez and Edmund J. True for Hartford, and Michael P. Rogin for Wisconsin, North Dakota, and South Dakota.[3]

In 1969, Jerome M. Clubb and Howard W. Allen published in the *American Historical Review* a provocative study of metropolitan areas, questioning the realigning influences of the 1928 contest. The authors found that for "the presidential vote alone in these areas . . . it is plausible to speak of an 'Al Smith Revolution.'" Their examination of voting for lesser offices, however, provided either "no support" for the occurrence of revolutionary change in 1928 or "at most inconclusive" evidence of such change. Clubb and Allen did not claim to have proved that "partisan realignment did not occur in 1928." Instead they judiciously concluded that their findings were "equally consistent" with the thesis of the "Al Smith Revolution," the "view that realignment came primarily in the 1930s," and the "suggestion that realignment came about in the course of a 'critical period.'"[4]

My study denies that the presidential election of 1928 was either a critical election or an important component of a realigning era of electoral change. Rather than forging durable new alignments of the American electorate, Smith's candidacy generated an intense conflict between Catholics and Protestants that only marginally affected subsequent patterns of politics. Electoral change during the 1930s was primarily influenced by the responses of Herbert Hoover and Franklin D. Roosevelt to challenges posed by the Great Depression. No election between 1916 and 1940 qualifies as a critical election, and taken together, these presidential contests form a more intricate pattern of stability and change than is predicted by critical election theory. Moreover, the theory itself lacks logical coherence and constricts our vision of American political history.

Since critical election theory provides the theoretical context for this reexamination of presidential politics, the theory's most prominent features need to be described.[5] Critical election theory has developed from ideas initially set forth by political scientist V. O. Key. According to Key, critical elections have occurred periodically in American history, generating high levels of voter interest, upsetting the previous balance of power among competing parties, and producing durable changes in the compositions of the voter coalitions supporting each party.[6]

Key's concept of critical elections has inspired scholars to formulate more complete typologies of American political contests. The most commonly used classification, first suggested by Angus Campbell and his coauthors of *The American Voter*, includes three categories of elections: critical or realigning elections; maintaining elections that do not significantly alter previous voting behavior; and deviating elections that produce sharp but temporary alterations in voter behavior.[7] Political scientist Gerald Pomper has further refined this typology by distinguishing between realigning or critical elections — those that alter both the distribution of power among parties and the composition of their voter coalitions—and "converting elections"— those that change only the composition of the parties' voter bases.[8]

Yet the working historian will have difficulty employing even Pomper's more complete schematic because it confuses analytically distinct categories of elections that may have different implications for American political history. The use of incomplete typologies is the most obvious logical weakness of critical election theory. If we follow previous theorists and divide into two mutually exclusive categories the three relevant variables of changes in party power, changes in voter coalitions, and the durability of change, a complete typology based upon these three dichotomies will have eight categories (the intersection of three two-category variables has 2^3 or eight categories).[9] This typology should include two types of maintaining elections, three types of deviating elections, and three types of realigning or critical elections. There are maintaining elections followed by stability and maintaining elections followed by change. There are deviating elections that produce temporary changes in party power, in the composition of voter coalitions, or in both of these variables. There are realigning elections that produce durable changes in party power, in the composition of voter coalitions, or in both of these variables. The first two types of deviating elections and the first type of critical election have not yet been incorporated into critical election theory.

Pomper also disputes Key's description of the statistical relationships that characterize critical or realigning elections. Pomper's statistical analysis of American electoral history does not identify particular elections in which "new and durable electoral groupings are formed"; he thus redefines critical elections as contests that disrupt the continuity of previously stable patterns of voter loyalty and herald (but do not begin) a period of stability. Pomper argues that "elections identified as critical do not show high correlations with later ballots," but contests following the critical election are highly correlated. Pomper also asserts that critical elections are preceded by "times of unease" and followed by a "period of assimilation." Although Pomper attributes his disagreement with Key partially to differences in statistical methods, the two authorities clearly offer substantively distinct descriptions of critical elections.[10]

As mentioned above, political scientists have further modified the concept of critical elections by asserting that electoral realignments may manifest themselves not only in a single critical election, but also in a critical or realigning era of electoral change. This is an important modification. As John L. Shover suggests, "The critical election model for description contains the latent assumption that changes in political behavior should be abrupt and sudden."[11] The notion of critical eras allows political change to occur more gradually and less uniformly.

Proponents of critical election theory generally assume that electoral realignments are determined by the influence of changes in party identification on changes in voter behavior. Long periods of stability in the party loyalties of American voters and thus in voter performance are shattered by the drastic upheavals of critical elections or critical eras and followed by new periods of stability characterized by new patterns of partisan commitment and voter behavior. Occasionally periods of continuity are punctuated by the short-term attitudinal changes that generate deviating elections. The electoral typologies of critical election theory are a simplified schematic expression of this underlying structure of party competition. If the structure did not exist, critical election typology would lose its raison d'être. The theory does not portray universal properties of electoral systems, but describes a particular configuration of temporal stability and change.

An examination of voter alignments in the presidential elections of 1916 to 1940 should disclose both the extent to which 1928 conforms to the description of a critical election and the compatability of this entire series of elections with the predictions of critical election theory. Pairs of elections with similar constituent coalitions should yield relatively strong associations, whereas pairs of elections with divergent coalitions should yield relatively weak associations. In theory, each election type (maintaining, deviating, critical) is characterized by a distinctive overall pattern of statistical associations with earlier and later elections. Maintaining elections should be strongly associated with preceding, but not necessarily with succeeding elections. Deviating elections should be weakly associated with both earlier and later elections. Critical elections should be weakly associated with preceding elections and either begin (Key's definition) or foreshadow (Pomper's definition) a succession of strongly associated elections.

Unfortunately, despite the appealing simplicity of these verbal descriptions, a historian cannot rigorously classify presidential elections on the basis of statistical associations. Critical election theory is sufficiently ambiguous that the typing of elections necessarily involves intuitive judgments. The theory includes no objective procedures for translating a set of statistical associations between elections into statements expressing the proper classification of each election. A historian will find to his consternation that critical election theory does not answer such questions as: What levels of association between election pairs characterize periods of stability? At what point do the associations between a particular election and previous contests become sufficiently tenuous to warrant classifying that election as either deviant or critical? How can an investigator distinguish between "temporary" and "durable" changes in electoral behavior?

What is the minimum length of the stable phase of a voting cycle? Although each type of election can be verbally described, the investigator has wide latitude in determining the statistical equivalent of each verbal description.[12]

The concept of critical or realigning eras is no less immune to these criticisms than are the standard categories of critical election theory. Theorists have provided no clear guidelines either for establishing the existence of such eras or for demarcating their boundaries. Although a laudable attempt to relax the rigidity of critical election theory, the notion of critical periods may easily be misused to gloss over divergences between empirical data and the fundamental assumptions of critical election models.

Descriptive statistical analysis detailed in the tables and text below suggests that 1928 was not a critical election according to either Key's or Pomper's sense of the term. Rather, voter coalitions in 1928 were skewed by a uniquely strong division between Catholics and Protestants and a lesser division between wets and drys. In actuality, a more significant turning point seems to occur in 1924 for the combined Davis-La Follette vote. Yet neither 1924 nor any other election of this period fulfills the description of a critical election and, overall, these elections do not conform to the predictions of critical election theory.

Table 9.1 portrays the relative stability of voter coalitions for all pairs of presidential elections between 1916 and 1940. Specifically, Table 9.1 is a matrix of regression (b) and squared correlation coefficients (r^2) for the presidential votes of 1916 to 1940. These coefficients are computed for all 2,058 counties outside the former Confederate South. Each percentage within Table 9.1 is a distinct variable. For each presidential election year, except 1924, the variable represents the Democratic percentage of the total presidential vote cast in each county. For the presidential election of 1924, two percentages are computed: the Democratic percentage of the vote and the combined Democratic-Progressive party percentage of the total vote. One set of entries in the table (b) represents the regression coefficient for the two corresponding percentages in the rows and columns of the table. The earlier election serves as the independent or explanatory variable, the later election as the dependent or response variable. Each regression coefficient estimates the responsiveness of the dependent variable to changes from county to county in the value of the independent variable. Since both variables are party percentages, the coefficient can be expressed as the percentage of change in the dependent variable produced by a 1 percent change in the independent variable. The value of the regression coefficient reflects stability and change in the composition of electoral groupings between two election years. The more stable the coalitions, the greater the value of the regression coefficient.[13] Included in parentheses with the regression coefficients are coefficients of determination (r^2, the square of the correlation coefficient) for each election pair. The coefficients of determination reveal the proportion of the county to county variation in the value of the dependent variable that can be predicted by its regression on the independent variable.[14] The value of r^2 varies from one to zero, with one indicating perfect prediction and zero indicating no improvement in prediction. Intermediate values of r^2 represent various other proportions of predicted variation.

Key states that a critical election establishes "new and durable groupings" of the electorate. This description suggests that it forms the beginning of a series of strongly interrelated elections that are weakly related to previous elections. Table 9.1 clearly reveals that Al Smith's 1928 vote fails to satisfy this requirement. In fact, the combined Democratic-Progressive vote of 1924 establishes a sharper turning point than the Democratic vote of 1928. This combined vote is more closely related to Democratic voting in 1928 to 1940 than to Democratic voting in 1920 or 1924. Moreover, although the continuity between elections should grow weaker as the time span between them increases, the Democratic-Progressive vote is a slightly more accurate precursor than the Al Smith vote of Roosevelt's 1932 performance, an equally good precursor of Roosevelt's 1936 performance, and a slightly less accurate precursor of Roosevelt's 1940 performance.[15]

Although the presidential election of 1928 does not fit Key's definition of a critical election, it may yet conform to Pomper's alternative definition. Pomper states that a critical election establishes a "break in electoral continuity" and is followed by, but not included in, a new "era of stability." This definition suggests that elections preceding a critical election should be strongly related to each other but weakly related to elections following the critical election. Elections succeeding the critical election should also be strongly related to each other and weakly related to preceding elections. The critical election itself should be weakly related to both preceding and succeeding elections. Once again, Table 9.1 reveals that the presidential election

Table 9.1. *Regression Coefficients (b) and Coefficients of Determination (r^2) for Presidential Elections: 2,058 Counties, 1916–1940 (in percent)*

	Dem 1916		Dem 1920		Dem 1924		Dem/Prog 1924	
	b	r^2	b	r^2	b	r^2	b	r^2
Dem 1916	1	(1)	.92	(.51)	.92	(.31)	.79	(.36)
Dem 1920			1	(1)	1.0	(.77)	.50	(.24)
Dem 1924					1	(1)	.38	(.23)
Dem/Prog 1924							1	(1)
Dem 1928								
Dem 1932								
Dem 1936								
Dem 1940								

of 1928 clearly fails to satisfy these requirements. Neither prior nor subsequent elections form a cohesive subgroup. And Al Smith's 1928 vote closely resembles Roosevelt's 1932 vote.

This evaluation of the regression coefficients reported in Table 9.1 demonstrates that 1928 does not fulfill either Key's or Pomper's notion of a critical election. Visual inspection of the table can be supplemented by the statistical technique of elementary linkage analysis. Linkage analysis identifies distinct groups of interrelated elections. The elections within each group are more strongly related to at least one other election in the group than to any election in any other group. An examination of the election groups generated by elementary linkage analysis provides another test of the hypothesis that a critical realignment of the electorate occurred in 1928.

If the Smith-Hoover confrontation were a critical election, the Democratic vote of 1928 should divide Table 9.1 into two groups of presidential votes. If it established "new and durable electoral groupings" (Key's definition), the 1928 Democratic vote should be included in the later group. If it disrupted previously stable electoral alignments and heralded but did not begin a new era of stability (Pomper's definition), the 1928 Democratic vote could be included as either the last election of the earlier group or the first election of the later group. It cannot form its own group because each group must include a minimum of two presidential votes.

The results of elementary linkage analysis do not reveal the

Dem 1928		Dem 1932		Dem 1936		Dem 1940	
b	r^2	b	r^2	b	r^2	b	r^2
.53	(.21)	.70	(.35)	.66	(.33)	.64	(.29)
.34	(.14)	.40	(.19)	.37	(.17)	.50	(.29)
.29	(.17)	.31	(.18)	.20	(.08)	.30	(.28)
.58	(.44)	.76	(.71)	.57	(.44)	.47	(.27)
1	(1)	.70	(.47)	.57	(.33)	.56	(.30)
		1	(1)	.70	(.53)	.55	(.30)
				1	(1)	.89	(.75)
						1	(1)

contest between Smith and Hoover to be a critical election according to either definition. The analysis generates three rather than two groups of presidential votes. The first group includes the Democratic votes of 1916, 1920, and 1924, the second group the Democratic-Progressive vote of 1924 and the Democratic votes of 1928 and 1932, and the third group the Democratic votes of 1936 and 1940.[16] Al Smith's 1928 vote does not either begin or end any of the three groups, but is included in the middle group along with the Demo-cratic-Progressive vote of four years earlier.

In terms of critical election theory, the presidential contest of 1928 would best be classified as a type of deviating election. The 1928 Democratic vote bears substantial resemblance only to the 1932 Democratic vote. Similarly, political scientists, using survey data, have found that in the presidential election of 1960, voter coalitions were once again skewed by reactions to the religion of the Democratic nominee.[17]

Yet it may be misleading to classify the presidential election of 1928 as a deviating election, or even to apply critical election termi-nology to any presidential election from 1916 to 1940, for these elec-tions do not exhibit the pattern of relationships predicted by critical election theory.

A careful examination of Table 9.1 reveals that no election be-tween 1916 and 1940 satisfies either Key's or Pomper's notion of a critical election. At first glance, Table 9.1 and the results of elementary linkage analysis suggest that an era of electoral stability may have begun in 1936 (this cannot be verified without extending the series) and that the election of 1932 is a critical election in Pomper's sense of the term. But 1932 is not a point of discontinuity. The Democratic vote of 1932 is a good precursor of the 1936 Democratic vote and is itself rather closely anticipated by the Democratic votes of 1916 and 1928 and the combined Democratic-Progressive vote of 1924.

The nature of the election groups identified by elementary linkage analysis might also suggest that a realigning or critical era began in 1924 and ended in 1936 (assuming that such a lengthy critical era is consistent with critical election theory). This hypothesis may also help to explain the instability that characterizes the so-called New Deal era of 1928–40. Compared to other regression coefficients in Table 9.1, the only coefficient from this period indicative of marked stability ($b = .89$) is obtained from the regression of Democratic voting in 1940 on Democratic voting in 1936. The regression relationships between the contiguous election pairs 1932–36 and 1936–40 are the only ones in which the composition of an earlier Democratic coalition can explain more than half the variation in a later Democratic coalition. Yet the pairwise relationships for the presidential elections of 1924 to 1940 do not demonstrate a gradual progression toward a stable situation. Moreover, the consistently strong relationship between Woodrow Wilson's 1916 percentage and later Democratic percentages undermines any assertion that 1924 began a critical era of electoral change.

The presidential election of 1916 presents a perplexing classification problem for any devotee of critical election theory. Compared to the vote cast in 1916, only the Democratic vote of 1936 better forecasts Democratic voting in 1940 and only the Democratic vote of 1932 better forecasts Democratic voting in 1936. These relationships preclude classifying 1916 as a maintaining election of the pre–New Deal era. But its relationships with the elections of 1920 and 1924 are much too strong to warrant classifying 1916 as a deviating election. Perhaps critical election theory requires us to argue that 1916 actually began the New Deal era of American politics (interrupted by the aberrations of World War I?). Perhaps we need to go even farther back in time to uncover the roots of the New Deal coalition.

However illuminating, descriptive statistical analysis of the contest between Al Smith and Herbert Hoover cannot disclose the causal influence of this election on the pattern of subsequent politics. This task requires additional quantitative analysis as well as the scrutiny of information derived from traditional historical sources.

The candidates and issues of an election and the interactions between the election and events such as war, depression, or demographic change can influence the outcome of later elections. Such influences can take many forms, for example, changes in the strength and structure of party organizations, in the party loyalties of the voting public, or in the images projected by political parties. Unfortunately, political theorists have failed to elaborate the causal dimensions of critical election theory. Although scholars frequently use the language of causality in their verbal descriptions of election types, they neither develop the theoretical implications of causal models of electoral change nor integrate methods of evaluating causality into their empirical investigations.[18] Political analysts generally focus their studies of election types on measures of statistical association that cannot in themselves establish the extent of the causal relationship between variables. Elections that ostensibly mark the beginning of new voting cycles may actually exert very little influence on the unfolding of these cycles, whereas elections that fulfill the statistical descriptions of maintaining or deviating elections may profoundly affect subsequent contests.

In delineating the social and economic composition of voter coalitions, multiple regression analysis provides important insight into the causality of electoral behavior. Analysis of all northern counties indicates that the major change wrought by Al Smith in the voter coalition established by Davis and La Follette was the creation of a wide rift between Catholics and non-Catholics and a lesser division between wets and drys. Yet the religious cleavages of 1928 resulted from the special circumstances of an election featuring the first Catholic to become a serious contender for the presidency. By 1932, religion was no longer an important independent influence on voting for president. This does not mean that Catholics deserted the Democratic party in droves between 1928 and 1932, but they no longer constituted the vanguard of the Democracy; Protestant groups were catching up. Although some Catholics undoubtedly joined the Democratic coalition in 1928 and remained loyal in later years, there is little reason to believe that Smith's candidacy was a decisive influence on their behavior during the Great Depression.

When the influence of social and economic variables on Democratic voting in 1928 is compared to their influence on Democratic, rather than Democratic and Progressive voting in 1924, religion is again far more important in 1928 than in 1924. In addition, between these two election years, foreign-stock heritage was transformed from a strong negative to a small positive influence on Democratic voting.

These results do not mean that Smith secured the loyalty of many foreign-stock Americans who might otherwise have continued to oppose Democratic presidential candidates. Further analysis discloses significant discontinuities in the behavior of foreign-stock voters between 1928 and 1932. Table 5.3 in Chapter 5 summarizes the results of a multiple regression analysis that substitutes for percent foreign stock nine variables representing membership in various nationality groups. The table reports the influence of each of these variables on the difference between the Democratic percentage of the presidential vote in 1932 and 1928. The coefficients displayed in the table demonstrate that the Democrats had different bases of ethnic support in 1928 and 1932. Independent of control variables, Germans and Scandinavians were stauncher supporters of FDR, and Italians, Poles, French Canadians, and Irish (the predominantly Catholic groups) stauncher supporters of Al Smith.

An analysis of ethnic voting also provides fresh insight into some of the most intriguing aspects of presidential voting between 1916 and 1940. Foreign-stock support for Democratic candidates sank to extraordinarily low levels in 1920 and 1924. Reacting against the policies of Woodrow Wilson and the tensions of post-World War I America, foreign-stock voters in 1920 deserted the Democratic party in far greater proportion than their native-stock counterparts. A major beneficiary of ethnic opposition to the Democratic candidate was Progressive party nominee Robert M. La Follette; independent of control variables, the vote for La Follette increased markedly as the percentage of foreign-stock voters likewise increased.

These findings have far-reaching implications. The repudiation of Democratic presidential candidates by foreign-stock voters in 1920 and 1924 helps explain why the vote attained by Woodrow Wilson in 1916 and by Davis and La Follette combined in 1924 forecast voting alignments in the first three Roosevelt elections far better than the vote attained by Cox in 1920 or Davis in 1924. Ethnic support for Al Smith, while skewed by reactions to his personal background, also represents, in part, a return to patterns of political allegiance that had been disrupted in 1920 and 1924. Thus it is not surprising that Lubell, Bernstein, and Degler should have observed dramatic increases between 1920 and 1928 in urban, ethnic support for the Democratic presidential candidate. The relationship of ethnic defections to national issues and presidential candidates may also help explain why such investigators as Burner, Clubb and Allen, and Alvarez and True found persisting Democratic strength in the vote for lesser offices throughout the 1920s.[19]

Franklin D. Roosevelt, of course, consolidated and extended ethnic support for the Democratic party. Yet his accomplishments cut across class, religious, and ethnic lines. During the 1930s, the Democratic party achieved impressive gains among groups outside the "new" America, notably blacks and both foreign- and native-stock Protestants.

Samuel Lubell and later commentators believe that the realignments of 1928 are linked to changes in the demographic composition of the electorate. The voters of 1928 surged to the polls in proportions unmatched since the Wilson era. Discussions of this large voter turnout emphasize how the candidacy of Al Smith mobilized previously apathetic and newly eligible voters, notably women, Catholic, urban, lower-class, and foreign-stock Americans. The new political participants of 1928 are considered the forerunners of the great Democratic majorities of the New Deal era.[20] Norman H. Nie, Sidney J. Verba, and John R. Petrocik's *The Changing American Voter*, a major reinterpretation of voter surveys taken by political scientists since 1952, seems to support this version of political history. According to a chapter on the New Deal realignment by Kristi Andersen, the ranks of Democratic voters in the late 1930s were swelled first by those "who came of political age" earlier in the 1920s, but were initially "mobilized to vote in 1928 or 1932 or 1936," and second by those who came "of age between 1928 and 1936" and voted as soon as they were legally able.[21]

Regression analysis offers support for this interpretation of voter turnout in 1928. Table 9.2 reveals that changes in turnout between 1924 and 1928 responded positively to increases from county to county in the percentage of women, Catholics, urbanites, and those who were foreign-born or had a foreign-born parent. Nonetheless, the interpretation should not be pressed too far. The magnitude of the regression coefficients for the percentage of city dwellers and for the percentage of immigrants and their children are sufficiently low (.02 and .05 respectively) to indicate little difference in turnout behavior for urbanites and rural dwellers or for native- and foreign-stock

Americans. The table also indicates that changes in participation responded positively to measures of economic status and to the percentage of home owners in a county. These results suggest that the electorate was becoming slightly more middle class in 1928 than it had been in 1924.

Emphasis on Smith's activation of new voters slights the boom in Republican votes that also occurred in 1928. The evidence does not sustain the assertion that those who came of age or were first mobilized to vote in 1928 were an advance guard of the New Deal coalition. Not only was Hoover an exceptionally attractive candidate, but politically inert Protestants voted in 1928 to uphold prohibition or to suppress Catholicism. Local politicians were well aware of the anti-Democratic vote elicited by the candidacy of Al Smith. Leo T. Crowley, chairman of the board of the Bank of Wisconsin, reported to Franklin D. Roosevelt on 6 December 1928: "On a normal vote Governor Smith received more than half the votes, however, the additional registration seemed to favor the Republicans more than the Democrats." William Fleet Palmer of California wrote FDR in November 1928: "It cannot be denied that many Democrats and many who had not heretofore been active in politics voted against Governor Smith because he was a Catholic." And in 1936, Clinton A. Anderson of New Mexico offered James A. Farley the following retrospective judgment: "In 1928 religion provided a strong personal interest and we

Table 9.2. *Influence of Explanatory Variables on the Percentage Change in Voter Turnout, 1924–1928: 2,058 Counties (in percent)*

	Regression Coefficient b	Standard Error
Catholic	.12	.014
Jewish	−.01	.038
Prot church	−.02	.013
Urban	.02	.006
Foreign stock	.05	.008
Economic status	.11	.043
Owners	.09	.015
Negro	.08	.025
Under 35	.14	.032
Female	.29	.046
Pop change	.09	.006

had a great vote in the Pecos Valley,—all of it wrong from my stand-point. These people got ashamed of themselves by the 1932 election and all turned around and voted against the man they had helped in 1928."[22]

The Republicans succeeded almost as well as the Democrats in boosting their total of votes between 1924 and 1928, and statistical analysis confirms that they did better than the Democrats among the newly eligible and newly activated voters. Historians and politi-cal scientists have tended to overlook the Republicans' accomplish-ments in gaining 5.67 million votes over 1924 compared to a gain of 6.63 million for the Democrats, despite the GOP's enormous lead over their rivals in 1924 and the correspondingly greater number of votes lost through normal attrition. In 1924, the Democrats' most disastrous year, the Republicans led by 7.33 million votes; in 1928, with no third party in the field, the GOP still led the Democrats by 6.38 million votes.

Relatively few of the new Republican voters actually came from the shrunken Davis coalition of 1924 or from the coalition put together by La Follette. They came primarily from those who had either chosen not to vote in 1924 or had first become eligible to vote for a president in 1928. Table 9.3 reports the results of an analysis using Leo Good-man's technique for estimating individual-level proportions from a multiple regression equation computed from aggregate data. The table shows the estimated proportion of Republican voters, Demo-cratic voters, La Follette voters, nonvoters and previously ineligible voters, who voted for Smith, voted for Hoover, or did not vote in

Table 9.3. Transition Probabilities for Voting in 1924 and 1928: 2,058 Counties (in percent)

	1928		
	Voted for Smith	*Voted for Hoover*	*Did Not Vote*
1924			
Voted for Davis	90	7	3
Voted for Coolidge	9	91	1
Voted for La Follette	56	31	13
Did not vote	11	15	74

1928. The percentages in the table reveal that although Smith lured a greater proportion of La Follette voters, Hoover gained a greater proportion of those who had not voted in 1924, the first-time voters of 1928. These percentages disclose that the proportion of former La Follette voters leaving the electorate was much larger than that of former Democratic or Republican supporters, perhaps indicating greater dissatisfaction with the electoral process among this group of voters. Very few of those who had voted for either Davis or Coolidge in 1924 failed to cast a ballot in 1928. The high rates of retention help explain the substantial turnout of 1928.

An examination of how changes in voter turnout between 1924 and 1928 influenced Al Smith's percentage of the presidential vote underscores the importance of anti-Smith sentiment in arousing the electorate of 1928. Independent of control variables, as the difference in voter turnout between 1928 and 1924 increases, the vote for Al Smith tends to decrease rather sharply. A 1 percent change in turnout rates generates a $-.29$ percent change in Al Smith's percentage (standard error = .035). Thus, when controlling for their demographic characteristics, newly activated voters were more inclined to favor Herbert Hoover than Al Smith. This result suggests that the new Protestant voters of 1928 were even more solidly behind Hoover than were Protestant voters who had participated in the previous election.

Responses to the Republican survey of party leaders (Appendix 3, Chart A3.8) indicate that Hoover performed quite well among individuals who voted for the first time in 1928. Only the report from John Richardson of Massachusetts suggests that a majority of first-time voters opted for Al Smith. Reports from every other respondent assert that these voters supported Hoover at least in proportion to the prevailing balance of party power within their localities. Many of the responding politicians, moreover, emphasize the party's great success in garnering the ballots of newly activated and newly eligible voters in 1928.

Further analysis reveals that independent of control variables, the younger voters of 1928 were not especially inclined to favor Al Smith. Controlling for other social and economic variables, a 1 percent change in the percentage of adults under 35 yields a $-.17$ percent change in Smith's percentage of the votes cast (standard error = .059), a $-.16$ percent change in Smith's percentage of the adult population (standard error = .041), and a $-.11$ percent change in Hoover's percentage of the adult population (standard error = .045). Similar results are obtained for the percentage of adults under 25—first-time voters in 1928.

Despite Andersen's claims, the data in her chapter of *The Changing American Voter* do not suggest that the Democrats were notably more successful than their Republican rivals in attracting new support during the campaign of 1928. Although the rhetoric of Andersen's chapter assures us that the election of 1928 was a key episode in mobilizing the New Deal coalition of later years, her data show that the Republicans activated as large a number of new supporters as did their Democratic rivals.[23] Andersen partitions the electorate of the 1920s into five groups: Democrats, Republicans, Independents, "Potential" Democrats, and "Potential" Republicans. For each presidential year, Democrats and Republicans are those who claimed in later surveys to have voted for and identified with each party, respectively. Potential Democrats and Republicans are eligible voters who claimed not to have voted in that year, but later to have identified with each party, respectively. Andersen's chart shows a gain of 4 percentage points for both Republicans and Democrats between 1924 and 1928. The proportion of Democrats increased from 16 to 20 percent of the electorate; the proportion of Republicans increased from 22 to 26 percent. Thus the Republicans were still the majority party in 1928, holding the same percentage point lead as in 1924. Only events of the 1930s profoundly changed the distribution of power between the Democratic and Republican parties.

Andersen's presentation might suggest a different conclusion since she contends that during the 1920s, the proportion of potential Democrats in the electorate was vastly greater than the proportion of potential Republicans. Andersen claims, for instance, that in 1928, 32 percent of the electorate were potential Democrats and only 13 percent were potential Republicans. Implicit in Andersen's analysis is the counterfactual argument that if those labeled potential Democrats had voted during the 1920s they would have opted for Democratic candidates.

Yet Andersen never offers the detailed historical analysis required for justifying her counterfactual claim. Instead she rests her case on the demonstration that in radically different circumstances, her potential Democrats later turned to the Democratic party.[24] Conceivably, Andersen could have tried to show that the potential Democrats of the 1920s were primarily immigrants and their children—men and women whose allegiances naturally would belong to the Democracy. This explanation, however, depends upon a demographic break-down of the potential Democrats that Andersen cannot provide. Moreover, previous analysis has demonstrated that immigrants and first-generation Americans were not solidly in the Democratic camp during the 1920s. Andersen's potential Democrats are decidedly not potential Democrats in the sense that if asked at the time they would have indicated a preference for the Democratic party. Only in retro-spect could Andersen label anyone as a potential Democrat or Re-publican; thus the proportion of potential Democrats and Republicans shown on her charts for 1928 does not represent the distribution that year of political opinion among nonvoters. From the vantage point of November 1928, few dared forecast a reversal of the balance of power between Democrats and Republicans. Both parties had made sub-stantial gains in the recruitment of new voters.

In developing the theory of the "Al Smith Revolution," Lubell argued that the presidential election of 1928 was causally significant because it led to an enduring division between urban and rural America. Those living in the city, of course, should naturally have responded more favorably to Al Smith than those residing in the country. In 1928, a greater proportion of Catholics and foreign-stock Americans lived in urban than in rural communities. Yet my Chapter 6 reveals major flaws in Lubell's arguments. Whether controlling for other variables or not, neither measures of the vote for Smith nor measures of the difference between his vote and the vote for previous Democratic candidates responds strongly to the urban-rural compo-sition of northern counties (considering both the census definition and a definition relying on the distinction between large cities and other communities). The Democratic percentage of the presidential vote became highly responsive to urban-rural residence only in the presidential election of 1936. Although the vote for Smith was pro-portionately more urban than the vote for Roosevelt in 1932, the vote for Roosevelt in 1936 and 1940 was proportionately more urban than the vote for Smith. These results, coupled with the analysis of major cities reported in Chapter 6, suggest that Roosevelt's strength in the cities was not based on the accomplishments of Al Smith.

The foregoing analysis helps isolate features of the 1928 contest that influenced segments of the voting population. Additional insight can be obtained through the scrutiny of measures of party loyalty. As was previously suggested, an election can be an important influence on later patterns of politics without engendering manifest changes in party affiliation. It can, for example, strengthen party organization or help shape a party image that is more attractive to independent voters. But changes in party loyalty can, of course, have a decisive influence on electoral competition and do constitute the almost exclusive focus of critical election theory.

For the period in question, party registration statistics are the best indicators of partisan affiliation. Such statistics are available from 1926 to 1940 for all 223 counties in New York, Pennsylvania, Oregon, and California and from 1928 to 1940 for all 55 counties in West Virginia as well. For each of these counties, the analysis considers the Democratic percentage of the major party registration, measured at two-year intervals. If Al Smith's candidacy realigned the American electorate, substantial changes in the percentage of registered Democrats and in the composition of the Democratic party coalition should have occurred either in 1928 or 1930.

To exploit these registration returns, a variety of statistical strategies must be employed. Party registration must be used both as a dependent or response variable and as an independent or explanatory variable. Analysis thus can consider the relationships between Democratic registration in earlier and later years as well as the relationships between registration and presidential voting. The statistical study also uses Democratic registration in later years as independent variables for presidential percentages in 1932 and 1936. Obviously, events taking place after an election cannot have influenced behavior in that election. But this statistical maneuver can indicate the extent to which the coalition of individuals registering as Democrats rather than Republicans resembles the Democratic voter coalitions of earlier years.

The analysis of registration data provides no support for the hypothesis that the presidential election of 1928 was associated with durable changes either in party power or party coalitions, but suggests that partisan realignment was confined to the 1930s. Inspection of the Democratic proportion of the two-party registration discloses that before 1932 the Democrats had not benefited from either a conversion of Republicans or a mobilization of newly eligible and previously inactive voters. In 1930 the Republicans were as dominant as they had been in 1926. For the sample of counties, Table 9.4 reveals remarkable stability in the percentage of Democratic registrants between 1926 and 1930. Not including West Virginia, the percentage of registered Democrats was 32 in 1926, 34 in 1928, and 31 in 1930. Not

Table 9.4. Democratic Percentage of the Two-Party Registration: Five States, 1926–1940

	1926	1928	1930	1932	1934	1936	1938	1940
California	24	28	22	43	52	60	62	62
New York	48	47	50	55	60	62	56	55
Oregon	28	28	27	33	39	46	49	50
Pennsylvania	22	23	20	22	35	44	48	44
West Virginia		42	45	49	55	55	58	58
Total	32	35	32	41	48	55	55	53
Total without W. Va.	32	34	31	40	48	55	55	53

until 1932 did a realignment in favor of the Democrats begin to take place. Moreover, these aggregate statistics do not conceal a raging "Al Smith Revolution" in large cities. Registration statistics for ten metropolitan counties within the sample (reported in Table 9.5) fail to disclose even the faint trace of a realignment in party power between 1926 and 1930. Again, in 1932, the Democrats first began to acquire new strength.

More detailed analysis also demonstrates that Al Smith's candidacy did not scramble the coalitions formed by Democratic and Republican registrants. According to Table 9.6, a matrix of regression and correlation coefficients for the Democratic percentage of the two-party registration, party coalitions in 1926, 1928, and 1930 are virtually indistinguishable. For each pair of party percentages, the value of the regression coefficient is .86 or more, and no earlier percentage explains less than 90 percent of the variation in a later percentage. Overall, the coefficients reported in Table 9.6 display no abrupt discontinuity, but a gradual transformation of partisan alignments during the 1930s.

A comparison of registration and voting statistics demonstrates that Democratic registration in 1928 and 1930 failed to foreshadow voter alignments in the presidential elections of 1932, 1936, and 1940. Table 9.7 reports regression and correlation coefficients for the influence of Democratic registration on Democratic voting. In each case, the voting percentage is the dependent variable and the registration percentage is the independent variable. The percentage of individuals registering as Democrats in 1928 and 1930 is very weakly related to the percentage of voters supporting Roosevelt. A 1 percent change in Democratic registration for either year generates no more than a .44 percent change in presidential voting, and variation in the percentage of registered Democrats explains no more than 34 percent of the variation in any of Roosevelt's percentages. Table 9.7 discloses that only in 1934 did the coalition of Democratic registrants begin to resemble more closely the voter coalitions forged by Roosevelt from 1932 to 1940.

For the 278 counties examined here, party registration seems to have been unaffected by Al Smith's candidacy. Both metropolitan and nonmetropolitan counties emerged unscathed from the "Revolution of 1928." Changes in the percentage of registered Democrats and in the composition of party coalitions began to take place only after 1930. The patterns of change portrayed in the statistical analysis suggest, however, that for partisan strength alone, the period between 1932 and 1936 could reasonably be regarded as a critical era. Yet for party coalitions, changes in regression and correlation coefficients during the 1930s take place so gradually that they might reflect the normal attenuation of relationships over time rather than the effects of electoral realignment.

Further insight into partisan allegiance can be gained through the scrutiny of primary election returns. For 850 counties this study

Table 9.5. Democratic Percentage of the Two-Party Registration: Nine Cities, 1926–1940*

	1926	1928	1930	1932	1934	1936	1938	1940
Buffalo	35	36	30	36	46	47	41	42
Los Angeles	25	27	22	44	56	62	65	64
New York	70	63	73	67	82	85	81	75
Oakland	16	21	15	34	43	55	56	57
Philadelphia	05	14	07	14	36	44	55	41
Pittsburgh	08	13	07	10	39	51	58	54
Portland	25	26	25	32	40	50	52	51
Rochester	16	17	16	17	42	40	26	26
San Francisco	19	31	15	47	53	65	66	66
Total	36	39	36	48	58	65	63	64

*Only cities from the five states of Table 9.4 are included. Percentages are computed for the county in which the city is located.

Table 9.6. Regression Coefficients (b) and Coefficients of Determination (r²) for the Democratic Percentage of the Two-Party Registration: 278 Counties, 1926–1940 (in percent)*

	Reg 1926		Reg 1928		Reg 1930		Reg 1932	
	b	r²	b	r²	b	r²	b	r²
Reg 1926	1	(1)	.86	(.92)	1.0	(.97)	.98	(.82)
Reg 1928			1	(1)	1.1	(.92)	1.1	(.86)
Reg 1930					1	(1)	.93	(.84)
Reg 1932							1	(1)
Reg 1934								
Reg 1936								
Reg 1938								
Reg 1940								

*Coefficients for Reg 1926 do not include the 55 counties of West Virginia.

measures the percentage of individuals participating in the Democratic rather than the Republican primaries. Data are reported for each presidential year from 1928 to 1940. Multiple regression analysis of Democratic primary voting in 1928 reveals that the key conflict of the general election also influenced voter behavior in the primaries. Smith's candidacy created a sharp religious cleavage of the primary electorate, but failed to undermine Republican dominance or to exert durable influence on primary voting behavior. Controlling for other social and economic factors, participation in the Democratic primaries increased as a county's proportion of Catholics increased. This religious division, however, did not persist in later primaries. Despite this temporary readjustment of the Democratic primary coalition, in 1928, a meager 21 percent of the electorate participated in the Democratic rather than the Republican primaries.

Political scientists have posited that the upheavals accompanying fundamental alterations in electoral behavior have certain characteristic effects. A comparison of these predicted effects with the historical realities of the Smith-Hoover confrontation further suggests that voter loyalties were not transformed in 1928.

Walter Dean Burnham, writing in 1970, presented a detailed enumeration of the concomitants of "the 'ideal-typical' form" of partisan realignment. First, "critical realignments are characterized by

Reg 1934		Reg 1936		Reg 1938		Reg 1940	
b	*r*^{2}	*b*	*r*^{2}	*b*	*r*^{2}	*b*	*r*^{2}
.83	(.66)	.67	(.49)	.63	(.38)	.57	(.32)
.95	(.74)	.77	(.57)	.75	(.47)	.70	(.41)
.79	(.69)	.62	(.50)	.58	(.39)	.55	(.34)
.87	(.87)	.74	(.73)	.72	(.61)	.70	(.58)
1	(1)	.88	(.89)	.86	(.76)	.84	(.72)
		1	(1)	1.0	(.87)	.97	(.83)
				1	(1)	.96	(.92)
						1	(1)

abnormally high intensity," which produces especially heavy voter turnout. Second, this intensity "spills over into the party nominating and platform writing machinery of the party most heavily affected by the pressures of realignment . . . accepted 'rules of the game' are flouted; the party's processes, instead of performing their usual integrative functions, themselves contribute to polarization." Third, partisan realignments lead to important ideological polarizations between the major parties. Fourth, such realignments "involve constitutional readjustments in the broadest sense of the term [and] they are associated with and followed by transformations in large clusters of policy. This produces correspondingly profound alterations in policy and influences the grand institutional structure of American government."[25]

The presidential election of 1928, however, clearly exhibits only the first of these characteristics of "the 'ideal-typical' form" of critical elections. There was intense voter interest in the Smith-Hoover confrontation and a large upsurge in voter turnout.

In 1928, hostility to the social and religious background of Al Smith was a source of some dissension within the Democratic party. Intraparty strife, however, was neither strongly ideological nor of lasting importance. Mutiny was largely confined to the South and involved very few of the major Democratic leaders in that region.

Table 9.7. Regression Coefficients (b) and Coefficients of Determination (r^2) for the Democratic Percentage of the Two-Party Registration, 1926–1940, and the Democratic Percentage of the Presidential Vote, 1936–1940: 278 Counties (in percent)*

	Reg 1926		Reg 1928		Reg 1930		Reg 1932	
	b	r^2	b	r^2	b	r^2	b	r^2
Dem 1932	.35	(.25)	.44	(.34)	.33	(.25)	.45	(.50)
Dem 1936	.18	(.06)	.29	(.12)	.17	(.06)	.32	(.21)
Dem 1940	.07	(.01)	.20	(.08)	.10	(.03)	.21	(.12)

*The registration percentage is always the independent variable; coefficients for Reg 1926 do not include the 55 counties of West Virginia.

Bolters quietly returned to the fold, and the South was a mainstay of the Democratic party throughout the Roosevelt years. During 1928, the "party's processes" effectively performed their "usual integrative functions." As was already noted, the Democrats actually abandoned several of their more controversial positions, including low-tariff doctrine and internationalism. Only a few diehard traditionalists opposed this pusillanimous strategy. The Democrats also papered over with compromise statements the ideological divisions within the party over such questions as prohibition and farm relief. It was in 1924 rather than 1928 when great upheaval occurred within the "party nominating and platform writing machinery" and polarization was so intense that the national convention divided into two warring camps. In 1928, the Democrats generally adhered to the "rules of the game," and party machinery fostered concord rather than conflict.

There was also very little ideological polarization between the two parties in 1928. On most important questions facing the American people, Democratic and Republican positions could not be distinguished. Only the prohibition question seemed to present voters with a clear-cut choice of alternative philosophies. Yet even this issue was deliberately obscured by the Republican and to a lesser extent by the Democratic party. Nor did prohibition become a basis for lasting divisions between the parties.

Finally, the presidential contest of 1928 was not "intimately associated with [or] followed by transformations in large clusters of policy." Neither did the election "produce correspondingly profound

Reg 1934		Reg 1936		Reg 1938		Reg 1940	
b	r^2	b	r^2	b	r^2	b	r^2
.52	(.58)	.61	(.67)	.58	(.70)	.58	(.71)
.44	(.35)	.59	(.53)	.62	(.66)	.61	(.66)
.32	(.24)	.44	(.39)	.48	(.52)	.49	(.54)

alterations in policy [or influence] the grand institutional structure of American government." During the campaign, Hoover promised faithfully to continue traditional Republican policies. Even when faced with the depression, he initiated little change in public policy, and generated no fundamental revisions in the structure of American government.[26]

The clash between Al Smith and Herbert Hoover does not resemble a presidential contest in which a basic realignment of the electorate was taking place. Increases in voter turnout are best explained by the intense controversy generated by Smith's Catholicism and to a lesser extent by his opposition to national prohibition. They were not the by-products of an electorate in the throes of realignment. The election did not significantly disrupt the normal processes of the two parties or produce ideological divisions that ultimately could lead to large-scale alterations in partisan commitments. And, during his incumbency, the winning candidate followed the traditional policies of his party.

It is extraordinarily difficult, however, to assess the implications for critical election models of the disparity between theoretical descriptions of "ideal-typical" realignments and the actualities of the Smith-Hoover confrontation. Political scientists have not carefully distinguished between descriptive and defining features of critical elections. Which of the factors isolated by Key and Burnham are necessary characteristics of critical elections? Are elections to be defined as critical strictly on the basis of their relationship to changes in party power and in the composition of voter coalitions (*The American Voter* typology, for example, is based only on these variables)? If so, what is the importance of such factors as intense voter interest, issue polarization, and new policy outcomes? Are they probable concomitants of elections otherwise identified as critical or realigning? Or are they merely developments that on a theoretical level political scientists believe to be associated with fundamental changes in the partisan alignments of the American electorate? The responses to these questions can determine our classification of presidential contests as well as our understanding of the relationship between electoral change and changes in government structure and public policy.

Traditional historical evidence does more than enable us to compare actual historical events with the predictions of political theory. It also provides a useful check on the findings of quantitative analysis. Such evidence discloses that contemporary Democratic politicians did not generally share the retrospective judgments of political authorities that the Democratic party was undergoing metamorphosis in 1928. Responses to inquiries about party affairs circulated by Franklin D. Roosevelt provide the best indication of how Democratic activists interpreted the politics of their times. Overall, these politicians did not suggest that Al Smith revolutionized the politics of their party. Several leaders argued that the election of 1928 gave the party an opportunity to secure the loyalties of Catholic voters. But others claimed that Catholics were bitterly disappointed with the Democratic party. Politicians from almost every state suggested that after the election the Democratic party was demoralized and disorganized.[27] James A. Farley recalled that the Smith-Hoover confrontation did not importantly influence the two elections he managed for Franklin Roosevelt. "In 1932," he states, "the only influence of the 1928 election was to eliminate Smith as the leading contender for the Democratic presidential nomination."[28]

Through multiple levels of analysis, using both quantitative and written evidence, my study shows that the presidential election of 1928 did not produce drastic, durable changes in the composition of electoral coalitions or in the balance of party power. The election did influence later Democratic successes in two ways. As a result of Hoover's victory, the GOP became associated with the horrors of depression. Smith's defeat, on the other hand, motivated Democratic leaders, for the first time, to keep the Democratic National Committee functioning in the interim between presidential elections. During the dark days of Hoover's incumbency, the Democratic organization was an important source of antiadministration propaganda.[29]

Undeniably, during the Great Depression, the balance of party power dramatically shifted in favor of the Democrats. For the 1920s and 1930s, changes in political power more neatly fit the critical election paradigm than do changes in the composition of voter coalitions. Between 1928 and 1936, the proportion of voters in the 850 sample counties participating in the Democratic rather than the Republican primaries increased twofold. Similarly, the proportion of voters registering as Democrats rather than Republicans increased by 72 percent in the 278 sample counties. Whether considered critical or maintaining by political theorists, however, each of the three presidential elections between 1932 and 1940 played an important role in the renaissance of the Democratic party.

In 1928, Herbert Hoover represented for many Americans the buoyant optimism of prosperity; four years later he symbolized the hardship and heartbreak of the depression. Eager for new leadership, a substantial majority of voters opted for the Democratic candidate, Franklin D. Roosevelt. Throughout the nation, according to correspondence received by the national headquarters of both parties, traditional Republicans planned to vote for Roosevelt in 1932.[30]

Yet Roosevelt's 1932 victory did not itself reverse the fortunes of the Democratic party. In 1932 the proportion of Democratic primary voters in the sample was 33 percent; in 1936, this proportion increased to 42 percent and remained at that level through 1940. Similarly, between 1932 and 1936 the proportion of Democratic registrants in the sample increased from 41 to 55 percent and remained roughly constant through 1940. Roosevelt's victory chiefly reflected the weakness of Herbert Hoover, not the strength of a burgeoning Democratic majority. Roosevelt raised few divisive issues in 1932. His campaign offered something for everybody and did not set forth a coherent alternative to the policies and ideology of the GOP.[31]

Changes in voting habits are not the inevitable result of social and economic change. Contrary to the mechanism implicit in most discussions of critical election theory, voting cycles do not ebb and flow with automatic, tidal regularity. Historical events create opportunities that can be exploited by shrewd political strategy and responsive policy or squandered by political blunders and unwise policy. During his first four years, Franklin D. Roosevelt effectively channeled public opinion in support of himself and his party. Roosevelt was an unusually charismatic and ebullient leader and a master of political persuasion. The programs of the New Deal and Roosevelt's spirited rhetoric provided the ideological and emotional foundation for a new Democratic majority.

Probably because the "New Deal coalition" seemed fully fashioned by 1936, political authorities have regarded the election of 1940 as a classic maintaining election that played no important role in realigning the electorate. More careful analysis reveals that events culminating in the clash between Franklin D. Roosevelt and Wendell Willkie were crucial to the maintenance of Democratic predominance. Public opinion polls conducted in 1938 and 1939 suggest that a majority of voters were disillusioned with the New Deal and hostile to the idea of a third term for President Roosevelt.[32] Had this gloomy situation failed to improve, it is unlikely that Roosevelt would have sought or could have attained reelection. The Democrats had no other promising candidate, and Republicans anticipated their first presidential victory since 1928. Some journalists even predicted that the aberrations of 1932 and 1936 had passed and the nation was returning to its normal Republican majority. The public opinion polls of 1940 suggest that only the events of World War II motivated Roosevelt to seek reelection and made a third term palatable to the American public.[33]

Although political scientists have not carefully analyzed the causes of critical elections, they have suggested that these elections generally accompany national crises that lead to fundamental conflicts over policy. They imply that the partisan realignments associated with critical election theory arise not from the personal appeals of competing candidates, but from reactions to these conflicts. Angus Campbell and his coauthors argue in the highly influential *Elections and the Political Order*: "Realigning elections have not been dominated by presidential candidates who came into office on a wave of great personal popularity. . . . The quality which distinguished the elections in which they came into power was the presence of a great national crisis, leading to a conflict regarding governmental policies and the association of the two major parties with relatively clearly contrasting programs for its solution."[34]

The presidential election of 1928 does not fit this pattern. The campaign occurred during a relatively tranquil period of American history, and the policy positions of the two parties presented few important contrasts. Its realigning influences are generally attributed to voter responses to Al Smith, allegedly the candidate of new-stock Americans not yet integrated fully into the American system of pluralist competition.

This study has demonstrated that there was no "Al Smith Revolution." Neither quantitative nor qualitative evidence reveals the presidential election of 1928 to have been a decisive turning point in American political history. Given the fleeting quality of the electoral alignments engendered by Smith's candidacy and the discontinuity of the depression, it is likely that had the Democrats nominated another party leader (Albert Ritchie, Thomas Walsh, Carter Glass) to oppose Herbert Hoover, the decision would scarcely have affected the next three presidential contests. The distinctive feature of the 1928 election was the appearance of a conflict between Protestants and Catholics. In causal terms, the election was important chiefly because the Democrats lost and a Republican administration presided over three years of depression.

By assigning the election of 1928 a bit part in the realignment drama of twentieth-century America, these results challenge accounts of electoral change that are keyed to ethnocultural conflict. Updated to the twentieth century, an ethnocultural interpretation must fasten on the contest between Smith and Hoover as a turning point in political history. In this view, realignment was not a response to economic distress, but the result of integrating millions of new immigrants and their children into the political system. Thus 1928 was part of a causally consistent process of realignment, based on major demographic shifts in the composition of America's electorate. Yet the evidence shows decisively that transformations of party power did not coincide with peaks of ethnocultural conflict and that the Roosevelt realignment did not neatly cleave the "old" and the "new" America. Changes in economic status or in the perception of economic opportunities seem to have been the prime generators of changes in political allegiance. Ethnic and religious differences produced great turmoil in the 1920s, but party power shifted only later, in response to economic crisis.

The present study also reevaluates critical election theory. Historical analysis can be enriched by the explicit use of such social science models as critical election theory. These models can help the historian interpret past events and enable him to use deductive reasoning to fill gaps in his empirical knowledge, but historians should treat them with open-minded skepticism. They should carefully evaluate a model's logical coherence and explanatory power, and they should realize that historical research can test the validity of a social science model. If the assumptions or predictions of a model do not conform to historical reality, the model itself should be modified or abandoned.

Voter behavior in the presidential elections of 1916 to 1940 does not neatly fit the predictions of critical election theory. There were both more stability and volatility in electoral coalitions than this political theory would suggest. No critical election or critical era obliterated earlier coalitions of voters and introduced a new period of stability. Yet there was instability in voter alignments throughout the period. Perhaps a modified version of the critical election story could be salvaged from the data by declaring the period from 1916 to 1936 a critical era of realignment. But to postulate a critical period encompassing twenty years and enormous diversity in the political, social, and economic life of the nation is not to verify critical election theory, but rather to illustrate the slipperiness of the critical era concept.

Conceptually, critical election theory does establish one useful perspective on American electoral history. Nonetheless, key features of the theory can impede our understanding of historical change. In its current form, critical election theory creates categories of elections that obscure important analytical distinctions. To solve this problem by increasing the refinement of electoral typologies is to aggravate the problem of classifying individual elections. Since there are no clear dividing lines between the various types of elections, the greater the number of subdivisions, the greater is the uncertainty faced by an investigator seeking to categorize particular contests. Additional uncertainty is created by the lack of guidelines for identifying critical eras of electoral change. Critical election theory lacks causal precision and thus can overemphasize the importance of some elections (for example, the presidential election of 1928), while obscuring the significance of others (for example, the presidential election of 1940). The theory also incorporates conflicting definitions of realigning elections and perpetuates mechanistic interpretations of electoral realignment that slight the importance of political leadership.

Even if these internal weaknesses could be shored up, critical election theory would still limit and even distort the analysis of American political history. By failing to distinguish between changes that simply reshuffle voter alignments and changes that alter the underlying basis of voter decisions, the theory blurs distinct varieties of electoral change. Critical election theory also incorporates dubious assumptions about the relationship between electoral change and changes in the broader context of American politics. Theoreticians and researchers have neither clearly specified nor empirically validated linkages between the rhythms of electoral realignment and transformations in political ideology, public policy, and government structure.

The results of this study also point toward new ways of periodizing American political history, which deserve mention even if they cannot be developed here. Voter behavior in the presidential elections of 1916 to 1940 reveals that seemingly moribund coalitions may prove highly tenacious, whereas the issues and personalities of particular elections can create considerable variation in voter alignments. This finding does not mean that historians should discard the notion that party loyalties remain relatively stable until jolted by a national crisis. But stability in party identification does not necessarily produce stability in presidential voting. While it has proved to be the best single predictor of voter choice, party loyalty is only one of the many influences on the decision to support one candidate rather than another. In the twentieth century, party identification may have become sufficiently tenuous and presidential elections sufficiently important and well publicized to produce substantial volatility in the response to presidential aspirants.[35]

The complex patterns of voter behavior in early twentieth-century presidential elections may reflect a systematic change in the American electoral system that occurred in the late nineteenth century. E. E. Schattschneider, Richard Jensen, and Walter Dean Burnham have argued that the political upheavals of the 1890s loosened the bonds of party loyalty and established a more fluid system of political competition. Their work suggests that in the twentieth century voter behavior is likely to be more susceptible to the issues and personalities of particular elections and electoral change less abrupt and decisive.[36]

Historians should distinguish between changes in electoral behavior that fit the contours of critical election theory and changes that influence determinants of the voting decision. If critical election theory itself more accurately describes nineteenth- than twentieth-century elections, the 1890s could be seen as a critical period, not in the traditional sense of the theory, but in the sense of introducing a qualitatively different era of electoral politics. Perhaps the complexity of temporal changes in voter behavior can be portrayed only through a new periodization of American political history. Historians need to reexamine the American past, searching not only for transitions that shuffled voter coalitions and shifted the balance of party power, but also for transitions that qualitatively changed the prevailing system of electoral politics.

Critical election theory may also apply better to twentieth-century congressional, state, and local elections than to presidential contests. Because the former elections generate less interest and information than presidential confrontations, voters may be more likely to rely on such rules of thumb as party identification.

Moreover, different localities and different subgroups of voters may experience critical realignments at different intervals of time and may exhibit qualitatively different patterns of voting behavior. The empirical analysis of the present study applies only to the nation as a whole (outside the old South) and to the entire voting population. Such factors as the special interests and outlook of class and ethnic groups, the strength of party organization in different localities, and the interactions between state, local, and national politics may produce distinct varieties of political behavior for various subgroups of the American electorate.[37]

Critical election theory applies a rigid determinism to the time and space of American politics. Movement across the American political universe may not only recast voter loyalties, but may also modify the causal forces underlying voter decisions. American political history is undoubtedly a multidimensional system, including at least the four dimensions of time, jurisdictional level, geographic location, and voter type. Not only must all dimensions be considered in a complete theory, but changes in one or more dimensions may require qualitatively different models of political behavior. Critical election theory, despite its impressive social science credentials, can blind historians to the rich variety of American electoral history.

Chapter 10

Conclusions

Prevailing interpretations of the encounter between Al Smith and Herbert Hoover have a stark and compelling simplicity. Two cultures clashed in the persons of these candidates, with the seeming victory of the older tradition marking the end of its dominance in the United States. In this view, the old politics perished in 1928, and a new era of American life began.

Yet analysis of the presidential election reveals that what appears to be a one-dimensional response to the candidates actually has many distinct, if related, dimensions. The coalitions forged by Al Smith and Herbert Hoover did not reflect a neat duality in the American electorate—the mind sets of the old and the new America. Multivariate analysis displays the distinct and intersecting paths of the different themes that run through the politics of 1928. And comparative study of electoral coalitions from 1916 to 1940 neither discloses the pattern predicted by theories of electoral realignment nor reveals 1928 as a turning point of political history.

Of all possible explanations for the distinctive political alignments of 1928, religion is the best. A bitter conflict between Catholics and Protestants emerged in the presidential election of 1928: religious considerations preoccupied the public, commanded the attention of political leaders, and sharply skewed the behavior of voters. Regardless of their ethnic background, their stand on prohibition, their economic status, and other politically salient attributes, Catholics and Protestants split far more decisively in 1928 than in either previous or subsequent elections. No other division of the electorate stands out so distinctively in that presidential year. This cleft between Catholics and Protestants was not confined to particular regions of the nation, to either city or country, to either church members or nominal Protestants. Both Protestants and Catholics responded to the religious tensions of 1928. Smith benefited from a pro-Catholic vote and Hoover from an anti-Catholic vote. Religion may also have interacted with ethnic background so that support for Smith would have been greater than expected among those who were both foreign stock and Catholic and less than expected among those who were both foreign stock and Protestant. Perhaps immigrants of Protestant heritage hesitated to support an otherwise attractive Catholic candidate, and perhaps Catholics of the second generation and beyond were not as beguiled by a Catholic candidate as were immigrants or first-generation Americans.

The diverse sources of anti-Catholicism that converged in 1928 cannot be forced into the model of the two Americas. Undoubtedly, many of those tabbed as stalwarts of the older America feared that the prestige of people like themselves and the culture they cherished was threatened by Catholics, immigrants, and the folkways of urban life. But reaction against Smith's religion also mirrored the heritage of immigrant groups, Protestant religious training, and doubts about the autonomy of a Catholic president.

Although anti-Catholic agitation abated after the defeat of Al Smith, historians have concluded too hastily that the election significantly advanced religious toleration in the United States. Attention both to the empirical evidence and to theory in social psychology suggests that the ebbing of overt hostility toward Catholics primarily meant that, with Smith's sound defeat, anti-Catholicism became temporarily less salient for most of the public. But Americans who objected to Smith's religion had not necessarily changed their views of the consequences of voting for a Catholic presidential candidate. Later evidence from surveys and from the presidential election of 1960 indicates that Protestant ideas about Catholic presidents were not transformed in 1928. These results underscore the importance of distinguishing changes in salience from changes in attitudes toward members of out-groups. They also point to the tenacity of prejudice and to the possible reappearance of intolerance toward particular groups long after tranquillity seemed to have been restored.

Each party responded to religious conflict according to strategic calculations. Hoover, the educator, was to remain aloof from controversies about religion, venturing only a brief affirmation of religious toleration in his acceptance address. Only adverse criticism compelled a later and more forceful statement. Other politicians identified with the Republican campaign were not to attack Smith on religious grounds; their task was to blame the Democrats for injecting religion into the presidential campaign. The activities of Republican chieftains behind the scene are, of course, much more difficult to ascertain. But the evidence suggests that both the local and national leadership of the party was heavily implicated in the effort to incite religious opposition to Al Smith. As the candidate of candor and blunt speech, Smith confronted the religious issue head-on. In a major address, he denounced anti-Catholic opposition to his candidacy and indicted the opposition for tacitly supporting the forces of religious bigotry. Other Democratic spokesmen were less circumspect in charging the Republicans with fomenting anti-Catholicism and in proclaiming that a ballot for Al Smith was a vote for religious toleration.

The wisdom of continuing to prohibit the manufacture and sale of alcoholic beverages was a major policy issue of the 1920s. Some historians have identified the dispute over prohibition as the prime mover of voting decisions in 1928. Yet prohibition had less influence than religion on all measures of the 1928 vote and on all deviation variables representing differences between this vote and the vote cast in other presidential contests. Seeking to minimize possible losses without sacrificing the ballots of likely supporters, both parties obscured the prohibition issue by adopting strategies that muddled distinctions between the positions taken by Hoover and Smith. The struggle to preserve prohibition in 1928 also became a convenient point of entry for those who objected to Smith's religion but sought to avoid charges of religious bigotry. To protect the Eighteenth Amendment, Assistant Attorney General Willebrandt appeared before church groups arguing for organized opposition to Al Smith. For Protestant churchmen taking part in the election, the defense of prohibition defined the limits of their moral concern with politics in the 1920s. As Donald B. Meyer wrote, the "living creed" of Protestantism in the 1920s naturally extended to the prohibition of alcohol but not to matters of economic or social justice.[1]

Historians such as Paul Kleppner, Richard Jensen, and Ronald Formisano, who have contended that the ethnic and cultural heritages of voters primarily shaped their behavior in the mid- and late nineteenth century, point to a clash of values between pietists and liturgicals. These ethnocultural historians see politics as a struggle between those who supported (pietists) and those who opposed (liturgicals) government control of personal morals. As perhaps a more discriminating version of the partitioning of America into two cultures, the rift between pietists and liturgicals fails as a synthesis of electoral conflict in 1928. The presidential election of 1928 was not fought across the trenches dividing these systems of competing values. Although more refined analysis is required to distinguish the behavior of individual denominations, the evidence suggests that opposition to Smith's Catholicism cut across the division between pietists and liturgicals. Indeed, Protestants without any church affiliation were at least as hostile to Smith as those with formal church membership. If the election had been a clash over notions about moral reform, then the split between wets and drys should have eliminated the distinction between Catholics and Protestants as a decisive factor distinguishing voter alignments in 1928 from those of earlier and later elections. The arguments about religion that appeared during the campaign did not tap the symbols associated with the competing world views of pietism and ritualism. Campaign rhetoric stressed a shared set of values and turned instead on disputes over matters of fact. What emerged in 1928 was an ethnocentric rather than an ethnocultural conflict between Catholics and Protestants—a matter of us versus them that did not pivot on any issue or constellation of issues that may have been at stake in the election.

A focus on the values and sensibilities of the two candidates also reveals no clear antipathy between pietism and ritualism or between the tradition-bound country and the libertarian, cosmopolitan city. Like Hoover, Al Smith believed in stable, close-knit family life, in loyalty to community, in discipline, sexual restraint, hard work, frugality, individual responsibility, and respect for private property. As Smith's participation in the postelection ritual illustrated, he endorsed the American dream and rejected the leadership of a movement outside the grooves of electoral politics. Although Al Smith opposed prohibition, Sunday closing laws, and other sumptuary legislation he believed to be aimed at his fellow Catholics, he neither disputed Victorian notions of vice nor automatically rejected government regulation of immoral behavior. He supported state laws to close lewd theatricals and to ban obscene literature irrespective of its literary merits.

No final reconciliation of the struggles over the toleration of divergent life styles and the use of government power to control personal behavior was achieved in 1928. Yet the conflict between the moral reformers and their opponents does not cleanly divide into those committed to the religious values of pietism and ritualism.

Recent work suggests that positions on issues involving personal freedom cannot be deduced from a set of religious principles. Also relevant are orientation toward nation or locality, religiosity per se, position in the social structure, and the stake in the particular battle being fought.[2]

Some of the historians taking an ethnocultural approach to politics of the nineteenth century may also have erred in equating the clash over moral reform to the opposing values of those tabbed as pietists or liturgicals. For Catholics, by far the largest group identified as liturgicals, church doctrine does not preclude state intervention in the moral sphere. Catholic teachings do stress the efficacy of conforming to ritual and the importance of the relationship between the individual and his priest. But, as Bernard J. Coughlin has noted, church dogma does not sharply separate the secular from the sacred, but stresses the infusion of religion into all aspects of the relationships among individuals. Indeed, anti-Catholic critics of Al Smith fastened on this element of Catholic thought to argue that his election posed a grave threat to the historic separation of church and state in America.[3]

Catholic positions on moral reform in the late nineteenth and early twentieth centuries were conditioned by the church's beleaguered, minority status. Catholics perceived their church as persevering within a state of siege during this period. Many of them feared that campaigns for particular kinds of moral reforms were directed against members of their religion and that expansion of government power would increase the firepower of weaponry that would be deployed against them.[4] By way of contrast, in European nations where Catholicism was the dominant religion, leaders of the church sought state backing for Catholic control of education and sponsored measures for the prohibition of gambling, prostitution, pornography, birth control, and divorce. The Catholic Church could thus take a so-called pietist stance on these moral issues. In the United States, a far more secure and confident Catholic hierarchy of the 1970s joined the forefront of the crusade to prohibit abortion. Ironically, when challenged to justify their involvement in this political campaign, Catholic prelates echoed the arguments used fifty years ago by Protestant clergy defending the prohibition of alcohol. At the same time, critics see the Catholic church emphasizing the single issue of abortion at the expense of concerns like civil rights and economic opportunity, just as the Protestant denominations had once done with prohibition.

The voting behavior of immigrants and first-generation Americans forms an intricate mosaic that can be fully understood only by looking at individual nationality groups. Overall, however, in 1920 and 1924, foreign-stock Americans rejected presidential candidates of the Democratic party even more emphatically than did those of native stock from the same social and economic strata. These findings contradict the widely held notion that demographic trends toward increasing numbers of foreign-stock voters inherently favored the Democratic party. Rather, the GOP failed to take advantage of widespread dissatisfaction among immigrants and their children with candidates put forth by the Democrats. Major beneficiaries of this Republican failure were Robert M. La Follette in 1924 and Al Smith in 1928. Historians have overlooked the heavily foreign-stock character of support for Robert M. La Follette; the senator's antiwar history and his brand of progressive politics seemed especially appealing to Americans of German, Scandinavian, and Russian descent.

In 1928, Al Smith reversed the trend of the two previous elections, with the result that immigrants and their children were slightly more likely to vote for him than were their counterparts of the second generation and beyond. Foreign-stock voters, however, did not form a relatively larger proportion of the coalition put together by Al Smith than of those forged by La Follette in 1924 and by Franklin D. Roosevelt in 1932. But the composition of foreign-stock support for the Democrats shifted between 1928 and 1932; predominantly Catholic ethnic groups were relatively stronger supporters of Smith and predominantly Protestant ethnic groups relatively stronger supporters of La Follette and Roosevelt.

Historians often identify the alleged uprising of the new America in 1928 as an awakening of the urban masses (or sometimes the *eastern*, urban masses). Although scholars have been careful not to equate the old America with the country and the new America with the city, their work implies that the division between city and country should be a good summary measure of discord in the presidential election of 1928. Yet statistical analysis reveals that urban-rural residence accounts for very little of the variation in measures of the vote for president in 1928 or of differences between this vote and the vote cast in other presidential years. The cleft between city and country discriminates best between the vote for Smith, on the one hand, and either the vote for La Follette in 1924 or the vote for Roosevelt in 1932 and in 1936 and 1940, on the other hand. Similar results derive from an analysis of how urban-rural residence affected the balloting for president, independent of religion, ethnic heritage, and other characteristics of voters. Again the split between city and country was an important influence only on differences between the vote for Smith and for La Follette and between the vote for Smith and for FDR. A comparison of the coalitions put together by Smith in 1928 and by La Follette in 1924 shows that the gap between the farm and the small-town vote was actually wider than the gap between the city and country vote. Thus what appears to be an urban-rural cleavage is best explained by a limitation on Smith's capacity to gain the votes of discontented agrarians. Comparison of the vote for Smith and the vote for Roosevelt reveals a striking pattern of change that likewise fails to uncover an urban revolt in 1928. Urban dwellers were a relatively larger component of Smith's 1928 tally than of Roosevelt's 1932 tally, but a relatively smaller component of Smith's 1928 tally than of Roosevelt's tally in either 1936 or 1940. Moreover, analysis of the metropolitan vote and of party registration in major cities discloses that Roosevelt did not build on accomplishments of Al Smith. These findings suggest that reasons for the urban emphasis of the New Deal vote must be found primarily in the politics and policies of the 1930s and not in the events of 1928.

Although accounts of the presidential election do not emphasize the behavior of black voters or strategies followed on racial issues, both parties ardently played the politics of race in 1928, and ripples of political change spread across black communities. Seizing the opportunity offered by a Democratic candidate who was both Catholic and wet, Herbert Hoover sought to purge the black leadership of his party's southern wing and fashion a lily-white organization that could compete for the votes of white supremacists. The Democrats responded in kind, seeking to stave off defeat in southern states by reminding voters that their party remained the most sturdy and reliable bulwark against changes in race relations. Abandoning traditional allegiances, prominent blacks defected from the Republican camp in 1928, urging voters to follow their lead. Republican performance during their years of dominance and the campaign strategies of 1928 convinced black leaders that the GOP was no longer a champion of black aspirations. Despite the unabated racism of the southern Democracy, they reasoned that it was better to support a candidate from another minority group than cling to faded memories of Republican benevolence. Only a modest percentage of black voters, however, heeded this call, and blacks were an even smaller proportion of the Democratic coalition four years later. The pull of old loyalties seemed stronger for ordinary blacks than for black elites. Not until 1936 did black voters shift their preferences to become stalwarts of the Democratic party.

American women, another neglected group in many accounts of the 1928 contest, led the upsurge in voter turnout that occurred between 1924 and 1928. The issues of religion and prohibition seem to have been most important in drawing out the woman voter. Although both Catholic and Protestant women were more likely to vote in 1928 than in previous elections, changes in the rate of voter turnout were greater for Catholic women than for their Protestant counterparts. Yet men as well as women increased their rates of participation in 1928, and these new voters included supporters of each candidate.

Women opted for Herbert Hoover in greater proportion than their male counterparts. Although explanations for this result can be fashioned from the issues of 1928 and the images of the rival candidates, in all three presidential elections following passage of the Nineteenth Amendment, women appear to have disproportionately favored the Republican nominee. If rank and file women did not simply vote the preferences of their fathers, husbands, and brothers, neither did they become the infantry of a renewed campaign for progressive reform.

Historians seem convinced beyond reasonable doubt that national prosperity guaranteed a Republican victory in the presidential election of 1928. Yet scholars have failed to reconcile this conviction with the undercurrent of poverty that flowed beneath the gilded surface of the 1920s. Greater attention must be paid to the means by which an ideology of prosperity was developed and maintained. The brief account offered in this study suggests that the schools, business, labor, media, and government all fostered public faith in the availability of economic opportunity and pinned responsibility for failure on the individual. Democrats throughout the nation reported to FDR that, in 1928, potential constituents of their party were mesmerized by the promise of Republican prosperity. Neither of the major political parties challenged the ideology of prosperity or sought to muster support for programs aimed at redistributing resources. Nor did other organized groups offer a strong institutional base for dissent from the prevailing order. Al Smith, tabbed by some as the working-man's candidate, firmly believed that America offered ample opportunity to the talented, the thrifty, and the industrious. His notion of social justice embraced only amelioration of the excesses of free enterprise and recognized no conflict of class interests. In 1928, he advanced policies designed to placate business and relied on his personal appeal to those who labored for a meager income.

Yet statistical analysis discloses in 1928 an economic alignment of the electorate, with a positive association between economic status and voting Republican. In addition, a positive relationship prevails between economic status and participation in the election. Economic divisions of the electorate cannot be traced to the issues raised in 1928 or the rhetoric used by the competing campaigns. These divisions seem to reflect divergent images of the two parties and go back at least to the presidential election of 1916. Historians need to reconsider conventional interpretations of the connections between class status and political affiliation in early twentieth-century America.

However fascinating and exciting, the presidential election of 1928 was not the harbinger of the next generation of politics. The contest was neither a critical election nor a key component of a critical era of voter realignment. The presidential election of 1928 is best viewed as an aberrant election that had little impact on later patterns of politics. Electoral alignments of the 1930s resulted primarily from the responses of Herbert Hoover and Franklin D. Roosevelt to challenges posed by the Great Depression. In many respects, theories that use models of critical elections or critical periods actually impede an understanding of American political history. Critical election theory incorporates systems of electoral classification that can badly distort the significance of particular elections. The theory suffers from conceptual weaknesses that create confusion and uncertainty. It includes a host of hidden assumptions, is insensitive to variations across time and space, and perpetuates a narrow, mechanistic interpretation of electoral realignment. Moreover, the presidential elections examined in this study point to more intricate patterns of voter behavior than would be predicted by critical election theory.

My reassessment of the contest of 1928 also challenges pluralist interpretations of twentieth-century history. Ethnocentric conflict in the election of 1928 cannot be explained away as the trauma of adjusting to a new process of pluralist competition in America. In 1928, the conflict between Catholics and Protestants and between blacks and whites cut across the boundaries of orderly competition drawn by pluralist theory. Not only did prejudice sway the behavior of voters, but both parties sought to turn religious and racial animosities to their political advantage. If anti-Catholicism lost its immediate salience with Hoover's victory, evidence from the 1930s and from 1960 denies that the election fostered or foreshadowed a stable era of toleration between Catholics and Protestants. Perhaps by the 1970s attitudes have been sufficiently transformed so that religion would not be as salient for voter behavior were another Catholic nominated by a major party. Yet ethnocentric divisions, independent of policy issues, would likely arise once again were a major party to nominate for president a black, a Puerto Rican, or even a Jew.

The findings of this study lead to the further conclusion that Smith could not have become a consensus candidate in 1928 by responding more sensitively to the fears and concerns of the old America. Abraham Moles's distinction between semantic and esthetic information helps sharpen this argument. Semantic information is designed to prepare an audience for particular actions and decisions. It appeals to rules of logic and a lexicon of symbols common to a society. Esthetic information, in contrast, does not represent the conscious intent of a communicator, but inheres in situations and events. It creates a state of mind that is especially sensitive to the knowledge, attitudes, and beliefs of individual receptors and is especially resistant to later modification.[5] Murray Edelman, who has pioneered the use of Moles's theory as a tool of political analysis, points out that semantic information might include "allegations of pressure groups about the impact of a proposed bill . . . assertions that a candidate for office will pursue particular policies, warnings that a particular form of welfare measure will detract from the incentive of its recipients to work." Esthetic information, however, may be quite different, as Edelman explains: "Police beating up bearded or black demonstrators, by contrast, is not a conscious effort to create different perceptions in different receptors according to their various repertories of knowledge, symbols, and a priori structurings, and serves to influence the attitudes of these people toward the demonstrators and toward the police . . . beliefs and perceptions created in this way are more resistant to debate and opposition and especially to doubt and ambivalence within the individual who holds them, than are those based on semantic information."[6]

In 1928, Al Smith's Catholicism was itself a form of esthetic information that generated a set of responses varying according to what people already felt and believed, and having no relation to anything the candidate sought or intended. Moreover, the evidence suggests that no conscious effort on his part could have significantly altered the state of mind he created merely by being a Catholic. Neither sympathetic rhetoric nor a refurbished public image would have sufficed. Contrary to the conventional view, the governor's provincialism was not an important component of Protestant opposition to his candidacy. Independent of control variables, neither residence in city or country nor regional location skewed voting patterns in ways predicted by historians. Regardless of where they lived, many Protestants repudiated Smith and many Catholics rallied to his support. Even in his home state of New York, Smith's candidacy opened a wide gap in the voting decisions of Protestants and Catholics.

Careful analysis of the presidential election of 1928 also suggests caution in hailing Smith's candidacy as the progenitor of a new reform tradition. As Michael Paul Rogin has perceptively noted, "The Smith election in this [pluralist] view contributed to and prefigured the New Deal coalition—a coalition differing sharply from previous reform movements." Rogin stressed that "pluralist history relies on this view of the 1928 campaign." He wrote, "For the pluralists, Smith's break with the past is a break with progressive moralism. Reform politics would now . . . capitalize on practical proposals to relieve economic distress, not on alienation from the industrial order."[7] Yet statistical analysis does not reveal a sharp break between the electoral base of Robert M. La Follette's brand of protest politics and the electoral base of the New Deal. The combined Democratic-Progressive vote of 1924 is about as accurate a precursor of the New Deal voting alignments as the Democratic vote of 1928. Moreover, the religious conflicts that highlighted the contest of 1928 hardly portend the sensible, tolerant pragmatism of new-style reform. As Rogin has argued, historians need to reevaluate carefully the connections among reform movements in twentieth-century American history.[8]

Al Smith did not emerge in the campaign of 1928 as an exemplar of the need to reform American society. His positions on national issues failed to challenge the status quo. Despite the governor's humble origins, his progressive record in state politics, his Catholicism, and his associations with the new immigrant, his policy proposals were scarcely more venturesome than those of Herbert Hoover. Smith never sought to offer the politics of redistribution as an alternative to Hoover's politics of distribution. His candidacy did not promise to improve the lives of ordinary Americans by altering the nation's lopsided distribution of wealth and power. Yet lower-class Catholics and members of some nationality groups believed that Smith was their champion because they could identify with the image he projected. He appealed to their longing to enter the mainstream of national life regardless of the terms. From this perspective, Smith's bid for the presidency was a conservative influence on American life.

Although Al Smith addressed himself specifically to the farmer and the worker, he did not define coherent and persuasive alternatives to Republican policies of the past eight years. Relying on his personal appeal to ordinary Americans, Al Smith never sought to develop issues that could forge a broad-based coalition of minority interests. From the first stages of platform building to the final orations of early November, the governor and other leading Democrats behaved more like front runners than longshots. They obfuscated or dodged issues that could conceivably have brought together a coalition of minorities and sought to dampen conflict and controversy. Although Al Smith was undoubtedly an underdog in 1928, the tactics he followed seemed most appropriate for a candidate who did not wish to burst the bubble of a majority coalition.

The old politics still guided the thinking of Democratic chieftains in 1928. Rather than transforming the structure of their party or devising new issues and strategies, they hoped and prayed that changing circumstances would sweep the Republicans from power and usher in an era of Democratic hegemony. In the meantime, party leaders sought to preserve their own bastions of power, to prevent further embarrassments in national elections, and, above all, to smother explosive issues that could shatter their party's delicate coalition of diverse interests and ideologies. For many Democrats, the presidential election of 1928 was undoubtedly a holding action and the nomination of Al Smith a necessary means of propitiating his ardent supporters and keeping the party from flying apart.

The Great Depression of the 1930s seemed to answer the prayers of worthy Democrats. During this decade, the Democratic party thoroughly dominated national politics and sponsored changes in the network of relationships involving business, government, and the public. Although immeasurably strengthened by a more robust party image, fresh leadership, accomplishments in domestic policy, and refurbished ideology, the Democratic party has remained an unstable compound of disparate elements. In the decades following the era of Franklin D. Roosevelt, the party has been forced to confront centrifugal forces similar to those that paralyzed Democratic politicians in 1928.

Taken together, the results of this study should unsettle prevailing views of linkages between the political world of the 1920s and the realignments of the 1930s. Although separated by twenty-five years, Samuel Lubell's creative speculations and Kristi Andersen's ingenious manipulations of survey data suggest that during the 1920s potential Democrats, mainly new immigrants and their descendants, were about to qualify for the franchise or to be aroused from their political slumbers. Yet analysis of both election statistics and manuscript sources reveals the volatility rather than the solidarity of foreign-stock voters during the 1920s. The election of 1928 was notable primarily for sparking religious strife, and it called forth more new Republican than new Democratic voters. Al Smith's bid for the presidency did not contribute significantly to the "Roosevelt Revolution" that cut across the division between Catholics and Protestants as well as those between new immigrants and other Americans. Data on party registration and primary voting show that realignment began only after the advent of depression and extended through Roosevelt's reelection to a second term. Although critical election theory cannot comfortably be imposed on politics of the early twentieth century, the depression and Roosevelt's leadership were the decisive events in shifting the balance of party power. America's Great Depression was a major discontinuity in the nation's electoral history. The politics of our own time are not traceable to events of the 1920s, but began to unfold after the stock market crashed in 1929.

This revised account of political change in the twentieth century questions the role of critical elections as guarantors of a beneficent, pluralist democracy. Realignment of the American electorate did not occur in response to the unmet needs of those sharing least in the prosperity of the 1920s. Party power shifted only in response to a national crisis that threatened the position and prospects of most Americans. Changes in partisan loyalties did not reflect the venting of demands pent up during the 1920s, but the creation of new demands that were not being met by the party in power during the crisis. The situation from 1929 to 1932 was strikingly similar to that of the 1890s, when the Cleveland administration failed to solve an economic emergency. The postponement of the New Deal realignment to after the crash means that since the Civil War party power has changed decisively only during a period of severe and prolonged depression. This result combined with criticisms of critical election theory itself suggest that periodic realignment of the electorate is not a dynamic inherent to the American political process.

The political demands of the 1930s called primarily not for the recasting of American society, but for the relief of distress and the restoration of opportunity. As historians such as Barton Bernstein and Paul Conkin have observed, Hoover failed and FDR succeeded as a conservator of American institutions. Robert H. Zieger, in a 1976 review of scholarship on Herbert Hoover, aptly noted that the "New Deal reforms were partial, frugally funded, closely in line with prevailing conceptions about the role of government, and extremely sensitive to the rhetoric of decentralization and local control to the disadvantage of minorities, working people, and the poor." Even the goals of New Deal liberalism, Zieger maintained, were "always more modest than those of other Western states."[9] With the revision of the conventional wisdom about electoral realignment in the 1920s and 1930s, the character of the New Deal becomes more consistent with the nature of political change in this period.

Finally, work by Richard Jensen and Paul Kleppner suggests that well before the clash of 1928, the Republican party already exemplified a beneficent pluralism that united diverse groups of Americans. According to Jensen, the victory of William McKinley ended Republican efforts to gain power through the mobilization of their diehard pietistic followers. Thereafter the party would seek to bring together a broad coalition of voter groups through the granting of political recognition and the merchandising of policy proposals tailored to the needs of those groups.

Republican political strategy in the 1920s, however, was not founded on this model of pluralist politics. The party failed to provide the political recognition and status sought by nationality groups and abandoned its black loyalists. Moreover, in 1928, the party's national campaign relied on the moralism and mass politics that pluralist theory condemns as dangerous and irresponsible. A fundamental deficiency of pluralist scholarship is its failure to deal with the mass-based moralistic appeals used by defenders of the status quo. As Rogin has maintained, such appeals are not limited to radical malcontents and pseudoconservatives isolated from the mainstream of

American life. They are used as well by those of power, wealth, and respectability, whose first loyalty is to American business and to whom moralism and mass politics are means of sustaining power and concealing from the general public the extent of their influence and authority.

This deficiency of pluralist scholarship flows not from slipshod research or sloppy analysis. Rather, it exposes the failure of pluralism to describe accurately the structure of American politics. The resort to moralistic and mass-appeal rhetoric, although not unique to business-oriented conservatives, has generally been characteristic of their participation in the electoral process. In situations such as legislative lobbying that do not require the ratification of decisions by popular majorities, elites can endorse the classic model of group competition. Their own groups possess the resources to compete effectively. Given the numerical insignificance of their immediate constituency, however, conservatives face grave disadvantages in the realm of electoral politics. They can no longer appear as the representatives of particular interest groups. Only their opponents can appeal to the interests of various groups in the redistribution of wealth and power. Business-oriented conservatives must reject the politics of redistribution in favor of appeals that cut across the group memberships of Americans. These appeals are most effective when they tap the emotions people invest in patriotic and moral symbols and exploit the common fears of the majority. And their impact is enhanced by the resources that the American business community can devote to political campaigns. Thus conservatives may fit the pluralist vision in the sense that they seek to advance their own wealth and status, rather than some abstract idea of the common good. But they do not necessarily conform to pluralist demands for eschewing moralism or extremism as techniques of persuasion.

The Republican presidential campaign of 1928 relied upon moralistic appeals to the mass of American voters. Not only did the Republicans appeal to the optimism of Americans and their faith in the economic system, but they also played upon the fear that a Democratic victory would destroy the nation's booming prosperity. They attempted to associate Al Smith with dangerous and un-American schemes for reconstructing society. And they exploited Protestant fears about the consequences of electing a Catholic president. In later campaigns, Republicans continued to rely on issues that cut across interest groups. During the New Deal, for example, the party unsuccessfully sought to counter FDR's welfare liberalism by invoking traditional values of American democracy.

Herbert Hoover directed the strategies and tactics of his presidential campaign of 1928. A diverse group of historians including William Appleman Williams, Donald R. McCoy, David Burner, Ellis M. Hawley, Joan Hoff Wilson, and Edgar Eugene Robinson have favorably reinterpreted Hoover's career—his leadership of the Commerce Department, his campaign for the presidency in 1928, his tenure as president, and his later years as dedicated public servant. One aspect of the new Hoover scholarship is an affirmation of the former president's integrity, his devotion to principle, and his unwillingness to engage in petty politics.[10] Recent studies of the campaign of 1928 implicitly or explicitly exonerate Hoover from responsibility for either anti-Catholicism or white racism.[11] These historians have mistakenly placed Hoover on a pedestal above the turmoil of presidential politics. In 1928, Hoover responded as a politician to the dictates of political advantage. He was a presidential candidate intent upon his own election, concerned with the fine details of his campaign, and willing to exploit the tensions of his society.

Appendix 1

Statistical Discussion

This Appendix supplements the methodological discussion presented in Chapter 2. It considers, in turn, the assumptions of regression analysis, the process of inferring individual-level behavior from aggregate-level data, and the use of nonlinear and interactive regression models.

The utility of multiple regression estimates of the relationship between variables depends, in part, on how well the data conform to certain assumptions. As previously indicated, if the error term of a regression equation is correlated with an independent variable, the partial regression coefficient for that variable will be biased. Even in the absence of bias, however, regression estimates may still not reflect the actual relationships between variables. In addition to systematic bias, random error in the selection of cases and the measurement of variables may produce misleading estimates. Methods for computing regression coefficients are designed to minimize random error and optimize the efficiency of estimation. But estimates will be most efficient only if the data fulfill certain assumptions. Theorists usually stress the assumptions that the variance of the residuals for each observation do not vary systematically (homoscedasticity), that the residuals are distributed independently of each other (nonautocorrelation of errors), that the residuals are normally distributed, and that variables are not linear combinations of one another.

If error terms are heteroscedastic rather than homoscedastic, standard methods of estimation may be inefficient and tests used to assess the reliability of regression estimates may be misleading. Heteroscedasticity is a common problem for the analysis of aggregate units with unequal populations; frequently the value of residuals will decrease as the population of units increases. To correct for this problem, all counties are weighted by the square root of the voting-age population in 1928. Nonetheless, for all 2,058 counties, the use of weighted rather than unweighted data (or weighting by the population rather than the square root of the population) yields only marginal changes in the value of regression estimates.[1]

The presence of outliers—cases whose values are far removed from the main body of data—also can generate heteroscedasticity. If sufficiently extreme, outliers can produce heteroscedasticity by tilting the regression plane away from the bulk of the observations. For this study, a reliance on percentages imposes limits on the values that can be assumed by variables and thus diminishes the problem of outliers. Regression equations based on the large number of cases are also less sensitive to the influence of outliers than are equations computed from relatively small samples. In addition, tests for outliers were conducted through the examination of frequency distributions, scattergrams between dependent and independent variables, and residual plots. No outliers were detected whose inclusion or exclusion alter regression estimates or the patterns formed by residuals.

Assumptions regarding nonautocorrelation and normality of residuals do not require extended discussion. Autocorrelation, which can also undermine the reliability of regression estimates and invalidate statistical tests, primarily affects the study of time series data. Residuals obtained from time series regression are likely to be correlated sequentially for the time period being considered.[2] Techniques have not been perfected, however, for judging the impact of autocorrelation on the cross-sectional analysis of widely dispersed geographic units. Departures from normality in the distribution of residuals primarily affect tests for the reliability of regression estimates. Fortunately, these procedures are not especially sensitive to violations of the normality assumption, especially for large samples. Moreover, the scrutiny of residual plots did not disclose substantial departures from normality.[3]

Multiple regression analysis, or any other multivariate procedure, is obviously inappropriate when independent variables are so highly correlated that they cannot be distinguished from one another. This situation represents an extreme form of the more general problem of multicollinearity. As was already noted, if explanatory variables are highly correlated, estimates of partial regression coefficients may be unreliable and their independent effects may not be separable. Multicollinearity is even more insidious if the data set includes distinct clusters of highly correlated variables. Small variations in the correlations within these sets or in the correlations of individual variables with the dependent variable can yield relatively large differences among the partial regression coefficients.[4] The correlations among the independent variables analyzed in this study are well below the levels generally found to undermine regression estimates.[5] In addition, the variables do not form highly correlated subdivisions and most coefficients have very low standard errors of estimate, another indication that multicollinearity is not a serious problem. Moreover, each variable entered in the regression equations has a distinct interpretation and a substantive rationale for its inclusion.

Although this study uses data collected for counties, it seeks to describe and explain the behavior of voter groups aggregated within these units. As was noted in Chapter 2, unstandardized measures like regression coefficients must be used for inference from the aggregate to the individual level of analysis. Not only correlation coefficients, but also standardized regression coefficients, often termed Beta weights (β), respond to fluctuations in the relative variation of variables produced by the process of grouping. Beta weights indicate the proportion of the variance in a response variable accounted for by changes in an explanatory variable when controlling for the influence of all other explanatory variables in an equation. Thus the examination of Beta weights might seem to be a way of ranking the importance of variables that influence the voting decision. Unfortunately, the value of a Beta weight is a function both of how behavior responds to attributes measured by explanatory variables and of how grouping alters the relative variance of explanatory and response variables. Beta weights are standardized by multiplying a partial regression coefficient by the ratio of the variance in the explanatory variable (X) to the variance in the response variable (Y): $\beta = b_{yx.z}[s_{(x)}/s_{(y)}]$, where Z represents a control variable. Thus even when the independent effect of X on Y does not change, the value of β can still change if aggregation alters $s_{(x)}/s_{(y)}$. Using an example taken from actual data, Laura I. Langbein and I found that, for individuals, Beta weights measuring the effects of race and parental education on student achievement had values of .35 and .31, respectively. After aggregation into groups according to the values of parental education, these values changed to .24 and .77, respectively, without corresponding changes in the unstandardized regression coefficients. For the present study, both explanatory and response variables are commonly measured in percentage units, so that comparisons can be made across variables without resort to the computation of Beta weights.[6]

Problems of cross-level inference, however, cannot be circumvented merely by the application of regression analysis. An additional strategy designed to bridge the gap between individual behavior and aggregate-level data is the proper specification of regression models. The most serious aggregation problems arise from the use of misspecified models of the response variable being considered. The grouping of individuals can alter specification bias and thus create significant differences in relations measured at the aggregate and individual levels of analysis. Each regression model analyzed in this study is specified as completely as possible, given the limitations of recorded data.[7]

Some investigators have sought to circumvent problems of ecological inference by looking at units roughly homogeneous for scores on a variable of interest. To determine, for example, the relationship between religion and voting for president in 1928, an investigator using this method would search for religiously homogeneous units. He would select counties, or some other unit, that have a very high proportion of Catholics, noting the proportion voting for the Democratic candidate in each. He may also select units that are highly Protestant, again noting the proportion that voted Democratic. By combining these proportions for a number of units, the investigator obtains an overall estimate of how Catholics and Protestants voted in 1928.

This study uses the method of homogeneous grouping only as an occasional supplement to regression analysis. Despite its widespread use, the method raises serious practical and theoretical problems. As a general technique for inferring individual behavior from group-level data, the examination of homogeneous units is not responsive to distortions created either by changes in relative variance or changes in specification bias.

First, for most variables relevant to voter behavior in 1928 it is impossible to generate a geographically dispersed sample of even roughly homogeneous units. The only alternative would be to lower the definition of a homogeneous unit to dangerously low levels. Even case studies of single cities or states have dropped their cutoff points to below 50 percent for dichotomous variables.

Second, leaving aside questions of measurement error and sampling variance, units homogeneous for one independent variable will have the same scores on the dependent variable only when this independent variable is the only cause of variation in the dependent variable or when all units have the same scores on all the other independent variables that also affect variation in the dependent variable. In practice, of course, neither condition is likely to hold.

To illustrate how these last two problems may affect the results of analyses based on homogeneous grouping, consider two studies of popular voting by David Burner and John M. Allswang.[8] Both investigators used the method of homogeneous grouping to determine the voting behavior of German-Americans, Polish-Americans, Jews, and Negroes by examining relatively homogeneous units in Chicago for the presidential elections of 1916 to 1932. Yet Table A1.1 reveals disturbing discrepancies in their results. The estimates of the proportion of each group voting for Democratic candidates varies by as much as 18 percentage points. The average divergence is 9.3 percentage points.

Third, individuals found in homogeneous units may behave quite differently from individuals found in heterogeneous units. Even if the method of homogeneous grouping yielded reliable estimates of proportions and correlations for individuals in homogeneous units, its utility would still be limited to inferences about homogeneous units. Specifically, the average scores of other independent variables of individuals living in homogeneous units may be different than the average scores of individuals from heterogeneous units. For example, German-Americans still residing in ethnic enclaves may tend to be of lower socioeconomic status than their counterparts residing in mixed neighborhoods. If socioeconomic status as well as ethnic background affects voting behavior, then the proportion of German-Americans from homogeneous units voting for a particular candidate or party will not be equal to the proportion of all German-Americans voting

Table A1.1. *Presidential Voting: Allswang versus Burner (in percent)*

Year	German		Jewish		Polish		Negro	
	All	*Burn*	*All*	*Burn*	*All*	*Burn*	*All*	*Burn*
1916	44	44	67	57	68	73	27	31
1920	18	11	15	31	39	53	11	6
1924	14	18	19	37	35	51	10	5
1928	58	45	60	78	71	83	23	29
1932	69	59	77	85	80	85	21	30

for the candidate or party. In addition, residence in a homogeneous community may itself be a contextual variable that influences the behavior being explored. For example, residence in a uniformly German-American community may reinforce traditional political allegiances, whereas residence in mixed communities may not.

Fourth, the method of homogeneous grouping does not generally permit the multivariate analysis necessary to determine the relationship between two variables independent of the confounding influences of other correlated variables. According to the logic of the technique, controls would be introduced by isolating units homogeneous on more than a single variable. To determine, for example, how German-Americans voted independent of their religious preferences, an investigator would look at German-American communities that are also Protestant and German-American communities that are also Catholic. In most cases, however, there will not be enough homogeneous units to control for even a single confounding variable, much less the several variables that often produce spurious effects.

Even when rigorously applied, the method of homogeneous grouping is not responsive to the sources of error in aggregate-level measures. In principle, problems created by changes in relative variance can be circumvented by examining random samples of group members and computing the proportion of the group exhibiting the behavior of interest. But the individuals residing in homogeneous units are not likely to represent a random sample of all group members. Moreover, because units that are homogeneous on one independent variable are unlikely to have similar values on related independent variables that also affect the dependent variable, correlations computed from such units are based on misspecified regression equations. And misspecification may be amplified by the failure of the approach to measure contextual effects.[9]

Table A1.2 summarizes the results of regression analysis for all 2,058 counties outside the former Confederate South. To adjust for population differences, each county is weighted according to the square root of its adult population in 1928. For each regression equation, the table reports the dependent variable, the set of explanatory variables, the partial regression coefficients and standard errors for each explanatory variable, and the coefficient of determination for the regression equation as a whole (R^2). The coefficient of determination measures the proportion of the variation from county to county in the response variable that can be predicted from knowing the values of all explanatory variables in the regression equation. Particular chapters of the text use portions of the results packed into this table.

As was noted in Chapter 2, regression equations can represent various forms of the relationship between a response variable and a set of explanatory variables. The equations in Table A1.2 are additive in form, with the influence of each variable best approximated by a straight rather than a curved line. Regression models can, however, be modified to include interactive and nonlinear relationships.

Although the general problem of nonlinear estimation is very complicated because there is such a large number of possible nonlinear forms, by adding the squares of independent variables to a regression equation, a researcher can approximate many of the more commonly occurring nonlinear relationships (for example, $Y = a + b_1 X_1 + b_2 X_1^2$). A coefficient for the squared term that is significantly different from zero would indicate that, independent of other variables in the equation, the relationship between explanatory variable X_1 and the response variable Y is better represented by a curved than by a straight line. For any value of X_1 the slope of this curved line is equal to $b_1 + 2b_2 X_1$, the first derivative of $b_1 X_1 + b_2 X_1^2$. If b_1 and b_2 have the same signs, the influence of X_1 on Y will increase until X_1 achieves its maximum value. If b_1 and b_2 have opposite signs, the influence of X_1 on Y will steadily decrease, until $2b_2 X_1$ exceeds b_1 and the direction of influence changes.

The appearance of a nonlinear relationship between the response variable and an explanatory variable would indicate that the ways in which individuals are grouped into units has a "contextual effect" on their behavior as voters. Contextual variables may have either a direct or an interactive effect on the behavior of individuals. For direct influence, an individual's behavior is expressed by the equation: $Y = a + b_1 X_1 + b_2 \bar{X}_1$, where $\bar{X}_1$ is the proportion of individuals with attribute X living in a community. At the aggregate level, however, the influence of X_1 and $\bar{X}_1$ will be indistinguishable; the equation representing the behavior of units will not be able to separate the effects of individual and the contextual variable: $\bar{Y} = a + (b_1 + b_2)\bar{X}_1$. Only for an interactive model of contextual influence can individual and contextual effects be separated. In this instance, an individual's behavior is expressed by the equation: $Y = a + b_1 X_1 + b_2 X_1 \bar{X}_1$. At the aggregate level, the behavior of units is represented by the equation $\bar{Y} = a + b_1 \bar{X}_1 + b_2 \bar{X}_1^2$, precisely the equation obtained from adding the square of the explanatory variable to the regression equation.[10]

Table A1.2. *Influence of Explanatory Variables on Measures of the Vote for President: 2,058 Counties (in percent)*

	Dem 1928		Dem 1928 total		Rep 1928 total	
	b	SE	b	SE	b	SE
Catholic	.37	.023	.32	.018	−.12	.019
Jewish	.41	.062	.17	.048	−.16	.053
Prot church	.17	.020	.18	.016	.03	.018
Urban	−.00	.010	−.03	.008	−.06	.009
Foreign stock	.09	.013	.01	.010	−.10	.012
Economic status	−.84	.071	−.23	.055	.95	.061
Owners	−.35	.024	−.13	.019	.26	.021
Negro	.41	.041	−.11	.032	−.05	.035
Under 35	−.17	.052	−.16	.041	−.11	.045
Female	−.30	.074	−.12	.058	.31	.064
Pop change	.00	.010	−.03	.008	−.07	.009
R^2	.39		.25		.46	

	Dem 1928 total minus Dem/Prog 1924 total		Dem 1928 total minus Prog 1924 total		Rep 1928 total minus Rep 1924 total	
	b	SE	b	SE	b	SE
Catholic	.26	.013	.46	.022	−.15	.014
Jewish	.07	.036	.48	.060	−.02	.038
Prot church	−.01	.012	.17	.020	.01	.013
Urban	.04	.006	.02	.010	.02	.006
Foreign stock	.05	.008	−.25	.013	.01	.008
Economic status	−.16	.042	−.38	.067	.11	.043
Owners	−.05	.014	−.16	.023	.10	.015
Negro	.13	.024	−.01	.039	−.08	.025
Under 35	−.09	.030	−.36	.049	.10	.031
Female	.15	.043	.19	.070	.05	.045
Pop change	.03	.006	.02	.010	−.06	.006
R^2	.46		.36		.23	

Dem 1928 minus Dem 1924		Dem 1928 minus Dem/Prog 1924		Dem 1928 minus Prog 1924		Dem 1928 total minus Dem 1924 total	
b	SE	b	SE	b	SE	b	SE
.11	.021	.37	.020	.62	.075	.13	.013
−.23	.059	.23	.056	.77	.089	−.24	.036
−.02	.019	−.02	.019	.20	.030	.01	.012
.02	.010	.03	.009	.04	.015	−.01	.006
.50	.013	.02	.012	−.38	.019	.31	.008
.07	.067	.04	.064	−.97	.101	−.01	.041
−.02	.023	−.06	.022	−.41	.035	−.02	.014
−.05	.038	.10	.037	.51	.058	.03	.023
.12	.049	−.22	.047	−.56	.075	.12	.030
−.68	.070	.21	.067	.45	.106	−.16	.043
.00	.010	.03	.009	.04	.015	−.00	.006
.71		.38		.49		.70	

Dem 1928 minus mean Dem 1916–24		Dem 1928 minus mean Dem 1916–20, Dem/Prog 1924		Dem 1928 minus Dem 1932		Dem 1928 minus mean Dem 1932–40	
b	SE	b	SE	b	SE	b	SE
.22	.018	.31	.017	.34	.018	.39	.018
.16	.050	.31	.045	.45	.049	.53	.049
.03	.017	.03	.015	.07	.016	.12	.016
−.02	.008	−.02	.008	.07	.008	−.07	.008
.38	.011	.22	.010	−.01	.011	.02	.011
−.41	.057	−.42	.052	−.08	.056	−.09	.056
−.12	.020	−.13	.018	.04	.019	−.05	.019
.03	.033	.08	.030	.14	.032	−.03	.032
.03	.042	−.08	.038	−.22	.041	−.29	.040
−.10	.060	.20	.054	.21	.058	.39	.058
.02	.008	.03	.007	−.02	.008	−.01	.008
.65		.57		.42		.38	

Nonlinear regression, however, offers only limited insight into how the composition of a community may alter the effects of explanatory variables; county-level percentages may not accurately represent the types of communities in which individuals reside.

Regression equations can also be adjusted to reveal interactions among explanatory variables. Two explanatory variables interact with one another when the value of the regression coefficient measuring the effect of one variable on the dependent variable changes according to the values of the other variable. For example, electoral decisions may be more responsive to a voter's religion in predominantly rural than in predominantly urban counties, causing the influence of religion on voter behavior to vary according to the value of a variable measuring urban-rural residence. A researcher can detect interaction by seeing how behavior responds to an explanatory variable for distinct categories of cases with different ranges of values for another variable. Following a procedure termed analysis of covariance, separate regression equations would, in effect, be computed for different levels of a control variable.[11] Interaction between urban-rural residence and religious preference, for example, might be disclosed by studying the relationship between the percentage of Catholics and the percentage of Democrats for counties with no urban population, counties that are up to 50 percent urban, and counties that are more than 50 percent urban. Changes in the relationship between religion and Democratic voting among the three categories would indicate interaction between religious affiliation and residence in city or country.

Various forms of interaction can also be expressed more efficiently through alteration of the regression equation itself. Interaction often assumes multiplicative form in which the joint influence of two or more explanatory variables is greater than expected when both have high values and less than expected when one has a low value. Religion, for example, might interact with urban-rural residence so that the percentage of Catholics has a much greater effect on voter behavior in heavily urban than in moderately urban or entirely rural counties. To represent joint effects that are multiplicative in form, new explanatory variables can be created by multiplying two potentially interacting variables. When this multiplicative variable is included in a regression equation along with the two initial variables, the resulting equation will portray both additive and interactive components of behavior (for example, $Y = a + b_1 X_1 + b_2 X_2 + b_3 X_1 X_2$). Higher-order interaction terms (for example, $X_1 X_2 X_3$) can likewise be created by multiplication and entered in the regression equation to express yet more complex forms of interaction. To judge the importance of interaction, a researcher should test the statistical significance of the interaction terms and determine their contribution to the predictive power of the regression equation as a whole.[12]

Interaction may also take the form of a purely multiplicative regression model that includes no additive component. Behavior, for example, might best be expressed by the following equation: $Y = aX_1^{b_1}X_2^{b_2}$, in which independent variables are raised to a power represented by the regression coefficient and then multiplied together. Since all explanatory variables are part of a single multiplicative term, their influences on the response variable are mutually dependent. The impact of any one variable is affected by the impact of every other variable included in the equation. When variables are added together in a regression model, each has a direct influence on the response variable that is exclusive of the influences of all other explanatory variables. By transforming all variables of a multiplicative model into their logarithms (for example, $\log Y = \log a + b_1(\log X_1) + b_2(\log X_2)$), with suitable adjustment for values of zero, this mutually dependent model can be set forth in linear, additive form. The multiplication of a logarithm by a constant is equivalent to raising the numerical counterpart of the logarithm to the power of the constant, and the addition of logarithms is equivalent to multiplying their numerical counterparts.[13]

To test for the presence of contextual effects and interactions among explanatory variables, the regression model was modified to include specific nonlinear and interactive components. The results of this analysis, however, must be considered tentative because of the very high correlations among the original variables, their squares, and their combination in multiplicative form.[14] Rather than launching a search through the several hundred possible interactions among the eleven explanatory variables included in Table A1.2, the analysis focuses on those forms of interaction that represent historians' verbal model that religion, ethnic heritage, urban-rural residence, and prohibition combined to produce voter responses to Al Smith and Herbert Hoover.

Looking at Smith's percentage of the presidential vote and the deviation of this vote from the average vote of the three previous Democratic candidates, three first-order interactions (the product of a two-variable combination) and one second-order interaction (the product of a three-variable combination) for the percentage of Catholics, urban dwellers, and foreign-stock residents are added to the regression equations. For the 471 counties with data from state-level referenda on prohibition, six first-order interactions, four second-order interactions, and one third-order interaction (the product of a four-variable combination) for the percentage of Catholics, urban dwellers, foreign-stock residents, and voters opposing prohibition are added to the equations for these same response variables. Also included in these expanded regression equations are the squares of the following variables: the percentages of Catholics, urbanites, immigrants and their children, voters opposing prohibition (for 471 counties), home owners, and radio owners (for ease of interpretation, the percentage of radio owners is substituted for the economic index). The addition of these squared variables probes for the presence of nonlinear relationships and adds additional controls to the test for interaction. Discussion of the nonlinear relationships was given in the substantive chapters.

The interactive and squared variables were added one by one to the additive models according to the statistical significance of their regression coefficients. The addition of variables ceased when no other variable could be included with a regression coefficient that was statistically significant at the .01 level. Tables A1.3 and A1.4 report the results of this analysis, recording the partial regression coefficients and the standard errors of estimate for each variable included in an equation. The omission of an interaction or a squared variable means that its regression coefficient was not statistically significant. Also included in the tables are coefficients for the linear, additive models and the coefficients of determination (R^2) for both models, adjusted for changes in the degrees of freedom. Inspection of R^2 reveals that for Smith's percentage of the vote, the addition of the squared and interactive variables adds very little to the predictive power of the regression equation. Slightly greater increases in predictive power are achieved for the difference between the vote for Smith and the average vote for the three previous Democratic candidates.

If the hypothesis regarding interaction were correct, the joint influences on voter behavior of the potentially interacting variables should be less positive than would be expected from the linear models when their values are low and more positive than would be expected when their values are high. Specifically, the variables measuring interaction should have positive signs, indicating that when religion,

Table A1.3. Regression Coefficients for Additive, Linear and for Interactive, Nonlinear Models of the Vote for President: 2,058 Counties (in percent)

	Dem 1928				Dem 1928 minus mean Dem 1916–24			
	Additive Linear		Interactive Nonlinear		Additive Linear		Interactive Nonlinear	
	b	SE	b	SE	b	SE	b	SE
Catholic	.38	.023	.16	.035	.23	.018	.08	.036
Jewish	.46	.063	.28	.068	.18	.051	.14	.055
Prot church	.19	.021	.22	.020	.04	.017	.06	.017
Urban	−.02	.010	−.13	.026	−.04	.008	−.07	.018
Foreign stock	.11	.014	−.04	.023	.38	.012	.29	.019
Radios	−.23	.021	−.47	.063	−.10	.017	−.35	.051
Owners	−.32	.024	−.30	.024	−.11	.020	−.14	.020
Negro	.41	.041	.39	.041	.04	.033	.01	.033
Under 35	−.17	.053	−.23	.053	.04	.043	−.01	.043
Female	−.28	.075	−.48	.075	−.10	.061	−.19	.061
Pop change	.01	.010	−.01	.010	.02	.008	.01	.008
Urban²			.09	.027				
Radios²			.37	.078			.35	.064
Cth-For			.83	.098			.65	.085
Cth-Urb							.31	.099
For-Urb			.21	.050			.21	.042
For-Urb-Cth			−.66	.124			−1.30	.213
R^{2*}	.38		.43		.64		.67	

*Adjusted for degrees of freedom.

foreign-stock heritage, urban-rural residence, and opposition to prohibition have their highest values, their impact on voting for president is substantially greater than would be indicated from the additive model alone. A low value for one or more of these variables, however, should substantially weaken their joint influence on how voters behaved.

The results of analysis fail to sustain these predictions, suggesting that variables do not cumulate into a mutually dependent set of characteristics that conditioned responses to Smith and Hoover. For the full sample of counties (Table A1.3), the two-variable interactions behave roughly as would be anticipated from the hypothesis. Only

Table A1.4. Regression Coefficients for Additive, Linear and for Interactive, Nonlinear Models of the Vote for President: 471 Counties (in percent)

| | Dem 1928 | | | | Dem 1928 minus mean Dem 1916–24 | | | |
| | Additive Linear | | Interactive Nonlinear | | Additive Linear | | Interactive Nonlinear | |
	b	SE	b	SE	b	SE	b	SE
Catholic	.39	.049	.49	.056	.24	.038	−.11	.115
Jewish	.71	.083	.26	.101	.14	.065	.06	.071
Prot church	.26	.051	.22	.048	.20	.039	.18	.037
Urban	.01	.020	−.03	.027	.00	.016	−.08	.036
Foreign stock	−.12	.034	−.57	.065	.28	.026	.21	.036
Radios	−.18	.041	.22	.125	−.11	.032	−.07	.031
Owners	−.04	.046	.49	.128	.04	.035	−.19	.036
Negro	.45	.115	.64	.110	.07	.089	.08	.085
Under 35	.05	.123	−.13	.117	.17	.095	.10	.093
Female	−.81	.179	−.74	.175	−.68	.139	−.79	.134
Pop change	.01	.016	.02	.016	.04	.012	.02	.012
Antiprohib	.23	.035	−.12	.051	.19	.027	.10	.038
Catholic²							.53	.176
Radios²			−.51	.151				
Owners²			−.55	.126				
Cth-For							.86	.189
Cth-Urb							−.36	.146
Urb-Proh							.41	.085
For-Proh			.97	.141				
Cth-For-Urb			−.85	.248				
For-Urb-Proh			.33	.124				
Cth-For-Urb-Proh							−1.3	.337
R^2*	.46		.48		.75		.82	

*Adjusted for degrees of freedom.

the product of a county's percentages of Catholics and of urbanites fails to have a positive, statistically significant regression coefficient for both response variables; its coefficient is not significant for Smith's percentage of the presidential vote. Yet, contrary to the hypothesis, the product of all three explanatory variables has a statistically significant but *negative* influence on both Smith's percentage and the deviation of this percentage from that of earlier candidates. This means that the product of all three variables that supposedly represent the new America actually deflates the vote for Smith and Smith's lead over the three previous Democratic contenders. In addition, when the new variables are added to the regression equations, the percentages of urbanites and of foreign-stock Americans have negative coefficients for Smith's tally, and the percentage of urbanites has a negative coefficient for the deviation variable.

More refined analysis of the coefficients in Table A1.3 discloses interaction in the expected direction only between religion and foreign-stock heritage. To test for the impact of interaction effects, values of the interacting variables are inserted into both the linear model and the model incorporating the interactive components. The joint effects of these variables on the response variable are then compared for the two models. The results of this procedure show that for both the vote for Smith and the deviation variable, the joint effects of religion, urbanism, and foreign-stock heritage are substantially greater for the interactive than for the linear model only when both percent Catholic and percent foreign stock have very high values and percent urban has a low value. *Decreasing* the value of either percent Catholic or percent foreign stock or *increasing* the value of percent urban will sharply decrease the joint effects of the interactive model.

Scrutiny of the regression models computed for the 471 referenda counties also fails to show that religion, foreign-stock heritage, urbanism, and prohibition combined into a single complex that influenced the vote for president. Again, interaction in the direction predicted by the model seems to emerge only for the combination of religion and foreign-stock heritage. For Smith's percentage of the vote, Table A1.4 reveals that one first-order interaction (the combination of prohibition and foreign-stock heritage) and two second-order interactions (the combination of religion, foreign-stock heritage, and urban-rural residence; and the combination of foreign-stock heritage, urban-rural residence, and prohibition) enter the regression equation. Both the interaction between foreign-stock heritage and prohibition and the interaction among foreign-stock heritage, urban-rural residence, and prohibition have positive signs (although the latter interaction is small in magnitude). Once again, however, the coefficient for the combination of religion, foreign-stock heritage, and urban-rural residence has a negative sign and a large magnitude. In addition, when interactive terms are added to the equation, percent foreign stock, percent urban, and percent antiprohibition all have negative signs. These results decisively rule out the interpretation that all four variables combined to influence the choices of voters. When the four variables assume their maximum values, their joint effects are actually greater for the additive than for the interactive regression model. Overall, the model does not reveal any significant interactive effects. The negative signs for the original variables combined with the negative sign for the combination of religion, ethnic background, and place of residence cancel the interactive influences of other combinations of variables.

Similar results are obtained for analysis of the model estimating the difference between the vote for Smith and the average votes of the three previous Democratic candidates. Three first-order and one third-order interaction term enter the regression equation for this response variable. Once again, the highest-order interaction term, that cumulating all four variables, has a negative sign, opposite of what would be predicted from the hypothesis of the two Americas. In this case, the interaction between urbanism and Catholicism is likewise negative. Again, the only variables that interact importantly in the expected direction are Catholicism and foreign-stock heritage.

Analysis of these interactive, nonlinear regression models can also help to test the hypothesis set forth in Chapter 6 that the prevalence of Smith supporters in large cities generated a nonlinear relationship between urbanism and measures of the vote for president. The coefficients of Tables A1.3 and A1.4 do not indicate that, independent of their social and economic characteristics, metropolitan voters rallied to support Al Smith. The square of a county's percentage of urban residents enters the regression equations only for Smith's percentage of the vote among the 2,058 counties. The regression coefficient for this squared variable is not statistically significant at even the .05 level for either of the two equations computed within the referenda counties or for the equation computed for the deviation variable within the full sample of counties.

Even when the squared variable enters the regression equation, however, the results fail to show a surge of big city support for Al Smith. In this case, Table A1.3 reveals that the regression coefficient for a county's percentage of urbanites has a value of $-.13$ and its square a value of .09. The easiest way to visualize the joint effects of these coefficients is to view the independent relationship between a county's percentage of Democrats and its percentage of urbanites as a line drawn on a graph, with the percentage of Democrats as its Y axis and the percentage of urban dwellers as its X axis. Such a line would slope downward at a decreasing rate until percent urban reaches a value of about 72.4 percent, when the line would begin to slope upward.[15] Despite this bend in the line, the joint influence of the urbanism variables on percent Democratic is still negative, even for counties that are 100 percent urban. Computation of this joint influence by multiplying the coefficient for percent urban by the proportion of urbanites in a county, multiplying the coefficient for percent urban squared by the proportion of urbanites squared, and adding the products, shows that an entirely urban county should be 4 percent less Democratic than an entirely rural county with the same demographic composition ($-.13 \times 1 + .09 \times 1^2 = -.04$).[16]

To supplement this analysis, the square of the percentages of urbanites was added by itself to all linear regression equations for response variables measuring Smith's performance and the difference between his performance and that of previous Democratic candidates. The results of this procedure, reported in Table A1.5, again fail to disclose nonlinear effects for any of the deviation variables that indicate how the coalition supporting Smith was different from the coalitions put together by Democratic candidates in earlier years. The

Table A1.5. Influence of Percentage of Urbanites and Percentage of Urbanites Squared on Measures of the Vote for President: 2,058 Counties (in percent)*

	Percent Urban		Percent Urban Squared	
	Regression Coefficient b	*Standard Error*	*Regression Coefficient b*	*Standard Error*
Dem 1928	−.10	.022	.12	.025
Dem 1928 minus Dem 1924	.01	.021	.00	.024
Dem 1928 minus Dem/Prog 1924	−.06	.020	.12	.023
Dem 1928 minus Dem 1916–24	−.04	.018	.03	.021
Dem 1928 minus Dem 1916–20 Dem/Prog 1924	−.07	.016	.07	.019

*Controlling for percentages of Foreign stock, Owners, Negro, Female, Under 35, Pop change, Jewish, Catholic, Prot church, and for Economic status.

regression coefficients for the square of the urbanism variable are statistically significant at the .001 level for Smith's percentages of the presidential vote and of the adult population. Even if the level of significance is raised to .05, the square of percent urban is not statistically significant for any of the other response variables listed in Table A1.5. For the two percentages of Smith's tally, percent urban has a negative sign and its square has a positive sign. Once again, the line depicting the independent relationship between Democratic voting and residence in urban communities slopes downward and then turns upward (at values of about 41.5 and 50 percent, respectively, for percent Dem 1928 and percent Dem 1928 total). For Smith's percentage of the vote cast, an entirely urban county would be 2 percentage points more Democratic than an entirely rural county with the same demographic composition ($-.10 \times 1 + .12 \times 1^2 = .02$). For his percentage of the adult population, an entirely urban county would have the same percentage of Democratic voters as an entirely rural county with the same demographic composition ($-.11 \times 1 + .11 \times 1^2 = 0$).

Appendix 2

Analysis of Seven Separate Regions

Chart A2.1. Regions Included in the Analysis

New England

Connecticut
Maine
Massachusetts
New Hampshire
Rhode Island
Vermont

Mid-Atlantic

Delaware
New Jersey
New York
Pennsylvania

East North Central

Illinois
Indiana
Michigan
Ohio
Wisconsin

West North Central

Iowa
Kansas
Minnesota
Missouri
Nebraska
North Dakota
South Dakota

Border

Kentucky
Maryland
Oklahoma
Tennessee
West Virginia

Mountain

Arizona
Colorado
Idaho
Montana
Nevada
New Mexico
Utah
Wyoming

Pacific

California
Oregon
Washington

Table A2.1. Regression Coefficients for Separate Regions, Response Variable:
Dem 1928 (in percent)

	New England		Mid-Atlantic		East North Central	
	b	SE	b	SE	b	SE
Catholic	.56	.09	.63	.08	.63	.05
Jewish	1.40	.34	.41	.10	1.63	.30
Prot church	−.25	.15	−.26	.10	.47	.04
Urban	.00	.05	−.01	.03	.01	.02
Foreign stock	−.02	.08	−.01	.06	− .04	.03
Economic status	.26	.31	−.36	.17	−1.23	.17
Owners	−.27	.14	−.40	.05	− .29	.05
Negro	−.86	.71	−.14	.12	− .43	.14
Under 35	−.60	.35	−.58	.20	.49	.15
Female	.03	.61	−.35	.43	.47	.29
Pop change	.03	.07	.10	.03	.01	.03
R^2	.92		.89		.51	

Table A2.2. Regression Coefficients for Separate Regions, Response Variable:
Dem 1928 Total (in percent)

	New England		Mid-Atlantic		East North Central	
	b	SE	b	SE	b	SE
Catholic	.48	.08	.60	.07	.51	.04
Jewish	.82	.30	.19	.08	.76	.24
Prot church	− .03	.13	−.31	.08	.40	.04
Urban	.01	.04	.00	.03	−.02	.02
Foreign stock	− .04	.07	−.13	.05	−.09	.02
Economic status	.59	.27	−.30	.14	−.89	.13
Owners	− .13	.12	−.14	.04	−.30	.04
Negro	−1.63	.62	−.09	.10	−.44	.12
Under 35	− .89	.30	−.90	.17	.18	.12
Female	− .46	.53	.24	.36	.51	.23
Pop change	.05	.06	.08	.02	−.01	.02
R^2	.83		.73		.52	

West North Central		Border		Mountain		Pacific	
b	SE	b	SE	b	SE	b	SE
.58	.04	.34	.13	.23	.04	.34	.10
.15	.23	1.54	.65	9.80	2.83	1.84	.62
.12	.04	.01	.08	.10	.03	.01	.13
.03	.02	−.11	.05	.04	.03	.02	.03
.05	.02	−.35	.16	.16	.04	.06	.06
−.94	.14	.01	.36	−.56	.21	−.07	.26
−.23	.05	−.39	.08	−.13	.05	−.00	.10
.36	.12	.48	.08	.61	.43	.82	.83
−.27	.11	.44	.13	.09	.12	−.31	.14
−.35	.20	.17	.16	−.67	.16	−1.25	.24
.02	.03	−.04	.03	.00	.02	−.03	.02
.40		.33		.35		.55	

West North Central		Border		Mountain		Pacific	
b	SE	b	SE	b	SE	b	SE
.47	.03	.56	.09	.22	.03	.07	.05
−.04	.17	.80	.47	5.22	2.23	.55	.35
.07	.03	−.01	.06	.14	.03	−.14	.07
−.02	.01	−.10	.03	−.02	.02	−.03	.02
.00	.02	−.22	.11	.13	.03	.12	.03
−.48	.10	.33	.25	−.01	.16	.26	.15
−.12	.04	−.09	.06	−.06	.04	.06	.06
.16	.09	.12	.06	−.81	.34	.32	.47
−.26	.08	−.25	.09	−.23	.09	−.23	.08
−.14	.15	−.21	.11	−.25	.13	−.18	.13
−.02	.02	−.03	.02	−.05	.02	−.03	.01
.40		.19		.45		.43	

Table A2.3. Regression Coefficients for Separate Regions, Response Variable:
Rep 1928 Total (in percent)

	New England		Mid-Atlantic		East North Central	
	b	SE	b	SE	b	SE
Catholic	− .07	.09	− .11	.08	− .23	.03
Jewish	− .50	.32	− .05	.09	−1.20	.20
Prot church	.34	.14	− .13	.10	− .06	.03
Urban	− .00	.04	.00	.03	− .03	.02
Foreign stock	− .02	.07	− .16	.05	− .06	.02
Economic status	.45	.29	.25	.16	.74	.12
Owners	.19	.13	.31	.05	− .05	.04
Negro	−1.02	.66	.11	.12	− .02	.10
Under 35	− .74	.32	−1.05	.20	− .59	.10
Female	− .55	.57	.50	.41	− .06	.20
Pop change	.05	.07	− .02	.02	− .04	.02
R^2	.85		.88		.63	

Table A2.4. Regression Coefficients for Separate Regions, Response Variable:
Dem 1928 Minus Dem 1924 (in percent)

	New England		Mid-Atlantic		East North Central	
	b	SE	b	SE	b	SE
Catholic	.47	.13	.36	.11	.28	.05
Jewish	1.10	.49	.28	.13	− .27	.31
Prot church	.02	.23	−.20	.14	.17	.05
Urban	.00	.07	−.00	.04	−.01	.02
Foreign stock	− .02	.11	.27	.08	.50	.03
Economic status	1.42	.45	−.15	.24	.17	.17
Owners	.21	.20	.17	.08	−.04	.06
Negro	−1.41	1.02	.23	.17	.19	.15
Under 35	.53	.50	.49	.29	.76	.15
Female	.35	.89	.32	.60	.48	.31
Pop change	− .26	.10	−.04	.04	−.10	.03
R^2	.74		.77		.77	

West North Central		Border		Mountain		Pacific	
b	SE	b	SE	b	SE	b	SE
−.30	.03	.09	.12	.04	.04	− .33	.07
−.25	.17	−1.24	.61	7.24	2.95	−1.10	.42
−.10	.03	− .07	.08	.04	.03	− .19	.09
−.09	.01	− .00	.04	− .11	.03	− .08	.02
−.07	.02	.35	.15	.07	.04	− .06	.04
.83	.10	.13	.32	.98	.21	.62	.18
.19	.04	.35	.08	− .12	.05	.11	.07
−.36	.09	− .38	.08	−1.93	.44	− .85	.57
.04	.08	.11	.12	− .35	.12	− .01	.10
.38	.15	− .39	.15	.60	.16	1.25	.17
−.07	.02	− .03	.03	− .09	.02	− .02	.01
.43		.31		.35		.69	

West North Central		Border		Mountain		Pacific	
b	SE	b	SE	b	SE	b	SE
.38	.04	.30	.07	.07	.04	.42	.10
−.15	.24	.22	.34	5.16	3.32	.29	.68
.00	.04	− .07	.04	−.06	.04	− .14	.14
.07	.02	.06	.02	.03	.03	.03	.04
.51	.02	.62	.08	.46	.05	.40	.07
−.50	.14	−1.30	.18	.02	.24	.39	.29
−.18	.05	.04	.04	−.10	.06	− .04	.11
−.35	.12	.14	.04	−.56	.50	3.56	.92
−.14	.12	.16	.06	.08	.14	− .40	.16
.58	.21	− .03	.08	−.48	.20	−1.33	.27
.08	.03	− .01	.02	−.04	.02	.02	.02
.76		.41		.53		.72	

Table A2.5. Regression Coefficients for Separate Regions, Response Variable: Dem 1928 Minus Dem/Prog 1924 (in percent)

	New England		Mid-Atlantic		East North Central	
	b	SE	b	SE	b	SE
Catholic	.44	.11	.47	.08	.25	.06
Jewish	.58	.41	.24	.10	.17	.33
Prot church	.10	.18	−.46	.10	−.25	.05
Urban	.02	.05	−.02	.03	.39	.03
Foreign stock	−.17	.09	.04	.06	−.09	.03
Economic status	.49	.37	−.16	.17	.02	.19
Owners	.23	.16	.20	.05	−.37	.06
Negro	.10	.85	.50	.12	.11	.16
Under 35	.70	.41	−.12	.20	−.66	.16
Female	.92	.73	.99	.43	−.54	.33
Pop change	−.10	.09	.01	.02	.11	.03
R^2	.61		.77		.32	

Table A2.6. Regression Coefficients for Separate Regions, Response Variable: Dem 1928 Minus Prog 1924 (in percent)

	New England		Mid-Atlantic		East North Central	
	b	SE	b	SE	b	SE
Catholic	.53	.10	.74	.11	.61	.08
Jewish	.89	.39	.37	.14	2.06	.47
Prot church	−.17	.17	−.52	.14	−.04	.07
Urban	.02	.05	−.03	.04	.06	.04
Foreign stock	−.18	.09	−.25	.08	−.63	.05
Economic status	−.67	.35	−.37	.24	−1.38	.26
Owners	−.25	.15	−.37	.08	−.61	.08
Negro	.64	.80	.13	.18	−.50	.23
Under 35	−.43	.39	−1.19	.29	−.93	.23
Female	.60	.69	.32	.61	−.56	.46
Pop change	.18	.08	.15	.04	.22	.05
R^2	.85		.67		.57	

West North Central		Border		Mountain		Pacific	
b	SE	b	SE	b	SE	b	SE
.43	.04	.34	.07	.29	.04	.32	.09
.44	.21	.19	.32	.91	3.40	.16	.56
.04	.04	.03	.04	.08	.04	−.20	.12
.04	.02	.04	.02	−.12	.03	−.04	.03
−.03	.02	.20	.08	.25	.05	.11	.06
−.11	.13	−1.33	.17	.66	.25	.20	.24
−.13	.05	.09	.04	.07	.06	−.11	.09
.20	.11	.18	.04	.62	.51	−.01	.76
−.39	.10	.14	.06	.33	.14	.12	.13
−.20	.19	− .04	.08	.38	.19	.20	.22
.11	.02	.00	.02	.00	.02	.03	.01
.29		.30		.30		.50	

West North Central		Border		Mountain		Pacific	
b	SE	b	SE	b	SE	b	SE
.64	.06	.38	.14	.46	.07	.24	.14
−.79	.35	1.51	.67	5.61	5.07	1.70	.89
.20	.06	.12	.09	.24	.06	− .05	.18
.04	.02	−.12	.05	−.11	.05	− .05	.05
−.51	.03	−.76	.16	−.04	.08	− .22	.09
−.64	.21	−.02	.36	.08	.37	− .26	.38
−.24	.08	−.34	.08	.03	.10	− .07	.14
.71	.18	.52	.09	1.80	.77	−2.83	1.20
−.66	.17	−.47	.13	.34	.21	.21	.20
−.38	.30	.16	.16	.19	.29	.28	.35
−.08	.04	−.03	.03	.04	.04	− .01	.02
.52		.41		.36		.17	

Table A2.7. Regression Coefficients for Separate Regions, Response Variable: Dem 1928 Minus Mean Dem 1916–1924 (in percent)

	New England		Mid-Atlantic		East North Central	
	b	SE	b	SE	b	SE
Catholic	.55	.11	.45	.09	.30	.05
Jewish	1.12	.41	.34	.10	−.11	.30
Prot church	.10	.18	−.40	.11	.27	.05
Urban	.03	.06	−.02	.03	−.06	.02
Foreign stock	.03	.09	.17	.06	.43	.03
Economic status	.85	.37	−.16	.18	−.55	.17
Owners	.36	.16	−.01	.06	−.32	.06
Negro	−.53	.85	.09	.13	−.04	.15
Under 35	.65	.41	.11	.22	−.60	.17
Female	.64	.73	.63	.46	.82	.30
Pop change	−.22	.09	.00	.03	−.04	.03
R^2	.80		.86		.67	

Table A2.8. Regression Coefficients for Separate Regions, Response Variable: Dem 1928 Minus Mean Dem 1916–1920, Dem/Prog 1924

	New England		Mid-Atlantic		East North Central	
	b	SE	b	SE	b	SE
Catholic	.54	.10	.48	.07	.29	.04
Jewish	.95	.39	.32	.09	.03	.25
Prot church	.12	.17	−.49	.09	.13	.04
Urban	.04	.05	−.03	.03	−.04	.02
Foreign stock	−.03	.09	.09	.05	.23	.02
Economic status	.54	.36	−.16	.16	−.61	.14
Owners	.37	.16	.01	.05	−.43	.04
Negro	−.03	.81	.18	.12	−.06	.12
Under 35	.71	.39	−.09	.19	.13	.12
Female	.83	.69	.85	.40	.48	.25
Pop change	−.17	.08	.02	.02	.03	.03
R^2	.82		.86		.56	

West North Central		Border		Mountain		Pacific	
b	*SE*	*b*	*SE*	*b*	*SE*	*b*	*SE*
.46	.04	.20	.06	.23	.03	.30	.08
.22	.21	.62	.32	6.60	2.62	.60	.50
.11	.04	− .11	.04	.02	.03	−.11	.10
.01	.01	.01	.02	.00	.02	.01	.03
.36	.02	.38	.08	.33	.04	.33	.05
−.96	.13	−1.29	.17	−.22	.19	.07	.21
−.20	.05	− .46	.04	−.06	.05	−.01	.08
−.16	.11	.13	.04	−.10	.40	1.12	.68
−.09	.10	.06	.06	.05	.11	−.18	.12
.12	.19	.03	.08	−.53	.15	−.80	.20
.06	.02	.00	.02	−.01	.02	.02	.01
.69		.34		.48		.70	

West North Central		Border		Mountain		Pacific	
b	*SE*	*b*	*SE*	*b*	*SE*	*b*	*SE*
.48	.03	.22	.06	.30	.03	.27	.07
.13	.20	.64	.31	5.17	2.40	.56	.44
.12	.03	− .08	.04	.07	.03	−.13	.09
.00	.01	.00	.02	−.05	.02	−.02	.02
.18	.02	.23	.08	.27	.03	.24	.04
−.83	.12	−1.27	.17	.00	.18	.01	.19
−.18	.05	− .03	.04	−.00	.05	−.03	.07
.03	.10	.15	.04	.29	.36	−.11	.59
−.17	.10	.07	.06	.14	.10	−.01	.10
.24	.17	.03	.07	.25	.14	.29	.17
.07	.02	− .00	.02	.00	.02	.03	.01
.52		.33		.46		.62	

Table A2.9. *Regression Coefficients for Separate Regions, Response Variable: Dem 1928 Minus Dem 1932 (in percent)*

	New England		Mid-Atlantic		East North Central	
	b	SE	b	SE	b	SE
Catholic	.29	.05	.38	.07	.28	.04
Jewish	.46	.20	.22	.09	.93	.22
Prot church	.29	.09	−.39	.09	.20	.03
Urban	.04	.03	.02	.03	.07	.02
Foreign stock	.06	.04	−.05	.05	−.03	.02
Economic status	.95	.18	.41	.16	−.32	.13
Owners	.15	.08	.11	.05	−.20	.04
Negro	−.89	.41	−.13	.11	.13	.11
Under 35	−.18	.20	−.45	.19	−.20	.11
Female	−.24	.35	.84	.39	−.04	.22
Pop change	−.01	.04	−.02	.02	−.00	.02
R^2	.89		.70		.39	

West North Central		Border		Mountain		Pacific	
b	*SE*	*b*	*SE*	*b*	*SE*	*b*	*SE*
.32	.02	.41	.09	.21	.03	.24	.07
.30	.15	.25	.46	3.78	2.00	− .35	.48
−.01	.02	.11	.06	.10	.02	− .09	.10
.06	.01	.10	.03	−.01	.02	.03	.03
−.01	.01	.15	.11	.22	.03	.11	.05
−.12	.09	−1.83	.25	.22	.14	.57	.21
.02	.03	.29	.06	.07	.04	− .04	.08
.23	.08	.32	.06	−.16	.30	−2.10	.65
−.37	.07	.18	.09	.21	.08	− .09	.11
.05	.13	− .02	.11	.12	.11	− .01	.19
.00	.02	.02	.02	−.03	.01	.00	.01
.43		.32		.54		.37	

Appendix 3

Transcripts of the Republican Party Survey of Local Leaders

Chart A3.1. *Comments on Protestant Voting from the Republican Survey**

Cleveland   We obtained the vote of perhaps 5% of normally Democratic women. Religion was the cause.

Los Angeles   While the Democrats gained by having a Catholic as a candidate among the Catholics, the Republicans gained among the Protestants by probably an offset vote.

Indiana   Religion, in a large measure, figured in the campaign but not openly, or through any organized efforts on the part of the political organization. It is certain that some claimed opposition to Smith because of his temperance views who were really actuated by religious motives.

Missouri (B)†   Religion cut a considerable figure in the returns. In Catholic centers there were many Catholics evidently influenced by the church question. In Protestant centers there was fully as large a percentage influenced by the religious question.

New Jersey (B)†   The religious issue gave us a big net gain inasmuch as a goodly number of Catholics in both parties voted for Hoover.

Rhode Island   It is apparent that the Catholic women voted for Smith and the Protestants came out strongly for Hoover. I do know that our women vote was large and also influenced to a great extent by the religious question.

Chart A3.2. *Comments on Catholic Voting from the Republican Survey*

Chicago   Religion certainly did cut a considerable figure in the campaign; but Governor Smith did not obtain a solid Catholic vote.

Cincinnati   The strong Catholic wards are also strong Democratic wards and were carried by Mr. Smith and his Democratic candidate for Governor, Mr. Davey. The 20th ward, however, was carried by Smith by approximately 5500 and by Davey by approximately 4400. Governor Smith did not obtain

*All charts in this appendix are direct quotations from reports filed in Presidential Campaign, Box 89, Herbert Hoover Papers.
†More than one report was submitted from these states.

the solid Catholic vote inasmuch as a number of our most prominent Catholic citizens were openly supporting Mr. Hoover.

Cleveland   Governor Smith obtained the solid Catholic vote.

Connecticut   The question of religion cut a very substantial figure, Governor Smith did not obtain the solid Catholic vote, if he had I doubt if we would have carried Connecticut.

Indiana   It is certain that Governor Smith did not obtain the solid Catholic vote.

Los Angeles   While the Democrats gained by having a Catholic as a candidate among the Catholics, the Republicans gained among the Protestants by probably an offset vote.

Maryland   I prefer not to discuss it (religion) except I will say Smith did not receive a solid denominational vote.

Massachusetts   Governor Smith obtained probably 90% of the Catholic vote.

Missouri (A)   Religion cut quite a figure. Practically all of the Catholics supported Smith.

Missouri (B)   Religion cut a considerable figure in the returns. In Catholic centers there were many Catholics evidently influenced by the church question.

New Hampshire   Governor Smith obtained a solid Democratic Catholic vote and 50% of the Republican Catholic vote.

New Jersey (A)   I don't think anybody under heaven can claim that Governor Smith obtained the solid Catholic vote.

New Jersey (B)   The religious issue gave us a big net gain inasmuch as a goodly number of Catholics in both parties voted for Hoover.

New Jersey (C)   Smith did not obtain the solid Catholic vote as many Republican Catholics openly claimed their support to Hoover. He did, however, undoubtedly receive a great majority.

Ohio   Religion did cut a figure in the returns, and was approximately 15% . . . Smith did NOT obtain the solid Catholic vote.

Oregon   The religious question was a very material issue and was the cause of changing more votes than any other one question. Generally 85% of the Catholic vote in Oregon is Republican, but this year I think you can safely say that 95% of them voted for Smith.

Rhode Island   In my opinion Smith obtained nearly the solid Catholic vote.

Wisconsin   There is evidence supporting the contention that Governor Smith received practically the unanimous Catholic vote. It is probable that Hoover would have obtained from 40,000 to 50,000 more votes had it not been for the religious issue.

Chart A3.3. Comments on the Prohibition Issue from the Republican Survey

Chicago   From our reports gathered, it is stated that [our net losses due to the prohibition issue were] about 30 percent. I am inclined to believe that this is a little too large, but am unable to fix any definite percentage.

Cincinnati In our opinion better than 80 percent of the Republican loss of votes in Hamilton County was due to the wet and dry issue. Hamilton County is notoriously wet and it was upon that basis that the Democrats were so confident prior to the election that Smith would carry Hamilton County. The fact that Smith made inroads into the strong Republican downtown wards was due primarily to the wet and dry issue, as was his strength among the German-Americans, Italians, and other foreign groups.

Cleveland In the city of Cleveland the Republican loss [due to the wet and dry issue] was undoubtedly 30 percent.

Connecticut It is impossible to estimate any percentage with reference to the result of the wet and dry issue. We lost and gained votes, the extent cannot be estimated.

Indiana Dry Democrats in the State at large bolted their ticket, and their loss was overwhelmingly large as compared with our loss; in other words, the Democratic drys voting for Hoover far outnumbered the Republican wets supporting Smith. In fact, many Republican wets found plenty of reason to support the ticket. The wet and dry issue did help immensely increasing the woman vote, which resulted in the largest total vote and also the largest Republican vote ever polled in Indiana.

Los Angeles I believe our greatest loss was due to the wet and dry issue, and I base this on the fact that our registration in Los Angeles County was distributed as follows:

600,000 Republicans	5,700 Socialists
217,000 Democrats	90,000 Declined to State
11,000 Prohibitionists	

In the final vote, the Chief in round figures received 515,000 while Smith received 209,000. This leads me to conclude that we lost quite a percentage of votes on the wet issue—I should say fifteen percent.

I believe that we gained probably fifteen percent of the Democratic vote, partly on account of the wet issue, and probably five percent more of the Democratic vote on a combination of the wet issue with the Tammany issue.

Maryland As to the extent of the Democratic loss and our gain due to the wet and dry issue, I would say that it would be difficult to dissever it from other issues, like the denominational issue and the prosperity issue, but I would say that while many wets were voting for us for prosperity reasons, many drys were voting for dry reasons so that it turned out we got quite an appreciable percentage of gain.

Massachusetts Loss due to the wet and dry issue expressed in terms of percentage of our normally Republican vote was 5 to 10 percent. Estimate of Democratic loss and our gain due to the wet and dry issue—probably two or three percent.

Missouri (A) The wet and dry issue was before us all the time. We lost some extreme wets although not a great many. We captured a lot of dry voters in the country where we made a special appeal for support of law enforcement.

Missouri (B)   In the city of St. Louis quite a large percentage of our losses from the Republican organization was due primarily to the wet and dry issue. Out in the state a very large percentage of Mr. Hoover's gain was due to the wet and dry issue.

New Hampshire   We did not obtain the usual support of the German-American vote, but on the other hand, our losses were 75 percent, the reason of the defection was the wet and dry issue. The other so-called foreign groups, Italian 50 percent loss, Poles, Greeks, etc. 75 percent, Jews 50 percent. The reason of the losses are attributed to the wet and dry issue and immigration. No other losses upon the wet and dry issue except as set forth above.

New Jersey (A)   As to question #4 "What was the extent of our loss due to the wet and dry issues?" Our answer is *none*, outside of the Italians. . . . The wet and dry issue never got anywhere with the great body of voters. Among our farmers the so-called wet and dry issue helped the Republican Party. All in all I should say that the Republicans gained throughout the state by the injection of the wet issue by Governor Smith.

New Jersey (B)   Lost five percent of our normal Republican vote on the prohibition issue but it was more than made up by our gains from dry Democrats.

New Jersey (C)   It is impossible to express in terms of percentage the loss of the Republican vote due to the wet and dry issue. However, there were a great deal of Republicans who voted for Smith because of this issue. [Democratic defections due to the wet and dry issue] were enough to carry three small counties for the Republican ticket.

Ohio   Extent of our loss due to the wet and dry issue, expressed in terms of percentage of our normally Republican vote was approximately 15 percent. Our gain, due to the wet and dry issue, was approximately 35 percent.

Oregon   Should say that 15 percent of the Republican registration voted for Smith on the wet and dry issue. Should say 25 percent of Democratic registration voted for Hoover on the wet and dry issue.

Rhode Island   I think that a small percentage of our normally Protestant Republican vote went for Smith on the wet-dry issue. . . . We have a large Italian population, normally 60 percent Republican; the men voted largely for Smith because he is wet and were influenced no doubt to some extent by his religion. The women voted for Smith more on account of his religion.

Wisconsin   The wet and dry question probably cost the Republican ticket 10 percent of its normal Republican strength. This was particularly true in Milwaukee, the largest city, and in many of the northern counties.

Chart A3.4. Comments on Ethnic Voting from the Republican Survey

Chicago

Our information is that a large majority of the German voters supported Mr. Hoover. At the beginning of the campaign it was considered impossible to receive but a small percentage. We are asked to consider the magnificent vote which Mr. Hoover received in New York, Cook County, State of Missouri, Nebraska, Wisconsin, and other great German-American centers.

We are also told that 35 percent of Democratic German-American women voted the Republican ticket; and it is estimated that 18 percent of our usual support for the presidential ticket was lost, on account of the Democratic propaganda that Hoover was pro-British.

There is every indication that the [other] so-called foreign groups were divided in accordance with their active participation in church affiliations.

Many Italians and Poles that are Roman Catholics were for Mr. Hoover notwithstanding their opposition to the prohibition cause.

Cincinnati

The German-American group in the 15th ward gave Hoover a majority of 400 votes and Cooper a majority of 700 votes. The 20th ward, which is normally Democratic and Catholic was carried by Smith by approximately 6,000 votes and by Davey by approximately 4600. The 23rd ward was carried by Hoover by 800 votes and carried by Davey by 500 votes. In 1924 Coolidge carried these wards by larger majorities and the opposition vote was divided between Davis and La Follette. The German vote is normally considered a wet vote in Cincinnati and with that thought in mind Smith did not receive the vote expected by his supporters from the German-Americans. They were possibly influenced more by the prosperity represented by Hoover. Also, the German-Americans are Protestants and were possibly influenced by that fact.

The Italians and similar groups voted in the main for Smith on the wet issue, and also because the majority of them are Catholics. We had occasion to talk to the minister of the Italian Presbyterian Church in Cincinnati both before and after the election and although he was for Hoover he said the majority of his members [Protestants] were for Smith because of their desire for their wine.

Cleveland

The German-American group voted for the Democratic Presidential candidate. We did not obtain as large a vote from that group as we usually receive. I am convinced that in the City of Cleveland, that we lost 30 percent of the vote we formerly received. One reason for the large defection was the fact that several raids were conducted on two large German-American clubs, shortly before the election. This alienated many thousands of German-American voters. Another reason was the fact that representatives of German-American organizations claimed to have been unable to arrange an interview with Mr. Hoover.

The Italians were predominantly for the Democratic candidate. Same with the Poles and same with the Bohemians, and Lithuanians. The reason for our loss among these groups was the wet and dry issue, and religion.

Indiana

The potential vote that may be classified as German-Americans totals 40,000 in Indiana, centered in Allen, Adams, Dearborn, DuBois, Franklin, Jackson, Wayne, and Vanderburgh Counties.

The majority voted the Republican ticket, but in less proportion and less number than in any election since the war.

This slump seems due to leaders of this group being inactive because of their pro-Smith sentiment due to his prohibition views, or their resentment of what they regarded as dictation of temperance fanatics. Some probably did not vote for Smith; they may have voted for Hoover—but they did [not] *work* for him like they did for Harding or for Coolidge.

All in all, Hoover's percentage of this vote was as large as that received by Coolidge, but smaller in both percentage and number than received by Harding. Hoover gained some German votes (Lutheran) in Allen and Adams and Jackson Counties, which fact seems apparent from precinct returns, but incapable of any real proof because no precinct is nearly solid German-American. As usual, Democratic Germans in such counties as Dearborn, DuBois, and Franklin voted for Smith, and some increase of their vote appears in the returns, these German-Americans being Catholic.

The only defection, as stated, was with certain leaders, and was inconsiderate, except that their failure to work cut down the vote.

Even "an approximate estimate" [of the vote of other foreign-born] groups would have little real basis of fact, and would be a rank guess if attempted by each nationality.

For one familiar with Indiana, it may be expressive to cite the returns of our one big county of foreigners (Lake County), as follows:

```
1928: Hoover received 45,297 or 64% of the total vote.
      Smith      "     35,284 or 36%  "   "   "   "
1924: Coolidge   "     30,990 or 76%  "   "   "   "
      Davis      "     10,918 or 24%  "   "   "   "
1920: Harding    "     26,296 or 78%  "   "   "   "
      Cox        "      7,136 or 22%  "   "   "   "
```

It is well known that we lost some foreign votes principally, if not wholly, because of religion, but the increased vote as indicated in the foregoing, makes it impossible of anything approaching accurate calculation.

St. Joe, another county, having a big foreign element, largely Catholic— voted Republican, as follows:

1928: Hoover received 36,844 or 57.7% of the total vote.
      Smith   "   26,846 or 42.3% "   "   "   "
1924: Coolidge   "   23,682 or 61%   "   "   "   "
      Davis   "   18,056 or 39%   "   "   "   "
1920: Harding   "   17,675 or 58.5% "   "   "   "
      Cox   "   12,355 or 41.5% "   "   "   "

From the foregoing tables on the two counties having a large foreign element, the conclusion seems justified that we held our own in 1928, making no gain and suffering no loss.

Los Angeles

We did not get the usual support of the German-American group. It is my feeling that that was almost entirely due to the wet and dry issue, and judging from my experiences here and talk with German-American people, I would say we lost almost twenty percent of that group.

It is my feeling that of the other foreign groups, those whom you naturally consider from countries where they do a great deal of drinking, leaned very much toward Smith. Among the other foreign groups, however, and particularly those groups where the Chief had done humanitarian work, I believe we gained considerably over normal vote.

Maryland

The German-American votes split. We probably did not obtain as large a percentage as usual. I prefer not to discuss the religious motives, but the split was to some extent along these lines.

As to the other foreign groups we held a good proportion of the Lithuanian votes but lost a good part of the Italians and Poles—not a loss, however, inasmuch as they generally vote the other way.

Massachusetts

GERMAN-AMERICANS
    1928 election: about 50% Republican
    1924 election: 85% Republican
    Reason for losses:
    a. Prohibition: About 85% for modification. . . . probably the most important factor. They want beer and cannot get it now in Massachusetts. They are making their own home brew which has a bad effect on their health. There are a couple of breweries in Connecticut which undoubtedly helped the German vote there.
    b. Textile depression: In Lawrence, for example, about 65% of the Germans are in textile mills.
    c. Religion: About ⅛ of the Germans are Catholic and with them religion was an added factor.

d. Lack of recognition of Germans by Republican party in the state. There are no judges.

ITALIANS

1928 election: 80% Democratic
1924 election: 70% Republican

In city districts formerly inhabited by the Irish, the vote ran as high as 20 to one, due to inherited Irish traditions and Irish boss leadership. In smaller cities and towns, the Republican vote was much higher.

Reason for losses:

a. In 1924 there was a great resentment against President Wilson on account of Dalmatia and the peace conference.

b. Ten or twelve years ago Italian settlements consisted of first generation immigrants, laborers, etc. dependent on employment from large industries. They believed that a Democrat meant lack of employment and forced repatriation. The expressions of good will by Roosevelt in connection with the Messina earthquake, Senator Lodge and Fiume, Hoover and the Reconstruction work in Italy all helped. The vote of this group might have been retained if work on them had been started in the summer of 1928, instead of October.

c. The Italians of the second generation have not participated in national elections to any extent until the 1928 election. This group is not dependent for employment on large business enterprises but rather on individual initiative. It includes lawyers, doctors, clerks and small tradesmen. It did not suffer under the Cleveland depression. This group has been ignored by Republicans but recognized by Democrats. Although it included the bootlegger, gangmen, and ne'er-do-well, it also included the future leaders.

d. Unemployment, prohibition, religion, and an Italian on the Democratic State Ticket.

POLISH VOTE

1928 election: 65% Republican
1924 election: 80% Republican

Reason for losses:

a. Religion: A great many copies of the *Fellowship Forum* were distributed among the Poles just before the election.

b. Business depression: A great many of the Poles work in textiles.

c. Prohibition: This did not have much to do with it.

SWEDES

1928 election: 70% Republican
1924 election: 85% Republican

Reason for losses:

a. Local rows among the Swedish Republican organizations.

JEWISH VOTE

1928 election: 55% Republican
1924 election: 75% Republican

1926 election: Senatorial election, Butler-Walsh, 50% Republican

The more intelligent Jewish people voted for Hoover. The less intelligent for Smith.

LITHUANIANS

1928 election: 80-20 Republican

1924 election: 80-20 Republican

Although there are many Catholics and many wets among the Lithuanians, all their leaders were for the Republican party because of their gratitude to Mr. Hoover.

LETTS

Normally strongly Republican and voted practically solidly this year.

GREEKS

1928 election: 60% Republican

1924 election: 75% Republican

Reason for losses:

a. The effectiveness of Governor Smith's campaign and the impression he gave of candor and courage as the leading issues and the fact that he had the interest of the people at heart.

b. Religious issue played no part.

Missouri (A)

The Lutherans, among the German-Americans, gave us their support, except a few who are extremely wet. We lost the German-Catholic vote almost entirely.

We lost some Italians and Poles on account of the immigration issue but not any great number.

Missouri (B)

As to the German group, Mr. Hoover received a very large vote among the Germans. There was quite a substantial percentage of Catholic Germans who were also opposed to prohibition who voted for Mr. Smith. Probably 95% of the Lutheran Germans voted for Hoover, some few voting for Smith on the ground of prohibition.

Practically all of the Italians voted for Smith upon the ground of prohibition, and religion may have cut some figure. Our information indicates that a very large percentage of the Poles voted for Mr. Hoover there being little misunderstanding among them as to Mr. Hoover's relief work in Poland. A large percentage of the Italians formerly voted the Republican ticket.

New Hampshire

We did not obtain the usual support of the German-American vote, but on the other hand our losses were 75%, the reason of the defection was the wet and dry issue.

The other so-called foreign groups, Italians 50% loss, Poles, Greeks, etc. 75%, Jews 50%. The reason of the losses are attributed to the wet and dry issue and immigration.

New Jersey (A)

The German-American group voted Republican and we had as large a percentage as usual in support of our Presidential ticket from that source.

In regard to the alignment of the so-called foreign group of voters, such as Italians, Poles, etc., I am forced to the conclusion that the Italians as a class were against us whereas in previous Presidential elections they were with us. The Poles stood by us. The Hungarians stood by us better than the Italians. The Italians went away from us because of the liquor issue raised by Mr. Smith. The religious issue and liquor had no effect apparently on the Poles. The liquor question did hurt us somewhat among the Hungarians.

New Jersey (B)

Lost 15% of our normal German-American vote due to the prohibition issue.

Lost 15% of our normal Italian vote, 20% of the Poles, and 12% of the Hungarian vote due to prohibition and religious issues.

New Jersey (C)

Many of the German-American group did not vote for President. They were not in sympathy with Smith, but were influenced by the prosperity issue, and while many of them did not vote, the result was that there was considerable defection among this class of voters.

There was a great loss of Republican votes among the Italians in some districts which ran over 50%, due to the wet and dry issue. The Polish voters were lost to Smith because they took the attitude that he was the son of an immigrant and that he was being punished for it and in that respect they had a bond of sympathy, and therefore were rallied to that standard.

Ohio

The Catholic-German vote was against us in the main; the non-Catholic German vote was for us in the main. We did not obtain as large a percentage as usual, but the defection was not as large as it might have been at one time under similar circumstances, because the old Catholic-German vote is not in the ascendancy in this day. The second and third generations are not as strong in Catholicism as were their fathers. The defection percentage, however, amounted to approximately 15%. Cause for the defection was prohibition and religion.

Alignments of the racial groups follow: Italians were practically a unit against us; Poles, 70% opposition; Hungarians, 65% opposition; Slovakians,

60% opposition; Rumanians, 60% opposition; Jews, almost evenly divided with edge to the opposition; Slavish, 60% opposition; Greeks, about evenly divided, with edge to the opposition. Prohibition and religion causes for defection.

Oregon

The Germans pretty generally voted our ticket, except the German Catholics and a few German farmers that were influenced by the preconvention propaganda sent out against Hoover. I figure that we got 75% of the German vote.

85% of Italians and Poles voted against us, the religious question dominating and Smith's personal appeal to Latin countries being very effective with them.

Rhode Island

We have not a large German-American group in this state.

We have a large Italian population, normally 60% Republican; the men voted largely for Smith because he is wet and were influenced no doubt by some extent by his religion. The women voted for Smith more on account of religion.

Wisconsin

A large part of Wisconsin's German-American vote until the war was normally Democratic. Since then they have voted largely the so-called Progressive Republican ticket. In the 1928 election many of the older men and women in this classification returned to their former political affiliation, voting for the Democratic nominee both for President and Governor. This, however, according to the last election observations was not true so extensively in the instance of the younger men and women of the German-American group with the result that the Hoover vote in most German-American counties showed almost normal Republican majorities.

Wisconsin's Italian vote is relatively small. Precincts where they are strong indicated defection from the Republican party, this being largely on the wet and dry issue. Careful estimates indicate a fifty-fifty break among Wisconsin Poles, showing some loss to Hoover. No good reason for this is assigned except that the church issue seemed to have crept in quite strongly. The Norwegians, Swedes and Danes, of whom there are many in Wisconsin, remained loyal to the Republican Party.

Chart A3.5. Comments on the Farm Relief Issue from the Republican Survey

Chicago On this farm relief question, we are told that about 20 percent of the normally Republican voters voted against Hoover on account of Coolidge vetoing the Farm Relief bill, but that about 20 percent of the farmers inclined to vote against Hoover were held in line on account of his stand on the dry question. There were included in this group many Democrats.

The statistics from the country districts indicate about 20 percent of dry farmers voting for Smith. These people that report are of the opinion that if the Democrats had nominated a dry candidate, Mr. Hoover would have had a very close race.

They believe that Smith's weakness was his failure to come out on the square for the equalization fee and also his position in regard to emigrants.

Connecticut   The farm relief issue was of little moment in Connecticut.

Indiana   Unquestionably [the farm relief issue] cut some figure in the results, but had nothing like the influence claimed before the election by leaders of the organized farmers.

With the record Republican vote being an increase in each of the ninety-two counties of the state and with the Democratic vote being an increase in forty-seven counties, it is virtually impossible to express in percent either the loss or gain due to a singular factor. It is noteworthy that the counties in which the Democratic vote slumped that many were agricultural and several of them were normally Democratic.

In Cass, Jasper, Park, Pulaski and Warren Counties, all of which were carried by us in both the last election and in 1924, it is noticeable that our majorities were one or two hundred votes less than four years ago despite the increase in the total state vote. This may be regarded as due to the farm issue. In none of the other counties does the farm influence seem apparent. For instance, Hoover's majority over Coolidge's majority was 900 votes in Benton County, 500 in Carroll, 900 in Fulton, 1450 in Hancock, 500 in Hendricks, 750 in Johnson, 300 in Newton, 500 in Noble, 1100 in Tipton and 250 in Warren. As you note, some of these counties are normally Republican while others are normally Democratic but all of them are predominately agricultural and yet the increased Hoover majority which would not be attributed to the farm relief issue but rather to other factors, notably prohibition which resulted in the big increased woman vote.

In conclusion it would seem fair to state that the Republican loss was only a minor fraction of the pre-election prediction made by the leaders of the organized farmers.

Los Angeles   I do not think we lost anything in California on the so-called farm relief issue.

Massachusetts   I doubt if there was any loss upon the farm relief issue.

Missouri (A)   We lost very few farmers. They came over gradually so that November 6th found them voting the Republican ticket.

Missouri (B)   Our information is that Mr. Hoover's loss of Republicans on account of the farm relief issue amounted to practically nothing. Mr. Hoover carried the State of Missouri by approximately 185,000. He lost St. Louis by approximately 14,000, giving him a clean majority in the whole state of a little more than 170,000.

New Hampshire   No loss upon the so-called farm relief issue.

New Jersey (B)   Farm issue of no importance. Netted us a gain if anything.
New Jersey (C)   No loss on the farm relief issue in New Jersey.
Ohio   No loss was caused by the so-called farm relief issue.
Oregon   No material gain or loss on farm relief issue.
Rhode Island   Farm relief did not enter the campaign to any extent.
Wisconsin   We do not believe the Republican ticket lost any of its normal farm strength as a result of the farm relief question.

Chart A3.6. Comments on Black Voting from the Republican Survey

Chicago   Concerning the negro vote, from my sources of information, it appears that for the most part the negro voted the straight Republican ticket, notwithstanding some newspaper reports to the contrary.

A larger percentage of the negroes this year voted for the National ticket than four years ago; yet there was a deflection. There was an increase in that population of more than 30 percent. The deflection is figured at about 10 percent.

Glowing promises of the Democratic party to right all wrongs for them and the use of money in great quantities played an important part.

The wet and dry issue and the religious issue played no particular part in the deflection of the vote.

The women's vote were increased about 15 percent.

Continual publicity by Tipper and other colored publishers advocating Hoover's election made it possible for our ward leaders to accomplish what was done.

Cincinnati   The negro vote was in majority naturally for Hoover, but Governor Smith made inroads into this vote. For instance in 1924, the 18th ward was five to one Republican, whereas Hoover carried the 18th ward 2½ to 1. Cooper carried this ward three to one. In 1924, the 16th ward was two and one-half to one Republican and this year about one and one-half to one. The 17th ward was carried by the Republicans by 600 votes in 1924 and this year carried by the Governor by 39 votes, whereas Cooper carried the same ward by 700 votes. Four colored precincts in the fourth ward, representing the better class negroes went Republican by approximately three to one, with Smith having a few more votes in each precinct than the Democratic candidate for governor.

The reason for the change in the negro vote, in our opinion, was based upon the wet and dry issue. The negroes were told that Smith was wet and would bring a return of liquor.

Cleveland   A major portion of the Negroes voted the Republican ticket. We did not obtain as large a percentage of the Negro vote as we have in previous Presidential elections. We lost approximately 30 percent of that vote. The reason of the defection was largely because of the wet and dry issue.

Connecticut   I feel we obtained over 90 percent of the negro vote. It was largely lost to us at the beginning of the campaign but we were more successful in getting this back than in many other cases.

Indiana   In Indiana, a majority of the negroes supported Republican candidates, in 1928, but in number not as large as predicted by political workers and in proportion certainly much less than popularly supposed.

For the state at large, it seems accurate to say that Mr. Hoover received about 60 percent of the negro vote and that the total negro vote cast both for Mr. Hoover and for Mr. Smith, was 30,000 to 35,000. In other words, 15,000 of the Indiana voting population did not vote.

Of course, the only accurate method of ascertaining the negro vote is to go into the precinct returns, and this has been attempted for Marion, Lake and Vanderburgh Counties, which have two-thirds of the total negro vote. In addition, informed persons in a half dozen other counties were solicited for their opinion (their answer was probably largely guess). For the three large centers, only precincts that are almost solid negro population were considered with the following results:

County	Precincts	Hoover		Smith	
		Vote	%	Vote	%
Lake	19	5251	63	3037	37
Marion	26	5560	46	6512	54
Vanderburgh	9	3685	76	1140	24
Total	54	14496	56.3	10689	44.7

In other counties, the vote was between 65 to 70 percent in favor of Mr. Hoover, which would increase the percent indicated above for the state as a whole.

The foregoing results are contrary to the poll in all three counties; for instance, the 30-day Marion County poll showed approximately 70 percent for Mr. Smith, and 30 percent for Mr. Hoover. Then, too, the vote (Marion County) was much smaller than might have been expected, apparently some Smith negroes failing to vote although in some instances taxicabs were used to transport negro voters.

Los Angeles   The results clearly indicate that we did not receive as large a percentage of the negro vote as normal. This was due to the temporary conditions, and it is my belief in the future that we can and will receive the normal or better than a normal so-called negro vote. This year, the strategy of the Al Smith campaign to appeal to prejudice, fears and discontent, together with the wet and dry issues, unquestionably affected the negro vote. We were able to neutralize these pleas during the latter part of the campaign, and had the election been a week later I believe our propaganda would have been more effective. It would be my guess that we lost in the neighborhood of fifteen percent of the normal negro vote for the above reasons.

Maryland   We organized thoroughly to hold the negro vote and did hold it in all the counties in Maryland, except St. Mary's and Charles Counties and to a lesser extent, Prince Georges County. In Baltimore City we probably lost 20 percent. We lost those in the counties largely on religious grounds but in both counties and city because of Smith's wetness and the efforts of the Democrats to connect up the Ku Klux Klan as being both against Smith and the negroes.

Massachusetts

THE NEGRO VOTE

1928 election: about 80 percent Republican

1924 election: about 90 percent Republican

Reason for losses:

a. Lack of employment due to closing of hotels, clubs, and restaurants on account of prohibition.

b. Few negroes Catholic, largely Portuguese and West Indians. On account of religion, plus the belief that the imprisonment and deportation of Marcus Garvey attributed to the Republican party was unjust.

c. The protest against the failure of the Republicans to remove segregation from all departments of the federal service.

d. The feeling that Mr. Coolidge has neglected the negroes, coupled with the fear as to what Hoover's attitude toward them would be.

Missouri (A)   We received our percent of the negro vote. During the first part of the campaign, the Democrats were using money freely with the negroes and it was a question how far we could go with them and accomplish anything, but after we were well started, got them back into line and think they stood by us as well as they ever do, which is practically one hundred percent.

Missouri (B)   It is our estimate that approximately 20 percent of the negroes of the state voted for Smith and that this was a much larger Democratic negro vote than we had four years ago. This defection we think was largely due to the large sums of money which appear to have been expended by Democratic Regional Headquarters in St. Louis, in charge of Senator Hawes. Some defection may have been due to the fact that Democrats nominated a negro for Congress against Congressman Dyer in the Twelfth District.

New Hampshire   The negro vote was for the National Republican ticket, defection too meagre to estimate in percentage.

New Jersey (A)   The answer is that the negroes in a large percentage this year voted with us. We had some trouble with what is known as (I understand this is confidential information) the purchaseable negro vote. Our Democratic friends used the Klan to scare others with but not very successfully, I am inclined to the belief that there was no appreciable percentage of the Negro vote lost.

New Jersey (B) Lost five percent of our normal negro support due to money used by the Democratic organization.

New Jersey (C) The negro vote this year was probably a little less than in previous elections due to the fact that the Democrats effected a stronger organization among the colored people. Apparently there was no other cause for a defection and whatever there was, was of a very small percentage.

Ohio Normally we have 85 percent of the negro vote in Ohio. This year, we had not to exceed 65 percent. (Their attitude was not "right"; it was contrary and stubborn, especially in the larger cities.) Therefore, we did not obtain as large a percentage of the negro vote this year as in previous presidential elections. Our loss was 20 percent. Reason for the defection was expenditure of opposition money among them; liberals among them wanting the return of liquor, and the feeling that Smith was friendly to them as he was supposed to be fighting the Klan.

Oregon I feel that at least 50 percent of the Negro voters in Oregon voted against us, as compared with not to exceed 10 percent in previous elections. Reasons for same were partially Ku Klux, but mostly a personal appeal made by Smith and no doubt a few were affected by a monetary consideration.

Wisconsin Wisconsin's colored population is not large. Figures from those precincts having negro votes in fairly large number indicate no defection as compared with the election of four years ago. Wisconsin's negro vote has been and still is largely Republican.

Chart A3.7. Comments on Female Voting from the Republican Survey

Chicago It is estimated here that 65 percent of the women voted the Republican ticket; and that we received many votes from Democratic women— possibly 25 percent; and that their reasons for affiliating themselves with the Republican party this time was on account of both the religious and prohibition issues.

Cincinnati The majority of women were for Hoover and the increase in voting from Cincinnati was largely represented by the registration and voting of women voters. The women were for Hoover because he was dry, because he represented prosperity and better living conditions to them, and because of his work in the food relief problem. The women were original Hoover boosters. A part of the women were for Hoover because they were opposed to Governor Smith, to Tammany Hall and to the wet platform, and a small majority we believe, were for Hoover because they admired Mrs. Hoover and thought that she would make a fitting "First Lady of the Land" and were opposed to the Smith's because of their supposed lack of cultural attainments.

Cleveland The women, except Catholic women, were very definitely aligned with the Republicans. The increase in the womens' vote was approximately 15 percent. We obtained the vote of perhaps 5 percent of normally Democratic women. Religion was the cause.

Connecticut   The work of the women contributed largely to the success of the campaign. . . . I think this was for two reasons, the wet and dry issue and the feeling that the Democratic candidate and his family did not represent a proper class to occupy the White House. In addition to this the Republican candidate was very strong with them.

Indiana   The increase in the women vote this year totaled 153,000 while the men vote was substantially the same as in 1924 and also in 1920.

The support of women was almost exclusively due to the wet and dry issue though of course there was to some degree a support of our candidate because of his policies as well as the dislike for the Democratic candidate and his policies.

Los Angeles   It is my belief that the women's vote almost neutralized the loss among the Republican men on the wet issue. I believe that the Democratic women stepped aside from their party affiliation primarily because of the personality of the candidate, strengthened in their views by their fears of the personality and policies of the Democratic candidate.

Maryland   We gained very decidedly by the women's vote. Probably 50,000 more women voted than in 1924. We got probably from 15 to 20 percent of the Democratic women. They supported our candidate for two reasons: Dislike of the opposition candidate and like for a humanitarian, like Hoover.

Massachusetts   Some normally Democratic women voted Republican this year—perhaps 5 percent. This was on the prohibition issue partly and partly on the particular appeal that Mr. Hoover makes to the women voters.

Among the so-called intelligent people, normally Republican, a great many husbands voted for Smith on the prohibition issue and their wives for Hoover.

The vote of women who were independent in politics was very largely Republican. This means such groups as the League of Women Voters, Womens' College Alumni Vote, etc.

Missouri (A)   More women voted with us than heretofore.

Missouri (B)   A very large percentage of the women voted for Hoover. Innumerable instances have been called to our attention where the husband of the family would be strongly supporting Smith while his wife supported Hoover with equal vigor. There was a large percentage of Democratic women who voted for Hoover. It would be very difficult to estimate the percentage. Most of the Democratic women who voted for Hoover did so on grounds of prohibition. A similar number did it on the ground of their hostility to Tammany Hall. And a very large percentage of them did it because of their strong admiration and devotion to Secretary Hoover.

We think the percentage of votes influenced on religious grounds was about a stand off in the two parties; the Protestant vote, however, being much larger in the state than the Catholic vote, Mr. Hoover received considerable advantage in the break.

New Hampshire We obtained for our Presidential ticket from women normally Democratic five percent, which was due to their confidence in the Republican candidate, inspired by his several years of activity, to their positive views in favor of prohibition, and to a slight extent upon the religious issue.

New Jersey (A) The women substantially aligned themselves with the Republican Party. . . . They were for Hoover first, last and all the time. I should say that we secured at least 30 percent of the normally Democratic women. Their reasons for stepping outside their party voting for Hoover were their belief in him from War times and his position on the liquor question as well as his general policies. I also believe that the Democratic women came over largely because of a dislike for the Democratic candidate and his policies.

New Jersey (B) We made a gain of over 30 percent to 40 percent in the women's vote. Women were with us to a very large degree. Many Democratic women voted for Hoover. Women who never voted before could not support Smith, some because of his stand on prohibition and some for other reasons.

New Jersey (C) It is estimated that about 100,000 more women voted in 1928 than in 1924. Most new voters among women voted the Republican ticket.

Ohio The women were with us approximately 65 percent. However, there was approximately 15 percent increase in the women's vote over 1924. The reason for women stepping outside of their Democratic Party was a combination of all circumstances—positive support of our candidate and his policies, prohibition and religion.

Oregon I should say that the increased registration was very marked among the women voters. While the women of our state held Mr. Hoover in very high regard, I think this applied also to the men. The personality of Governor Smith and his religious and wet and Tammany affiliations had a marked effect on the voters of the state.

Rhode Island It is apparent that the Catholic women voted for Smith and the Protestants came out strongly for Hoover. I do know that our women vote was large and also influenced to a great extent by the religious question.

Chart A3.8. Comments on First-Time Voters from the Republican Survey

Chicago The reports are so conflicting on the question of first voters that it would be quite hard to arrive at any percentage.

Cincinnati The first voters as represented by the college group were in a great majority for Hoover, because Hoover was a college man and Smith was not. Hoover also appealed to that group because of his ability and Smith did not appeal to them because of his associations with Tammany Hall and professional politics. The other first voters as nearly as we could discover lined up in the main with their parents.

Cleveland   A great effort was made to have the first voters align themselves with the Republican party, and I am under the impression that the Republicans secured a major portion of that vote.

Connecticut   I feel that the first voters divided along the lines of the political sentiment in their respective communities. For instance, in the large cities and more populous centers the Democrats gained, while through the rural communities where a large Republican vote is found, they were about two to one Republican.

Indiana   In the broad sense of first voters being all persons voting for the first time regardless of their age, then it is certain that the Republicans obtained a very larger percentage of such votes than did the Democrats. This is true largely that women who had never voted before voted for Mr. Hoover.

Confining first voters to those men and women who have just had their 21st birthday, it would seem fair to say that having better local organization than the Democrats that we got the best part of these votes, but of course there is no way of proving such a claim.

Los Angeles   It is my feeling that fully 60 percent of the first voters aligned themselves with the Chief.

Maryland   I think we had a considerable advantage of the first voters alignment.

Massachusetts   Our first voters were made up partly of those who had just reached 21 and partly of older people who had not heretofore registered. In regard to the older people, I believe that the majority of those registered were Democrats. . . .

The new young voters, of course, generally followed their parents but I had a number of reports to the effect that young voters whose parents were Republican were going to vote Democrat practically entirely on the prohibition issue. I also think that Governor Smith's free and easy style had an especial appeal to the younger element.

Missouri (A)   First voters were about fifty-fifty. We received what we were entitled to and the Democrats received what they were entitled to except where the religious issue entered.

Missouri (B)   It appears that a very large percentage of the first voters aligned themselves with Hoover.

New Hampshire   The relative percentage of the party registrations were fairly equal.

New Jersey (A)   My observation is that the first voters aligned themselves largely with the Republican party. These young men and women were brought up on Hoover. They knew Hoover during the War when his work for food conservation was saving the world.

New Jersey (B)   The first voters generally were with us, especially the older group of first voters.

New Jersey (C)   First voters it is estimated were divided one-third for Smith and two-thirds for Hoover.

Ohio   The first voters aligned themselves largely with our side.

Oregon   First voters aligned themselves in about the same proportion to registration.

Rhode Island   It is my opinion that the first voters aligned themselves exactly in accordance with the above (the behavior of previous voters).

Wisconsin   We believe that 66 percent of the first voters were for Hoover.

Appendix 4

Sources of the Statistical Data

Statistic	Source
Population, 1920	U.S. Department of Commerce, Bureau of the Census, *Fourteenth Census of the United States, Population, 1920*, Vol. III, Table 9.
Population, 1930* Females* Foreign-born* Native-born, foreign parent* Negroes* Urban residents* Rural farm residents*	U.S. Department of Commerce, Bureau of the Census, *Fifteenth Census of the United States, Population, 1930*, Vol. III, Table 13.
Foreign-born, by country of origin*	Ibid., Table 18.
Nonfarm families, 1930 Nonfarm owner families Median home valuations (nonfarm) Median rental costs (nonfarm)	U.S. Department of Commerce, Bureau of the Census, *Fifteenth Census of the United States, Families, 1930*, Vol. VI, Table 19.
Farm families, 1930 Farm families owning homes Median home valuations (farms)	Ibid., Table 20. The housing values variable used in this study is the mean (weighted according to number of families)
Median rental costs (farm) Families reporting radios (farm and nonfarm)	Nonfarm median home valuations, nonfarm median rental costs, farm median home valuations and rental costs, transformed into common units by multiplying weekly rents by 100.

*These statistics were obtained from the Inter-University Consortium for Political Research, Ann Arbor, Michigan. Unless otherwise indicated, all other statistics were collected and computerized by the author.

Statistic	*Source*
Church members, 1926 Catholic church members Jewish church members	U.S. Department of Commerce, Bureau of the Census, *Religious Bodies, 1926*, Vol. I, Table 32.
Church members, 1936 Catholic church members Jewish church members	U.S. Department of Commerce, Bureau of the Census, *Religious Bodies, 1936*, Vol. I, Table 32. Statistics for 1928 were obtained by a linear interpolation of the statistics for 1926 and 1936.
Retail sales, 1929	U.S. Department of Commerce, Bureau of the Census, *Fifteenth Census of the United States, Distribution, 1930*, Vol. I, Retail Distribution, Table 13. For 1939 statistics, the Magazine Marketing Service determined the number of retail purchases in each country of the nation. The retail purchases variable used in this study was obtained by multiplying retail sales in 1929 by the ratio of retail purchases to retail sales in 1939. For an analysis of the Magazine Marketing Service, *M. M. S. County Buying Power Index* (New York, 1942), pp. 1–50. Estimates of retail purchases were used in preference to reports of retail sales because they better indicate the economic status of a county's residents. Statistics for retail sales will overestimate the economic status of individuals in counties that tend to attract buyers from other counties and underestimate the status of individuals in counties that tend to lose buyers to other counties.
High school graduates, 1940*	U.S. Department of Commerce, Bureau of the Census, *Sixteenth Census of the United States, Population, 1940*, Table 21.
Taxpayers, 1928	U.S. Treasury Department, Internal Revenue Service, *Individual Income Tax Returns for 1928* (Washington, D.C., 1930). A county's adult population was used as the base of its percentage of taxpayers.
Telephone owners, 1930	Unpublished data obtained from American Telephone and Telegraph Co., New York, N.Y.

Statistic	*Source*
Presidential election returns, 1916, 1920	Edgar Eugene Robinson, *The Presidential Vote, 1896–1932* (Stanford, Calif., 1932).
Presidential election returns, 1924–40*	Inter-University Consortium for Political Research.
Primary election statistics, 1928–40	Illinois, Secretary of State, *The Illinois Blue Book* (Springfield, 1929–41). Iowa, *Official Register* (Des Moines, 1929–41). Michigan, Secretary of State, *Michigan Official Directory and Legislative Manual* (Lansing, 1929–41). Missouri, Secretary of State, *Official Manual* (Jefferson City, 1929–41). New Jersey, *Manual of the Legislature of New Jersey* (Trenton, 1929–41). Pennsylvania, *Pennsylvania Manual* (Harrisburg, 1929–41). South Dakota, *South Dakota Legislative Manual* (Pierre, 1929–41). Vermont, Secretary of State, *Vermont Legislative Directory* (Montpelier, 1929–41). Statistics were also obtained from newspapers and the unpublished records of state governments.
Returns for state-level referenda on prohibition	Illinois, *Blue Book, 1927*, p. 903. Missouri, *Official Manual*, pp. 294–95. New York, Secretary of State, *Legislative Manual* (Albany, 1928), pp. 889–90. Wisconsin, *The Wisconsin Blue Book* (Madison, 1929), p. 873. Statistics for California and Colorado were obtained from the unpublished records of the state governments.
Party registration, 1926–40	California Secretary of State, *Statement of the Vote* (Sacramento, 1926–40). Commonwealth of Pennsylvania, *The Pennsylvania Manual* (Harrisburg, 1927–41). New York Secretary of State, *Manual for the Use of the Legislature* (Albany, 1927–41). State of Oregon, *The Oregon Blue Book* (Portland, 1927–41). West Virginia Clerk of the Senate, *Legislative Handbook and Manual* (Charleston, 1928–40).

Notes

Chapter 1

1. *New York Times*, 8 Nov. 1928, p. 1.

2. Ibid., pp. 1, 8. Allan J. Cigler and Russell Getter, "Conflict Reduction in the Post-Election Period," pp. 363–76, point to the lack of study on efforts to resolve conflicts after an election.

3. For a sampling of the scholarly literature on Herbert Hoover, see David Burner, *Herbert Hoover*; Joan Hoff Wilson, *Herbert Hoover*; Elliot A. Rosen, *Hoover, Roosevelt and the Brains Trust*; Harris G. Warren, *Herbert Hoover and the Great Depression*; Albert U. Romasco, *The Poverty of Abundance*; Carl N. Degler, "The Ordeal of Herbert Hoover," pp. 563–83; Joseph S. Davis, "Herbert Hoover, 1874–1964, Another Appraisal," pp. 295–318; Craig Lloyd, *Aggressive Introvert*; Martin L. Fausold and George T. Mazuzan, eds., *The Hoover Presidency*; J. Joseph Huthmacher and Warren I. Sussman, eds., *Herbert Hoover and the Crisis of American Capitalism*; Ellis W. Hawley, "Herbert Hoover, the Commerce Secretariat and the Vision of an 'Associative State,' 1921–1928," pp. 116–40; Gary Dean Best, *The Politics of American Individualism*; Edgar Eugene Robinson and Vaughn Davis Bornet, *Herbert Hoover*.

4. Herbert Hoover, *American Individualism*, p. 32.

5. Ibid., p. 35.

6. Herbert Hoover, *The New Day*, pp. 155–56.

7. E. N. Carpenter to Henry P. Fletcher, 14 Sept. 1928, Box 14, Henry P. Fletcher Papers; Brice Clagget to William Gibbs McAdoo, 4 Oct. 1928, Box 340, William Gibbs McAdoo Papers; Henry F. Pringle, "Hubert Work, MD," *Outlook* (5 Sept. 1928), p. 724.

8. The absence of personal papers has meant that the serious literature on Al Smith is extremely thin. See, for example, Oscar Handlin, *Al Smith and His America*; Matthew Josephson and Hannah Josephson, *Hero of the Cities*; Richard O'Connor, *The First Hurrah*; David R. Colburn, "Governor Alfred E. Smith and Penal Reform," pp. 315–27; Paula Eldot, "Alfred E. Smith, Reforming Governor,"; Martin I. Feldman, "An Abstract of the Political Thought of Alfred E. Smith"; Donn Charles Neal, "The World beyond the Hudson."

9. Quoted in Paul A. Carter, *Another Part of the Twenties*, pp. 184–85. Although this book is a scattered collection of insights rather than a sustained analysis of themes, it modifies some of the views expressed in Carter's earlier work on Al Smith and the 1920s. For efforts to synthesize Victorian culture in America and describe its critics in the 1920s, see, respectively, Daniel Walker

Howe, "American Victorianism as a Culture," pp. 507–32; Stanley Coben, "The Assault on Victorianism in the Twentieth Century," pp. 604–25.

    10. David Burner, *The Politics of Provincialism*, pp. 189–90.

    11. Alfred E. Smith, *The Campaign Addresses of Governor Alfred E. Smith*, p. 236.

Chapter 2

    1. Samuel Lubell, *The Future of American Politics*; William E. Leuchtenburg, *The Perils of Prosperity, 1914–32*, Paul A. Carter, "The Campaign of 1928 Re-examined," pp. 263–72; David Burner, *The Politics of Provincialism*. This interpretation also appears in recent dissertations dealing with the election, for example, Leah Marcile Taylor, "Democratic Presidential Politics," p. vii; John Sword Hunter Smith, "Al Smith and the 1928 Campaign in Idaho, Nevada, Utah, and Wyoming," pp. 3–4.

    2. Walter Lippmann, *Men of Destiny*, p. 8.

    3. Lee Benson, *The Concept of Jacksonian Democracy*; Paul Kleppner, *The Cross of Culture*; Richard J. Jensen, *The Winning of the Midwest*; Ronald P. Formisano, *The Birth of Mass Political Parties*; John M. Allswang, *A House for All Peoples*.

    4. James E. Wright, "The Ethnocultural Model of Voting," p. 36. For methodological critiques of "ethnocultural" history, see J. Morgan Kousser, "The 'New Political History,'" pp. 1–14; Allan J. Lichtman and Laura I. Langbein, "Regression vs. Homogeneous Units," pp. 180–83.

    5. Richard L. McCormick, "Ethnocultural Interpretations of Nineteenth Century American Voting Behavior," pp. 352, 358–71.

    6. Burner, *Politics*, pp. 94–95.

    7. Lubell, *Future*, p. 36.

    8. V. O. Key, Jr., "A Theory of Critical Elections," p. 4.

    9. Angus Campbell, Philip E. Converse, Warren E. Miller, and Donald E. Stokes, *The American Voter*, pp. 531–35; Gerald M. Pomper, "Classification of Presidential Elections," pp. 535–66; Walter Dean Burnham, *Critical Elections and the Mainsprings of American Politics*.

    10. Campbell et al., *American Voter*, pp. 534–35; Duncan MacRae, Jr., and James A. Meldrum, "Critical Elections in Illinois," p. 681; Charles Sellers, "The Equilibrium Cycle in Two-Party Politics," p. 23; John L. Shover, "The Emergence of a Two-Party System in Republican Philadelphia, 1924–1936," pp. 1000–1002.

    11. Bernard Sternsher, "The Emergence of the New Deal System," pp. 142–43.

    12. For examples of pluralist scholarship, see: David B. Truman, *The Governmental Process*; Edward Shils, *The Torment of Secrecy*; Daniel Bell, *The End of Ideology*; Seymour Martin Lipset, *Political Man*; Robert A. Dahl, *Who Governs?*; Gabriel A. Almond and G. Bingham Powell, Jr., *Comparative Politics*. For examples of critical commentary, see: Henry S. Kariel, *The Decline of*

American Pluralism; Charles A. McCoy, ed., *Apolitical Politics*; Theodore Lowi, *The End of Liberalism*; William E. Connolly, *The Bias of Pluralism*; Michael Paul Rogin, *The Intellectuals and McCarthy*.

13. Richard Hofstadter, *The Age of Reform*; Daniel J. Boorstin, *The Americans*; Lubell, *Future*.

14. John Higham, "The Cult of the 'American Consensus,'" p. 100.

15. Gabriel Kolko, *The Triumph of Conservatism*; William Appleman Williams, *The Tragedy of American Diplomacy*.

16. Leuchtenburg, *Perils*, p. 240.

17. Carter, "Campaign of 1928," p. 272.

18. Burner, *Politics*, pp. 179–215. For similar arguments, see Kent Schofield, "The Public Image of Herbert Hoover in the 1928 Campaign," pp. 292–93; Taylor, "Democratic Presidential Politics," p. 282; Smith, "Al Smith," pp. 77–78, 213.

19. Pluralists rely upon a distinction between competition and conflict. Competition is an orderly process consistent with well-established rules of the game. Conflict, on the other hand, is characterized by a disregard for established rules and procedures.

20. For further explication of this argument, see Rogin, *Intellectuals*, pp. 80–81.

21. Burnham, *Critical Elections*, pp. 191–92. James F. Ward, "Toward a Sixth Party System?" pp. 385–413, is a provocative critique of Burnham's work.

22. Benjamin Ginsberg, "Elections and Public Policy," p. 49. For a sampling of the recent literature on critical election theory and policy choice, see: Thomas P. Jahnige, "Critical Elections and Social Change," pp. 465–500; Benjamin Ginsberg, "Critical Elections and the Substance of Party Conflict, 1844–1968," pp. 603–25; Richard W. Boyd, "Popular Control of Public Policy," pp. 429–49; Richard Furston, "The Supreme Court and Critical Elections," pp. 795–811; Carl D. Tubbesing, "Predicting the Present," pp. 478–503; Barbara Deckard Sinclair, "Party Realignment and the Transformation of the Political Agenda," pp. 940–53, and "The Policy Consequences of Party Realignment," pp. 83–105.

23. William F. Ogburn and Nell Snow Talbot, "A Measurement of the Factors in the Presidential Election of 1928," p. 178.

24. Ruth C. Silva, *Rum, Religion, and Votes*, p. 43.

25. Inclusion of counties from the former Confederate South would have greatly expanded the size of the sample without commensurate benefit. With the exception of 1928, there was very little variation in the voting of southern counties from 1916 to 1940, yet the sources of these aberrations could not be measured reliably. The formerly Confederate South was overwhelmingly Protestant and native stock, with very little variation from county to county in the values of religious and ethnic variables. Moreover, states of the Old South did not conduct referenda on prohibition during the 1920s. The unique political patterns of the region merit separate study by procedures adapted to its demographic profile.

26. These arguments are thoroughly developed in the following sources: Hubert M. Blalock, Jr., *Causal Inferences in Non-Experimental Research*, pp. 102–7, and "Causal Inferences," pp. 130–36; John W. Tukey, "Causation, Regression and Path Analysis"; Allan J. Lichtman, "Correlation, Regression, and the Ecological Fallacy," pp. 418–20; Laura Irwin Langbein and Allan J. Lichtman, *Ecological Inference*, pp. 33–38. Langbein and Lichtman note that these problems of grouping distort not only correlation coefficients, but all "standardized measures like correlation coefficients and beta weights" (p. 33).

27. Hubert M. Blalock, Jr., *Social Statistics*, pp. 361–506, is an excellent introduction to regression analysis. For more advanced work there is no substitute for consulting the econometrics literature. Edward J. Kane, *Economic Statistics and Econometrics*, can be mastered without mathematical training. Jan Kmenta, *Elements of Econometrics*, and John Johnston, *Econometric Methods*, are more detailed, demanding texts.

28. For a guide to the analysis of residuals, see Norman R. Draper and H. Smith, *Applied Regression Analysis*, pp. 86–103.

29. James M. Sakoda, Burton H. Cohen, and Geoffrey Beall, "Test of Significance for a Series of Statistical Tests," pp. 172–75. Given, however, that the results tested in the study are not independent of one another, the problem of multiple tests is less severe than their analysis would indicate. Moreover, the decision rules outlined in the text are based on two-tailed tests in which the direction of departure from zero is not specified. For one-tailed tests, in which direction is specified, the level of statistical significance is lowered by one-half for a given decision rule.

30. David Gold, "Significance Tests and Substantive Significance," p. 46.

31. This is the standard correction for heteroscedasticity when studying aggregate units of varying population.

32. Lichtman, "Correlation, Regression," pp. 430–31; Langbein and Lichtman, *Ecological Inference*, pp. 58–59; Leo Meltzer, "Comparing Relationships of Individual and Average Variables to Individual Response," pp. 117–23; Robert D. Putnam, "Political Attitudes and the Local Community," pp. 640–54; Tapani Valkonen, "Individual and Structural Effects," pp. 53–68; C. Neal Tate, "Individual and Context Variables in British Voting Behavior," pp. 1656–62.

33. Political File, 1928, Alben W. Barkley Papers.

34. Copies of the questionnaire and the responses received are filed in Presidential Campaign, Box 89, Herbert Hoover Papers.

35. The responses to Roosevelt's circular letter are briefly summarized in the *National Political Digest, 1928*. The actual letters are filed according to their state of origin in Before Convention, Democratic National Campaign Committee Correspondence, 1928–33. For an example of a study using this information, see Earland I. Carlson, "Franklin D. Roosevelt's Post-Mortem of the 1928 Election," pp. 298–308.

36. Richard J. Bernstein, *The Restructuring of Social and Political Theory*, p. 235.

Chapter 3

1. George W. Norris to John F. Cordeal, 13 Nov. 1928, Tray 1, Box 5, George W. Norris Papers.

2. Robert Moats Miller, *American Protestantism and Social Issues, 1919–1939*, p. 51.

3. Paul A. Carter, "The Campaign of 1928 Re-examined," p. 272.

4. Leo A. Goodman, "Some Alternatives to Ecological Correlation," pp. 622–25. To illustrate Goodman's procedure, consider the problem of estimating the proportion of Catholics voting Democratic in the presidential election of 1928. Assume that the regression equation takes the form $Y = a + b_1 X_1 + \ldots + b_k X_k$, where X_1 is the proportion of Catholics in a county. In this case, the intercept a of the equation represents the proportion of non-Catholics voting Democratic when the proportion of Catholics in a county and all other independent variables are set at zero. The regression coefficient b_1 represents the independent effect of religion on voting; its value is the difference between the proportion of Catholics and non-Catholics voting Democratic when controlling for the influence of included variables. To estimate the proportion of Catholics voting Democratic in a particular county, the investigator adds a, b, and $b_2 X_2$ through $b_k X_k$. A weighted sum of these proportions for all counties yields an overall estimate of the proportion of Catholics opting for the Democratic candidate. For further discussion of the technique, see Laura Irwin Langbein and Allan J. Lichtman, *Ecological Inference*, pp. 50–58.

5. This technique involves, first, estimating the parameters of the multiplicative model from the log-linear regression equation. Second, the values of the response variables are estimated from the multiplicative equation, using these parameters. The power of this equation to predict variation in the response variable is then compared to the predictive power of the additive equation. For a succinct statement of the technique, see David Seidman, "On Choosing between Linear and Log-Linear Models," pp. 461–66. Walter Dean Burnham and John Sprague, "Additive and Multiplicative Models of the Voting Universe," pp. 471–90, and Glaucio Soares and Robert T. Hamblin, "Socio-Economic Variables and Voting for the Radical Left," pp. 1053–65, also compare the predictive power of additive and multiplicative models to test theories about voter behavior.

6. Milton M. Gordon, *Assimilation in American Life*, pp. 216–20.

7. Republican National Committee, "Summary Report on the 1928 Campaign," Pre-Presidential, Box 89, Hoover Papers. For additional information on the reaction of German Lutherans to Smith's candidacy, see Douglas C. Strange, "Al Smith and the Republican Party at Prayer," pp. 347–64; Richard L. Kolbe, "Culture, Political Parties and Voting Behavior," p. 264.

8. David Burner, *The Politics of Provincialism*, pp. 220–21.

9. Gordon W. Allport, "The Composition of Political Attitudes," pp. 230–38; Harwood L. Childs, "Ranking Motives in Voting," pp. 59–66. Childs

does not indicate when he conducted his survey, but undoubtedly his canvass was completed several years prior to the publication date of 1935.

10. Hadley Cantril and Mildred Strunk, eds., *Public Opinion*, p. 95.

11. W. H. O'Keefe to Franklin D. Roosevelt, 14 Jan. 1929, Box 717, Democratic National Campaign Committee Correspondence, 1928–33.

12. These reports also offer an opportunity to assess the accuracy of the predictions made by the Kentucky chairmen. For sixty-eight of the seventy-three reports, the county of origin can be identified and estimated vote totals can be compared with the actual vote cast for Hoover and Smith. Sixty-six of the sixty-eight chairmen underestimated the Republican vote; forty-eight overestimated the Democratic vote. Underestimations of the Republican tally ranged from 2 to 58 percent of the actual vote cast with a mean of 21.6 percent and a median of 21.4 percent. The three overestimations of the Republican vote were 1, 2, and 14 percent. Overestimations of the Democratic vote ranged from .3 to 205 percent with a mean of 34.2 percent and a median of 23.0 percent. The disparity between the mean and median indicates skewness to the high side of the distribution. Underestimations of the Democratic vote ranged from .1 to 24 percent with a mean of 7.5 percent and a median of 6.5 percent. For all estimates of both Republican and Democratic totals, the mean error in the chairmen's estimations was 24.1 percent (computed from the absolute values of both over and underestimations).

13. William Gibbs McAdoo to J. H. O'Neil, 10 Oct. 1928, Box 230, William Gibbs McAdoo Papers; Carter, "Campaign of 1928," p. 272, and Paul A. Carter, "The Other Catholic Candidate," pp. 1–8. On the Walsh candidacy, see also Peter L. Peterson, "Stopping Al Smith," pp. 439–54.

14. Thomas J. Walsh to R. E. Blackwell, 21 July 1932, Box 382, Thomas J. Walsh Papers.

15. The letters of Norris of Nebraska provide considerable insight into the intensity of religious conflict during the campaign: Tray 1, Norris Papers. See also Michael Williams, *The Shadow of the Pope*; Edmund A. Moore, *A Catholic Runs for President*; Lawrence H. Fuchs, "The Election of 1928," pp. 2585, 2609; James H. Smylie, "The Roman Catholic Church, the State and Al Smith," pp. 321, 327–41.

16. For examples of how major Catholic media dealt with the religious issue in 1928, see "Religion in the Campaign," *America*, 20 Oct. 1928, p. 29; "Politics and Bigotry," *America*, 3 Nov. 1928, p. 77; "Appalled by the Extent of Bigotry in Campaign," *Catholic News*, 27 Oct. 1928, p. 5.

17. *Fellowship Forum*, 6 Oct. 1928, p. 2; 27 Oct. 1928, p. 5.

18. P. T. Vaughan to Franklin D. Roosevelt, 17 Dec. 1928, Box 298, Democratic National Campaign Committee Correspondence, 1928–33; Franklin D. Roosevelt to Nicholas Roosevelt, 28 Jan. 1929, in Elliot Roosevelt, *Franklin D. Roosevelt*, 1:28.

19. Victor Short, "The Documents of Intolerance," *Commonweal*, 7 Oct. 1928, p. 14.

20. *New York Times*, 7 Sept. 1928, p. 22. Moore, *A Catholic*, pp. 90–91. On

behalf of the Democratic National Committee, former presidential candidate John W. Davis sought to persuade Postmaster General Harry S. New to prohibit the mailing of anti-Catholic propaganda (John W. Davis to Harry S. New, 4 Oct. 1928, Box 23, John W. Davis Papers; Harry S. New to John W. Davis, 6 Oct. 1928, Box 23, Davis Papers).

21. Michael Williams, "Plain Facts for Americans," *Commonweal*, 31 Oct. 1928, p. 564. Cordell Hull to Wirt Courtney, 19 Sept. 1928, Box 22, Cordell Hull Papers; T. M. Hodgman to Thomas J. Walsh, 5 Nov. 1928, Box 377, Walsh Papers; Alfred M. Landon, Personal Interview; *New York Times*, 29 Oct. 1928.

22. Quoted in *New York Times*, 7 Sept. 1928, p. 2. For detailed studies of anti-Catholic arguments in newspapers and periodicals, see Elias Macropoulos, "The Treatment with Reference to the Roman Catholic Issue of Democratic Candidates in the Presidential Election of 1928 and 1960 by Selected Periodicals"; Donald F. Heath, "The Presidential Campaign of 1928."

23. *Los Angeles Times*, 1 Oct. 1928, p. 3. Culbertson's argument may have been strangely prophetic. If elected in 1928, Smith probably would not have been much more successful than Hoover in combating the depression, and surely many Americans would have blamed the president's subservience to the Catholic church for that disaster.

24. Charles C. Marshall, *The Roman Catholic Church in the Modern State*; Winfred Ernest Garrison, *Catholicism and the American Mind*; for the original exchange of letters, see Charles C. Marshall, "An Open Letter to the Honorable Alfred E. Smith," *Atlantic Monthly* 139 (April 1927): 540–49; Alfred E. Smith, "Catholic and Patriot: Governor Smith Replies," ibid. (May 1927): 721–28.

25. "The Religious Issues," *Christian Century*, 18 Oct. 1928, p. 1252.

26. Herbert Hoover, *The New Day*, p. 36.

27. Press Conference, 21 Sept. 1928, Pre-Presidential, Box 961, Hoover Papers.

28. Joan Hoff Wilson, *Herbert Hoover*, p. 15.

29. Henry J. Allen to Mark L. Requa, 22 Sept. 1928, Box C134, Henry J. Allen Papers; Henry J. Allen, Press Release, 21 Aug. 1928, Pre-Presidential, Box 1, Hoover Papers; William A. White to Herbert Hoover, no date, Pre-Presidential, Box 25, Hoover Papers; William A. White to Henry J. Allen, 13 Sept. 1928, Box C12, Allen Papers.

30. Hiram Johnson to Harold Ickes, 29 Sept. 1928, Box 33, Harold L. Ickes Papers.

31. Mabel W. Willebrandt to Hubert Work, 27 Sept. 1928, Pre-Presidential, Box 26, Hoover Papers.

32. Alfred M. Landon, Personal Interview.

33. John Sword Hunter Smith, "Al Smith and the 1928 Campaign in Idaho, Nevada, Utah, and Wyoming," pp. 95–96.

34. *Los Angeles Times*, 2 Nov. 1928, p. 1.

35. Merrill A. Symonds, "George Higgins Moses of New Hampshire," pp. 268–69.

36. C. M. Haskell to Franklin D. Roosevelt, 21 Dec. 1928, Before Convention, Box 621, Democratic National Campaign Committee Correspondence, 1928–33.

37. Mrs. C. M. Caldwell to Mrs. C. W. Harris, 24 Sept. 1928, Pre-Presidential, Box 5, Hoover Papers; Henry J. Allen to George Ackerson, 26 Sept. 1928, Pre-Presidential, Box 1, Hoover Papers; *Los Angeles Times*, 2 Oct. 1928, p. 7.

38. Allen to Ackerson, 26 Sept. 1928.

39. Diary of Breckinridge Long, Box 4, Breckinridge Long Papers.

40. Herbert Henry Lehman, The reminiscences of Herbert Henry Lehman, p. 228, Columbia University Oral History Collection; see also Joseph M. Proskauer, The reminiscences of Joseph M. Proskauer, p. 130, ibid.

41. Alfred E. Smith, *The Campaign Addresses of Governor Alfred E. Smith*, p. 56. For a detailed analysis of this famous speech, see Elton H. Wallace, "Alfred E. Smith, the Religious Issue."

42. Henry Van Dyke, *In Defense of Religious Liberty*.

43. See, for example, John W. Davis, *Religion and Politics*; Nellie Tayloe Ross, *Tolerance and Governor Smith*; Harry B. Hawes, *Election of Smith Would End Intolerance*.

44. Examples include Bishops Warren A. Candler and Collins Denny of the Methodist Episcopal church, South; S. Parkes Cadman, president of the Federal Council of Churches of Christ in America; Dan S. Brummitt, a prominent leader of the Methodist Episcopal church, North; Bishop John Palmerston Anderson of the Protestant Episcopal church; and several ad hoc committees of Protestant clergymen and divinity students.

45. John J. Raskob to Michael Williams, 22 Sept., 4 and 16 Oct. 1928, File 457, John J. Raskob Papers.

46. Lehman, Reminiscences, p. 228.

47. Radio address, Station WTFF, published in *Fellowship Forum*, 15 Sept. 1928, p. 7; ibid., 8 Sept. 1928, p. 6. See also Lydia Hansen, "Tolerance," *Kourier Magazine* 4 (August 1928): 30–33.

48. For an illuminating discussion of the issues raised by the nominations of a Catholic and of a Quaker, see the exchanges of letters between Walter Lippman and Charles C. Marshall in Box 20, Folder 794, Walter Lippman Papers.

49. Gordon W. Allport, *The Nature of Prejudice*, p. 226.

50. Charles H. Anderson, *White Protestant American*.

51. Respondents to both the survey of the Republican National Committee and Franklin D. Roosevelt's circular letters comment on the anti-Catholicism of Protestant immigrant groups.

52. Bernhard E. Olson, *Faith and Prejudice*, pp. 28–29, 385–422.

53. John Higham, *Strangers in the Land*.

54. Social scientists have debated at length the interactions between attitudes and behavior. For a sampling of the vast literature, see: Allport, *Nature of Prejudice*, pp. 463–80; Allen Liska, ed., *The Impact of Attitudes on*

Behavior; Walter Mischel, *Personality and Assessment*; Philip Zimbardo and Ebbe E. Ebbesen, *Influencing Attitudes and Changing Behavior*; Alan C. Acock and Melvin L. DeFleur, "A Configurational Approach to Contingent Consistency in the Attitude-Behavior Relationship," pp. 714–26; Richard D. Alba, "Ethnic Networks and Tolerant Attitudes," pp. 1–16; Irving Crespi, "What Kinds of Attitude Measures Are Predictive of Behavior," pp. 327–34; A. G. Davey, "Attitudes and the Prediction of Social Conduct," pp. 11–22; Norman S. Endler, "The Person versus the Situation," pp. 287–303; Steven Jay Gross and C. Michael Niman, "Attitude-Behavior Consistency," pp. 358–68; Thomas A. Heberlein and J. Stanley Black, "Attitudinal Specificity and the Prediction of Behavior in a Field Setting," pp. 474–79; Stanley H. Jones and Stuart W. Cook, "The Influence of Attitude on Judgments of the Effectiveness of Alternative Social Policies," pp. 762–73; Russell Middleton, "Regional Differences in Prejudice," pp. 94–117; Dennis T. Regan and Russell H. Fazio, "On the Consistency between Attitudes and Behavior," pp. 28–45; Irwin G. Sarason, Ronald E. Smith, and Edward Diener, "Personality Research," pp. 199–204; Mark Snyder and Elizabeth Decker Tanke, "Behavior and Attitude," pp. 501–17; Mark Snyder and William B. Swann, "When Actions Reflect Attitudes," pp. 1034–42; Alan G. Weinstein, "Predicting Behavior from Attitudes," pp. 355–60; Alan W. Wicker, "An Examination of the 'Other Variables' Explanation of Attitude-Behavior Inconsistency," pp. 18–30.

55. Jane W. Ferrar, "The Dimensions of Tolerance," pronounces "the concept of tolerance" to be "in a state of disarray" (p. 63). Ferrar argues for the application of a "multidimensional" model similar to the one suggested here (p. 78).

56. Allport, *Nature of Prejudice*, p. 66. The most familiar explanation for variation in the proclivity to reject out-groups is the psychoanalytic one, stressing the role of ego defense. T. W. Adorno, Else Frenkel-Brunswik, Daniel J. Levinson, and R. Nevitt Sanford, *The Authoritarian Personality*, is the classic statement of this viewpoint. Other explanations emphasize the importance of such factors as educational background, life experience, and social structure. For a sampling of the vast literature on this subject, see: Allport, *Nature of Prejudice*; Milton Rokeach, *The Open and Closed Mind* and *Beliefs, Attitudes, and Values*; Don Stewart and Thomal Hoult, "A Social-Psychological Theory of 'The Authoritarian Personality,'" pp. 274–79; James G. Martin, *The Tolerant Personality*; Donald J. Treiman, "Status Discrepancy and Prejudice," pp. 651–64; George E. Simpson and J. Milton Yinger, *Racial and Cultural Minorities*; John P. Kirscht and Ronald C. Dillehay, *Dimensions of Authoritarianism*; Harold J. Ehrlich, *The Social Psychology of Prejudice*; Christopher Orpen, "Authoritarianism in an 'Authoritarian' Culture," pp. 119–20; John C. Brigham, "Ethnic Stereotypes," pp. 15–38; Harold Sigall and Richard Page, "Current Stereotypes," pp. 247–55; Howard Gabennesch, "Authoritarianism as World View," pp. 857–75; Louis Mezei, "Perceived Social Pressure as an Explanation of Shifts in the Relative Influence of Race and Belief on Prejudice across Social Interactions," pp. 69–81; Jack M. Feldman and Robert J. Hilter-

man, "Stereotype Attribution Revisited," pp. 1177–88; Ferrar, "Dimensions," pp. 63–81.

57. Eugene L. Hartley, *Problems in Prejudice*, p. 99.

58. Higham, *Strangers*, pp. 329, 110–11.

59. T. M. Hodgman to Thomas J. Walsh, 5 Nov. 1928, Box 377, Walsh Papers.

60. For accounts of Catholic-Protestant tension in the early twentieth century, see Higham, *Strangers*, pp. 158–330; Lerond Curry, *Protestant-Catholic Relations in America, World War I through Vatican II*, pp. 1–25; Donn Charles Neal, "The World beyond the Hudson," pp. 244–58.

61. John L. Thomas, *The Catholic Family*, pp. 106ff.; William Michael Halsey, "The Survival of American Innocence," pp. 122–23.

62. David J. O'Brien, *American Catholics and Social Reform*, p. 45.

Chapter 4

1. The simple correlation coefficient (r) between the percentage of Catholics in a county and the percentage of voters opposing prohibition in state-level referenda is +.49.

2. Andrew Sinclair, *Era of Excess*, pp. 23–24; Joseph Gusfield, *Symbolic Crusade*, pp. 222ff. For a mild dissent against this view, see Norman H. Clark, *Deliver Us from Evil*, pp. 186–88.

3. Robert Moats Miller, *American Protestantism and Social Issues, 1919–1939*, p. 51; Ruth C. Silva, *Rum, Religion, and Votes*, p. 43.

4. Republican National Committee, "Summary Report on the 1928 Campaign," Republican National Committee, Pre-Presidential, Box 89, Hoover Papers.

5. Kirk H. Porter and Donald Bruce Johnson, *National Party Platforms, 1840–1964*, pp. 276–88.

6. Democratic National Committee, "Official Report of the Proceedings of the Committee on Platform and Resolutions, Executive Session," Box 149, Key Pittman Papers.

7. Ibid., pp. 67, 69.

8. Democratic National Committee, *Official Report of the Proceedings of the Democratic National Convention of 1928*, p. 185.

9. Democratic National Committee, "Official Report of the Committee on Platform and Resolutions," p. 60.

10. Democratic National Committee, *Official Report of the Democratic National Convention*, pp. 201–4.

11. Democratic National Committee, *Campaign Book of the Democratic Party, Candidates and Issues in 1928*, pp. 188–89; Al Smith's daughter Emily Smith Warner notes in *The Happy Warrior*, pp. 201–2, that Smith spontaneously dispatched this telegram in outraged reaction to the neutral plank on prohibition adopted by the convention. Contrary to this widely accepted view, Ralph Hayes wrote during the convention that Joseph Proskauer,

Walter Lippmann, and Smith had earlier decided on the strategy "that the Governor's views on prohibition be stated in answer to a telegram from Houston after the platform had been adopted and he had been nominated, but before the Convention had closed" (Hayes to John H. Clarke, 28 June 1928, Box 115, Newton D. Baker Papers). Three days earlier, on 25 June, Walter Lippmann had written to Belle Moskowitz that he had "given a lot of thought to the telegram which the Governor proposes to send when he is notified of his nomination." Lippmann noted that "the part dealing with prohibition seems to me fine, and ought not to be changed" (Lippmann to Moskowitz, Box 21, Folder 845, Walter Lippmann Papers).

12. Herbert Hoover, *The New Day*, pp. 29–30.

13. Virginius Dabney, *Dry Messiah*, pp. 178–79.

14. Sinclair, *Era of Excess*, pp. 300, 449.

15. Carter Glass to George Fort Milton, 3 Aug. 1928, Box 339, William Gibbs McAdoo Papers; italics added.

16. Mortimer C. Rhone to Franklin D. Roosevelt, 26 Dec. 1928, Pre-Convention, Box 648, National Democratic Campaign Committee Correspondence, 1928–33; Sam T. Spears to Franklin D. Roosevelt, 3 Dec. 1928, ibid., Box 778; C. A. Lord to Franklin D. Roosevelt, 14 Dec. 1928, ibid., Box 360.

17. Democratic National Committee, *Campaign Book, 1928*, pp. 184–96.

18. Sinclair, *Era of Excess*, p. 64.

19. *Christian Advocate*, 23 July 1928, pp. 1–2; *Congregationalist*, 12 July 1928, pp. 38–39, and 19 July 1928, pp. 68–70; *Presbyterian Magazine* 34 (Oct. 1928): 525–26.

20. Rembert Gilman Smith, *Politics in a Protestant Church*, p. 34.

21. Cushing Strout, *The New Heavens and New Earth*, p. 231; other relevant literature includes: Paul A. Carter, *The Decline and Revival of the Social Gospel*; Donald B. Meyer, *The Protestant Search for Political Realism*, pp. 1–123; Miller, *American Protestantism*; Robert T. Handy, *A Christian America*, pp. 184–207; Martin E. Marty, *Righteous Empire*, pp. 177–220.

22. Ferenc M. Szasz, "The Progressive Clergy and the Kingdom of God," pp. 3–20.

23. Alfred E. Smith, *The Campaign Addresses of Governor Alfred E. Smith*, pp. 13–15.

24. Hoover, *New Day*, pp. 47–62, 149–76.

25. This analysis relies heavily on the insights of Charles Merz, *The Dry Decade*, pp. 228–31. For specific examples of how politicians blurred the prohibition issue, see the following citations from the *New York Times*: 14 Aug. 1928, p. 1; 24 Aug., pp. 4, 6; 7 Sept., pp. 2, 3; 12 Sept., pp. 2, 6; 16 Sept., III:4; 19 Sept., p. 1; 25 Sept., p. 30; 28 Sept., p. 6; 24 Oct., pp. 2, 3; 29 Oct., p. 23; 31 Oct., p. 26. See also James B. Hoey to Royal S. Copeland, 15 Aug. 1928, Box 18, Royal S. Copeland Papers; Samuel L. Wilson, "Is Prohibition a Paramount Issue?" (undated manuscript), Wilson Family Collection; George Akerson to Henry J. Allen, 11 Aug. 1928, Box C2, Henry J. Allen Papers; Thomas W. Lamont to Charles D. Hilles, 16 Oct. 1928, Box 194, Charles D. Hilles Papers.

26. Frank Fabian, "Analyzing the Election Results," *Current History* (Dec. 1928): 370–73.

27. For contrary arguments, see Miller, *American Protestantism*, p. 51; Paul A. Carter, "The Campaign of 1928 Re-examined," p. 266.

28. For an account of how people mask opinion that is not socially acceptable, see Hans Toch, *The Social Psychology of Social Movements*, pp. 20–21.

29. B. E. Haney to Franklin D. Roosevelt, 4 Dec. 1928, Pre-Convention, Box 635, National Democratic Campaign Committee Correspondence, 1928–33.

30. George N. Peek to General Hugh S. Johnson, 4 Oct. 1928, George N. Peek Papers.

31. *New York Times*, 29 Sept. 1928, p. 5.

32. Quoted in *Commonweal* 8 (24 Oct. 1928): 623.

33. Dabney, *Dry Messiah*, pp. 185–86.

34. Quoted in *New York Times*, 24 Sept. 1928, p. 2.

35. Quoted in "Mrs. Willebrandt's Appeal to the Methodists," *Literary Digest* 98 (29 Sept. 1928): 14.

36. *New York Times*, 26 Sept. 1928, p. 2.

37. Presidential Press Conference, 25 Sept. 1928, Pre-Presidential, Box 96, Hoover Papers.

38. Harold Ickes to Hiram Johnson, 6 Sept. 1928, Box 33, Harold Ickes Papers.

39. Key Pittman to Fred W. Johnson, 27 Oct. 1928, Key Pittman to H. H. McPike, 25 Oct. 1928, Box 11, Pittman Papers.

40. Memo to Kirchofer, undated, unsigned, Pre-Presidential, Box 19, Hoover Papers.

Chapter 5

1. Samuel Lubell, *The Future of American Politics*, p. 41. Ruth C. Silva, *Rum, Religion, and Votes*, p. 43. Silva defines "percent foreign stock" as the percentage of individuals in a state who are foreign-born or have a foreign-born parent. William F. Ogburn and Nell Snow Talbot, "A Measurement of Factors in the Presidential Election of 1928," p. 178.

2. Frank Freidel supports the first interpretation. Citing an unpublished study by Robert Friedman of the University of Illinois, Freidel argues that "there is nothing to indicate anti-league Irish and Germans deserted the Democratic party in any greater proportions than the population as a whole" (Frank Freidel, *Franklin D. Roosevelt*, 2:88). For a similar point of view, see R. A. Burchell, "Did the Irish and German Voters Desert the Democrats in 1920?" pp. 153–64. Most scholars at least implicitly support the third interpretation for Germans, Irish, and Italians. See, for example, J. Joseph Huthmacher, *Massachusetts People and Politics, 1919–1933*, pp. 43–47; Wesley M. Bagby, *The Road to Normalcy*, pp. 159–61; Louis L. Gerson, *The Hyphenate in*

Recent American Politics and Diplomacy, pp. 100–108. Despite the presentation of considerable statistical evidence on the behavior of ethnic Americans in the election of 1920, no clear position is taken by either David Burner, *The Politics of Provincialism*, or John M. Allswang, *A House for All Peoples*. See pp. 250–52 for criticism of the methods used by these historians to discover the behavior of ethnic voters.

3. John A. Hawgood, *The Tragedy of German-America*, p. 292; Joseph P. O'Grady, "Introduction" to Joseph P. O'Grady, ed., *The Immigrants' Influence on Wilson's Peace Policies*, pp. 5–29 (see also the essays on individual ethnic groups); Gerson, *Hyphenate*, pp. 59–61, 73–95.

4. Edward George Hartmann, *The Movement to Americanize the Immigrant*, pp. 189–266; John Higham, *Strangers in the Land*, pp. 253–62.

5. For accounts of the Red Raids, see Robert K. Murray, *Red Scare*; William Preston, Jr., *Aliens and Dissenters*, pp. 208–37; Stanley Coben, "A Study in Nativism," pp. 52–75.

6. Hartmann, *Movement*, p. 258.

7. Ray Stannard Baker and William E. Dodds, eds., *The Public Papers of Woodrow Wilson*, 1:319–21, 2:77–79, 368–69, 389, 400.

8. Austin J. App, "The Germans," pp. 39–55; Gerson, *Hyphenate*, pp. 101–2; Carl Wittke, *German-Americans and the World War*, pp. 203–9; Richard O'Connor, *The German-Americans*, pp. 429–33.

9. Gerson, *Hyphenate*, p. 106.

10. Henning Friis, *Scandinavia*, pp. 140–253, 337–41; Charles H. Anderson, *White Protestant American*, pp. 55, 67, 69.

11. Allswang, *A House for All Peoples*, pp. 113–14.

12. Jerome Davis, *The Russian Immigrant*, pp. 163–72.

13. Joseph P. O'Grady, "The Irish," pp. 57–84; William V. Shannon, *The American Irish*, pp. 325–33.

14. William M. Leary, Jr., "Woodrow Wilson, Irish-Americans, and the Election of 1916," p. 57; Edward Cuddy, "Irish-Americans and the 1916 Election," pp. 228–43.

15. John B. Duff, "The Italians," pp. 111–39.

16. Dennis J. McCarthy, "The British," pp. 85–110.

17. O'Connor, *German-Americans*, pp. 408–10; Belle Case La Follette and Fola La Follette, *Robert M. La Follette*, 1:657–66, 2:732–37, 905–84, 1078–79; David P. Thelen, *Robert M. La Follette and the Insurgent Spirit*, pp. 125–54.

18. *New York Times*, 15 Oct. 1924, p. 9.

19. Kenneth Campbell MacKay, *The Progressive Movement of 1924*, pp. 162–70; Russell B. Nye, *Midwestern Progressive Politics*, pp. 339–40; Thelen, *La Follette*, pp. 189–90; Robert K. Murray, *The 103rd Ballot*, pp. 239–40.

20. Norman C. Meier, "Motives in Voting," pp. 199–212.

21. *New York Times*, 25 Oct. 1924, p. 6.

22. La Follette and La Follette, *Robert M. La Follette*, pp. 922–24; Davis, *Russian Immigrant*, pp. 72–73; Thelen, *La Follette*, p. 191.

23. Moses Rischin, *Our Own Kind*, p. 9; George Q. Flynn, *American*

Catholics and the Roosevelt Presidency, 1932–1936, pp. 50–51; Peter H. Odegard, "Catholicism and Elections in the United States," pp. 121–22; Oscar Handlin, *Al Smith and His America*, pp. 83, 84; Shannon, *American Irish*, p. 330; Jerome A. Petitti to Herbert Hoover, 10 Jan. 1929, Pre-Presidential, Box 20, Herbert Hoover Papers; Frank J. Kohout to Herbert Hoover, undated, Pre-Presidential, Box 15, Ernest L. Klein, editorial excerpt, Before Convention, Box 583, Democratic National Campaign Committee Correspondence, 1928–33.

24. Shannon, *American Irish*, p. 330.

25. *New York Times*, 9, 23, 24 Aug. 1924, all on p. 1.

26. Republican National Committee, "Summary Report on the 1928 Campaign," Pre-Presidential, Box 89, Hoover Papers.

27. Constantine Panunzio, "The Foreign-Born and Prohibition," p. 147.

28. Robert A. Divine, *American Immigration Policy, 1924–1952*, pp. 20–25.

29. Kirk H. Porter and Donald Bruce Johnson, *National Party Platforms, 1840–1964*, pp. 276, 289; "Proceedings of the Democratic National Committee, Committee on Platform and Resolutions, Executive Session," p. 55, Box 149, Key Pittman Papers.

30. Alfred E. Smith, *The Campaign Addresses of Governor Alfred E. Smith*, p. 25; Divine, *American Immigration Policy*, pp. 26, 27; Herbert Hoover, *The New Day*, p. 25.

31. In his discussion of the 1928 campaign, Divine incorrectly implies that Smith supported immigration restriction only in "speeches in the South" (Divine, *American Immigration Policy*, p. 41). In fact, Smith's speeches in the following cities included statements favoring immigration restriction: St. Paul, Minnesota (27 September); Nashville, Tennessee (12 October); Louisville, Kentucky (13 October); Newark, New Jersey (31 October); New York, New York (3 November) (Smith, *Campaign Addresses*, pp. 102–3, 147–48, 156, 267, 291).

32. *Governor Smith WRONG on Immigration*. Also see statements by Republican campaigners quoted in the *Los Angeles Times*, 27 Oct. 1928, p. 5, and 28 Oct. 1928, p. 5.

33. Allswang, *A House for All Peoples*, p. 132.

34. See, for example, Burrell Russel to Franklin D. Roosevelt, 8 Dec. 1928, Pre-Presidential, Box 584; George Law Currey to Roosevelt, 10 Dec. 1928, Pre-Presidential, Box 635; Ernest F. Smith to Roosevelt, 17 Dec. 1928, Pre-Presidential, Box 717, National Democratic Campaign Committee Correspondence, 1928–33.

35. William E. Leuchtenburg, *The Perils of Prosperity, 1914–32*, p. 231.

36. Lubell, *Future*, pp. 29–41.

37. "Intolerance," *Interpreter* 8 (Oct. 1928): 6.

38. Maxcy R. Dickson, "The War Comes to All"; Eugene Lyons, *Herbert Hoover*, pp. 122–37.

39. Hill is quoted by the *New York Times*, 6 June 1928, p. 3; Hearst is quoted by Vaughn Davis Bornet, *Labor Politics in a Democratic Republic*, p. 73.

40. "Report of the Division for Foreign Language Publicity and Advertis-

ing of the Republican National Committee," Pre-Presidential, Box 15, Hoover Papers.

41. Peter H. Odegard, "Political Parties and Group Pressures," p. 80.

42. There are few useful works on the foreign-language press. This analysis is based mainly on: Robert E. Park, *The Immigrant Press and Its Control*; Robert E. Park, "The Foreign Language Press and Social Progress," pp. 493–500; Joseph S. Roucek, "The Foreign-Language and Negro Press," pp. 369–83; Yaroslav Chyz, "Number, Distribution and Circulation of the Foreign Language Press in the United States," pp. 290–97.

43. Porter and Johnson, *National Party Platforms*, pp. 250–51.

44. "Proceedings of the Committee on Platform and Resolutions," pp. 13–43.

45. Ibid., pp. 19–20. For Baker's reflections on this aspect of the platform, see Newton Baker to Frank Baker, 11 July 1928, Box 36, Newton D. Baker Papers.

46. Franklin D. Roosevelt to Clark M. Eichelberger, 20 July 1928, Franklin D. Roosevelt Campaign Correspondence, Box 5; Newton D. Baker to Harry M. Ayres, 19 July 1928, Box 32, Baker Papers.

47. O'Connor, *German-Americans*, p. 386.

48. *New York Times*, 10 Oct. 1928, p. 4.

49. Statement by C. W. Sypniewski, censor of the Polish National Alliance, 3 Oct. 1928, Pre-Presidential, Box 10, Hoover Papers.

50. Harold J. Abramson's study of Catholic ethnic groups indicates that the French-Canadians had an especially strong commitment to Catholicism. The strength of the influence on Al Smith's vote of membership in various Catholic nationality groups closely conforms to Abramson's analysis of the intensity of their religious commitment ("Ethnic Diversity within Catholicism," pp. 359–88).

51. Will Herberg, *Protestant, Catholic, Jew*, p. 35.

Chapter 6

1. Samuel Lubell, *The Future of American Politics*, p. 36.

2. Richard Hofstadter, *The Age of Reform*, pp. 298–301; Paul A. Carter, "The Campaign of 1928 Re-examined," pp. 263–72; William E. Leuchtenburg, *The Perils of Prosperity, 1914–32*, pp. 225–40; Andrew Sinclair, *Era of Excess*, pp. 292–306. For other work with a similar point of view, see: Don S. Kirschner, *City and Country*, pp. 50–53; Berton Dulce and Edward J. Richter, *Religion and the Presidency*, pp. 96–97; David Burner, *The Politics of Provincialism*, pp. 215–16, 228–31; Irving Bernstein, *The Lean Years*, pp. 76–80; Carl N. Degler, "American Political Parties and the Rise of the City," pp. 52–56; James H. Shideler, "*Flappers and Philosophers*, and Farmers," pp. 283–99; Leah Marcile Taylor, "Democratic Presidential Politics"; John Sword Hunter Smith, "Al Smith and the 1928 Campaign in Idaho, Nevada, Utah, and Wyoming."

3. These findings on turnout corroborate results reported for a later

period by Alan D. Monroe, "Urbanism and Voter Turnout," pp. 71–78. Monroe notes that "most general treatments either ignore the urban-rural dimension . . . or else repeat the oft-cited but seldom documented generalization that turnout is higher in more urban areas" (p. 71).

4. Burner, *Politics*, p. 215, italics added; Smith, "Al Smith," p. 213, after studying the 1928 campaign in the mountain states, also indicts the governor for failing to transcend his regional image.

5. Table 4.2, Chapter 4.

6. James A. Farley, Personal Interview.

7. Chart A3.7, Appendix 3.

8. For a thorough development of this argument, see Allan J. Lichtman and Valerie French, *Historians and the Living Past*, pp. 44–77.

9. Pitirim Sorokin and Carle C. Zimmerman, *Principles of Rural-Urban Sociology*, pp. 289–90.

10. Ibid., p. 484.

11. Kenneth T. Jackson, *The Ku Klux Klan in the City, 1915–1930*, pp. 233–34.

12. Robert Moats Miller, "The Ku Klux Klan," pp. 215–55. For other work on the Klan, see Charles C. Alexander, *The Ku Klux Klan in the Southwest*; David M. Chalmers, *Hooded Americanism*; Arnold S. Rice, *The Ku Klux Klan in American Politics*; Robert A. Garson, "Political Fundamentalism and Popular Democracy in the 1920's," pp. 219–33.

13. The relative solidarity of ethnic groups in city and country has not been reliably determined. See, for example, Andrew F. Rolle, *The Immigrant Upraised*, pp. 335–36; Samuel Koenig, "Second and Third Generation Americans," p. 481; Michael Parenti, "Ethnic Politics," pp. 267–83; Milton M. Gordon, "Assimilation in America," pp. 24–44.

14. Richard A. Watson, "Religion and Politics in Mid-America," p. 49.

15. For analyses of the image projected by Hoover in the 1928 campaign, see Kent Schofield, "The Public Image of Herbert Hoover in the 1928 Campaign," pp. 278–93, and "The Figure of Herbert Hoover in the 1928 Campaign"; Clair E. Nelson, "The Image of Herbert Hoover as Reflected in the American Press," pp. 20–25.

16. More than forty years of controversy in psychology and sociology suggests that historians should be wary of any facile generalizations (see note 3 for an example) about the effects of urban and rural environments on attitudes or behavior. Social scientists dispute whether important urban-rural effects have existed and, if so, precisely what they are and how they might be affected by different circumstances. For an introduction to the now voluminous literature, see Mark Abrahamson, "The Social Dimensions of Urbanism," pp. 376–84; Richard Dewey, "The Rural-Urban Continuum," pp. 60–66; Claude S. Fischer, "The Effect of Urban Life on Traditional Values," pp. 420–32, and "Toward a Subcultural Theory of Urbanism," pp. 1319–41; Herbert Gans, "Urbanism and Suburbanism as Ways of Life," pp. 625–48; Albert Hunter, "The Loss of Community," pp. 537–52; George D. Lowe and

Charles W. Peek, "Location and Lifestyle," pp. 392–420; Leo F. Schnore, "The Rural-Urban Variable," pp. 129–43; J. C. Van Es and J. E. Brown, Jr., "The Rural-Urban Variable Once More," pp. 373–91; Ferne H. Weiner, "Altruism, Ambiance, and Action," pp. 112–24; Louis Wirth, "Urbanism as a Way of Life," pp. 1–24.

17. Sorokin and Zimmerman, *Principles*, p. 407; Charles N. Glaab, "Metropolis and Suburb," p. 401.

18. Sorokin and Zimmerman, *Principles*, pp. 616–17; John D. Black, *Agricultural Reform in the United States*, p. 58.

19. Peter J. Schmitt, *Back to Nature*, p. 188; Charles N. Glaab and A. Theodore Brown, *A History of Urban America*, p. 289.

20. Robert R. Dykstra, "Town-Country Conflict," p. 195. For evidence of town-country conflict during the early twentieth century, see Edmund deS. Brunner, Gwendelyn S. Hughes, and Marjorie Patten, *American Agricultural Villages*, pp. 96–112; Harlan P. Douglas, *The Little Town*; T. Lynn Smith, "The Role of the Village in American Rural Society," pp. 10–21; Garin Burbank, "Two Defenses of Community."

21. Anselm L. Strauss, *Images of the American City*; Frederick Lewis Allen, *Only Yesterday*, pp. 172–75.

22. Strauss, *Images*, pp. 120–23.

23. Quoted in Robert L. Cole, "The Democratic Party in Washington State, 1919–1933," p. 204.

24. Quoted in Franklin Dean Mitchell, "Embattled Democracy," pp. 201–2.

Chapter 7

1. See, for example, Harold F. Gosnell, *Negro Politicians*, pp. 27–30; John M. Allswang, "The Chicago Negro Voter," pp. 244–54; Ernest M. Collins, "Cincinnati Negroes and Presidential Politics," pp. 131–37; David Burner, *The Politics of Provincialism*, pp. 237–41.

2. For descriptions of those aspects of the campaign relevant to racial issues, see William F. Nowlin, *The Negro in American National Politics*, pp. 82–83; Paul Lewinson, *Race, Class, and Party*, pp. 171–76; Henry Lee Moon, *Balance of Power*, pp. 105–8; Elbert Lee Tatum, *The Changed Political Thought of the Negro*, pp. 100–109; Richard B. Sherman, *The Republican Party and Black America*, pp. 229–33.

3. Alain Locke, "The New Negro," pp. 3–16; John Hope Franklin, *From Slavery to Freedom*, pp. 498–522; August Meier, *Negro Thought in America, 1880–1915*, pp. 256–78 (Meier tries to trace the roots of the "new Negro" back to the era of Booker T. Washington); Robert A. Bone, *The Negro Novel in America*, pp. 53–64; Gilbert Osofsky, *Harlem*, pp. 179–87; Florette Henri, *Black Migration*, pp. 332–43.

4. One of the most ambitious attempts to describe the lives of nonelite, northern blacks in the early twentieth century relies almost entirely on in-

formation from the "articulate elite": David Gordon Nielson, *Black Ethos*.

5. Gosnell, *Negro Politicians*, p. 36; Collins, "Cincinnati Negroes," pp. 131–32.

6. E. Franklin Frazier, "American Negroes' New Leaders," pp. 55–59; Ralph J. Bunche, *The Political Status of the Negro in the Age of FDR*; Nathan Irvin Huggins, *Harlem Renaissance*, pp. 30–51; Martin L. Kilson, Jr., "Political Change in the Negro Ghetto," pp. 167–92.

7. Bunche, *Political Status*, p. 92.

8. United States Department of Commerce, *The Statistical History of the United States from Colonial Times to the Present*, p. 218; Monroe N. Work, ed., *The Negro Handbook*, pp. 111–12.

9. Nowlin, *The Negro*, pp. 82–83.

10. "Color Discrimination in Government Service," *Crisis* 35 (Nov. 1928): 369, 387–89; August Meier and Elliot Rudwick, "The Rise of Segregation in the Federal Bureaucracy, 1900–1930," pp. 178–84.

11. Kelly Miller to Herbert Hoover, 4 Oct. 1928, Pre-Presidential, Box 7, Herbert Hoover Papers. For general discussions of Republican policies and the reactions of black leaders, see Sherman, *Republican Party*, pp. 174–223; John L. Blair, "A Time for Parting," pp. 177–99; William Griffin, "Black Insurgency in the Republican Party of Ohio, 1920–1932," pp. 25–45.

12. Charles H. Martin, "Negro Leaders, the Republican Party, and the Election of 1932," p. 85.

13. Stanley P. Hirshson, *Farewell to the Bloody Shirt*, p. 253.

14. Lewinson, *Race, Class, and Party*, pp. 171–73; *New York Times*, 5 June 1928, p. 6; *Afro-American*, 16 June 1928, p. 1, 20 Oct. 1928, p. 5; *Cleveland Gazette*, 30 June 1928, p. 1; *Amsterdam News*, 20 June 1928, p. 1.

15. Miller to Hoover; *Afro-American*, 23 June 1928, p. 2.

16. Kirk H. Porter and Donald Bruce Johnson, *National Party Platforms, 1840–1964*, p. 290.

17. Lewinson, *Race, Class, and Party*, p. 173; Sherman, *Republican Party*, pp. 230–32; *Afro-American*, 23 June 1928, pp. 1–2, 21 July 1928, pp. 1, 5, 6, 28 July 1928, p. 1, 11 Aug. 1928, p. 1; *Norfolk Journal and Guide*, 23 June 1928, pp. 1–2; *Cleveland Gazette*, 30 June 1928, p. 1, 21 July 1928, p. 1, 1 Sept. 1928, p. 1; *Amsterdam News*, 20 June 1928, p. 2, 27 June 1928, p. 16, 18 July 1928, p. 1, 1 Aug. 1928, p. 16.

18. Henry J. Allen to George Ackerson, 26 Sept. 1928, Henry J. Allen to Mark L. Requa, 24 and 26 Sept. 1928, all in Box C 134, Henry J. Allen Papers.

19. Sam F. Woolard to Henry J. Allen, 11 Aug. 1928, Henry J. Allen to Sam F. Woolard, 18 Aug. 1928, Box C 134, Allen Papers.

20. Henry J. Allen to George Ackerson, 26 Sept. 1928, Henry J. Allen to Herbert Hoover, 28 Aug. 1928, Pre-Presidential, Box 1, Hoover Papers.

21. Herbert Hoover, *The New Day*, p. 106.

22. L. M. Osborne to Herbert Hoover, 28 Aug. 1928, Pre-Presidential, Box 19, Herbert Hoover to L. M. Osborne, 31 Aug. 1928, George Ackerson to K. C. Barnard, 20 Oct. 1928, Pre-Presidential, Box 22, Hoover Papers.

23. *Afro-American*, 21 July 1928, p. 6; *Norfolk Journal and Guide*, 28 July 1928, p. 1; *Cleveland Gazette*, 1 Sept. 1928, p. 1.

24. *Afro-American*, 28 July 1928, p. 1; *Norfolk Journal and Guide*, 8 Sept. 1928, p. 1.

25. Herbert Hoover to Hubert M. Work, 18 July 1928, Pre-Presidential, Box 26, Hoover Papers.

26. *Afro-American*, 25 Aug. 1928, p. 1; *Norfolk Journal and Guide*, 25 Aug. 1928, p. 1.

27. *Chicago Defender*, 20 Oct. 1928, p. 3.

28. *Afro-American*, 16 June 1928, pp. 1–2, 30 June 1928, p. 1.

29. The findings of several state-level studies suggest that, in 1928, these tactics prevented a more significant erosion of Democratic support in the Old South: Hugh D. Reagan, "Race as a Factor in the Presidential Election of 1928 in Alabama," pp. 5–19; Ben G. Edmunson, "Pat Harrison and Mississippi in the Presidential Elections of 1924 and 1928," pp. 333–50; William Foy Lisenby, "Brough, Baptists, and Bombast," pp. 120–31; Donald B. Kelley, "Deep South Dilemma," pp. 63–92.

30. *New York Times*, 26 Oct. 1928, p. 11.

31. Bernard Baruch to Walter F. George, 23 Aug. 1928, Selected Correspondence, 1912–1945, vol. 20, Bernard Baruch Papers.

32. Editorial, *Messenger* 10 (May–June 1928): 110.

33. Diary of Breckinridge Long, Box 4, Breckinridge Long Papers; Appendix I, reports from Chicago, Indiana, Missouri, and Oregon.

34. *Afro-American*, 22 Sept. 1928, p. 2.

35. Ibid., p. 3.

36. Nowlin, *The Negro*, p. 92.

37. *Afro-American*, 3 Nov. 1928, p. 3; *Amsterdam News*, 24 Oct. 1928, p. 1, 31 Oct. 1928, p. 1.

38. William E. Leuchtenburg, *The Perils of Prosperity, 1914–32*, p. 235; Burner, *Politics*, p. 229; Samuel Lubell, *The Future of American Politics*, p. 40.

39. Stuart A. Rice and Malcolm M. Willey, "A Sex Cleavage in the Presidential Election of 1920," pp. 519–20, and "American Women's Ineffective Use of the Vote," pp. 641–47.

40. Republican National Committee, "Summary Report on the 1928 Campaign," Pre-Presidential, Box 89, Hoover Papers.

41. Thomas E. Cashman to Franklin D. Roosevelt, 14 Dec. 1928, Pre-Convention, Box 360, Democratic National Campaign Committee Correspondence, 1928–33.

42. Emma M. May to Franklin D. Roosevelt, 5 Dec. 1928, Pre-Convention, Box 193, Democratic National Campaign Committee Correspondence, 1928–33.

43. For discussion of American feminism during the 1920s, see: William Henry Chafe, *The American Woman*, pp. 3–22; William L. O'Neill, *Everyone Was Brave*, pp. 225–359; J. Stanley Lemons, *The Woman Citizen*; Jill Conway, "Women Reformers and American Culture, 1870–1930," pp. 164–72; Es-

telle B. Freedman, "The New Woman," pp. 372–93; Anne F. Scott, "After Suffrage," pp. 298–318; Allis Rosenberg Wolfe, "Women, Consumerism, and the National Consumers' League in the Progressive Era, 1900–1923," pp. 378–92; David E. Kyvig, "Women against Prohibition," pp. 464–82.

44. Aileen S. Kraditor, *The Ideas of the Woman Suffrage Movement*, pp. 38–63; Emily Stoper and Roberta Ann Johnson, "The Weaker Sex and the Better Half," p. 193.

45. O'Neill, *Everyone Was Brave*, p. 354.

46. O'Neill's book indicates some of the key issues and offers some interesting conclusions. Much more study, however, is clearly required.

Chapter 8

1. Variables measuring economic status do not identify people's place in the occupational structure or indicate their subjective consciousness of class. For recent discussions of subjective class consciousness and its implications for politics, see: Richard F. Curtis and Elton F. Jackson, *Inequality in American Communities*, pp. 83–116, 221–49; Isaac D. Balbus, "The Concept of Interest in Pluralist and Marxian Analysis," pp. 151–77; Avery M. Guest, "Class Consciousness and American Political Attitudes," pp. 496–510; Mary R. Jackman and Robert W. Jackman, "An Interpretation of the Relation between Objective and Subjective Social Status," pp. 569–82; Sidney Verba and Kay Lehman Schlozman, "Unemployment, Class Consciousness, and Radical Politics," pp. 291–323.

2. David Burner, *The Politics of Provincialism*, p. 217.

3. The percentage of high school graduates within each county is first available in 1940.

4. A. B. McDaniel to Herbert Hoover, undated, Pre-Presidential, Box 1, Herbert Hoover Papers; James A. Farley, Personal Interview.

5. Republican National Committee, "Summary Report on the 1928 Campaign," Pre-Presidential, Box 89, Hoover Papers.

6. Abraham Epstein, "How Real Was Our Prosperity?" pp. 550–56.

7. Simon Kuznets, *National Income and Its Composition, 1919–1938*, pp. 314–15. Kuznets offers the following breakdown by industry group of average annual compensation: agriculture, 14 percent of all employees, $646; mining, 4 percent, $1,514; manufacture, 34 percent, $1,500; construction, 3 percent, $1,934; utilities, 12 percent, $1,656; trade, 15 percent, $1,526; finance, 3 percent, $1,885; service, 7 percent, $1,229; government, 9 percent, $1,673.

8. Ewan Clague and Anne G. Geddes, "Why We Need a Social Security Program," p. 9. The estimates are from the Alexander Hamilton Institute, the American Federation of Labor, and the National Industrial Conference Board.

9. David Weintraub, "Unemployment and Increasing Productivity," p. 70.

10. Consumer credit, however, was a mixed blessing. Epstein reports

that three hundred thousand automobiles were repossessed in 1923–26 and that the situation was similar for other commodities ("How Real Was Our Prosperity?" p. 556).

11. Irving Bernstein, *The Lean Years,* pp. 68–69.

12. These studies are summarized in Weintraub, "Unemployment and Increasing Productivity," pp. 83–84.

13. James H. Shideler, *Farm Crisis,* is an intensive study of agricultural depression in the aftermath of World War I.

14. Donald C. Blaisdell, *Government and Agriculture,* pp. 5–6. Especially illuminating are the statistics reported in United States Department of Agriculture, *Yearbook of Agriculture,* 1923–30.

15. Shideler, *Farm Crisis,* pp. 152–88; Murray R. Benedict, *Farm Policies of the United States, 1790–1950,* pp. 200–238; John D. Black, *Agricultural Reform in the United States,* pp. 69–77; Alice M. Christenson, "Agricultural Pressure and Governmental Response, 1919–1929," pp. 33–37.

16. Black, *Agricultural Reform,* pp. 232–54; Darwin N. Kelley, "The McNary-Haugen Bills, 1924–1928," pp. 170–80; Henry L. Rofinot, "Normalcy and the Farmer," pp. 202–28; Christenson, "Agricultural Pressure," pp. 37–42.

17. "The Democratic Tariff Plank," *Protectionist* 40 (Aug. 1928): 180.

18. "Official Report of the Proceedings of the Democratic National Convention, 1928, Committee on Platform and Resolutions, Executive Session," pp. 2, 25, Box 149, Key Pittman Papers.

19. "Injunctions Planks Need Clarifications," *American Federationist* 25 (Aug. 1928): 916.

20. George F. Milton to Oswald Garrison Villard, 28 July 1928, Box 339, William Gibbs McAdoo Papers.

21. Roy V. Peel and Thomas C. Donnelly, *The 1928 Campaign,* pp. 34–40; *New York Times,* 28 Oct. 1928, p. 25; "Forecasts by Nationally Known Business Men," *Forum* 80 (Nov. 1928): 746–54; Campaign Memo, Box 1, Franklin D. Roosevelt 1928 Campaign Correspondence, Franklin D. Roosevelt Papers.

22. Treasurer of the Republican State Committee, New York State, to John J. Raskob, 21 Dec. 1927, Chairman of the Finance Committee, Republican National Committee to Raskob, 6 Nov. 1922, Secretary of the Finance Committee, Republican National Committee to Raskob, 20 Dec. 1924, Chairman of the National Contributions Committee, Republican National Committee to Raskob, 19 Nov. 1924, File 1947, John J. Raskob Papers.

23. John J. Raskob to Irenée Du Pont, 19 July 1928, File 677, Raskob Papers.

24. For Smith's activities during the 1930s, see Samuel B. Hand, "Al Smith, Franklin D. Roosevelt, and the New Deal," pp. 366–81, and Jordan A. Schwartz, "Al Smith in the Thirties," pp. 316–30.

25. For a seminal discussion of the politics of distribution and redistribution, see Theodore J. Lowi, "American Business, Public Policy, Case Studies, and Political Theory," pp. 677–715.

26. John Dickson to William G. McAdoo, 3 Aug. 1928, McAdoo Papers.

27. Richard O'Connor, *The First Hurrah*, p. 155.

28. Frank Freidel, *Franklin D. Roosevelt*, 2:246.

29. See Frances Fox Piven, "The Social Structuring of Political Protest," pp. 297–326, for an illuminating discussion of the relationships among political protest, consciousness, and social structure.

30. In their reanalysis of data from a 1939 Roper survey, Sidney Verba and Kay Lehman Schlozman, "Unemployment, Class Consciousness, and Radical Politics," pp. 291–323, found that even after a decade of economic depression, only a small proportion of wage earners and unemployed Americans were fully class conscious. Yet even those with a highly developed consciousness of class generally shared the American dream of "rugged individualism and optimism about the future" (p. 322). Versions of the American dream conducive to political quiescence, moreover, need not deny the presence of inequality or affirm the possibility of a transition from "rags to riches." People need only believe that opportunities are available for a decent life, perhaps for their children if not for themselves, and that individuals are primarily responsible for their own situations. Evidence from recent surveys suggests that this version of the American dream was prevalent among ordinary Americans of the period following World War II (although perhaps less so among the working class than among the middle and upper classes). See, for example, Ely Chinoy, *Automobile Workers and the American Dream*; Joan Huber and William H. Form, *Income and Ideology*; Curtis and Jackson, *Inequality*, pp. 83–106; G. David Garson, "Automobile Workers and the Radical Dream," pp. 163–77; Kay Lehman Schlozman, "Coping with the American Dream," pp. 241–63. Comparing the results of more contemporary surveys with the reanalysis of the 1939 Roper data, Schlozman (pp. 260–61) suggests that since the Great Depression people's aspirations may have shifted from an emphasis on opportunity, risk, individualism, and continuing advancement to a stress on job security and a stable family life.

31. Department of Commerce, United States Bureau of the Census, *The Statistical History of the United States from Colonial Times to the Present*, p. 301; Donald Day, ed., *The Autobiography of Will Rogers*, p. 201.

32. Seymour Feshbach and Irving L. Janis, "Effects of Fear Arousing Communications," pp. 78–92; Kay H. Smith and Barrie Richards, "Effects of a Rational Appeal and of Anxiety on Conformity Behavior," pp. 122–26; Saundra F. Zimmerman, Kay H. Smith, and Darhl M. Pederson, "The Effect of Anticonformity Appeals on Conformity Behavior," pp. 93–103; Victor A. Harris and Jerald M. Jellison, "Fear-arousing Communications, False Physiological Feedback, and Acceptance of Recommendations," pp. 269–79; Ronald W. Rogers and Ronald C. Mewborn, "Fear Appeals and Attitude Change," pp. 54–61. See Clyde Hendrick, Martin Glesen, and Richard Borden, "False Physiological Feedback and Persuasion," pp. 196–214, for the view that only the arousal of fear is important for behavior.

33. Ruth Miller Elson, *Guardians of Tradition*; Henry J. Perkinson, *The*

Imperfect Panacea, pp. 67–191; Robert H. Wiebe, "The Social Functions of Public Education," pp. 147–64; David K. Cohen, "Immigrants and the Schools," pp. 13–27; Alexander Rippa, *Education in a Free Society*, pp. 158–230; Lawrence A. Cremin, *The Transformation of the School*; Michael B. Katz, *Class, Bureaucracy, and the Schools*, pp. xvii–125.

34. For evidence on the favorable image of businessmen during the 1920s, see Russel B. Nye, *Midwestern Progressive Politics*, pp. 320–21; James W. Prothro, *The Dollar Decade*, pp. 222–37; Robert H. Wiebe, *Businessmen and Reform*, pp. 221–22.

35. Comments on the press in Roosevelt's correspondence are summarized in the "National Political Digest, 1928," National Democratic Campaign Committee Correspondence, 1928–33.

36. John W. Davis to Claude Meeher, 7 Nov. 1928, Box 27, John W. Davis Papers.

37. The following works are relevant in evaluating progressivism during the 1920s: Leroy Ashby, *The Spearless Leader*; Clarke A. Chambers, *Seedtime of Reform*; Otis L. Graham, Jr., *The Great Campaigns*, pp. 97–169; Richard Lowitt, *The Persistence of a Progressive*, pp. 124–486; J. Stanley Lemons, *The Woman Citizen*; Burl Noggle, *Into the Twenties*, pp. 179–99; Stuart Rochester, *American Liberal Disillusionment in the Wake of World War I*; Karel Denis Bicha, "Liberalism Frustrated," pp. 19–28; Paul W. Glad, "Progressives and the Business Culture of the 1920s," pp. 75–89; Alan R. Havig, "A Disputed Legacy," pp. 44–64; J. Stanley Lemons, "Social Feminism in the 1920's," pp. 83–91; Arthur S. Link, "What Happened to the Progressive Movement in the 1920's?" pp. 833–51; Herbert F. Margulies, "Recent Opinion on the Decline of the Progressive Movement," pp. 250–68; Robert S. Maxwell, "The Progressive Bridge," pp. 83–102; Jackson K. Putnam, "The Persistence of Progressivism in the 1920's," pp. 395–411; Stanley Shapiro, "The Great War and Reform," pp. 323–44; Ferenc M. Szasz, "The Progressive Clergy and the Kingdom of God," pp. 3–20; George B. Tindall, "Business Progressivism," pp. 92–106; Donald L. Winters, "The Persistence of Progressivism," pp. 109–20; Allis Rosenberg Wolfe, "Women, Consumerism, and the National Consumers League in the Progressive Era, 1900–1923," pp. 378–92; Robert H. Zieger, "Herbert Hoover, the Wage-Earner, and the 'New Economic System,' 1919–1929," pp. 161–89, and "Labor Progressivism, and Herbert Hoover in the 1920's," pp. 196–208.

38. Bernstein, *Lean Years*, pp. 97–143; Noggle, *Into the Twenties*, pp. 89–115; William Preston, Jr., *Aliens and Dissenters*, pp. 88–272; James Weinstein, *The Decline of Socialism in America, 1912–1925*, pp. 119–339. Kenneth Campbell MacKay, *The Progressive Movement of 1924*, pp. 219–64; David P. Thelen, *Robert M. La Follette and the Insurgent Spirit*, pp. 179–94; James H. Shideler, "The Disintegration of the Progressive Party Movement of 1924," pp. 189–201.

39. David Brody, "The Rise and Decline of Welfare Capitalism," pp. 151–57; Zieger, "Herbert Hoover," pp. 182–83.

40. George L. Berry to Franklin D. Roosevelt, 6 Dec. 1928, Pre-Conven-

tion, Box 716, National Democratic Campaign Committee Correspondence, 1928–33.

41. Caroline Bird, *The Invisible Scar*, p. 39.

42. E. H. Casterlin to Franklin D. Roosevelt, 12 Dec. 1928, Pre-Convention, Box 148, National Democratic Campaign Committee Correspondence, 1928–33. For expressions of similar views, see L. W. Powers to Franklin D. Roosevelt, 23 Nov. 1929, ibid., Box 208, and Charles R. Bell to Franklin D. Roosevelt, 26 Dec. 1928, ibid., Box 232.

43. Bryant Putney, *Labor in Politics*, pp. 8–11; John David Greenstone, *Labor in American Politics*, pp. 30–35.

44. Executive Council of the AFL, quoted in Putney, *Labor*, p. 11.

45. Matthew Josephson and Hannah Josephson, *Hero of the Cities*, pp. 222–30, 287–91, 328–31.

46. For a summary of the closed-door deliberations of AFL leaders over the question of endorsing Smith, see Vaughn Davis Bornet, *Labor Politics in a Democratic Republic*, pp. 130–38.

47. John P. Frey, The reminiscences of John P. Frey, p. 322, Columbia University Oral History Collection.

48. Robert H. Zieger, *Republicans and Labor, 1919–1929*, pp. 87–277; Bornet, *Labor Politics*, pp. 146–48; Joseph S. Davis, "Herbert Hoover, 1874–1964, Another Appraisal," pp. 304–5.

49. Zieger, *Republicans and Labor*, pp. 190–277, "Herbert Hoover," pp. 161–89, and "Labor," pp. 196–208.

50. Bernstein, *Lean Years*, pp. 97–105; Zieger, "Herbert Hoover," pp. 181–82.

51. Bornet, *Labor Politics*, pp. 259, 229.

52. Ibid., pp. 276–80.

53. Berry to Roosevelt, 6 Dec. 1928.

54. Bernstein, *Lean Years*, pp. 84–90.

55. Gilbert C. Fite, *George N. Peek and the Fight for Farm Parity*, pp. 205–6; Theodore Salautos and John D. Hicks, *Agricultural Discontent in the Middle West, 1900–1939*, pp. 402–3; William Hirth to Royal S. Copeland, 29 June 1928, Royal S. Copeland Papers; George N. Peek to Adam McMullen, 23 July 1928, Folder 445, George N. Peek Papers.

56. Alfred E. Smith, *The Campaign Addresses of Governor Alfred E. Smith*, pp. 27–42.

57. Fite, *George N. Peek*, p. 215.

58. Herbert Hoover, *The New Day*, pp. 17–24.

59. Fite, *George N. Peek*, p. 212; James W. Gerard to George N. Peek, 30 Aug. 1928, Folder 413, Chester C. Davis Papers; George N. Peek and Joseph Proskauer to John J. Raskob, 22 Aug. 1928, Folder 241, Peek Papers.

60. Fite, *George N. Peek*, p. 215–16; reprints of press comments in *Literary Digest* 99 (6 Oct. 1928): 7.

61. Fite, *George N. Peek*, pp. 207–11.

62. In a 1926 study of newspapers and public opinion in Seattle, Washington, George Lundberg found no important correlation between the opin-

ions of newspapers and their readers on particular candidates and issues. Lundberg does, however, cite impressionistic evidence of a relationship between newspaper endorsement and candidate preference in rural areas. Lundberg's study also fails to control for the social, economic, and political characteristics of the newspaper readers included in the survey. See George A. Lundberg, "The Newspaper and Public Opinion," pp. 709–15.

63. *New York Times,* 10 Oct. 1928, p. 4.

64. George N. Peek to Hugh Craig, 13 Nov. 1928, Folder 252, Peek Papers.

65. Political File, 1928, Alben W. Barkley Papers.

66. Republican National Committee, "Summary Report on the 1928 Campaign," Pre-Presidential, Box 89, Hoover Papers.

67. For a thorough treatment of the political significance of party images, see Richard Trilling, *Party Image and Electoral Behavior.*

68. Arthur F. Burns, "Ideology of Businessmen and Presidential Elections," pp. 230–36.

69. Ibid.

70. Ibid., p. 235. In particular, the Republicans effectively manipulated the fear that, despite their platform declaration, the Democrats would undermine the protective tariff. The Democrats' concern over this issue is exemplified by the telegram sent by John J. Raskob and Millard E. Tydings to all Democratic House and Senate candidates asking them to pledge commitment to a carefully worded statement on the tariff. John J. Raskob and Millard E. Tydings to Royal S. Copeland, 20 Oct. 1928, Copeland Papers.

71. Newton D. Baker to Ralph Hayes, 7 Nov. 1928, Box 115, Newton D. Baker Papers.

72. Louise Overacker, *Money in Elections,* p. 75.

73. The business elite, this analysis suggests, served as a "non-membership reference group" for the middle class—that is, a group to which the individual does not belong but which influences his behavior because he wishes to emulate group members. See Raymond L. Schmitt, *The Reference Other Orientation.* Of course, only surveys of individual opinion that are unavailable for the 1920s could reliably test this hypothesis. But considerable impressionistic evidence from contemporary observers could be marshaled in its support.

74. Robert S. Lynd and Helen Merrell Lynd, *Middletown,* p. 415.

75. See, for example, Edmund A. Moore, *A Catholic Runs for President,* p. 158.

76. Farley interview.

77. Lee Benson, *The Concept of Jacksonian Democracy,* p. 165.

Chapter 9

1. William L. Langer, "The Next Assignment," pp. 283–304.

2. See Allan J. Lichtman and Valerie French, *Historians and the Living Past,* pp. 122–52, for a discussion of the new history.

3. V. O. Key, Jr., "A Theory of Critical Elections," p. 4; Samuel Lubell, *The Future of American Politics*, p. 36. An argument similar to Lubell's is presented by Samuel J. Eldersveld in "The Influences of Metropolitan Party Pluralities in Presidential Elections since 1920," pp. 1189–1206. Irving Bernstein, *The Lean Years*, pp. 75–82; Carl N. Degler, "American Political Parties and the Rise of the City," pp. 41–59; Gerald M. Pomper, "Classification of Presidential Elections," p. 554; W. Phillips Shively, "A Reinterpretation of the New Deal Realignment," pp. 621–24; William H. Flanigan and Nancy H. Zingale, "The Measurement of Electoral Change," pp. 49–82. Flanigan and Zingale applied analysis of variance methods to state-level voting returns for the presidential elections of 1824–1968. They used these procedures to distinguish between changes in party power termed "realigning surge" and changes in voter coalitions termed "realigning interactive change." They also examined separately Republican and Democratic percentages of the presidential vote; 1928, they concluded, "involved a substantial interactive realignment for the Democratic vote" (p. 71). Their methodology, however interesting, is applicable only to long series of elections and not to the intensive analysis of a relatively limited time span. Duncan MacRae, Jr., and James A. Meldrum, "Critical Elections in Illinois," pp. 669–83; John M. Allswang, *A House for All Peoples*; Marc V. Levine, "Standing Political Decisions and Critical Realignment," p. 317; Walter Dean Burnham, *Critical Elections and the Mainsprings of American Politics*, pp. 50–57; John L. Shover, "The Emergence of a Two-Party System in Republican Philadelphia, 1924–1936," p. 1000; John L. Shover, "Was 1928 a Critical Election in California?" pp. 196–204; Charles M. Dollar, "Innovation in Historical Research," pp. 144–49; David J. Alvarez and Edmund J. True, "Critical Elections and Partisan Realignment," pp. 563–76; Michael Paul Rogin, *The Intellectuals and McCarthy*, pp. 81, 126–27, 151–56.

4. Jerome M. Clubb and Howard W. Allen, "The Cities and the Election of 1928," pp. 1205–20.

5. Critical election theory is not a precise, formal system of thought. It is a general perspective on electoral change shared by many political theorists. In order to use and evaluate the theory this study synthesizes concepts put forth by various scholars. It does not attempt to describe, in detail, the work of any individual theorist.

6. Key, "Theory of Critical Elections," p. 4. In another article, Key suggests that realignment may also take place through "processes of long-term or secular" change (V. O. Key, Jr., "Secular Realignment and the Party System," pp. 198–99).

7. Angus Campbell, Philip E. Converse, Warren E. Miller, and Donald E. Stokes, *The American Voter*, pp. 531–34.

8. Pomper, "Classification of Presidential Elections," pp. 537–38.

9. If we postulate that both temporary and durable changes can be associated with an election (for example, a temporary change in party power and a durable change in the composition of voter coalitions), the typology

expands further. There is some dispute over whether durable changes in party power must produce a new majority party. See, for example, Burnham, *Critical Elections*, pp. 32–53.

10. Pomper, "Classification of Presidential Elections," pp. 537–38.

11. Shover, "Emergence of a Two-Party System," p. 1002.

12. Few social science theories can be made operational with precision. It is important, however, to minimize the gap between the concepts expressed in a theory and the ways in which these concepts can be empirically tested.

13. Because of problems of measurement error as well as problems inherent to a reliance on aggregate-level data, changes in coefficients computed for counties only approximate changes in the underlying voter coalitions.

14. Since presidential percentages are measured using the total vote rather than the potential electorate as the base, the regression and correlation coefficients do not necessarily register changes in voter turnout. These measures would, however, reflect changes in turnout that influenced the county to county specification of voter coalitions.

15. The importance of the 1924 contest is also noted at the local level by Bruce Stave in "The 'La Follette Revolution' and the Pittsburgh Vote, 1932," pp. 244–51.

16. The same groupings are obtained whether linkage analysis is applied to correlation or regression coefficients. Factor analysis of the correlation coefficients also fails to disclose groups of elections neatly divided by the 1928 contest.

17. Angus Campbell, Philip E. Converse, Warren E. Miller, and Donald E. Stokes, *Elections and the Political Order*, pp. 96–124.

18. Shover, "Emergence of a Two-Party System," attempts to resolve this problem by simply asserting that critical election theory is purely descriptive in nature.

19. David Burner, *The Politics of Provincialism*, pp. 159–60; Clubb and Allen, "The Cities and the Election of 1928," pp. 1210–18; Alvarez and True, "Critical Elections," pp. 566–75.

20. See, for example, Burner, *Politics*, p. 228.

21. Kristi Andersen, "Generation, Partisan Shift, and Realignment," pp. 74–95.

22. Leo T. Crowley to Franklin D. Roosevelt, 6 Dec. 1928, Pre-Convention, Box 785, William Fleet Palmer to Franklin D. Roosevelt, 28 Nov. 1928, Pre-Convention, Box 30, Democratic National Campaign Committee Correspondence, 1928–33; Clinton A. Anderson to James A. Farley, 8 Sept. 1936, Franklin D. Roosevelt, Box 82, President's Official File 300, Franklin D. Roosevelt Papers.

23. Andersen, "Generation," p. 93.

24. Not only Norman H. Nie, Sidney J. Verba, and John R. Petrocik, *The Changing American Voter*, but other major books by political scientists on past elections fail to cite a single manuscript source in support of their analysis. Burnham, *Critical Elections*, Campbell et al., *American Voter*, and James L.

Sundquist, *Dynamics of the Party System*, all neglect the historical sources that lend insight into the contemporary meaning of past events. These comments suggest my profound disagreement with Richard J. Jensen, "History from a Deck of IBM Cards," pp. 229–34; Jensen implies approval of an approach to political history that emulates social science by "the total absence of references to newspapers, speeches, manuscripts or documents" and by the failure to consider "the hopes, fears, needs, ambitions, ideas, prejudices, and achievements of people who lived long ago" (p. 233). If the "new political history" is to be explanatory as well as descriptive, it must draw upon these written sources and consider people's intentions and motivations. Quantitative and traditional history should be complementary, not competitive.

25. Burnham, *Critical Elections*, pp. 6–10.

26. The most thorough analysis of Hoover's policies is provided by Harris G. Warren, *Herbert Hoover and the Great Depression*.

27. Before Convention Collection, Democratic National Campaign Committee Correspondence, 1928–33.

28. James A. Farley, Personal Interview.

29. See, for example, Charles Michelson, *The Ghost Talks*.

30. Before Election Collection, Democratic National Campaign Committee Correspondence, 1928–33; Presidential Subject File, Herbert Hoover Papers.

31. Roy V. Peel and Thomas C. Donnelly, *The 1932 Campaign*, pp. 123–79; William E. Leuchtenburg, *Franklin D. Roosevelt and the New Deal, 1932–1940*, pp. 9–17.

32. In December 1939, for example, the Gallup Poll reported that 70 percent of a national cross section of potential voters opposed a third term for President Roosevelt (George H. Gallup, *The Gallup Poll*, 1:129).

33. Gallup found that in October 1940, 53 percent of a national cross section claimed that they would favor Wendell Willkie rather than Franklin D. Roosevelt if "there were no war in Europe today" (ibid., p. 247).

34. Campbell et al., *Elections*, p. 76.

35. Recent work in political science on the period since World War II questions the stability of party identification and the strength and direction of its connection with voter behavior. See, for example, Robert Axelrod, "Where the Votes Come From," pp. 11–20; Douglas Dobson and Douglas St. Angelo, "Party Identification and the Floating Vote," pp. 481–90; Edward C. Dreyer, "Change and Stability in Party Identification," pp. 712–23; Morris P. Fiorina, "An Outline for a Model of Party Choice," pp. 601–25; Michael Margolis, "From Confusion to Confusion," pp. 31–43; Kenneth J. Meier, "Party Identification and Vote Choice," pp. 496–505; Samuel Popkin, John W. Gorman, Charles Phillips, and Jeffrey A. Smith, "What Have You Done for Me Lately?" pp. 779–805; David Repass, "Issue Saliency and Party Choice," pp. 389–400; Mark A. Schulman and Gerald M. Pomper, "Variability in Electoral Behavior," pp. 1–18; Donald U. Searing, Joel J. Schwartz, and Alden E. Lind, "The Structuring Principle," pp. 415–32.

36. E. E. Schattschneider, *The Semisovereign People*, pp. 78–85; Richard J. Jensen, *The Winning of the Midwest*, pp. 306–8; Burnham, *Critical Elections*, and "Theory and Voting Research," pp. 1002–23. Other authorities suggest that changes in the legal framework of electoral competition (for example, adoption of the Australian ballot) were the critical factor in generating a more fluid system of electoral politics. See, for example, Jerrold G. Rusk, "The Effect of the Australian Ballot Reform on Split-Ticket Voting," pp. 1220–38, and "The American Electoral Universe," pp. 1028–49.

37. This statement does not imply an endorsement of Key's view that 1928 was a critical election for New England. An analysis of the New England region similar to the analysis performed here for the nation suggests no important differences in interpretation. Moreover, with regard to Massachusetts, Key's best example of a state undergoing realignment in 1928, a careful study by Robert K. Massey, Jr., "The Democratic Laggard," pp. 553–74, demonstrates that increases in Democratic voting in 1928 were due primarily to the unique issue of that election (religion) and that Massachusetts was a laggard rather than a leader in the Democratic resurgence of the 1930s. In light of my study it is hardly surprising that a heavily Irish Catholic state should provide unusually high levels of support for Al Smith. Key's similar findings for New Hampshire can likewise be explained by the high incidence of French Canadians in that state. Indeed, multiple regression analysis of Democratic voting in 1928 demonstrated that of all predominantly Catholic ethnic groups, Irish Catholics were Al Smith's strongest supporters and French Canadians his second strongest supporters. Once again, electoral trends of the 1930s cannot be attributed to the same causal forces that produced the political patterns of 1928.

Chapter 10

1. Donald B. Meyer, *The Protestant Search for Political Realism, 1919–1941*, p. 122.

2. For a variety of views, see: Richard D. Alba, "Ethnic Networks and Tolerant Attitudes," pp. 1–16; David Fairbanks, "Religious Forces and 'Morality' Policies in the American States," pp. 411–17, Dean R. Hoge and Jackson W. Carroll, "Religiosity and Prejudice in North and South," pp. 181–97; Richard T. Santee and Jay Jackson, "Cultural Values as a Source of Normative Sanctions," pp. 439–54; W. Clark Roof, "The Local-Cosmopolitan Orientation and Traditional Religious Commitment," pp. 1–15; Richard H. White, "Toward a Theory of Religious Influence," pp. 23–28; Robert Wuthnow, "Religious Commitment and Conservatism," pp. 117–32.

3. Bernard J. Coughlin, *Church and State in Social Welfare*, pp. 28–29; see also J. Milton Yinger, *Religion in the Struggle for Power*, pp. 142–44.

4. Jay P. Dolan, "A Critical Period in American Catholicism," pp. 523–36; Philip Gleason, *The Conservative Reformers*, pp. 14–45; David J. O'Brien, *American Catholics and Social Reform*, p. 45; James W. Sanders, *The Education of an Urban Minority, Catholics in Chicago*, pp. 17–39.

5. Abraham A. Moles, *Information Theory and Esthetic Perception*, pp. 131–32.

6. Murray Edelman, *Politics as Symbolic Action*, pp. 35–36.

7. Michael Paul Rogin, *The Intellectuals and McCarthy*, p. 80.

8. Ibid., pp. 1–31, 261–82.

9. Barton J. Bernstein, "The New Deal," pp. 264–82; Paul K. Conkin, *The New Deal*; Robert H. Zieger, "Herbert Hoover," pp. 808–9.

10. See, for example, William Appleman Williams, "What This Country Needs . . . ," pp. 7–11; David B. Burner, "Before the Crash," pp. 50–65; Donald R. McCoy, "To the White House," pp. 29–49; Ellis W. Hawley, "Herbert Hoover, the Commerce Secretariat, and the Vision of an 'Associative State,' 1921–1928," pp. 116–40; Joan Hoff Wilson, *Herbert Hoover*; Edgar Eugene Robinson and Vaughn Davis Bornet, *Herbert Hoover*.

11. McCoy, "To the White House," p. 36; Wilson, *Herbert Hoover*, pp. 127–29.

Appendix 1

1. For discussions of heteroscedasticity see Hubert M. Blalock, Jr., *Social Statistics*, pp. 367–69; Edward J. Kane, *Economic Statistics and Econometrics*, pp. 355–79; John Johnston, *Econometric Methods*, pp. 214–21; Jan Kmenta, *Elements of Econometrics*, pp. 249–69. Scrutiny of residuals failed to reveal other significant patterns of heteroscedasticity.

2. Kane, *Economic Statistics*, pp. 355–79; Johnston, *Econometric Methods*, pp. 243–66; Kmenta, *Elements*, pp. 269–97.

3. Kmenta, *Elements*, pp. 247–48.

4. Blalock, *Social Statistics*, p. 457; Johnston, *Econometric Methods*, pp. 159–68; Kmenta, *Elements*, pp. 380–91.

5. The largest r^2 between any pair of independent variables in Table A1.2 is .45; the second largest is .25.

6. Laura Irwin Langbein and Allan J. Lichtman, *Ecological Inference*, pp. 33–38.

7. On the importance of specification, see ibid., pp. 12–33; Laura Irwin and Allan J. Lichtman, "Across the Great Divide," pp. 411–39; Allan J. Lichtman and Laura Irwin Langbein, "Regression vs. Homogeneous Units," pp. 172–93; Allan J. Lichtman, "Correlation, Regression, and the Ecological Fallacy," pp. 417–33.

8. David Burner, *The Politics of Provincialism*; John Allswang, *A House for All Peoples*.

9. See note 32, Chapter 2.

10. Langbein and Lichtman, *Ecological Inference*, pp. 58–59.

11. For a lucid discussion of analysis of covariance, see Blalock, *Social Statistics*, pp. 473–506.

12. Ibid., pp. 463–64.

13. David Seidman, "On Choosing between Linear and Log-Linear Models," pp. 461–66.

14. See Blalock, *Social Statistics*, pp. 463–64.

15. The rate change in the line is the first derivative of $-.13X_1 + .09X_1^2$ or $-.13 + .18X_1$. This derivative has a value of zero when X_1 is approximately .724. For higher values of X_1, the derivative will have a positive value, indicating that the line is now sloping upward.

16. Although the line is now sloping upward at a rate of .05, the effects of percent urban on Democratic voting are still negative, as the equation in the text indicates. This calculation, of course, does not attempt to assess urbanism's possible joint effects with other variables.

Bibliography

Manuscript Collections

ANN ARBOR, MICHIGAN
   Bently Library
      Royal S. Copeland Papers
BERKELEY, CALIFORNIA
   Bancroft Library, University of
      California
      Hiram Johnson Papers
BUFFALO, NEW YORK
   Buffalo and Erie County Historical
      Society
      Norman E. Mack Papers
COLUMBIA, MISSOURI
   University of Missouri Library
      Chester C. Davis Papers
      George N. Peek Papers
HYDE PARK, NEW YORK
   Franklin D. Roosevelt Presidential
      Library
      National Democratic Campaign
         Committee Correspondence,
         1928–33
      Franklin D. Roosevelt Papers
LEXINGTON, KENTUCKY
   University of Kentucky Library
      Alben W. Barkley Papers
      Jouett Shouse Papers
      Wilson Family Collection
NEW HAVEN, CONNECTICUT
   Yale University Library
      John W. Davis Papers
      Charles D. Hilles Papers
      Walter Lippmann Papers

NEW YORK, NEW YORK
   Columbia University Library
      Frances Perkins Papers
   New York Public Library
      Frank P. Walsh Papers
PRINCETON, NEW JERSEY
   Princeton University Library
      Bernard Baruch Papers
WASHINGTON, D.C.
   Georgetown University Library
      Robert F. Wagner Papers
   Library of Congress
      Henry J. Allen Papers
      Newton D. Baker Papers
      William Borah Papers
      Josephus Daniels Papers
      James A. Farley Papers
      Henry P. Fletcher Papers
      Harold L. Ickes Papers
      Breckinridge Long Papers
      William Gibbs McAdoo Papers
      Charles McNary Papers
      George W. Norris Papers
      Key Pittman Papers
      Thomas J. Walsh Papers
WEST BRANCH, IOWA
   Herbert Hoover Presidential
      Library
      Herbert Hoover Papers
WILMINGTON, DELAWARE
   Eleutherian Mills Historical Library
      John J. Raskob Papers

Books

Abell, Aaron I. *American Catholicism and Social Action*. New York, 1960.

Abramson, Harold S. *Ethnic Diversity in Catholic America*. New York, 1973.

Abramson, Paul R. *Generational Change in American Politics*. Lexington, Mass., 1975.

Adorno, T. W.; Frenkel-Brunswik, Else; Levinson, Daniel J.; and Sanford, R. Nevitt. *The Authoritarian Personality*. New York, 1950.

Alexander, Charles C. *The Ku Klux Klan in the Southwest*. Lexington, Ky., 1965.

Allen, Frederick Lewis. *Only Yesterday: An Informal History of the Nineteen-Twenties*. New York, 1931.

Allport, Gordon W. *The Nature of Prejudice*. Reading, Mass., 1954.

Allswang, John M. *A House for All Peoples: Ethnic Politics in Chicago, 1890–1936*. Lexington, Ky., 1971.

Almond, Gabriel A., and Powell, G. Bingham, Jr. *Comparative Politics: A Developmental Approach*. Boston, 1966.

Anderson, Charles H. *White Protestant American: From National Origins to Religious Group*. Englewood Cliffs, N.J., 1970.

Apter, David E., ed. *Ideology and Discontent*. New York, 1964.

Ashby, Leroy. *The Spearless Leader: Senator Borah and the Progressive Movement in the 1920's*. Urbana, Ill., 1972.

Bagby, Wesley M. *The Road to Normalcy: The Presidential Campaign and Election of 1920*. Baltimore, 1962.

Bailey, Harry A., and Katz, Ellis, eds. *Ethnic Group Politics*. Columbus, Ohio, 1969.

Baker, Ray Stannard, and Dodds, William E., eds. *The Public Papers of Woodrow Wilson*. 6 vols. New York, 1927.

Bell, Daniel. *The End of Ideology: On the Exhaustion of Political Ideas in the Fifties*. 2d rev. ed. New York, 1962.

Benedict, Murray R. *Farm Policies of the United States, 1790–1950*. New York, 1966.

Benson, Lee. *The Concept of Jacksonian Democracy: New York as a Test Case*. Princeton, N.J., 1961.

Berelson, Bernard; Lazarsfeld, Paul F.; and McPhee, William N. *Voting: A Study of Opinion Formation in a Presidential Campaign*. Chicago, 1954.

Bernstein, Irving. *The Lean Years: A History of the American Worker, 1920–1933*. Boston, 1960.

Bernstein, Richard J. *The Restructuring of Social and Political Theory*. Philadelphia, Pa., 1976.

Berthoff, Rowland. *Unsettled People: Social Order and Disorder in American History*. New York, 1971.

Best, Gary Dean. *The Politics of American Individualism: Herbert Hoover in Transition, 1918–1921*. Westport, Conn., 1975.

Bird, Caroline. *The Invisible Scar*. New York, 1966.

Black, John D. *Agricultural Reform in the United States*. New York, 1929.

Blaisdell, Donald C. *Government and Agriculture: The Growth of Federal Farm Aid.* New York, 1940.

Blalock, Hubert M., Jr. *Causal Inferences in Non-Experimental Research.* Chapel Hill, N.C., 1964.

————. *Social Statistics.* 2d ed. New York, 1972.

Bogue, Allan G., ed. *Emerging Theoretical Models in Social and Political History.* Beverly Hills, Calif., 1973.

Bone, Robert A. *The Negro Novel in America.* Rev. ed. New Haven, Conn., 1965.

Boorstin, Daniel J. *The Americans.* 3 vols. New York, 1958–73.

Bornet, Vaughn Davis. *Labor Politics in a Democratic Republic: Moderation, Division, and Disruption in the Presidential Election of 1928.* Washington, D.C., 1964.

Braeman, John; Bremner, Robert; and Brody, David, eds. *Change and Continuity in Twentieth Century America: The 1920's.* Columbus, Ohio, 1968.

Brown, Francis J., and Roueck, Joseph S., eds. *One America: The History and Present Problems of Our Racial and National Minorities.* New York, 1945.

Brunner, Edmund deS.; Hughes, Gwendelyn S.; and Patten, Marjorie. *American Agricultural Villages.* New York, 1927.

Buenker, John D. *Urban Liberalism and Progressive Reform.* New York, 1973.

Bunche, Ralph J. *The Political Status of the Negro in the Age of FDR.* Edited by Dewey Grantham. Chicago, 1973.

Burner, David. *Herbert Hoover: The Public Life.* New York, 1978.

————. *The Politics of Provincialism: The Democratic Party in Transition, 1918–1932.* New York, 1968.

Burnham, Walter Dean. *Critical Elections and the Mainsprings of American Politics.* New York, 1970.

Campbell, Angus; Converse, Philip E.; Miller, Warren E.; and Stokes, Donald E. *The American Voter.* New York, 1960.

————. *Elections and the Political Order.* New York, 1966.

Cannon, James. *Bishop Cannon's Own Story.* Edited by Richard L. Watson, Jr. Durham, N.C., 1955.

Cantril, Hadley, and Strunk, Mildred, eds. *Public Opinion: 1935–1946.* Princeton, N.J., 1951.

Carter, Paul A. *Another Part of the Twenties,* New York, 1977.

————. *The Decline and Revival of the Social Gospel: Social and Political Liberalism in American Protestant Churches, 1920–1940.* Ithaca, N.Y., 1954.

————. *The Twenties in America.* New York, 1968.

Chafe, William Henry. *The American Woman: Her Changing Social, Economic, and Political Roles, 1920–1970.* New York, 1972.

Chalmers, David M. *Hooded Americanism: The First Century of the Ku Klux Klan, 1865–1965.* Garden City, N.Y., 1965.

Chambers, Clarke A. *Seedtime of Reform: American Social Service and Social Action, 1918–1933.* Minneapolis, 1963.

Chinoy, Ely. *Automobile Workers and the American Dream.* Garden City, N.Y., 1955.

Clark, Norman H. *Deliver Us from Evil: An Interpretation of American Prohibition.* New York, 1976.

Clubb, Jerome M., and Allen, Howard W., eds. *Electoral Change and Stability in American Political History.* New York, 1971.

Conkin, Paul K. *The New Deal.* New York, 1967.

Connolly, William E. *The Bias of Pluralism.* New York, 1969.

Coughlin, Bernard J. *Church and State in Social Welfare.* New York, 1965.

Cremin, Lawrence A. *The Transformation of the School: Progressivism in American Education, 1876–1957.* New York, 1961.

Curry, Lerond. *Protestant-Catholic Relations in America, World War I through Vatican II.* Lexington, Ky., 1972.

Curtis, Richard F., and Jackson, Elton F. *Inequality in American Communities.* New York, 1977.

Dabney, Virginius. *Dry Messiah: The Life of Bishop Cannon.* New York, 1949.

Dahl, Robert A. *Who Governs? Democracy and Power in an American City.* New Haven, Conn., 1961.

Davis, Jerome. *The Russian Immigrant.* New York, 1922.

Day, Donald, ed. *The Autobiography of Will Rogers.* Boston, 1949.

Democratic National Committee. *Campaign Book of the Democratic Party, Candidates and Issues in 1928.* New York, 1928.

_____. *Official Report of the Proceedings of the Democratic National Convention of 1928.* Indianapolis, Ind., 1928.

Divine, Robert A. *American Immigration Policy, 1924–1952.* New Haven, Conn., 1957.

Dogan, Mattei, and Rokkan, Stein, eds. *Quantitative Ecological Analysis in the Social Sciences.* Cambridge, Mass., 1969.

Douglas, Harlan P. *The Little Town.* New York, 1919.

Draper, Norman R., and Smith H. *Applied Regression Analysis.* New York, 1966.

Dulce, Berton, and Richter, Edward J. *Religion and the Presidency: A Recurring American Problem.* New York, 1962.

Edelman, Murray. *Politics as Symbolic Action: Mass Arousal and Quiescence.* Chicago, 1971.

_____. *The Symbolic Uses of Politics.* Urbana, Ill., 1964.

Ehrlich, Howard J. *The Social Psychology of Prejudice: A Systematic Theoretical Review and Propositional Inventory of the American Social Psychology of Prejudice.* New York, 1973.

Elder, Glen H., Jr. *Children of the Great Depression: Social Change in Life Experience.* Chicago, 1974.

Elson, Ruth Miller. *Guardians of Tradition: American Schoolbooks of the Nineteenth Century.* Lincoln, Neb., 1964.

Fausold, Martin L., and Mazuzan, George T., eds. *The Hoover Presidency: A Reappraisal.* Albany, 1974.

Fine, Nathan. *Labor and Farmer Parties in the United States, 1828–1928.* New York, 1928.

Fite, Gilbert C. *George N. Peek and the Fight for Farm Parity.* Norman, Okla., 1954.

Flynn, George Q. *American Catholics and the Roosevelt Presidency, 1932–1936.* Lexington, Ky., 1968.

Formisano, Ronald P. *The Birth of Mass Political Parties: Michigan, 1827–1861.* Princeton, N.J., 1971.

Franklin, John Hope. *From Slavery to Freedom: A History of Negro Americans.* 3d ed. New York, 1967.

Freidel, Frank. *Franklin D. Roosevelt.* 4 vols. Boston, 1952–73.

Friis, Henning. *Scandinavia: Between East and West.* Ithaca, N.Y., 1950.

Gallup, George H. *The Gallup Poll: Public Opinion, 1935–1971.* 3 vols. New York, 1972.

Garrison, Winfred Ernest. *Catholicism and the American Mind.* Chicago, 1928.

Gerard, James W. *My First Eighty-Three Years in America.* New York, 1951.

Gerson, Louis L. *The Hyphenate in Recent American Politics and Diplomacy.* Lawrence, Kan., 1964.

Glaab, Charles N., and Brown, A. Theodore. *A History of Urban America.* New York, 1967.

Gleason, Philip. *The Conservative Reformers: German-American Catholics and the Social Order.* Notre Dame, Ind., 1968.

Gordon, Milton M. *Assimilation in American Life: The Role of Race, Religion, and National Origins.* New York, 1964.

Gosnell, Harold F. *Machine Politics: Chicago Model.* 2d ed. Chicago, 1968.

———. *Negro Politicians: The Rise of Negro Politics in Chicago.* Chicago, 1935.

Graham, Frank. *Al Smith: American.* New York, 1945.

Graham, Otis L., Jr. *An Encore for Reform: The Old Progressives and the New Deal.* New York, 1967.

———. *The Great Campaigns: Reform and War in America, 1900–1928.* Englewood Cliffs, N.J., 1971.

Greenstone, John David. *Labor in American Politics.* New York, 1969.

Gusfield, Joseph. *Symbolic Crusade: Status Politics and the American Temperance Movement.* Urbana, Ill., 1963.

Handlin, Oscar. *Al Smith and His America.* Boston, 1958.

Handy, Robert T. *A Christian America: Protestant Hopes and Historical Realities.* New York, 1971.

Harbaugh, William H. *Lawyer's Lawyer: The Life of John W. Davis.* New York, 1973.

Hartley, Eugene L. *Problems in Prejudice.* New York, 1946.

Hartmann, Edward G. *The Movement to Americanize the Immigrant.* New York, 1948.

Hawgood, John A. *The Tragedy of German-America: The Germans in the United States of America during the Nineteenth Century—and After.* New York, 1940.

Hawkins, Brett W., and Lorinskas, Robert A. *The Ethnic Factor in American Politics.* Columbus, Ohio, 1970.

Henri, Florette. *Black Migration: Movement North, 1900–1920.* New York, 1975.

Herberg, Will. *Protestant, Catholic, Jew: An Essay in American Religious Sociology*. Garden City, N.Y., 1955.

Hicks, John D. *Republican Ascendancy, 1921–1933*. New York, 1960.

Higham, John. *Strangers in the Land: Patterns of American Nativism, 1860–1925*. 2d ed. New York, 1975.

Hirshson, Stanley P. *Farewell to the Bloody Shirt: Northern Republicans and the Southern Negro, 1877–1893*. Chicago, 1968.

Hofstadter, Richard. *The Age of Reform: From Bryan to F.D.R.* New York, 1955.

Hoover, Herbert. *American Individualism*. Garden City, N.Y., 1922.

———. *The New Day: The Campaign Speeches of Herbert Hoover*. Stanford, Calif., 1928.

Huber, Joan, and Form, William H. *Income and Ideology: An Analysis of the American Political Formula*. New York, 1973.

Huggins, Nathan Irvin. *Harlem Renaissance*. New York, 1971.

Huthmacher, J. Joseph. *Massachusetts People and Politics, 1919–1933*. Cambridge, Mass., 1959.

———, and Sussman, Warren I., eds. *Herbert Hoover and the Crisis of American Capitalism*. Cambridge, Mass., 1973.

Jackson, Kenneth T. *The Ku Klux Klan in the City, 1915–1930*. New York, 1967.

Jensen, Richard J. *The Winning of the Midwest: Social and Political Conflict, 1888–1896*. Chicago, 1971.

Johnston, John. *Econometric Methods*. 2d ed. New York, 1972.

Josephson, Matthew, and Josephson, Hannah. *Hero of the Cities: A Political Portrait of Alfred E. Smith*. Boston, 1969.

Kane, Edward J. *Economic Statistics and Econometrics: An Introduction to Quantitative Economics*. New York, 1968.

Kariel, Henry S. *The Decline of American Pluralism*. Stanford, Calif., 1961.

Katz, Michael B. *Class, Bureaucracy, and Schools: The Illusion of Educational Change in America*. New York, 1971.

Key, V. O., Jr., with the assistance of Milton C. Cummings, Jr. *The Responsible Electorate: Rationality in Presidential Voting, 1936–1960*. Cambridge, Mass., 1966.

Kirschner, Don S. *City and Country: Rural Responses to Urbanization in the 1920s*. Westport, Conn., 1970.

Kirscht, John P., and Dillehay, Ronald C. *Dimensions of Authoritarianism: A Review of Research and Theory*. Lexington, Ky., 1967.

Kleppner, Paul. *The Cross of Culture: A Social Analysis of Midwestern Politics, 1850–1900*. New York, 1970.

Kmenta, Jan. *Elements of Econometrics*. New York, 1971.

Knoke, David. *Change and Continuity in American Politics: The Social Bases of Political Parties*. Baltimore, 1976.

Kolko, Gabriel. *The Triumph of Conservatism: A Re-interpretation of American History, 1900–1916*. New York, 1963.

Kraditor, Aileen S. *The Ideas of the Woman Suffrage Movement, 1890–1920*. New York, 1965.

Krug, Edward A. *The Shaping of the American High School.* 2 vols. New York, 1964–72.

Kuznets, Simon. *National Income and Its Composition, 1919–1938.* New York, 1941.

Ladd, Everett C., and Hadley, Charles D. *Transformations of the American Party System: Political Coalitions from the New Deal to the 1970's.* New York, 1975.

La Follette, Belle Case, and La Follette, Fola. *Robert M. La Follette: June 14, 1855–June 18, 1925.* 2 vols. New York, 1953.

Lane, Robert E. *Political Ideology.* New York, 1962.

Langbein, Laura Irwin, and Lichtman, Allan J. *Ecological Inference.* Quantitative Applications in the Social Sciences, no. 10. Beverly Hills, Calif., 1978.

Laumann, Edward V. *Bonds of Pluralism.* New York, 1973.

Lemons, J. Stanley. *The Woman Citizen: Social Feminism in the 1920's.* Urbana, Ill., 1973.

Leuchtenburg, William E. *Franklin D. Roosevelt and the New Deal, 1932–1940.* New York, 1963.

———. *The Perils of Prosperity, 1914–32.* Chicago, 1958.

Levine, Edward M. *The Irish and Irish Politicians: A Study of Cultural and Social Alienation.* Notre Dame, Ind., 1966.

Lewinson, Paul. *Race, Class, and Party: A History of Negro Suffrage and White Politics in the South.* New York, 1932.

Lichtman, Allan J., and French, Valerie. *Historians and the Living Past: The Theory and Practice of Historical Study.* Arlington Heights, Ill., 1978.

Lippmann, Walter. *Men of Destiny.* New York, 1927.

Lipset, Seymour Martin. *Political Man: The Social Bases of Politics.* Garden City, N.Y., 1960.

Liska, Allen, ed. *The Impact of Attitudes on Behavior: The Attitude-Behavior Consistency Controversy.* New York, 1975.

Lloyd, Craig. *Aggressive Introvert: A Study of Herbert Hoover & Public Relations Management, 1912–1932.* Columbus, Ohio, 1973.

Lowi, Theodore. *The End of Liberalism: Ideology, Policy, and the Crisis of Public Authority.* New York, 1969.

Lowitt, Richard. *George W. Norris: The Persistence of a Progressive, 1913–1933.* Urbana, Ill., 1971.

Lubell, Samuel. *The Future of American Politics.* 2d ed. New York, 1955.

Lynd, Robert S., and Lynd, Helen M. *Middletown: A Study in Contemporary American Culture.* New York, 1929.

Lyons, Eugene. *Herbert Hoover: A Biography.* Garden City, N.Y., 1964.

Marshall, Charles C. *The Roman Catholic Church in the Modern State.* New York, 1928.

Martin, James G. *The Tolerant Personality.* Detroit, 1964.

Marty, Martin E. *Righteous Empire: The Protestant Experience in America.* New York, 1970.

McCoy, Charles A., ed. *Apolitical Politics: A Critique of Behavioralism.* New York, 1967.

MacKay, Kenneth Campbell. *The Progressive Movement of 1924*. New York, 1947.

Meier, August. *Negro Thought in America, 1880–1915: Racial Ideologies in the Age of Booker T. Washington*. Ann Arbor, Mich., 1963.

Merz, Charles. *The Dry Decade*. Garden City, N.Y., 1931.

Meyer, Donald B. *The Protestant Search for Political Realism, 1919–1941*. Berkeley, Calif., 1960.

Michelson, Charles. *The Ghost Talks*. New York, 1944.

Miller, Robert Moats. *American Protestantism and Social Issues, 1919–1939*. Chapel Hill, N.C., 1958.

Mischel, Walter. *Personality and Assessment*. New York, 1968.

Moles, Abraham A. *Information Theory and Esthetic Perception*. Translated by Joel E. Cohen. Urbana, Ill., 1968.

Moon, Henry Lee. *Balance of Power: The Negro Vote*. Garden City, N.Y., 1948.

Moore, Edmund A. *A Catholic Runs for President: The Campaign of 1928*. New York, 1956.

Morgan, David. *Suffragists and Democrats: The Politics of Woman Suffrage in America*. East Lansing, Mich., 1971.

Murphy, John C. *Analysis of the Attitudes of American Catholics toward the Immigrant and the Negro, 1825–1925*. Washington, D.C., 1940.

Murray, Robert K. *The 103rd Ballot: Democrats and the Disaster in Madison Square Garden*. New York, 1976.

_____. *The Politics of Normalcy: Governmental Theory and Practice in the Harding-Coolidge Era*. New York, 1973.

_____. *Red Scare: A Study in National Hysteria, 1919–1920*. Minneapolis, 1955.

Nie, Norman H.; Verba, Sidney J.; and Petrocik, John R. *The Changing American Voter*. Cambridge, Mass., 1976.

Nielson, David G. *Black Ethos: Northern Urban Negro Life and Thought, 1890–1930*. Westport, Conn., 1977.

Niemi, Richard G., and Weisberg, Herbert F. *Controversies in American Voting Behavior*. San Francisco, 1976.

Noggle, Burl. *Into the Twenties: The United States from Armistice to Normalcy*. Urbana, Ill., 1974.

Nowlin, William F. *The Negro in American National Politics*. Boston, 1931.

Nye, Russell B. *Midwestern Progressive Politics: A Historical Study of Its Origins and Development, 1870–1950*. East Lansing, Mich., 1951.

O'Brien, David J. *American Catholics and Social Reform: The New Deal Years*. New York, 1968.

O'Connor, Richard. *The First Hurrah: A Biography of Alfred E. Smith*. New York, 1970.

_____. *The German-Americans: An Informal History*. Boston, 1968.

O'Grady, Joseph P., ed. *The Immigrants' Influence on Wilson's Peace Policies*. Lexington, Ky., 1967.

Olson, Bernhard E. *Faith and Prejudice: Intergroup Problems in Protestant Curricula*. New Haven, Conn., 1963.

O'Neill, William L. *Everyone Was Brave: The Rise and Fall of Feminism in America.* Chicago, 1969.

Osofsky, Gilbert. *Harlem: The Making of a Ghetto, Negro New York, 1890–1930.* New York, 1966.

Overacker, Louise. *Money in Elections.* New York, 1932.

Park, Robert E. *The Immigrant Press and Its Control.* New York, 1922.

Peel, Roy V., and Donnelly, Thomas C. *The 1928 Campaign: An Analysis.* New York, 1931.

———. *The 1932 Campaign: An Analysis.* New York, 1935.

Perkinson, Henry J. *The Imperfect Panacea: American Faith in Education, 1865–1965.* New York, 1968.

Pomper, Gerald M. *Voters' Choice: Varieties of American Electoral Behavior.* New York, 1975.

Porter, Kirk H., and Johnson, Donald B., comps. *National Party Platforms, 1840–1964.* Urbana, Ill., 1966.

Preston, William, Jr. *Aliens and Dissenters: Federal Suppression of Radicals, 1903–1933.* New York, 1963.

Proskauer, Joseph M. *A Segment of My Years.* New York, 1950.

Prothro, James W. *The Dollar Decade: Business Ideas in the 1920's.* Baton Rouge, La., 1954.

Putney, Bryant. *Labor in Politics.* New York, 1940.

Rice, Arnold S. *The Ku Klux Klan in American Politics.* Washington, D.C., 1962.

Rippa, Alexander. *Education in a Free Society: An American History.* New York, 1972.

Rischin, Moses. *Our Own Kind.* Santa Barbara, Calif., 1960.

Robinson, Edgar Eugene, and Bornet, Vaughn Davis. *Herbert Hoover: President of the United States.* Stanford, Calif., 1975.

Rochester, Stuart. *American Liberal Disillusionment in the Wake of World War I.* University Park, Pa., 1977.

Rogin, Michael Paul. *The Intellectuals and McCarthy: The Radical Specter.* Cambridge, Mass., 1967.

Rokeach, Milton. *Beliefs, Attitudes, and Values: A Theory of Organization and Change.* San Francisco, 1968.

———. *The Open and Closed Mind: Investigations into the Nature of Belief Systems and Personality Systems.* New York, 1960.

Rolle, Andrew F. *The Immigrant Upraised: Italian Adventurers and Colonists in an Expanding America.* Norman, Okla., 1968.

Romasco, Albert U. *The Poverty of Abundance: Hoover, the Nation, the Depression.* New York, 1965.

Roosevelt, Elliot. *Franklin D. Roosevelt: His Personal Letters, 1928–1945.* Vol. 1. New York, 1970.

Rosen, Elliot A. *Hoover, Roosevelt, and the Brains Trust: From Depression to New Deal.* New York, 1977.

Saloutos, Theodore, and Hicks, John D. *Agricultural Discontent in the Middle West, 1900–1939.* Madison, Wisc., 1951.

Sanders, James W. *The Education of an Urban Minority: Catholics in Chicago, 1833–1965*. New York, 1977.

Schattschneider, E. E. *The Semisovereign People: A Realist's View of Democracy in America*. New York, 1960.

Schlesinger, Arthur M., Jr., ed. *The Coming to Power: Critical Presidential Elections in American History*. New York, 1971.

––––––. *The Crisis of the Old Order, 1919–1933*. Boston, 1957.

––––––, and Israel, Fred L., eds. *History of American Presidential Elections, 1789–1968*. New York, 1971.

Schmitt, Peter J. *Back to Nature: The Arcadian Myth in Urban America*. New York, 1969.

Schmitt, Raymond L. *The Reference Other Orientation: An Extension of the Reference Group Concept*. Carbondale, Ill., 1972.

Shannon, William V. *The American Irish*. New York, 1963.

Sherman, Richard B. *The Republican Party and Black America: From McKinley to Hoover, 1896–1933*. Charlottesville, Va., 1973.

Shideler, James H. *Farm Crisis: 1919–1923*. Los Angeles, 1957.

Shils, Edward A. *The Torment of Secrecy: The Background and Consequences of American Security Policies*. Glencoe, Ill., 1956.

Silbey, Joel H., and McSeveney, Samuel T. *Voters, Parties, and Elections: Quantitative Essays in the History of American Popular Voting Behavior*. Lexington, Mass., 1972.

Silva, Ruth C. *Rum, Religion, and Votes: 1928 Re-examined*. University Park, Pa., 1962.

Simpson, George E., and Yinger, J. Milton. *Racial and Cultural Minorities*. 3d ed. New York, 1965.

Sinclair, Andrew. *Era of Excess: A Social History of the Prohibition Movement*. New York, 1964.

Smith, Alfred E. *The Campaign Addresses of Governor Alfred E. Smith*. Washington, D.C., 1929.

Smith, Rembert Gilman. *Politics in a Protestant Church*. Atlanta, 1930.

Sorokin, Pitirim, and Zimmerman, Carle C. *Principles of Rural-Urban Sociology*. New York, 1929.

Soule, George H. *Prosperity Decade*. New York, 1952.

Stark, Rodney, and Glock, Charles Y. *American Piety: The Nature of Religious Commitment*. Berkeley, Calif., 1968.

Sternsher, Bernard. *Consensus, Conflict, and American Historians*. London, 1975.

––––––, ed. *The Negro in Depression and War: Prelude to Revolution, 1930–1945*. Chicago, 1969.

Strauss, Anselm L. *Images of the American City*. New York, 1961.

Strout, Cushing. *The New Heavens and New Earth: Political Religion in America*. New York, 1974.

Sundquist, James L. *Dynamics of the Party System*. Washington, D.C., 1973.

Tatum, Elbert Lee. *The Changed Political Thought of the Negro, 1915–1940*. New York, 1951.

Thelen, David P. *Robert M. La Follette and the Insurgent Spirit*. Boston, 1976.

Thomas, John L. *The American Catholic Family*. Englewood Cliffs, N.J., 1956.

Timberlake, James H. *Prohibition and the Progressive Movement, 1900–1920*. Cambridge, Mass., 1963.

Toch, Hans. *The Social Psychology of Social Movements*. Indianapolis, 1965.

Trilling, Richard. *Party Image and Electoral Behavior*. New York, 1976.

Truman, David B. *The Governmental Process: Political Interests and Public Opinion*. New York, 1951.

United States Department of Agriculture. *Yearbook of Agriculture*. Washington, D.C., 1923–30.

United States Department of Commerce, Bureau of the Census. *The Statistical History of the United States from Colonial Times to the Present*. Stamford, Conn., 1965.

_____. *Statistical Abstract of the United States*. Washington, D.C., 1931.

Warner, Emily Smith. *The Happy Warrior: A Biography of My Father*. Garden City, N.Y., 1956.

Warren, Harris G. *Herbert Hoover and the Great Depression*. New York, 1959.

Weinstein, James. *The Decline of Socialism in America, 1912–1925*. New York, 1967.

White, William Allen. *Masks in a Pageant*. New York, 1928.

Wiebe, Robert H. *Businessmen and Reform: A Study of the Progressive Movement*. Cambridge, Mass., 1962.

Williams, Michael. *The Shadow of the Pope*. New York, 1932.

Williams, William Appleman. *The Tragedy of American Diplomacy*. Rev. ed. New York, 1962.

Wilson, Joan Hoff. *Herbert Hoover: Forgotten Progressive*. Boston, 1975.

_____, ed. *The Twenties: The Critical Issues*. Boston, 1972.

Wittke, Carl. *German-Americans and the World War*. Columbus, Ohio, 1936.

Work, Monroe N., ed. *The Negro Handbook*. Tuskegee, Ala., 1937.

Yinger, J. Milton. *Religion in the Struggle for Power: A Study in the Sociology of Religion*. New York, 1961.

Zieger, Robert H. *Republicans and Labor, 1919–1929*. Lexington, Ky., 1969.

Zimbardo, Philip, and Ebbesen, Ebbe E. *Influencing Attitudes and Changing Behavior: A Basic Introduction to Relevant Methodology, Theory, and Applications*. Reading, Mass., 1969.

Articles

Abrahamson, Mark. "The Social Dimensions of Urbanism." *Social Forces* 52 (1974): 376–83.

Abramson, Harold J. "Ethnic Diversity within Catholicism: A Comparative Analysis of Contemporary and Historical Religion." *Journal of Social History* 4 (1971): 359–88.

Acock, Alan C., and DeFleur, Melvin L. "A Configurational Approach to Contingent Consistency in the Attitude-Behavior Relationship." *American Sociological Review* 37 (1972): 714–26.

Alba, Richard D. "Ethnic Networks and Tolerant Attitudes." *Public Opinion Quarterly* 42 (1978): 1–16.

Allport, Gordon W. "The Composition of Political Attitudes." *American Journal of Sociology* 35 (1929): 220–38.

Allswang, John M. "The Chicago Negro Voter." In *The Negro in Depression and War*, edited by Bernard Sternsher. Chicago, 1969.

Alvarez, David J., and True, Edmund J. "Critical Elections and Partisan Realignment: An Urban Test Case." *Polity* 5 (1973): 563–76.

Andersen, Kristi. "Generation, Partisan Shift, and Realignment: A Glance Back to the New Deal." In *The Changing American Voter*, by Norman H. Nie, Sidney J. Verba, and John R. Petrocik. Cambridge, Mass., 1976.

Andrews, William. "American Voting Participation." *Western Political Quarterly* 19 (1966): 639–52.

App, Austin J. "The Germans." In *The Immigrants' Influence on Wilson's Peace Policies*, edited by Joseph P. O'Grady. Lexington, Ky., 1967.

Axelrod, Robert. "Where the Votes Come From: An Analysis of Electoral Coalitions, 1952–1968." *American Political Science Review* 66 (1972): 11–20.

Baggaley, Andrew R. "Religious Influences on Wisconsin Voting, 1928–1960." *American Political Science Review* 56 (1962): 66–70.

Balbus, Isaac D. "The Concept of Interest in Pluralist and Marxian Analysis." *Politics and Society* 1 (1971): 151–77.

Beck, Paul Allen. "Environment and Party: The Impact of Political and Demographic County Characteristics on Party Behavior." *American Political Science Review* 68 (1974): 1229–44.

Bem, Daryl J., and Allen, Andrea. "On Predicting Some of the People Some of the Time: The Search for Cross-Situational Consistencies in Behavior." *Psychological Review* 81 (1974): 506–20.

Bernstein, Barton J. "The New Deal." In *Toward a New Past: Dissenting Essays in American History*, edited by Barton J. Bernstein. New York, 1968.

Bicha, Karel Denis. "Liberalism Frustrated: The League for Independent Political Action, 1928–1933." *Mid-America* 48 (1966): 19–28.

Blair, John L. "A Time for Parting: The Negro during the Coolidge Years." *Journal of American Studies* 3 (1971): 177–99.

Blalock, Hubert M., Jr. "Causal Inferences, Closed Populations, and Measures of Association." *American Political Science Review* 61 (1967): 130–36.

Boyd, Richard W. "Popular Control of Public Policy: A Normal Vote Analysis of the 1968 Election." *American Political Science Review* 66 (1972): 429–49.

Bradford, Richard H. "Religion and Politics: Alfred E. Smith and the Election of 1928 in West Virginia." *West Virginia History* (1975): 213–21.

Brigham, John C. "Ethnic Stereotypes." *Psychological Bulletin* 76 (1971): 15–38.

Brody, David. "The Rise and Decline of Welfare Capitalism." In *Change and Continuity in Twentieth-Century America: The Twenties*, edited by John Braeman, Robert Bremner, and David Brody. Columbus, Ohio, 1968.

Burbank, Garin. "Two Defenses of Community: The Oklahoma Klan and Its Opposition." Paper presented at the 1978 Meeting of the Organization of American Historians.

Burchell, R. A. "Did the Irish and German Voters Desert the Democrats in 1920? A Tentative Statistical Answer." *Journal of American Studies* 6 (1972): 153–64.

Burner, David B. "The Brown Derby Campaign." *New York History* 66 (1965): 356–80.

————. "Before the Crash: Hoover's First Eight Months in the Presidency." In *The Hoover Presidency: A Reappraisal*, edited by Martin L. Fausold and George T. Mazuzan. New York, 1974.

Burnham, J. C. "New Perspectives on the Prohibition Experiment of the 1920's." *Journal of Social History* 2 (1968): 51–68.

Burnham, Walter Dean. "Theory and Voting Research: Some Reflections on Converse's Change in the American Electorate." *American Political Science Review* 68 (1974): 1002–23.

————, and Sprague, John. "Additive and Multiplicative Models of the Voting Universe: The Case of Pennsylvania, 1960–1968." *American Political Science Review* 64 (1970): 471–90.

Burns, Arthur F. "Ideology of Businessmen and Presidential Elections." *Southwestern Political and Social Science Quarterly* 10 (1929): 230–36.

Carleton, William G. "The Popish Plot of 1928: Smith-Hoover Presidential Campaign." *Forum* 112 (1949): 141–47.

Carlson, Earland I. "Franklin D. Roosevelt's Post-Mortem of the 1928 Election." *Midwest Journal of Political Science* 8 (1964): 298–308.

Carter, Paul A. "The Campaign of 1928 Re-examined: A Study in Political Folklore." *Wisconsin Magazine of History* 46 (1963): 263–72.

————. "The Other Catholic Candidate: The 1928 Presidential Bid of Thomas J. Walsh." *Pacific Northwest Quarterly* 55 (1964): 1 8.

Casey, Ralph D. "Scripps-Howard Newspapers in the 1928 Presidential Campaign." *Journalism Quarterly* 7 (1930): 207–31.

Childs, Harwood L. "Ranking Motives in Voting." *American Journal of Sociology* 41 (1935): 59–66.

Christenson, Alice M. "Agricultural Pressure and Governmental Response, 1919–1929." *Agricultural History* 11 (1937): 33–42.

Chyz, Yaroslav. "Number, Distribution and Circulation of the Foreign Language Press in the United States." *Interpreter Releases* 20 (1943): 290–97.

Cigler, Allan J., and Getter, Russell. "Conflict Reduction in the Post-Election Period: A Test of the Depolarization Thesis." *Western Political Quarterly* 30 (1977): 363–76.

Clague, Ewan, and Geddes, Anne E. "Why We Need a Social Security Program." *Annals of the American Academy of Political and Social Science* 202 (1939): 8–21.

Clubb, Jerome M., and Allen, Howard W. "The Cities and the Election of 1928: Partisan Realignment?" *American Historical Review* 74 (1969): 1205–20.

Coben, Stanley. "The Assault on Victorianism in the Twentieth Century." *American Quarterly* 27 (1975): 604–25.

————. "A Study in Nativism: The American Red Scare of 1919–1920." *Political Science Quarterly* 79 (1964): 52–75.

Cohen, David K. "Immigrants and the Schools." *Review of Educational Research* 40 (1970): 13–27.

Colburn, David R. "Governor Alfred E. Smith and Penal Reform." *Political Science Quarterly* 91 (1976): 315–27.

Collins, Ernest M. "Cincinnati Negroes and Presidential Politics." *Journal of Negro History* 41 (1956): 131–37.

Conway, Jill. "Women Reformers and American Culture, 1870–1930." *Journal of Social History* 5 (1971–72): 164–77.

Crespi, Irving. "What Kinds of Attitude Measures are Predictive of Behavior." *Public Opinion Quarterly* 35 (1971): 327–34.

Cuddy, Edward. "Irish-Americans and the 1916 Election: An Episode in Immigration Adjustment." *American Quarterly* (1969): 228–43.

Davey, A. G. "Attitudes and the Prediction of Social Conduct." *British Journal of Social and Clinical Psychology* 15 (1976): 11–22.

Davis, Joseph S. "Herbert Hoover, 1874–1964, Another Appraisal." *South Atlantic Quarterly* 68 (1969): 295–318.

Degler, Carl N. "American Political Parties and the Rise of the City: An Interpretation." *Journal of American History* 51 (1964): 41–59.

_____. "The Ordeal of Herbert Hoover." *Yale Review* 52 (1963): 563–83.

Dewey, Richard. "The Rural-Urban Continuum: Real But Relatively Unimportant." *American Journal of Sociology* 66 (1960): 60–66.

Dobson, Douglas, and St. Angelo, Douglas. "Party Identification and the Floating Vote: Some Dynamics." *American Political Science Review* 69 (1975): 481–90.

Doherty, Herbert J., Jr. "Florida and the Presidential Election of 1928." *Florida Historical Quarterly* 26 (1947): 174–86.

Dolan, Jay P. "A Critical Period in American Catholicism." *Review of Politics* 35 (1973): 523–36.

Dollar, Charles M. "Innovation in Historical Research: A Computer Approach." *Computers and the Humanities* 3 (1969): 139–51.

Dreyer, Edward C. "Change and Stability in Party Identification." *Journal of Politics* 35 (1973): 712–23.

Duff, John B. "The Italians." In *The Immigrants' Influence on Wilson's Peace Policies*, edited by Joseph P. O'Grady. Lexington, Ky., 1967.

Dykstra, Robert R. "Town-Country Conflict: A Hidden Dimension in American Social History." *Agricultural History* 38 (1964): 195–204.

Edmunson, Ben G. "Pat Harrison and Mississippi in the Presidential Elections of 1924 and 1928." *Journal of Mississippi History* 33 (1971): 333–50.

Eldersveld, Samuel J. "The Influences of Metropolitan Party Pluralities in Presidential Elections since 1920: A Study of Twelve Cities." *American Political Science Review* 43 (1949): 1189–1206.

Endler, Norman S. "The Person versus the Situation—A Pseudo Issue? A Response to Alker." *Journal of Personality* 41 (1973): 287–303.

Fairbanks, David. "Religious Forces and 'Morality' Policies in the American States." *Western Political Quarterly* 30 (1977): 411–17.

Farris, Charles D. "Prohibition as a Political Issue." *Journal of Politics* 23 (1961): 507–25.

Feldman, Jack M., and Hillerman, Robert J. "Stereotype Attribution Revisited: The Role of Stimulus Characteristics, Racial Attitude, and Cognitive Differentiation." *Journal of Personality and Social Psychology* 31 (1975): 1177–88.

Ferrar, Jane W. "The Dimensions of Tolerance." *Pacific Sociological Review* 19 (1976): 63–81.

Fesbach, Seymour, and Janis, Irving L. "Effects of Fear Arousing Communications." *Journal of Abnormal and Social Psychology* 48 (1953): 78–92.

Fiorina, Morris B. "An Outline for a Model of Party Choice." *American Journal of Political Science* 21 (1977): 601–25.

Fischer, Claude S. "The Effect of Urban Life on Traditional Values." *Social Forces* 53 (1975): 420–32.

————. "Toward a Subcultural Theory of Urbanism." *American Journal of Sociology* 80 (1975): 1319–41.

Fite, Gilbert C. "The Agricultural Issue in the Presidential Campaign of 1928." *Mississippi Valley Historical Review* 37 (1951): 653–72.

Flanigan, William H., and Zingale, Nancy H. "The Measurement of Electoral Change." *Political Methodology* 1 (1974): 49–82.

Frazier, E. Franklin. "American Negroes' New Leaders." *Current History* 28 (1928): 55–59.

Freedman, Estelle B. "The New Woman: Changing Views of Women in the 1920's." *Journal of American History* 61 (1974): 372–93.

Furston, Richard. "The Supreme Court and Critical Elections." *American Political Science Review* 69 (1975): 795–811.

Gabennesch, Howard. "Authoritarianism as World View." *American Journal of Sociology* 77 (1972): 857–75.

Gans, Herbert. "Urbanism and Suburbanism as Ways of Life: A Re-evaluation of Definitions." In *Human Behavior and Social Processes: An Interactionist Approach*, edited by Arnold M. Rose. Boston, 1962.

Garson, G. David. "Automobile Workers and the Radical Dream." *Politics and Society* (1973): 163–77.

Garson, Robert A. "Political Fundamentalism and Popular Democracy in the 1920's." *South Atlantic Quarterly* 76 (1977): 219–33.

Ginsberg, Benjamin. "Critical Elections and the Substance of Party Conflict, 1844–1968." *Midwest Journal of Political Science* 16 (1972): 603–25.

————. "Elections and Public Policy." *American Political Science Review* 70 (1976): 41–49.

Glaab, Charles N. "Metropolis and Suburb: The Changing American City." In *Change and Continuity in Twentieth Century America: The 1920's*, edited by John Braeman, Robert Bremner, and David Brody. Columbus, Ohio, 1968.

Glad, Paul W. "Progressives and the Business Culture of the 1920s." *Journal of American History* 53 (1966): 75–89.

Gold, David. "Statistical Tests and Substantive Significance." *American Sociologist* 4 (1969): 42–46.

Goldsmith, Selma F. "The Relation of Census Income Distribution Statistics to Other Income Data." In *Income and Wealth*. vol. 23. Conference on Research in Income and Wealth, National Bureau of Economic Research, Princeton, N.J., 1958.

Goodman, Leo A. "Some Alternatives to Ecological Correlation." *American Journal of Sociology* 64 (1959): 610–25.

Gordon, Milton M. "Assimilation in America: Theory and Reality." In *The Ethnic Factor in American Politics*, edited by Brett W. Hawkins and Robert A. Lorinskas. Columbus, Ohio, 1970.

Gordon, Rita Werner. "The Change in the Political Alignment of Chicago's Negroes During the New Deal." *Journal of American History* 56 (1969): 584–603.

Gordon, Robert A. "Issues in Multiple Regression." *American Journal of Sociology* 73 (1968): 592–616.

Greer, Scot. "Urbanism Reconsidered: A Comparative Study of Local Areas in a Metropolis." *American Sociological Review* 21 (1956): 19–25.

Griffin, William. "Black Insurgency in the Republican Party of Ohio, 1920–1932." *Ohio History* 82 (1973): 25–45.

Gross, Steven Jay, and Niman, C. Michael. "Attitude-Behavior Consistency: A Review." *Public Opinion Quarterly* 39 (1975): 358–68.

Guest, Avery M. "Class Consciousness and American Political Attitudes." *Social Forces* 52 (1974): 496–510.

Hand, Samuel B. "Al Smith, Franklin D. Roosevelt, and the New Deal: Some Comments on Perspective." *Historian* 27 (1965): 366–81.

Harris, Victor A., and Jellison, Jerald M. "Fear-arousing Communications, False Physiological Feedback, and Acceptance of Recommendations." *Journal of Experimental Social Psychology* 7 (1971): 269–79.

Hattery, John W. "The Presidential Election Campaigns of 1928 and 1960: A Comparison of *The Christian Century* and *America*." *Journal of Church and State* 9 (1967): 36–50.

Havig, Alan R. "A Disputed Legacy: Roosevelt Progressives and the La Follette Campaign of 1924." *Mid-America* 53 (1971): 44–64.

Hawley, Ellis W. "Herbert Hoover, the Commerce Secretariat, and the Vision of an 'Associative State,' 1921–1928." *Journal of American History* 61 (1974): 116–40.

Heberlein, Thomas A., and Black, J. Stanley. "Attitudinal Specificity and the Prediction of Behavior in a Field Setting." *Journal of Personality and Social Psychology* 33 (1976): 474–79.

Hendrick, Clyde; Giesen, Martin; and Borden, Richard. "False Physiological Feedback and Persuasion: Effect of Fear Arousal versus Fear Reduction on Attitude Change." *Journal of Personality* 43 (1975): 196–214.

Higham, John. "The Cult of the 'American Consensus': Homogenizing Our History." *Commentary* 27 (1959): 93–100.

Hofstadter, Richard. "Could a Protestant Have Beaten Hoover in 1928?" *Reporter* 22 (1960): 31–33.

Hoge, Dean R., and Jackson, W. Carroll. "Religiosity and Prejudice North and South." *Journal for the Scientific Study of Religion* 12 (1973): 181–97.

Howe, Daniel Walker. "American Victorianism as a Culture." *American Quarterly* 27 (1975): 507–32.

Hunt, Thomas C. "Public Schools, 'Americanism,' and the Immigrant at the Turn of the Century." *Journal of General Education* 26 (1974): 147–55.

Hunter, Albert. "The Loss of Community: An Empirical Test through Replication." *American Sociological Review* 40 (1975): 537–52.

Irwin, Laura, and Lichtman, Allan J. "Across the Great Divide: Inferring Individual Level Behavior from Aggregate Data." *Political Methodology* 4 (1976): 411–39.

Jackman, Mary R., and Jackman, Robert W. "An Interpretation of the Relation between Objective and Subjective Social Status." *American Sociological Review* 38 (1973): 569–82.

Jahnige, Thomas P. "Critical Elections and Social Change: Towards a Dynamic Explanation of Natural Party Competition in the United States." *Polity* 3 (1971): 465–500.

Jennings, M. Kent, and Niemi, Richard G. "Party Identification at Multiple Levels of Government." *American Journal of Sociology* 72 (1966): 86–101.

Jensen, Richard J. "History from a Deck of IBM Cards." *Reviews in American History* 6 (1978): 229–34.

Jones, Stanley H., and Cook, Stuart W. "The Influence of Attitude on Judgments of the Effectiveness of Alternative Social Policies." *Journal of Personality and Social Psychology* 32 (1975): 762–73.

Kelley, Darwin N. "The McNary-Haugen Bills, 1924–1928." *Agricultural History* 14 (1940): 170–80.

Kelley, Donald B. "Deep South Dilemma: The Mississippi Press in the Presidential Election of 1928." *Journal of Mississippi History* 25 (1963): 63–92.

Key, V. O., Jr. "Secular Realignment and the Party System." *Journal of Politics* 21 (1959): 198–210.

————. "A Theory of Critical Elections." *Journal of Politics* 17 (1955): 3–18.

Kilson, Martin L., Jr. "Political Change in the Negro Ghetto, 1900–1940s." In *Key Issues of the Afro-American Experience*, edited by Nathan L. Huggins, Martin L. Kilson, Jr., and Daniel M. Fox. New York, 1971.

Kirschner, Don S. "Conflicts and Politics in the 1920's: Historiography and Prospects." *Mid-America* 48 (1966): 219–33.

Koenig, Samuel. "Second and Third Generation Americans." In *One America: The History and Present Problems of Our Racial and National Minorities*, edited by Francis J. Brown and Joseph C. Roucek. New York, 1945.

Kolbe, Richard L. "Culture, Political Parties and Voting Behavior: Schuykill County." *Polity* 8 (1975): 241–68.

Kousser, J. Morgan. "The 'New Political History': A Methodological Critique." *Reviews in American History* 4 (1976): 1–14.

Kyvig, David E. "Women against Prohibition." *American Quarterly* 28 (1976): 464–82.

Langer, William L. "The Next Assignment." *American Historical Review* 63 (1958): 283–304.

Leary, William M., Jr. "Woodrow Wilson, Irish-Americans, and the Election of 1916." *Journal of American History* 54 (1967): 57–72.

Lemons, J. Stanley. "Social Feminism in the 1920s: Progressive Women and Industrial Legislation." *Labor History* 14 (1973): 83–91.

Levine, Marc V. "Standing Political Decisions and Critical Realignment: The Pattern of Maryland Politics, 1872–1948." *Journal of Politics* 38 (1976): 292–325.

Lichtman, Allan J. "Correlation, Regression, and the Ecological Fallacy: A Critique." *Journal of Interdisciplinary History* 4 (1974): 417–33.

_____. "Critical Election Theory and the Reality of American Presidential Politics, 1916–1940." *American Historical Review* 81 (1976): 317–51.

_____, and Langbein, Laura I. "Regression vs. Homogeneous Units: A Specification Analysis." *Social Science History* 2 (Winter 1978): 172–93.

Lindeen, James W. "Longitudinal Analysis of Republican Presidential Electoral Trends, 1896–1968." *Midwest Journal of Political Science* 16 (1972): 102–22.

Link, Arthur S. "What Happened to the Progressive Movement in the 1920's?" *American Historical Review* 64 (1959): 833–51.

Lisenby, William Foy. "Brough, Baptists, and Bombast: The Election of 1928." *Arkansas Historical Quarterly* 32 (1973): 120–31.

Locke, Alain. "The New Negro." In *The New Negro*, edited by Alain Locke. New York, 1925.

Lowe, George D., and Peek, Charles W. "Location and Lifestyle: The Comparative Explanatory Ability of Urbanism and Rurality." *Rural Sociology* 39 (1974): 392–420.

Lowi, Theodore J. "American Business, Public Policy, Case Studies, and Political Theory." *World Politics* 16 (1964): 677–715.

Lundberg, George A. "The Newspaper and Public Opinion." *Social Forces* 4 (1926): 709–15.

McCarthy, Dennis J. "The British." In *The Immigrants' Influence on Wilson's Peace Policies*, edited by Joseph P. O'Grady. Lexington, Ky., 1967.

McCormick, Richard L. "Ethno-Cultural Interpretations of Nineteenth-Century American Voting Behavior." *Political Science Quarterly* 89 (1974): 351–77.

McCoy, Donald R. "To the White House: Herbert Hoover, August 1927—March 1929." In *The Hoover Presidency: A Reappraisal*, edited by Martin L. Fausold and George T. Mazuzan. New York, 1974.

MacRae, Duncan, Jr., and Meldrum, James A. "Critical Elections in Illinois: 1888–1958." *American Political Science Review* 54 (1960): 669–83.

Marcus, Robert D. "Presidential Elections in the American Political System." *Review of Politics* 33 (1971): 3–23.

Margolis, Michael. "From Confusion to Confusion: Issues and the American Voter (1956–1972)." *American Political Science Review* 71 (1977): 31–43.

Margulies, Herbert F. "The Election of 1920 in Wisconsin: The Return to 'Normalcy' Reappraised." *Wisconsin Magazine of History* 41 (1957): 15–22.
———. "Recent Opinion on the Decline of the Progressive Movement." *Mid-America* 45 (1963): 250–68.
Martin, Charles H. "Negro Leaders, the Republican Party, and the Election of 1932." *Phylon* 32 (1971): 85–93.
Massey, Robert K., Jr. "The Democratic Laggard: Massachusetts in 1932." *New England Quarterly* 44 (1971): 553–74.
Maxwell, Robert S. "The Progressive Bridge: Reform Sentiment in the United States between the New Freedom and the New Deal." *Indiana Magazine of History* 63 (1967): 83–102.
May, Henry F. "Shifting Perspectives on the 1920's." *Mississippi Valley Historical Review* 43 (1956): 405–27.
Meier, August, and Rudwick, Elliot. "The Rise of Segregation in the Federal Bureaucracy, 1900–1930." *Phylon* 28 (1967): 178–84.
Meier, Kenneth J. "Party Identification and Vote Choice: The Causal Relationship." *Western Political Quarterly* 28 (1975): 496–505.
Meier, Norman C. "Motives in Voting: A Study in Public Opinion." *American Journal of Sociology* 31 (1925): 199–212.
Meltzer, Leo. "Comparing Relationships of Individual and Average Variables to Individual Response." *American Sociological Review* 28 (1963): 117–23.
Mezei, Louis. "Perceived Social Pressure as an Explanation of Shifts in the Relative Influence of Race and Belief on Prejudice across Social Interactions." *Journal of Personality and Social Psychology* 19 (1971): 69–81.
Middleton, Russell. "Regional Differences in Prejudice." *American Sociological Review* 41 (1976): 94–117.
Miller, Arthur H.; Miller, Warren E.; Raine, Alden S.; and Brown, Thad A. "A Majority Party in Disarray: Policy Polarization in the 1972 Election, with Comments and Rejoinder." *American Political Science Review* 70 (1976): 753–849.
Miller, Robert Moats. "A Footnote to the Role of the Protestant Churches in the Election of 1928." *Church History* 25 (1956): 145–59.
———. "The Ku Klux Klan." In *Change and Continuity in Twentieth-Century America: The 1920s*, edited by John Bracman, Robert Bremmer, and David Brody. Columbus, Ohio, 1968.
Monroe, Alan D. "Urbanism and Voter Turnout: A Note on Some Unexpected Findings." *American Journal of Political Science* 21 (1977): 71–78.
Neal, Nevin E. "The Smith-Robinson Campaign of 1928." *Arkansas Historical Quarterly* 19 (1960): 3–11.
Noggle, Burl. "The Twenties: A New Historiographical Frontier." *Journal of American History* 52 (1966): 299–324.
Odegard, Peter H. "Catholicism and Elections in the United States." In *Religion and Politics*, edited by Peter H. Odegard. New Brunswick, N.J., 1960.
———. "Political Parties and Group Pressures." *Annals of the American Academy of Political and Social Science* 179 (1935): 68–81.

Ogburn, William F., and Talbot, Nell Snow. "A Measurement of the Factors in the Presidential Election of 1928." *Social Forces* 8 (1929): 175–83.

O'Grady, Joseph P. "The Irish." In *The Immigrants' Influence on Wilson's Peace Policies*, edited by Joseph P. O'Grady. Lexington, Ky., 1967.

Orpen, Christopher. "Authoritarianism in an 'Authoritarian' Culture: The Case of Afrikaans-Speaking South Africa." *Journal of Social Psychology* 81 (1970): 119–20.

Panunzio, Constantine. "The Foreign-Born and Prohibition." *Annals of the American Academy of Political and Social Science* 163 (1932): 147–54.

Parenti, Michael. "Ethnic Politics and the Persistence of Ethnic Identification." In *Ethnic Group Politics*, edited by Harry A. Bailey and Ellis Katz. Columbus, Ohio, 1969.

Park, Robert E. "The Foreign Language Press and Social Progress." *Proceedings of the National Conference of Social Work* 47 (1920): 493–500.

Peterson, Peter L. "Stopping Al Smith: The 1928 Democratic Primary in South Dakota." *South Dakota History* 4 (1974): 439–54.

Pierce, John C. "Party Identification and the Changing Role of Ideology in American Politics." *Midwest Journal of Political Science* 14 (1970): 25–42.

Piven, Frances Fox. "The Social Structuring of Political Protest." *Politics and Society* 6 (1976): 297–326.

Pollock, James K., Jr. "Campaign Funds in 1928." *American Political Science Review* 23 (1929): 59–69.

Pomper, Gerald M. "The Classification of Presidential Elections." *Journal of Politics* 29 (1967): 533–66.

_____. "The Decline of the Party in American Elections." *Political Science Quarterly* 92 (1977): 21–41.

_____. "From Confusion to Clarity: Issues and American Voters, 1956–1968." *American Political Science Review* 66 (1972): 415–28.

Popkin, Samuel; Gorman, John W.; Phillips, Charles; and Smith, Jeffrey A. "What Have You Done for Me Lately? Toward an Investment Theory of Voting." *American Political Science Review* 70 (1976): 779–805.

Price, Douglas. "Critical Elections and Party History: A Critical View." *Polity* 4 (1971): 236–42.

Przeworski, Adam. "Contextual Models of Political Behavior." *Political Methodology* 1 (1974): 44–50.

Putnam, Jackson K. "The Persistence of Progressivism in the 1920's: The Case of California." *Pacific Historical Review* 35 (1966): 395–411.

Putnam, Robert D. "Political Attitudes and the Local Community." *American Political Science Review* 60 (1966): 640–54.

Ray, J. J. "Do Authoritarians Hold Authoritarian Attitudes?" *Human Relations* 29 (1976): 307–25.

Reagan, Hugh D. "Race As a Factor in the Presidential Election of 1928 in Alabama." *Alabama Review* 19 (1966): 5–19.

Regan, Dennis T., and Fazio, Russell. "On the Consistency between Attitudes and Behavior: Look to the Method of Attitude Formation." *Journal of Experimental Social Psychology* 13 (1977): 28–45.

Repass, David. "Issue Saliency and Party Choice." *American Political Science Review* 65 (1971): 389–400.

Rice, Stuart A., and Willey, Malcolm M. "American Women's Ineffective Use of the Vote." *Current History* 20 (1924): 641–47.

————. "A Sex Cleavage in the Presidential Election of 1920." *Journal of the American Statistical Association* 29 (1928): 519–20.

Rogers, Ronald W., and Mewborn, Ronald C. "Fear Appeals and Attitude Change: Effects of a Threat's Noxiousness, Probability of Occurrence, and the Efficacy of Coping Responses." *Journal of Personality and Social Psychology* 34 (1976): 54–61.

Roof, W. Clark. "The Local-Cosmopolitan Orientation and Traditional Religious Commitment." *Sociological Analysis* 33 (1972): 1–15.

Roucek, Joseph S. "The Foreign-Language and Negro Press." In *One America: The History and Present Problems of Our Racial and National Minorities*, edited by Francis J. Brown and Joseph C. Roucek. New York, 1945.

Rusk, Jerrold G. "The American Electoral Universe: Speculation and Evidence." *American Political Science Review* 68 (1974): 1028–49.

————. "The Effect of the Australian Ballot Reform on Split-Ticket Voting: 1876–1908." *American Political Science Review* 64 (1970): 1220–38.

Sakoda, James M.; Cohen, Burton H.; and Beall, Geoffrey. "Test of Significance for a Series of Statistical Tests." *Psychological Bulletin* 51 (1954): 172–75.

Santee, Richard T., and Jackson, Jay. "Cultural Values as a Source of Normative Sanctions." *Pacific Sociological Review* 20 (1977): 439–54.

Sarason, Irwin G.; Smith, Ronald E.; and Diener, Edward. "Personality Research: Components of Variance Attributable to the Person and the Situation." *Journal of Personality and Social Psychology* 32 (1975): 199–204.

Schlozman, Kay Lehman. "Coping with the American Dream: Maintaining Self-Respect in an Achieving Society." *Politics and Society* 6 (1976): 241–63.

Schnore, Leo F. "The Rural-Urban Variable: An Urbanite's Perspective." *Rural Sociology* 31 (1966): 129–43.

Schofield, Kent. "The Public Image of Herbert Hoover in the 1928 Campaign." *Mid-America* 51 (1969): 278–93.

Schulman, Mark A., and Pomper, Gerald M. "Variability in Electoral Behavior: Longitudinal Perspectives from Causal Modeling." *American Journal of Political Science* 19 (1975): 1–18.

Schwartz, Jordan A. "Al Smith in the Thirties." *New York History* (1964): 316–30.

Scott, Anne F. "After Suffrage: Southern Women in the Twenties." *Journal of Southern History* 30 (1964): 298–318.

Searing, Donald U.; Schwartz, Joel J.; and Lind, Alden E. "The Structuring Principle: Political Socialization and Belief System." *American Political Science Review* 17 (1973): 415–32.

Seidman, David. "On Choosing between Linear and Log-Linear Models." *Journal of Politics* 38 (1976): 461–66.

Sellers, Charles. "The Equilibrium Cycle in Two-Party Politics." *Public Opinion Quarterly* 29 (1965): 16–38.

Shapiro, Stanley. "The Great War and Reform: Liberals and Labor, 1917–1919." *Labor History* 12 (1971): 323–44.

Shideler, James H. "The Disintegration of the Progressive Party Movement of 1924." *Historian* 13 (1951): 189–201.

_____. "*Flappers and Philosophers*, and Farmers: Rural-Urban Tensions of the Twenties." *Agricultural History* 47 (1973): 283–99.

_____. "The La Follette Progressive Party Campaign of 1924." *Wisconsin Magazine of History* 33 (1950): 444–57.

Shively, W. Phillips. "A Reinterpretation of the New Deal Realignment." *Public Opinion Quarterly* 35 (1971–72): 621–24.

Shover, John L. "The Emergence of a Two-Party System in Republican Philadelphia, 1924–1936." *Journal of American History* 60 (1974): 985–1002.

_____. "Was 1928 a Critical Election in California?" *Pacific Northwest Quarterly* 58 (1967): 196–204.

Sigall, Harold, and Page, Richard. "Current Stereotypes: A Little Fading, A Little Faking." *Journal of Personality and Social Psychology* 18 (1971): 247–55.

Simrell, V. E. "Oratory of the 1928 Presidential Campaign." *Quarterly Journal of Speech* 15 (1929): 128–34.

Sinclair, Barbara Deckard. "Party Realignment and the Transformation of the Political Agenda: The House of Representatives, 1925–1938." *American Political Science Review* 71 (1977): 940–53.

_____. "The Policy Consequences of Party Realignment—Social Welfare Legislation in the House of Representatives, 1933–1954." *American Journal of Political Science* 22 (1978): 83–105.

Smith, Kay H., and Richards, Barrie. "Effects of a Rational Appeal and of Anxiety on Conformity Behavior." *Journal of Personality and Social Psychology* 5 (1967): 122–26.

Smith, T. Lynn. "The Role of the Village in American Rural Society." *Rural Sociology* 7 (1942): 10–21.

Smylie, James H. "The Roman Catholic Church, the State and Al Smith." *Church History* 29 (1960): 321–43.

Snyder, Mark, and Swann, William B. "When Actions Reflect Attitudes: The Politics of Impression Management." *Journal of Personality and Social Psychology* 34 (1976): 1034–42.

_____, and Tanke, Elizabeth Decker. "Behavior and Attitude: Some People Are More Consistent Than Others." *Journal of Personality* 44 (1976): 501–17.

Soares, Glaucio, and Hamblin, Robert T. "Socio-Economic Variables and Voting for the Radical Left: Chile, 1952." *American Political Science Review* 61 (1967): 1053–65.

Stave, Bruce Martin. "The 'La Follette Revolution' and the Pittsburgh Vote, 1932." *Mid-America* 49 (1967): 244–51.

Sternsher, Bernard. "The Emergence of the New Deal System: A Problem in Historical Analysis of Voter Behavior." *Journal of Interdisciplinary History* 6 (1975): 127–49.

Stewart, Don, and Hoult, Thomal. "A Social-Psychological Theory of 'The Authoritarian Personality.' " *American Journal of Sociology* 65 (1959): 274–79.

Stoper, Emily, and Johnson, Roberta Ann. "The Weaker Sex and the Better Half: The Idea of Women's Moral Superiority in the American Feminist Movement." *Polity* 10 (1977): 192–217.

Strange, Douglas C. "Al Smith and the Republican Party at Prayer: The Lutheran Vote—1928." *Review of Politics* 32 (1970): 347–64.

Szasz, Ferenc M. "The Progressive Clergy and the Kingdom of God." *Mid-America* 55 (1973): 3–20.

Tate, C. Neal. "Individual and Context Variables in British Voting Behavior: An Exploratory Note." *American Political Science Review* 68 (1974): 1656–62.

Thomas, D. R. "Conservatism, Authoritarianism, and Child Rearing Practices." *British Journal of Social and Clinical Psychology* 14 (1975): 97–98.

Tindall, George B. "Business Progressivism: Southern Politics in the Twenties." *South Atlantic Quarterly* 62 (1963): 92–106.

Treiman, Donald J. "Status Discrepancy and Prejudice." *American Journal of Psychology* 71 (1966): 651–64.

Tubbesing, Carl D. "Predicting the Present: Realigning Elections and Redistributive Policies." *Polity* 7 (1975): 478–503.

Tukey, John W. "Causation, Regression, and Path Analysis." In *Statistics and Mathematics in Biology*, edited by Oscar Kempthorne; Theodore A. Bancroft; John W. Gowen; and Jay L. Lush. Ames, Iowa, 1954.

Valkonen, Tapani. "Individual and Structural Effects in Ecological Research." In *Quantitative Ecological Analysis in the Social Sciences*, edited by Mattei Dogan and Stein Rokkan. Cambridge, Mass., 1969.

Van Es, J. C., and Brown, J. E., Jr. "The Rural-Urban Variable Once More: Some Individual Level Observations." *Rural Sociology* 39 (1974): 373–91.

Verba, Sidney, and Schlozman, Kay Lehman. "Unemployment, Class Consciousness, and Radical Politics: What Didn't Happen in the Thirties." *Journal of Politics* 39 (1977): 291–323.

Ward, James F. "Towards a Sixth Party System? Partisanship and Political Development." *Western Political Quarterly* 26 (1973): 385–413.

Watson, Richard A. "Religion and Politics in Mid-America: Presidential Voting in Missouri, 1928 and 1960." *Midcontinental American Studies Journal* 5 (1964): 33–55.

Watson, Richard L., Jr. "A Political Leader Bolts—F. M. Simmons in the Presidential Election of 1928." *North Carolina Historical Review* 37 (1960): 516–43.

Weeks, O. Douglas. "The Election of 1928." *Southwest Political and Social Science Quarterly* 9 (1928): 337–48.

Weiner, Ferne H. "Altruism, Ambiance, and Action: The Effects of Rural and Urban Rearing on Helping Behavior." *Journal of Personality and Social Psychology* 34 (1976): 112–24.

Weinstein, Alan G. "Predicting Behavior from Attitudes." *Public Opinion Quarterly* 36 (1972): 355–60.

Weinstein, James. "Radicalism in the Midst of Normalcy." *Journal of American History* 52 (1966): 773–90.

Weintraub, David. "Unemployment and Increasing Productivity." In *Report of the Subcommittee on Technology to the National Resources Committee, Technological Trends and National Policy.* Washington, D.C., 1937.

Wesser, Robert F. "Charles Evans Hughes and the Urban Sources of Political Progressivism." *New York Historical Society Quarterly* 40 (1966): 365–400.

White, Richard H. "Toward a Theory of Religious Influence." *Pacific Sociological Review* 10 (1968): 23–28.

Wicker, Allan W. "An Examination of the 'Other Variables' Explanation of Attitude-Behavior Inconsistency." *Journal of Personality and Social Psychology* 19 (1971): 18–30.

Wiebe, Robert H. "The Social Functions of Public Education." *American Quarterly* 21 (1969): 147–64.

Winters, Donald L. "The Persistence of Progressivism: Henry Cantwell Wallace and the Movement for Agricultural Economics." *Agricultural History* 41 (1967): 109–20.

Wirth, Louis. "Urbanism as a Way of Life." *American Journal of Sociology* 44 (1938): 1–24.

Witt, Hugh P., and Nelson, Hart M. "Residence, Moral Traditionalism, and Tolerance of Atheists." *Social Forces* 54 (1975): 328–40.

Wolfe, Allis Rosenberg. "Women, Consumerism, and the National Consumers' League in the Progressive Era, 1900–1923." *Labor History* 16 (1975): 378–92.

Wolfinger, Raymond E. "The Development and Persistence of Ethnic Voting." *American Political Science Review* 59 (1965): 896–908.

Wright, Gerald C., Jr. "Contextual Models of Electoral Behavior: The Southern Wallace Vote." *American Political Science Review* 71 (1977): 497–508.

Wright, James E. "The Ethnocultural Model of Voting." In *Emerging Theoretical Models in Social and Political History*, edited by Allan G. Bogue. Beverly Hills, Calif., 1973.

Wuthnow, Robert. "Religious Commitment and Conservatism." In *Religion in Sociological Perspective: Essays in the Empirical Study of Religion*, edited by Charles Y. Glock. Belmont, Calif., 1973.

Zieger, Robert H. "Herbert Hoover: A Reinterpretation." *American Historical Review* 81 (1976): 800–810.

_____. "Herbert Hoover, the Wage-earner, and the 'New Economic System,' 1919–1929." *Business History Review* 51 (1977): 161–89.

_____. "Labor, Progressivism, and Herbert Hoover in the 1920's." *Wisconsin Magazine of History* 58 (1975): 196–208.

Zimmerman, Saundra F.; Smith, Kay H.; and Pederson, Darhl M. "The Effect of Anticonformity Appeals on Conformity Behavior." *Journal of Social Psychology* 81 (1970): 93–103.

Newspapers

Afro-American (Baltimore)
Amsterdam News (New York)
Chicago Defender (Chicago)
Christian Advocate (Nashville)
Cleveland Gazette (Cleveland)

Congregationalist (Boston)
Fellowship Forum (Washington, D.C.)
Los Angeles Times (Los Angeles)
New York Times (New York)
Norfolk Journal and Guide (Norfolk, Va.)

Magazines

America
American Federationist
Atlantic Monthly
Catholic News
Christian Century
Commonweal
Contemporary Review
Crisis
Fortnightly
Forum
Harper's
Interpreter

Kourier Magazine
Literary Digest
Messenger
Nation
New Republic
North American Review
Outlook
Plain Talk
Presbyterian Magazine
Protectionist
United Presbyterian

Campaign Pamphlets 1928

Davis, John W. *Religion and Politics*. Democratic National Committee.
Hawes, Harry B. *Election of Smith Would End Intolerance*. Central Regional Headquarters, Democratic National Committee.
Hoover for President Labor Council, *Governor Smith WRONG on Immigration*. Republican National Committee.
Ross, Nellie Tayloe. *Tolerance and Governor Smith*. Western States Smith for President Association.
Van Dyke, Henry. *In Defense of Religious Liberty*. Democratic National Committee.

Columbia University Oral History Collection

The reminiscences of John Philip Frey, 1955.
The reminiscences of James Watson Gerard, 1950.
The reminiscences of Herbert Henry Lehman, 1961.
The reminiscences of Frances Perkins, 1955.
The reminiscences of Joseph M. Proskauer, 1961.

Personal Interviews

James A. Farley, New York, N.Y., 27 January 1971.
Alfred M. Landon, Topeka, Kansas, 18 December 1972.

Dissertations

Carlson, Earland I. "Franklin D. Roosevelt's Fight for the Presidential Nomination, 1928–1932." University of Illinois, 1955.
Cole, Robert L. "The Democratic Party in Washington State, 1919–1933." University of Washington, 1972.
Dickson, Maxcy R. "The War Comes to All: The Story of the United States Food Administration as a Propaganda Agency." George Washington University, 1942.
Eldot, Paula. "Alfred E. Smith, Reforming Governor." Yale University, 1961.
Feldman, Martin I. "An Abstract of the Political Thought of Alfred E. Smith." New York University, 1963.
Halsey, William Michael. "The Survival of American Innocence: Catholicism in an Era of Disillusionment, 1920–1940." Graduate Theological Union, 1977.
Heath, Donald F. "The Presidential Campaign of 1928: Protestants' Opposition to Al Smith as Reflected in Denominational Periodicals." Vanderbilt University, 1973.
Johnson, Dorothy E. "Organized Women and National Legislation, 1920–1941." Western Reserve University, 1960.
Jones, Bartlett C. "The Debate over National Prohibition, 1920–1933." Emory University, 1961.
Macropoulos, Elias. "The Treatment with Reference to the Roman Catholic Issue of Democratic Candidates in the Presidential Elections of 1928 and 1960, by Selected Periodicals." New York University, 1967.
Mitchell, Franklin Dean. "Embattled Democracy: Missouri Democratic Politics, 1918–1932." University of Missouri, 1964.
Neal, Donn Charles. "The World beyond the Hudson: Alfred E. Smith and National Politics, 1918–1928." University of Michigan, 1973.
Neal, Nevin E. "A Biography of Joseph T. Robinson." University of Oklahoma, 1957.
Nelson, Clair E. "The Image of Herbert Hoover as Reflected in the American Press." Stanford University, 1956.
Rofinot, Henry L. "Normalcy and the Farmer: Agricultural Policy under Harding and Coolidge, 1920–1928." Columbia University, 1958.
Schofield, Kent M. "The Figure of Herbert Hoover in the 1928 Campaign." University of California at Riverside, 1966.
Shideler, James H. "The Neo-Progressives: Reform Politics in the United States, 1920–1925." University of California at Berkeley, 1945.
Smith, John Sword Hunter. "Al Smith and the 1928 Campaign in Idaho,

Nevada, Utah, and Wyoming: A Media Perspective." University of Utah, 1976.

Smith, William David. "Alfred E. Smith and John F. Kennedy: The Religious Issue during the Presidential Campaigns of 1928 and 1960." Southern Illinois University, 1964.

Symonds, Merrill A. "George Higgins Moses of New Hampshire—The Man and the Era." Clark University, 1955.

Taylor, Leah Marcile. "Democratic Presidential Politics: 1918–1932." Louisiana State University, 1973.

Thielbar, Gerald W. "Localism-Cosmopolitanism: Social Differentiation in Mass Society." University of Minnesota, 1966.

Wallace, Elton H. "Alfred E. Smith, the Religious Issue: Oklahoma City, September 20, 1928." Michigan State University, 1965.

Index

359